THE WISE WORLD TRAVELER

Becoming a Part of All that You Meet

James E. Harf
Lawrence J. R. Herson

Agapy®

First published in the USA in January 2015 by Agapy LLC, www.agapy.com.

International Standard Book Number: 978-1-938522-01-7

Library of Congress Control Number: 2014952501

To my first traveling companion, my daughter Marie Harf, who began her overseas journeys with me when only three years old and who now travels the globe three decades later in her chosen work as a force for peace.

—James E. Harf

To my wife, Libby Herson, as always, the center of my life.

—Lawrence J. R. Herson

CONTENTS

PREFACE: THE SHAPE OF THINGS TO COME

We live in an age of global travel, an age marked by the death of distance, as technology has shrunk the planet both physically and psychologically. Jumbo jets and giant cruise ships make travel increasingly easier and affordable. And many people, particularly those from industrialized societies, now venture abroad every year in numbers hundreds of times greater than a short fifty years ago. Most travel solely as tourists, going from place to place rather quickly, racking up miles, counting up cities, taking countless pictures on their digital cameras, listening to canned lectures by tourist guides. That is, they rely on the *act* of traveling for whatever knowledge they will carry from their journeys. In contrast, those who go as *travelers*, wise travelers, bring knowledge to their travels. As a consequence, in the words of English writer Samuel Johnson, they will take knowledge from their travel in direct proportion to the knowledge they bring to it.

This book is dedicated to helping travelers follow the wisdom of Johnson's words. Simply put, the more you know, the more you learn. You don't know what you see until you know what you are seeing. Based on this truth, the book is designed to move travelers' experiences beyond a simple "look and see" to an appreciation of how what they are seeing came to be in the first place. *The Wise World Traveler* is for the discerning traveler of any age and generation who seeks a deeper travel experience. It is for those who yearn to experience what English poet Lord Alfred Tennyson claims for Ulysses: "I am a part of all that I have met."

The Wise World Traveler emerges from the authors' ideas about how the world works, why things happen, and how history unfolds. It is shaped by our experiences as professors, writers, and travelers in the library, on the Web, and in the world. We are lifelong travelers and have made more than 300 trips abroad, sometimes as representatives of government in peace and war, sometimes as researchers, often as tourists, and often as teachers with hordes of eager young college students or older adults in hand. Wise world travel is education wrapped around explanation—learning and teaching about other people and the places where they lived. In so doing, we also learn about ourselves and the culture that has shaped us.

We cannot really know our own culture until we have experienced another. This is true in part because every place on the globe is part of a larger enterprise, similar to a spider's web. Countries are intricately woven together. Trace one strand, and it will lead to every other. Touch one strand, and the entire web vibrates, country after country and culture after culture. Merriam-Webster defines culture as the "customary beliefs, social forms, and material traits of a ...group... The characteristic features of everyday existence."[1]

The Frenchman Alexis de Tocqueville, who came to the young United States in the 1830s to study this newly created phenomenon of a nation, offered a simpler definition. He summed up culture with a wonderful phrase, "habits of the heart." Habits of the heart are what we illuminate throughout this book, by looking at seven major strands of culture: language; religion; ideology; geography; social, political, and economic systems; ways of making a living; and history.

The web and its strands are laced in theory, a word with the same roots as the word theater, from the Greek word that means "to behold." What we behold in a theory is a set of causes and consequences, an assertion that X causes Y. For example, widespread poverty results in communal violence. Stated this way, theory *explains.* And explanation *satisfies.* It is the building block of knowledge and understanding. Theory and explanation go hand in glove; both involve the connection between cause and consequence.

Science and philosophy offer many ways of testing the connections between cause and consequence. The laboratory experiment is one way. Statistical connection or correlation—

---

[1] *Merriam Webster Online*, s.v. "Culture," accessed August 2, 2014, http://www.merriam-webster.com/dictionary/culture.

where a change in one variable is associated with a commensurate change in one or more other variables—is another. And still a third way is by seeking general patterns and searching for exceptions to the patterns. Setting out instances of a general pattern is what lawyers call the weight of evidence. And the search for exceptions tests the rule. As Aristotle put it, the exception proves, or tests, the rule.

The Wise World Traveler mostly asserts its theories and explanations by looking at patterns and the evidence supporting them. Such theories cast a wide net. They offer insight into politics, economics, and history. They explain much about people and places. But they are imprecise, because connections are rarely simple and direct. Other causes may intervene. As T.S. Eliot once said, "Between the idea and the reality, there falls the shadow."[2] So, the observer's obligation is to account for the likelihood of shadows—of intervening variables or factors. And sometimes, theories explain too much. As the old warning states, if a theory explains everything, it risks explaining nothing. Even so, broad theories are useful, so we include them as much as we can.

We can illustrate how theory works through the cultural strand of language. Those who share a language share not only words and meanings; they also share a universe of memories, a history of success and failure, of good times and bad. As the scholar Benedict Anderson says, a nation "is an imagined community," and language is considered the bedrock of that community.[3] The Swiss psychiatrist, Carl Jung, put it another way: "language is the folk warehouse of subconscious ideas, tracings on the mind that give those who share a language a sense of common identity and a sense of proper and improper behavior."[4] Based on these ideas, one theory of language asserts that a connection between nation and culture can be found in the totality of the ways of living by a group of individuals, which is passed on from one generation to another.

Consider another strand, geography. It is often remarked that geography is destiny. And one of the theories based on this aphorism is as follows: Cultures that emerge in the vast expanse of plains and steppes are likely to develop as despotisms. Examples include China, Russia, and ancient Egypt. "You can run but you can't hide," is the simple explanation. Or, as

---

[2] T.S. Eliot, "The Hollow Men" (Poem), 1925.

[3] Benedict Anderson, *Imagined Communities: Reflections on the Origin and Spread of Nationalism*, 2nd edition (New York: Verso, 2006), 6.

[4] Anthony Storr, *C. G. Jung* (New York: Viking Adult, 1973), vii.

Catherine the Great famously remarked, the ruler of Russia must be an autocrat, as no other form of government suits the vastness of Russia.

Another aspect of geography is latitude. We sometimes say that latitude is attitude. People and cultures cover the globe from the equator to about eighty degrees north latitude and to about sixty degrees south latitude. Climate is the obvious variable that helps to relate latitude to cultural and political development. Societies in temperate climates differ from those in tropical climates. One major difference is that societies in temperate climates have been the architects of industry and technology, while equatorial societies have not. Why is this the case? Enter the spider web of connections and explanations. In equatorial societies, heat and insect-borne diseases weaken resistance; the presence of dangerous animals requires constant vigilance. Problems of survival are permanent and paramount. Equatorial societies did not have the energy, levels of education, and technological skills necessary for industrialization. Equally important, the soil in equatorial lowland societies is mostly poor, unsuited for sustained farming. And animals of tropical forests and savannas do not domesticate. As Jared Diamond learned from European settlers in Kenya and Tanzania, "you cannot plow a field behind a rhinoceros. And you cannot ride to the next village on a zebra. Zebras are rarely domesticated. They bite and do not let go."[5] As a result, equatorial tribes live by hunting and gathering and by traveling on foot.

The Wise Traveler is divided into nine parts. The first part explores what it means to be a wise traveler in terms of the cultural strands mentioned above, which will help readers to master the questions and theories that make up the wise traveler's knowledge base and mindset. The remaining eight parts are organized according to popular travel destinations around the globe. We explore these by showing how we use the seven strands of culture not only to appreciate tourist attractions but also to extend our canvass of broad theories. So, as we bring to life many of the best tourist sites, from the wonders of Michelangelo to the Pyramids of Giza, we will also explore things like the effect of Protestantism on the rise of capitalism, and the connection between industrialization and colonialism. With this blend of fact and theory, storytelling and history, we show the radical differences in outlook between an ordinary tourist and a wise traveler.

---

[5] Even so, Diamond recounts the story of a London aristocrat, Lord Walter Rothschild, who drove through the streets of London in a carriage pulled by zebras. Jared Diamond, *Germs, Guns, and Steel: The Fates of Human Societies* (New York: W.W. Norton & Co, 1999), 171.

But for now, as Alice said in Wonderland, let's begin at the beginning—with the Gifts of Travel.

We wish to thank Wendy Williamson, president of Agapy LLC, for her encouragement, support, and tireless efforts to bring this book to publication. She understood that there were "wise travelers" out there who would greatly benefit from this knowledge.

We also wish to thank Miriam Murray for the arduous undertaking of making certain that the photographs and prints used in this book met copyright standards.

THE WISE TRAVELER REVEALED

1. The Gifts of Travel

I am a part of all that I have met.
—Lord Alfred Tennyson, "Ulysses"

The *American College Dictionary* defines travel in less than a half-dozen words. The core definition is simple: to go from place to place. The *Oxford English Dictionary*, which, in the words of Simon Winchester, tells us "the meaning of everything," uses several hundred words to define travel. But the full meaning of travel eludes even the magisterial *OED*. Travel, particularly global travel, is more than a journey, much more. It is an experience of sights, sounds, and emotions. It is an act of discovery in which travelers learn about themselves, other people, and the world. As when the English Romantic poet John Keats says, "Much have I travell'd in the realms of gold, / And many goodly states and kingdoms seen,"[1] the wise reader knows that the realms of gold and goodly states are really metaphors for the wealth of ideas and memories that travelers, particularly global travelers, take from their journeys. They are in essence the *raison d'être,* or ultimate reason, for travel abroad.

---

[1] John Keats, "On First Looking Into Chapman's Homer," 1816, http://www.theguardian.com, accessed September 11, 2014.

The wise traveler also knows that travel is addictive. The happier the travel experience, the greater the yearning to travel again, to store in one's memory new ideas and experiences. Tennyson's Ulysses speaks for us all:

> Yet all experience is an arch wherethro'
> Gleams that untravell'd world, whose margin fades
> For ever and for ever when I move.[2]

THE GIFT OF LANGUAGE

Few things please the wise traveler more than discovering that each journey has many layers of experience, that each experience can lead to greater knowledge, and that every layer and level of knowledge connect to an expanding web of information and ideas. Consider, for example, language. Language is the principal method of human communication. It is usually in spoken form although writing is considered communication as well. But like travel, the idea of language extends far beyond a dictionary's definition. Language is a universe of shared meanings and memories—of historic struggles and of shared triumphs and defeats. Language is thus a principal component and shaper of a country's culture.

Most strangers in a foreign country know that language is a cornerstone of culture. These visitors observe how people of the local culture easily and comfortably communicate through the spoken word, often accompanied by various gestures perfectly understood by fellow citizens, however mysterious to outsiders. Many travelers, for example, have observed the accentuated use of hands and arms by Italians deep in conversation, and mistakenly thought that they were arguing rather than simply communicating normally. For the traveler, then, even a rudimentary understanding of a foreign language can give clues to a country's culture. In many languages, forms of address delineate the barriers among social classes and between genders. In similar fashion, the use of obscenities and other expressions that defame marks the speaker's social class along with what is traditionally called "good breeding."

But the wise traveler also knows that a country's language is part of a larger family of languages. He or she has observed natives of one European country, for example, conversing with those of another, with each speaking bits and pieces of each other's language learned from previous interactions or from years in the classroom. For example, French, Spanish, Italian, and

[2] Alfred Lord Tennyson, "Ulysses," in *Poems, In Two Volumes* (London: Moxon, 1842).

Portuguese are offshoots of Latin, each a local variant established and evolved during the centuries in which the countries that became France, Spain, and other western European nations were part of the Roman Empire. During those centuries, Latin was the language of Rome's administrators and of the Roman legions that had conquered the country and, after their term of enlistment, married local women and settled in their province.

With these ideas in mind, imaginative and wise travelers can construct mental maps that place language families across the globe. The Germanic languages, for example, include English, Dutch, German, Norwegian, Swedish, and Danish. Each group of related languages shares somewhere in its history a conquest and settlement by a group of warriors, who were also language carriers. So it is not surprising that many European languages have much in common and sound so much alike. The history of Europe is one of conquest and occupation.

Language families also share patterns known as morphology and syntax: how, for example, plural words are formed, how verbs are conjugated, and where adjectives are placed in a sentence. These families also share many closely related words. For example, the word *pater* (father) in Latin moved to German as *vater* and to English as *father*. When the Vikings, who spoke Old Norse, conquered large parts of the British Isles, they left linguistic traces of their invasions: *jarl* as an English title of nobility (now *earl*) and *thrall* for slave (which still commands our attention as the word *enthrall*). *Berserk* reminds us that Viking warriors wore a short shirt, a *sark*, overlaid by a bearskin. The four days of the week entered the English language from the Latin of the Roman legions. Sunday, the first day of the week and the Christian Sabbath, is from the Latin *dies solis*, the day of the sun. Monday honors the moon; Tuesday salutes Mars, the god of war; and Saturday is dedicated to Saturn, the Roman god of agriculture. The remaining three days of the week commemorate Viking gods: Thursday is Thor's day, the god of thunder; Wednesday salutes Wodin, the father god; and Friday honors Freya, his wife and mother goddess. And so, in the roundabout ways of language, those who exclaim, "Thank God it's Friday!" are returning to the Viking roots of their language.

These word changes and similarities were first set down by nineteenth-century philologists, including Jacob Grimm (yes, one of the two German brothers who compiled their now-famous book of fairy tales). These philologists were inspired by the work of an English magistrate in far-off India. In 1786 Sir William Jones, in his address to the Bengal Asiatic Society, argued that Sanskrit was the common source for ancient Greek and Latin. Following Jones's lead, other philologists began tracing modern European languages to the forerunner of ancient Sanskrit, a hypothetical founding language called Proto-Indo-European. From these origins, sometime around 7000 BCE and somewhere around the Caspian Sea, the ancestors of modern languages were carried to India, Europe, and the Near East.

The details of other language journeys differ, but each language family is assumed to have been carried outward from a linguistic cradle. Thus, Proto-Malay speakers sailed west to Madagascar and east to the Philippines and Polynesia. Proto-Chinese speakers moved into Southeast Asia and northwest to Korea and Japan. Also, 20,000 to 30,000 years ago, during the last interglacial period when the Arctic seas gave way to a land bridge between Siberia and Alaska, migrants from Asia carried to the Americas the Proto-Amerind language. And from somewhere in Africa, possibly from the Great Rift Valley, proto languages began their journeys to all of equatorial Africa.

OTHER CULTURAL MARKERS

Language is one level of knowledge, but curious eyes and ears find other cultural clues. Traditional and tribal dress in large cities indicates the presence of migrants from the hinterlands. Or, if traditional dress is widely worn, it may in fact mirror resistance to cultural globalization. In parallel fashion, the presence and number of veiled women in Europe say much about religious tensions and the extent to which Muslims have chosen not to integrate into the general European culture. And the response of some national governments, such as in France, in turn suggests recognition that such behavior is an attack on a country's national identity and even on its sovereignty.

Still other clues can be found. How are people dressed on the streets, in shops, and in places to eat? Are they in well-made, stylish clothes or in baseball caps, T-shirts, and jeans? Clothes are indicators of poverty and affluence. Of course, young people who wear baseball caps and jeans may or may not be poor, but their clothes suggest in this instance that they are significantly influenced by western lifestyles.

How people move about (cars, buses, trams, on foot) are rough guides to wealth and poverty. The same holds true for the condition (new or old) of motorized transport. How goods are bought and sold is another rough guide to wealth and poverty. The kind of goods on sale is also a window on the local culture, as is the nature of face-to-face business transactions. Is the latter via fixed prices or through bargaining? The places where goods are sold are further clues to the extent to which the national economy is integrated or decentralized. What dominates—street vendors, small shops, department stores, bazaars, or malls?

Architecture is another important cultural marker. Slums speak for themselves, as do the location and style of well-kept buildings. Are palaces and great houses now public property or still occupied by wealthy families? Gated communities surrounded by barbed wire and armed police say much about both racial tension and the wide income gap between rich and poor. Communal longhouses in Borneo and compounds in rural Vietnam mark societies with strong family and clan ties. In large cities around the world skyscraper apartments point to anonymity and social distance.

Statues tell their own stories. Who are honored by public statues? Warriors usually speak to a critical period in a country's history, such as a war for independence, the overthrow of tyranny, or the apogee of an empire. And if the same historical figure crowds the statuary landscape, a dictator's secret police may be keeping tabs on the tourist.

Restaurants also tell us much about a culture, not just what is on the menu but how it is prepared and served. What food is offered? Who eats where? When do people typically eat? How long does a meal usually last? What is considered the main meal of the day? And how do prices compare with those in the traveler's home city? In fact, we can use one particular food to compare the cost of living in various cities around the world with our own country. For years, the *Economist* has given its readers a rough guide to world prices by comparing the cost of a Big Mac hamburger. All over the world, the Big Mac is built around a set of specifications: a certain weight of meat, size of bun, uniform leaves of lettuce, etc. By comparing the price of a Big Mac in one's hometown with the price, say, in Moscow, in Oslo, or some other faraway city, one has a fairly accurate guide to the cost of living in any "Big Mac city."

THE GIFT OF CULTURAL DIVERSITY

> For the Colonel's Lady an' Judy O'Grady
> Are sisters under their skins
> —Rudyard Kipling, "The Ladies"[3]

> All the people like us are We,
> And every one else is They.
> —Rudyard Kipling, "We and They"[4]

The world population has recently topped seven billion. This vast aggregate of individuals speaks something on the order of 7,000 languages, of which about 700 are predominant. The

[3] Rudyard Kipling, "The Ladies," (Poem), 1896.

[4] Ibid., "We and They," (Poem), 1926.

United Nations, which mirrors the world's cultural diversity, contains 193 member states. What, then, accounts for the striking differences in the vast array of cultures, their contrasting and competing habits of the heart? And what should the wise traveler know about this cultural array?

A remarkable conclusion drawn from genetic science is that all people share more than 99 percent of the same genetic code. If proof were needed, consider that humans are "inter-fertile"; that is, human offspring are born wherever and whenever people mate. What, then, accounts for striking racial differences in skin color and facial features? Centuries-long adaptation to the environment is the most widely accepted evolutionary answer. For example, a random genetic mutation, light skin, might have been an adaptation that helped migrants survive in colder climates. The large body mass of many Polynesians suggests that they descend from ancestors whose girth enabled them to survive long sea voyages to the remote islands of the Pacific. The compact body mass and metabolism of the Eskimos enable them to conserve body heat in Arctic temperatures. In each of the above cases, what may have been a random mutation helped to assure the survival of those who inherited the mutation. And with this idea, we return to a familiar theme: geography is destiny.

As far as is presently known, everyone on earth has descended from ancestral bands of humans living three to five million years ago in eastern Africa. Half a million years ago, *Homo erectus* (upright man) "lived and hunted in suitable areas throughout the Old World from China to Germany and in North and East Africa."[5] Ten thousand years ago, plants and animals were domesticated in the Near East, and permanent dwellings replaced tribal wandering in search of game and wild foods: "...Upland valleys offered good water supplies, often fertile soil, and their natural configuration made it easier for men to confine their herds and to move them between summer and winter pastures."[6]

During these long centuries, cultural separations took place. Gods and myths of creation became increasingly localized. As language developed, it, too, was centered in specific geographic areas. Tools, weapons, shrines, dwellings, and paintings on the walls of caves give evidence of cultures separated by time and place. Among the many contributors to cultural separation, and thus to diversity, the most prominent are language, religion, and geography.

---

[5] Jaquetta Hawkes, *The Atlas of Early Man* (New York: St. Martin's Press, 1976), 17.

[6] Ibid., 39-40.

THE GIFT OF PERSPECTIVE

The distinguished anthropologist Ralph Linton once remarked that the last thing a fish probably thinks about is water until, of course, it is taken from its life-giving habitat. A foreign culture, especially an exotic one, prompts the traveler to think about his or her own society. Why is my culture different from this one? What has made us what we are? Here, we touch the greatest gift of travel: a deeper understanding of our own society. Forced to confront another culture, we return to our own with a better understanding of it.

For students of American culture, geography lies near the center of the American experience. Rufus Miles writes of the consequences of a "virgin continent":

> Settlers of the North American continent found incalculable riches—seemingly inexhaustible sources of food, fiber, hides, woods, and minerals with which to fashion all the necessities and most of the amenities of life…Never again can human beings stumble upon so mammoth an area of rich, sparsely populated, undercultivated and easily exploitable land.[7]

In historian David Potter's observation, Americans were born a people of plenty. As a consequence, it is customary to link American economic development with the optimism that has dominated American culture.[8] More important, the easy availability of land for taking (and conquering) gave America one of its most powerful social memories and our mythic age—the westward movement, the frontier. The frontier, with land to be farmed, forested, and mined, also gave opportunities for accumulating wealth. As Alexis de Tocqueville wrote about America in the 1830s, "I know of no country, indeed, where the love of money has taken stronger hold on the affections of men."[9]

The frontier also fostered a sense of self-reliance, resistance to intrusive government, and the importance of private property. Over time, we would make our system a market-based, or capitalist, political economy. And perhaps most important of all, the availability of land meant that the new America could escape European and Asian feudal systems. This is why Karl Marx observed that America is the great exception to feudal social, political, and economic organiza-

---

[7] Rufus Miles, *Awakening From the American Dream: The Social and Political Limits to Growth* (New York: Universe Books, 1976), 23.

[8] See David Potter, *People of Plenty: Economic Abundance and the American Character* (Chicago: University of Chicago Press, 1954).

[9] Alexis de Tocqueville, *Democracy in America* (New York: A.A. Knopf, 1945). 2 vols (New York: Alfred A. Knopf, 1957) I, 51.

tion. Lacking that feudal history, America turned its back on an ascriptive society, that is, a society in which rank and social privilege are inherited. As is often said, a democratic outlook and a demand for democratic government are rooted in American geography.

Figure 1.1. Alexis de Tocqueville

This observation, of course, overstates the case. It sums up American culture as we wish it to be, not as it has always been. Thomas Jefferson claimed that in writing The Declaration of Independence, he had merely given voice to sentiments already in the air. But the Declaration's assertion that "all men are created equal" came from a slave-owner. And the assertion of "unalienable rights" smoothes over a long colonial history of Indian massacres, censored speech, witch hunts and hangings, as well as a long, long struggle to make our society color-blind. Even so, the Declaration serves as the American Creed, goading us to "achieve a more perfect union." As English poet Robert Browning says, "A man's reach should exceed his grasp / Or what's a heaven for."[10]

The American experience also has its impediments and its critics. Americans take pride in what is often called "American exceptionalism," the idea that the United States is qualitatively different from other nations. For the most part, Americans have been free of the social and po-

[10] Robert Browning, "Andrea del Sarto" (poem), 1855, http://www.poetryfoundation.org, accessed September 11, 2014.

litical constraints that blighted the life and spirit of other societies. This has created an attitude of separation based on individualism, egalitarianism, and liberty. In 1630 the Puritan John Winthrop, who helped to found the Massachusetts Bay Colony, spoke of America as a beacon, a "city on a hill" bringing light to the rest of the world. In his "Letters from an American Farmer" (1782), French-American writer Hector de Crèvecœur spoke of the spirit of equality that sets Americans apart from all others. Thomas Jefferson called America "the world's best hope."

But, as the eighteenth-century Scottish poet Robert Burns once wrote, "O wad some Pow'r the giftie gie us / To see oursels as others see us"[11] (Oh would some power give us the gift of seeing ourselves as others see us). As the wise and perceptive traveler soon learns, people in other countries may admire our technology and imitate our popular culture, but many deny that America is a city on a hill, a place worthy of emulation. In growing measure, people in other countries resist and resent the spread of the American way of life, especially in foreign affairs and international dealings. To see ourselves as others see us, however painful, is also a gift of travel.

THE GIFT OF AN OPEN MIND

The late James Michener, novelist and travel writer (*Tales of the South Pacific, The Bridges of Toko Ri*), warns us against rejecting people and cultures that are different from our own: "If you reject the food, ignore the customs, fear the religion, and avoid the people, you might better stay home. You are like a pebble thrown into the water; you become wet on the surface but you are never part of the water."[12]

Michener is telling us to travel with an open mind. He warns us to be cautious in judging other societies against our own. Some principles of the American Creed, of course, are not to be compromised. Self-government, honesty in public affairs, freedom of expression, and compassion for the less fortunate are worthwhile standards by which other societies are to be judged. But the open mind is also forgiving of shortcomings and failures. And that is yet another wonderful gift of travel. To understand that gift a bit better, let us now take a look at one of the most celebrated wise travelers in the history of western civilization.

---

[11] Robert Burns, "To a Louse: On Seeing a Lady's Bonnet at Church" (Poem), 1785, http://www.scottishpoetry.org.uk, accessed August 10, 2014.

[12] *Holiday Magazine*, (March, 1956): 40-51.

2. The First Wise Traveler to the West

> They all laughed at Christopher Columbus
> When he said the world was round...
> But who's got the last laugh now
> — Ira and George Gershwin[1]

Christopher Columbus, so popular legend suggests, discovered America. When all of Europe said the world was flat, Columbus claimed the world was round. To finance his voyage of discovery, Queen Isabella pawned her jewels, and when news of his discovery reached Europe, scholars were so amazed and so given to doubting Columbus's accomplishment that geographers named the newfound lands after an altogether different person, Amerigo Vespucci.

So much for legend. The truth is less romantic. With royal consent, money for the voyage came from the coffers of the Spanish Inquisition. The experience of sailors brought evidence that the world was round. Many had sailed to the horizon; none had fallen off the earth, even at its farthest horizon. And the name given to the New World—"America"—came from the Latin version of Amerigo Vespucci, a Florentine nobleman who followed Columbus's westward route in 1501, kept charts more accurate than those of Columbus, and did what Columbus failed to do—explore the mainland of both North and South America. The 400th anniversary of Columbus's arrival in the Americas (1992) was a time to challenge the Columbus legend. A

---

[1] Ira Gershwin and George Gershwin, "They All Laughed" (Song), 1937.

Norwegian flotilla of replica Viking longboats crossed the Atlantic to call attention to Leif Erikson's landing in Canada in the year 1000. Spokespersons for Native Americans decried the name Columbus had bestowed on them: he called them Indians, in his mistaken belief that he had arrived in the Indies, the generic term for the Far East.

Native Americans objected to the myth that Columbus had "discovered" them. "We were here and had been here for 30,000 years! If anyone was lost, it was Columbus!" they sneered. They demanded apologies from descendants of the Europeans who had come to the "New World" after 1492, newcomers who robbed and killed Native Americans, threw them off their land, and broke the harmony with nature in which they had once lived. Scholars (Native Americans and others) have also offered credit-debit statements of what Native Americans gained and lost through contact with Europe's settlers.

WHO WAS CHRISTOPHER COLUMBUS?

But what of the man who started it all, Christopher Columbus? His biographers offer conflicting portraits. To some, he is a hero, an inspired thinker, a brilliant navigator. To others, he is vain, arrogant, grasping, and a paranoid twister of truth. Most all agree that he is not an easy man to know.

The child who became Christopher Columbus was born in Genoa in 1421, the son of Domenico Colombo, a wool merchant and weaver, and his wife, Susanna Fontanarosa. The baptismal records carry the son's name as Cristoforo Colombo. By tradition, sons followed fathers into the family trade. But Cristoforo shipped out to sea sometime between the ages of ten and fourteen. His early years are recorded by his second son, Ferdinand, whose tomb is at the foot of his father's in the great Cathedral in Seville.

According to Cristoforo's own account, the great turning point in his life was a pirate attack in 1476 off the coast of Portugal. Cristoforo was age twenty-five, and with bravery and stamina he swam many leagues to shore and made his way to Lisbon, where his brother Bartholomew (Bartolomeo) worked as a chart maker. The man who emerged from the sea was striking in appearance. In an age when most Mediterranean Europeans were short in stature, Cristoforo stood more than six feet tall. He had reddish, blond hair and grey eyes. He was never heard speaking the Genoa dialect but did write and converse in related languages: Portuguese, Castilian, and Latin, the language of the learned. In Lisbon, Cristoforo displayed a talent that would serve him all his life. He was a charming and persuasive speaker, and he accomplished an unheard-of leap, changing his status from an ordinary sailor to a member of the Portuguese aristocracy by marrying a woman considerably above his social station, Beatriz Perestrello. They went to Madeira, where Beatriz's brother was hereditary ruler of Santos, one of the small Madeiras. And it is there that Cristoforo conceived what he would call the Enterprise of the Indies.

Cristoforo never called himself Christopher Columbus. After reaching the New World and mindful of his mission to bring Christianity to the natives of the region, he began to call himself Cristobal Colon—bringer of Christianity to the colonies. As to his current recognizable name, that is a coinage that followed the American Revolution. The new nation needed a hero who was neither English nor too European. The answer seems to have been provided by Washington Irving, the author of *The Legend of Sleepy Hollow*. Cristobal Colon became Christopher Columbus, a name that seizes the popular imagination.

WHY THE ENTERPRISE OF THE INDIES?

The Enterprise of the Indies has its roots in the Great Crusades. In 1095, on a hillside in Clermont, France, Pope Urban called on Christian warriors to liberate the Holy Land from its Muslim overlords. Urban's motives were unclear and are still debated, but the Crusades that followed were an uneven amalgam of religious piety, secular greed and ambition, and a lust for war and adventure.

The First Crusade stormed into Jerusalem in 1098, horses knee-deep in blood and knights slaughtering enemies and innocents alike. European invaders established kingdoms all across the Near East (Latin Kingdoms: Frankish kingdoms is their usual name), building great castles to defend their regimes. From triumph in 1098 to the final Muslim counter-conquest in 1291, the knightly classes of Europe grew accustomed to the luxury goods of the East: porcelain, playing cards, silks, and spices. To an aristocracy who had once eaten from lead platters and wooden trenches (hence, our word for big eater, trencherman), porcelain was an ultimate domestic luxury. It was outdone only by silk, a cloth so fine and so beautifully dyed that some thought it had a sorcerer's provenance. And spices? Spices were magic medicines: cloves for stomach disorders, oil of clove for toothaches, cinnamon for fevers, nutmeg for flavor (an ingredient of Coca Cola), and above all, pepper. Pepper was a remedy for fatigue (it helped build Egypt's pyramids), and it gave flavor to food. Some historians assert that pepper also made putrid meat palatable.

No European knew precisely where these trade goods came from, only that they came from the far-off Indies. Arabs knew, because Arab traders carried it in their dhows across the ocean from India, Malay, and China. And Muslim lips were sealed. No European yet knew about the monsoon, that steady wind that blows from west to east for six months and then reverses direction for the rest of the year. Venice had received papal dispensation to trade with the Muslim East, and Venice grew rich with the trade. As Wordsworth said of Venice, "Once she did hold the gorgeous East in fee / And was the Safeguard of the West."[2]

Figure 2.1. Entry of the Crusaders into Constantinople (Gustave Doré)

Pepper had come across the oceans from India, silks by way of the Silk Road across desert and mountains from China, and spices from a tiny cluster of islands (The Spiceries) from the Indonesian archipelago. At every caravansary, at each trans-shipping point, the cost of cargo

[2] William Wordsworth, "On the Extinction of the Venetian Republic," (Poem), 1802.

increased. Goods bought for copper at their points of origin sold for gold at their final destination. Where would men not go for pepper? For a bag of pepper, writes Joseph Conrad in *Lord Jim,* they "would cut each other's throats without hesitation and would foreswear their souls...defy death...and strange diseases..."[3] Venice was the conduit of the luxury trade, and Portugal, the maritime nation at the western edge of Europe, schemed to break the conduit.

WHY THE PORTUGUESE?

As Ralph Waldo Emerson famously said, "An Institution is the lengthened shadow of but one man."[4] The institution was Sagres, and the man was Prince Henry, known to history as Henry the Navigator. Henry was a younger son of the King of Portugal. His mother was English, Philippa of Gaunt. Pious and humorless, he wore a hair shirt as a reminder of man's obligation to foreswear frivolity and sin. As a young man, Henry fought against the Moors of North Africa. Later, he aimed to outflank Islam in North Africa, sail south down the West African coast, use whatever riches he found there to wage war on Muslims, and perhaps ally Portugal to the legendary Christian kingdom of Prester John.

To pursue these ends, Henry established an observatory and Europe's first school for navigators at Sagres (meaning sacred) near Cape St. Vincent on a promontory jutting into the Atlantic. All incoming Portuguese sea captains were required to report to Sagres and share charts and sailing information. A ship for inshore sailing (the caravel) was designed at Sagres. About seventy foot at keel and twenty-five foot at beam, the caravel had a triangular sail at its foremast (a lateen sail) that could be pulled quickly from starboard to port to starboard to take advantage of offshore breezes and sail close to the wind. The caravel was so efficient in design that it became the favored ship for 200 years of exploration. (In 1492, two of Columbus's ships were caravels.)

Henry's navigators discovered Madeira in 1420. In 1434 they rounded the forbidding Cape Bojador, and in 1446 they reached the mouth of the Gambia River. Henry died in 1460, but the Sagres navigators pressed on. Africa's Gold Coast and Ivory Coast began to make Portugal rich (and finance further expeditions). In 1488 the resolute Bartolomeu Dias rounded southernmost Africa, calling it (for understandable reasons) The Cape of Good Hope. Ten

---

[3] Joseph Conrad, *Lord Jim* (New York: McCure, Phillips and Co., 1905), 211.

[4] Ralph Waldo Emerson, "On Self-Reliance," *Essays: First Series* (1841), Reprinted in Tony Adams and David Widger, *The Project Gutenberg EBook of Essay,* First Series (EBook #2944) (December 1, 2008).

years later, Vasco da Gamma gave Portugal its greatest triumph of discovery, East Africa, and from there, across the Indian Ocean to Calicut, India, still home to the finest pepper in the world (and home to the cloth called calico).

HOW DID MARCO POLO HELP COLUMBUS?

To reward Portugal for its attempt to outflank and outfight Islam, the Pope gave Portugal authority to colonize and otherwise rule all non-Christian nations that lay on its seaward path to the Indies. On at least two occasions Columbus tried to convince the Portuguese king that a faster route to the Indies lay across the Western Sea to China. Columbus built his case by relying on the travels of Marco Polo, who went overland to China in 1273 and stayed twenty-five years in the service of the Great Khan. Columbus also fudged his geographic calculations in order to place China (or better still, Cipango/Japan) within sailing range of Iberian ships. As fate would have it, Columbus was alongside the River Tagus when Dias returned to Lisbon; he had brought news of the likely African route to the Indies. Secure in his belief in his own great destiny, Columbus then traveled north to the court of Ferdinand and Isabella, the embattled and ambitious monarchs of Aragon and Castille, to make his case for the westward route to the Indies.

WHY WAS COLUMBUS A REMARKABLE NAVIGATOR?

Columbus was a secretive soul. As he grew older he walked the narrow ridge that often separates the visionary from the mentally unhinged. In late life he wrote of an angelic choir that would sing his praises for eternity. A more pragmatic explanation for his vision comes from his days as a sailor on a Genoese ship making the Atlantic run to Britain, Ireland, and possibly Iceland. Somewhere off Galway, Ireland, came a report of Asian-appearing men, dead, in a small oar-driven craft (Indians in a dugout canoe?). Whether Columbus saw the dead sailors or merely heard about them is not known. But perhaps that, as well as driftwood carried eastward on Atlantic currents, provided Columbus with his vision.

By the time he sailed on his historic voyage, Columbus was familiar with the trade winds: turn southwest at the Canaries to find a westward-moving wind; to return to Europe, sail northward to the Azores and then back east to reach home. As far as is known, Columbus never mastered any navigational tools more complex than the cross-staff for sighting the angle of the sun over the horizon. But service on Genoese ships most likely gave him an understanding of dead reckoning: use cloud drift to estimate wind force; use an hourglass to calculate location. The compass, which made its way from China to Europe around 1250, provided overall directions. Sailors' experience provided handy navigational rules for latitude. (Find the angle of the sun over the horizon or above the ship's mast at noon each day; ditto the angle of the North Star.) With whatever navigational tools he possessed, Columbus was a remarkable navigator. On his second voyage to the Caribbean, he arrived precisely where he wished to be—on the island of Hispaniola.

Figure 2.2. Columbus (Ridolfo Ghirlandaio painting)

HOW DID HIS DREAM BECOME REALITY?

Probably through his wife's aristocratic connections, Columbus twice put his proposal to the Portuguese court. Both times it was rejected. Court advisors may have seen through Columbus's misleading geography. Whether by accident, ignorance, or design, he had shaved off 25 percent from the circumference of the earth. Or court advisors may have concluded (even if his calculations of distances were correct) that he and his ships would run out of food and water long before reaching the intended shores.

Columbus then traveled north to Spain to try to convince the Spanish court. By coincidence, luck, or perhaps because he was an engaging and persuasive speaker, Columbus was passed along from one influential Spaniard to another until he was able to offer his dream and his services to the court of Aragon and Castile. Ferdinand and Isabella took advice from the

University of Salamanca, Europe's foremost center of geography and navigation. Its professors were not convinced. The royal court did not dismiss Columbus outright; it gave him a small stipend for living expenses. So Columbus lived on his dreams and the royal pittance for five years. Time to move on, he then set out for the French court. And just as he was about to cross the border into France, there came a wonderfully dramatic moment. A Spanish courier rode up and commanded him to return to court.

WHAT DID COLUMBUS DEMAND OF HIS SOVEREIGNS?

Ever proud (some would say preposterously so) and convinced that he was a man of destiny, Columbus asked for a written contract covering his proposed voyage. One biographer expresses astonishment that a penniless sailor, standing before the haughtiest thrones of Europe, never known to have captained a vessel or to have discovered any new lands, demanded that if his voyage were successful, he be made a hereditary nobleman of title and rank (Admiral of the Ocean Sea), be governor of all lands discovered, entitled to 10 percent of all the wealth obtained from those lands, and permitted to invest one-eighth in subsequent voyages. (The monetary claims of the soon-to-be Admiral would tie up the Spanish courts for years.) Such were the formally titled Capitulations of Santa Fe.

Money for the voyage was provided by the coffers of the Society of Hermandad (the treasury of the Inquisition), and the town of Palos, having incurred royal displeasure, was ordered to furnish the ships. Three ships (as might be imagined) were grudgingly offered up, and in another instance of Columbus's long string of good fortune, two resourceful and experienced captains, the Pinzon brothers, joined the expedition. Those three ships, soon to sail into greatness, were not in the most seaworthy condition. And their names have been glossed over. They were dedicated to the whores of Palos. Nina means little girl; Pinta is a painted woman; and "Santa Maria" revised the original name of Maria Galante, or Naughty Mary.

WHAT WAS COLUMBUS'S ROUTE?

Ordinarily, Columbus might have sailed from Seville, Spain's chief southern port, but he was forced to sail out of Palos. On sailing day, August 23, the Seville harbor was jammed with ships carrying Jews into exile. The Spanish court had given them three hard choices: leave, convert, or face the Inquisition.

Columbus sailed to the Spanish Canary Islands, named not for any species of bird but for the fierce wild dogs (Latin, *canis*) that once roamed the islands. The tiny fleet anchored in Las Palmas for refitting and reprovisioning. Backstairs history offers Columbus (now a widower with a mistress in Spain) a liaison with Beatriz de Paraza, widow of the governor of Las Palmas. For whatever reason, the fleet spent more time than might be ordinarily required for refitting, and on September 8 it sailed on the trade winds "bound for glory."

Figure 2.3. Ships of Columbus

The fateful adventure ended on October 12, 1492, after thirty-three days at sea. As a tribute to Columbus's seamanship, not a sailor was lost during the crossing. The fleet landed somewhere in the Bahamas; the best reconstruction puts the landing at Watlings Island. In thanks for deliverance, Columbus called his landfall San Salvador. At that moment, Columbus became an Admiral and, in the name of his sovereigns and with appropriate words and ceremony, took possession of the island. Sword in hand, brandishing the flag of his sovereigns, Columbus invented the protocols of discovery. (An American flag signed by President Richard Nixon stands firmly planted on the moon.)

Always goal-driven, Columbus kept two logs on his voyage. One was his secret but accurate estimates of daily progress, and the other was a false log to calm his crew's fears that they had sailed too far. Ironically, the false log is truer to course than the secret but presumably accurate one.

OCTOBER 12, 1492: HOW DID THE WORLD CHANGE?

> Let the great world spin forever,
> Down the ringing grooves of change.
> — Lord Alfred Tennyson[5]

Columbus's New World landing set vast changes in motion. Genetic changes, cultural changes, material changes, intellectual changes, and pathogenic consequences are only four that nest inside the vast catalog of intermingled consequences flowing from Columbus's voyages. Let us elaborate on these.

Some nine months after his crew first came ashore, a new race came into the world, an admixture of European and Native American genes came forth. *Mestizo*, Spanish for mixed, became the new race, now dominant in many parts of Latin America: around 60 percent of Mexico's present population, about 65 percent of the population of Ecuador, and 58 percent of Colombia. In this admixture, many students of Latin American politics find the roots of Latin America's perennial political corruption—a subservient *mestizo* population, long dominated by a powerful landed class, long accepting that class's right to rule. Students of Latin American politics also link Latin America's constant cycle of revolution and military dictatorship to *mestizo* presence—the patient, long-suffering *mestizo* who at long last explodes into violence. (As the Spanish philosopher Ortega y Gasset observes, "Violence is reason exasperated."[6]) And in parallel fashion, sociologists attribute to the *mestizos* the master-and-servant culture that is the foundation for the top-heavy (asymmetrical) distribution of Latin American wealth. Brazil is the extreme case. About 10 percent of the population controls over 40 percent of the nation's wealth.

The material and cultural consequences of the New World discoveries were inordinate in Spain's first 150 years in Latin America. It is estimated that a half-million pounds of gold and thirty-five million pounds of silver were taken from the ground directly or stolen from the Indians. This newfound wealth brought the first round of inflation to Europe (too much money chasing after too few goods). Privateers and pirates cruised the Caribbean, attempting to intercept Spain's treasure fleet. Money that leaked out of Spain helped to spur northern Europe's Industrial Revolution. New World gold helped build the Spanish Armada, whose defeat in

---

[5] Lord Alfred Tennyson, "Locksley Hall," (Poem), 1835.

[6] José Ortega y Gasset, *The Revolt of the Masses*, translation (New York: W. W. Norton, 1932), 74.

1588 emboldened England and Holland to sail east and west to establish their own colonial empires. As the Spanish monarchy weakened, one hundred years of wars followed, with Britain, France, Prussia, and almost all the rest of Europe scrambling and fighting to dominate Spain and its New World wealth. From the War of Spanish Succession in 1701 to the Battle of Waterloo in 1815, Europe was rarely at peace. War followed war, spreading far beyond Europe to India, Canada, and the English settlements in North America. And perhaps most important of all, British incursions into North America led to the first large-scale, long-lived democratic regimes since the early Greeks sailed from their mother republics to carry democratic banners westward to Sicily. In poetic terms, Columbus's arrival in the New World set in motion a chain of events that carried democracy to the modern world.

As far as is known, there are three major sources of human knowledge: God's revelations, human experience, and human reason. Divine revelation comes as God's message to humanity. ("And God said, let there be light...") Experience, also called empirical knowledge from the Greek word for experience, teaches us that the sun rises every day in a place we call the East. And reason is humankind's capacity to move from evidence to inference, from premise to conclusion. (To journey east, walk in the morning toward the sun.) We can move from premise to conclusion by following well-tried rules of reasoning: chiefly, induction and deduction and a combination of both. And we are guided in reasoning by remembering notable and useful empirical conclusions. (Isaac Newton's third law: for every action there is an opposite and equal reaction; Alexander Hamilton's observations on the short-lived republics of the Italian Renaissance.)

Throughout the Middle Ages the most important sources of knowledge were said to be reason and revelation, with reason second to revelation. But following October 12, 1492, experience came gradually to assume greater and greater importance. There was nothing in the Bible about geographic worlds yet to be discovered. Nor did Aristotle, one of the most revered ancient philosophers, suggest the existence of lands far beyond the horizon of the western sea. And yet, they were undeniably there. Modern science builds on experience, on careful observation (ideally made several times and shared with others) combined with reasoning. Experience opens the gates of scientific truth, and October 12, 1492, thus stands as a milestone in the great journey of modern science.

WHAT IS THE GREAT COLUMBIAN EXCHANGE?

Thomas Jefferson once remarked that there is no greater gift to mankind than the discovery of a new food. Consider, then, the New World's gifts of food. For more than 10,000 years the Native Americans of the Andes have been cultivating a root that we know as the potato. Remarkably adaptive, the potato grows at different elevations and in an astonishing variety of climates, from temperate to subtropical, from an altitude of 13,000 feet to sea level. It grows in varied soils, from rich loam to stony clay. Unlike most of the staples known to Europeans and Asians before 1492, potato seeds and cuttings can be pushed into the ground with nothing more than a stick—no need for plow and turning board and no need for draft animals or humans to pull the plow. More remarkable still, the potato does not need harvesting within a few critical days at maturity. It can be kept in the soil for considerable time after maturing and pulled from the ground, one or two potatoes at a time. For cooking, potatoes need no pots or fireplaces; a simple fire will do, a considerable gift for peasants in hovels. It also has high nutritional value, containing vitamin C and numerous minerals necessary for health. Parts not eaten, such as the peelings, can nourish pigs, the animal companions of people who live at the very margins of nutritional existence.

Figure 2.4. Irish Immigrants to America

The potato gained acceptance in Europe only slowly. It elicited fear and loathing when first encountered because a widespread theory of disease held that plants caused a disease associated with their appearance. And unfortunately for the potato, its eyes and skin suggested the skin lesions of leprosy. But by the 1600s, potatoes were common in northern Europe. Now, with a new and ready source of food, Europe's population began a steady climb. Population grew not only because of the potato's nutritional value but because it spared Europe's peasants the starvation that followed foraging armies and rapacious tax collectors, who seized grains stored in barns and sheds. The potato could remain hidden underground, safe from prying eyes and grasping hands.

But as Ralph Waldo Emerson says, every credit has its debit side. By 1800, rural Ireland was totally dependent on the potato. Most households ate nothing but potatoes, as much as fourteen pounds of potatoes per person per day.[7] Sustained by the potato, Ireland's population grew in Malthusian fashion (500 percent) from 1715 to 1815. The population increased by 172 percent from 1779 to 1840. By 1845, the population had swelled to eight million. Then disaster struck. In the years 1845, 1846, and 1848, a fungus attacked the potato. Rotting, inedible plants were everywhere. Starving families walked the roads and lanes begging for food, with desperate mothers clutching dead babies as they traveled. Families, too weak to move, lay dead in the doorways of their huts. By the end of the Great Hunger, more than a million had died of starvation and starvation-induced disease. And one million more emigrated, mostly to Canada and the United States. Desperate to escape death, those who could borrow the four or five pounds' passage against future wages crammed aboard poorly provisioned, unseaworthy ships—coffin ships, they were called. Just one example of their toll: of the 89,738 people who sailed to Canada in 1847, 15,330 perished. Those who accomplished the Great Migration carried, and their descendants still carry, bitter memories of the English landlords and the British government that did too little and too late to stem the rising tide of death during the Great Famine.

FOOD, GLORIOUS FOOD

Corn is another life-sustaining gift from the New World. Originally cultivated in Middle America, corn is that rare plant that nourishes both humans and livestock. Corn is so adaptable (and welcome as foodstuff) that it made its way (by routes unknown) into China in the early 1500s. And maize, as corn is called in many parts of the world, became an important source of

---

[7] See Cecil Woodham Smith, *The Great Hunger--Ireland: 1845-1849* (New York: Harper & Row, 1962).

food in the high Balkan Mountains. Sustaining Greek and Slavic populations in mountain valleys, corn served to feed and fuel the Balkans revolts against their Ottoman overlords. One might claim poetically that Greek independence in the 1820s began centuries earlier in corn-cultivating Middle America.

The list of the New World's food bounty unfolds rhythmically: tomatoes, squash, pumpkin, sweet potatoes, peanuts (now a leading cash crop of Africa), and pecan and cashew nuts. Chili peppers, cultivated in Mexico before 3500 BCE, were brought to Spain by Columbus to bolster his claim that he had reached the pepper-rich Indies. Sunflowers, source of another alternative to cooking with olive oil, is among the New World's gifts to the rest of the world, as are the far-roving pineapple, avocado, and blueberry.

To this list we add flora of pleasure and pain. Tobacco and cocoa are American gifts. So, too, is quinine, an antidote for malaria and the first effective agent for reducing fever. Quinine is derived from the powdered bark of an Amazon tree, the Cinchona. Given to Jesuits by the Indians, the powdered bark was long known as Jesuit powder. Oliver Cromwell, ill with fever, refused to have anything to do with Popish medicine and died as a consequence. King Charles II had no such concerns. He took the powder from an illiterate peddler, Robert Talbot, and when the powder made the king well, he appointed Talbot Royal Physician, no doubt the beginnings of a long tradition wherein doctors' prescriptions are set down in a seeming illiterate scrawl. And perhaps as a penultimate benefit of Jesuit's powder, in 1858 an enterprising Englishman, Erasmus Bond, obtained a patent for quinine water. Today, more than 500 pharmaceuticals originate in the Amazon.

The sap of another Amazon tree yields chewing gum. And the milky sap (hence the word latex from the Spanish word for milk) from another Amazon tree, *hevea brasiliensis*, gives us rubber, used for automobile tires, rainproof clothes, and round balls indispensable for sports. *Homo ludens*, playful man, became even more playful when rubber came to Europe. Rubber owes its name to chemist Joseph Priestly, who discovered in 1759 that a ball of rubber could rub out graphite pencil marks on paper.

Perhaps as a grace note, national cuisines have become inseparable from New World food. England, Germany, and Scandinavia build their cuisines around the potato. The cuisine of Italy is firmly rooted in the tomato. Perhaps most distinctive, Hungarian goulash is made from a paprika (Hungarian for pepper) sauce made from a variety of chilis. *Capsicum annuum*, to use its Latin name, is grown worldwide and more commonly called pimento. And pause for a moment to toast the contribution of potatoes to Vodka and of corn to American bourbon!

SATAN'S MASK

The great Columbus Exchange also wore Satan's mask, through the dark gifts of pathogens traveling from Europe to the Americas. Native Americans had lived in viral isolation for 30,000 years. Their immune systems were no match for smallpox and diphtheria, measles and mumps. These diseases came close to killing off the Native Americans. Henry Hobhouse suggests that 50 to 90 percent of the Indians of North and South America died of diseases introduced from Europe.[8] And only a few years after 1492, what may be an American pathogen, syphilis, raced around the world all the way to Canton China.

THE WAY OF THE GAUCHO AND THE COWBOY

The Spanish brought horses to America in 1493 on Columbus's second voyage; cattle followed. The Spanish came as conquerors, and the horse greatly assisted the conquest. Horses terrified the Indians; they had never before seen any large, four-legged animals, with the exception of the llama and alpaca. It was also the case that Andalusia was the one place in Europe that practiced large-scale horse and cattle rearing. *Caballero* (one who rides a horse) is the Spanish word for gentleman. *Vaquero* is the word for cattle drover. The two words came together on the great *pampas*, or grasslands, of South America (today's Argentina and Uruguay), perfect places for continuing and expanding the Andalusian tradition. The term *gaucho* was given to the cowboys of the South American *pampas*.

Leather was the plastic and rubber of the fifteenth, sixteenth, and seventeenth centuries. It was used for shoes, hats, belts, saddles, reins, carriage springs, door hinges, and body armor. There was a ready market for South American hides, and in 1510 the first shipload of 100,000 hides left South America for Spain. The *vaquero* rode the grasslands, and the vocabulary of his subculture embedded itself in New World Spanish: *lasso, corral, chaps, sombrero, pistolero*, and *hombre*. As the cattle-ranching culture moved northward into what became the United States, *vaquero* became cowboy, and Spanish vocabulary entered the American English language. More significant, the cowboy became America's mythic symbol: the solitary rider on the plains, slow to anger, deadly when aroused, a straight shooter, defender of the weak, a man of honor, and a man of justice. The cowboy became America's cultural icon long before Hollywood discovered him and put him on the screen, but once there, he traveled the world—as an American

---

[8] See Henry Hobhouse, *Seeds of Change: Six Plants That Transformed Mankind* (Berkeley: Counterpoint Press, 2005).

can discover in remote China and Borneo, where boys rush him in pantomime challenges to a quick-draw shootout!

Figure 2.5. Gaucho (OSU Special Collections & Archives)

By 1600, horses had made their way north beyond the Rio Grande. Plains Indians took to the horse gracefully and with alacrity. Warfare on the plains was revolutionized by the horse; raids and cavalry charges became the new style of war. The buffalo hunt also changed—less exhausting and less dangerous for the hunter who no longer had to creep on foot with bow, arrow, and spear to kill his prey. Indians quickly became dependent on their horses, so much so that they came to believe that the horse had always been with them. "The Great Father in the sky gave us the horse" was a common refrain of the day.

AFTER 1492, WHAT NEXT DID COLUMBUS DO?

Columbus's great achievement is his voyage of discovery. He made three more voyages to the New World, but after 1492 his career and reputation went on a downward slide. He claimed to have been only a few leagues from the Asian mainland, but he never sailed west to make good his claim. Instead, he kept threading through Caribbean waters. As to why he did this, a few explanations suggest themselves. As a God-driven explorer, perhaps Columbus had received a divine message as to his routes. Perhaps he knew in his heart that he had arrived in new lands but was too proud (or frightened) to admit it. Or perhaps he shared a not-uncommon belief that gold was to be found in hot climates. The Portuguese had found gold in Africa.

Through no fault of Columbus, the Santa Maria ran aground Christmas Day, 1492, and split at the seams. Columbus took the ship's loss as a divine sign that he was to colonize the island of Hispaniola. So he put his mistress's cousin in charge of the shipwrecked crew, and he sailed for Spain.

Homeward bound, with parrots and captive Indians, Columbus composed a letter to his sovereigns that would soon set Europe's imagination racing. As the ultimate sign of grace and favor, the Admiral of the Ocean Sea was permitted to kiss his sovereigns' hands and to sit in their presence. A second, triumphal expedition was mounted in 1493: seventeen ships, 1,500 men, and numerous horses set out to colonize and conquer the new possessions. But trouble had come to paradise. There was no sign of the crew left behind in 1492 or of the wealth of the Indies. In desperation, the Admiral threatened to lash any seamen and to cut out the tongues of any boys who denied that they were now in Cathay. Contrary to expectations and promises to his sovereigns, only chili peppers could be paraded as tantamount to the spices of the Indies. Only the Indians' gold ornaments could be brought to Spain. Spanish overlords began to brutalize and kill the Indians. To fulfill the promise of riches, Columbus committed what some historians call the first sin of the New World. He put Indians in chains and carried them as slaves to Spain. But Queen Isabella was offended and set them free.

Columbus captained a third voyage in 1498 with six ships, but when reports of mismanaged New World colonies reached Spain (Columbus was an excellent navigator but a miserable manager of men), the third voyage was cut short when a court-appointed overlord arrived to put Columbus in shackles and send him back to Spain. With the demeanor of a martyr, the Admiral appeared at court still wearing his bonds. And a pitying Queen set him free.

Columbus was permitted a fourth voyage in 1502. Despite the promises of the Capitulation of 1492, he went not to govern but only to explore. With his gift of self-importance and belief that he was divinely inspired, Columbus called this his High Voyage. He journeyed to the Orinoco and, perhaps as a measure of his piety or perhaps as a sign of his mental deterioration, he claimed to have seen Eden, with Adam and Eve disporting in that wondrous garden. He was shipwrecked on Jamaica, and when news of his plight reached the governor of Hispaniola, no attempt at rescue was made for seven months.

Columbus died in Vallodolid, Spain in 1506, ill and knowing that he had been ill-used, never conceding the failure of his mission to reach the Indies. In 1520 Hernan Cortes (Cortez) landed on the American mainland, and at long last the gold and silver that Columbus had promised began pouring into Spain, making it rich beyond the dreams of avarice. For every *mirvadi* (a copper coin) invested in the voyage of 1492, Spain received 200 million percent in return.

WHY DOES THE U. S. LEAD THE WORLD IN ITS REVERENCE FOR COLUMBUS?

When the American War for Independence ended, the new nation yearned for non-English heroes. Christopher Columbus was an obvious choice, an English language approximation of the name that Cristoforo Colon had chosen for himself (Christ Bearer to the Colonies). In 1781 King's College changed its name to Columbia (the feminine form of Columbus). In 1791 the American Congress agreed on a location for the country's new capital and named it after two heroes, Washington and the District of Columbia. In 1792 the Boston sloop Columbia, rounding South America, entered a river at the Washington-Oregon border. That river was named in honor of the sloop. In 1803 President Jefferson commissioned a Corps of Discovery led by Lewis and Clark to explore the newly acquired Louisiana Territory. Fittingly, their westward journey ended at the Columbia River.

Memorializing Columbus in Latin America began after the Spanish colonies won their freedom, the decade that began in 1811. Colombia, the country, and Cristobal, at the Atlantic side of the Panama Canal, honor Columbus, as do seven Colons. In the United States, commemorating Christopher Columbus began almost at the beginning of the republic and has never stopped. The first recorded celebration of October 12 occurred in 1792, and it became a national holiday in 1892. In 1888 American Roman Catholics, barred by Church decree from joining Masonic orders, created their own equivalent to Freemasonry, the Knights of Columbus. Columbus is memorialized by place name as well. In the United States the names Columbus, Columbia, Columbiana, and Colon are listed thirty-nine times in *Rand McNally's Atlas of World Geography*. And when the United States entered the space age, what better name to bestow on the first shuttle to orbit the earth than The Columbia?

3. On the World's Seas and Oceans

While the lands of this great planet yield much joy and learning, the earth's oceans and seas also offer fertile exploration for the wise traveler. Ancient countries that wished to be thought of as regional or global powers sought to develop a sea presence, both in terms of a military navy and commercial vessels. And while the heartland of Europe enticed early explorers, it was really lands across the seas that beckoned the bravest of adventurous souls. By the time of the nation-state international system, which began around 1500, pursuit of sea power was still a novel idea.

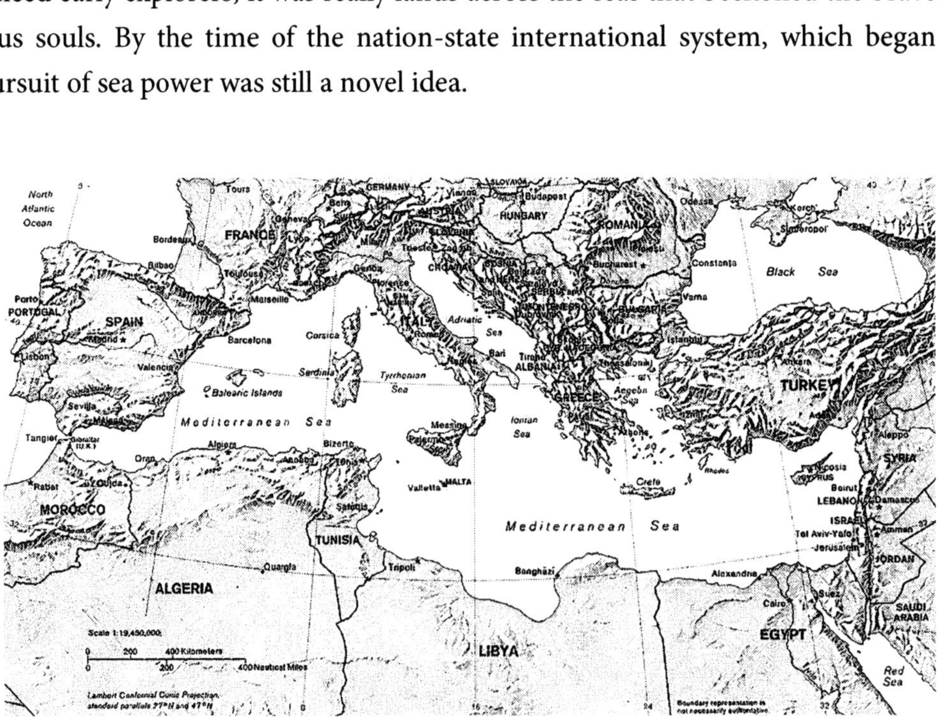

Figure 3.1. Mediterranean Sea

Near the end of the nineteenth century, Alfred Mahan, American historian and naval officer, presented the case for sea power in his *The Influence of Sea Power Upon History, 1600-1783*. The radical idea of controlling the seas was advanced as an essential foreign policy goal of any country that wished to be taken seriously. Today, as the world has seen exploration everywhere and events in its farthest corners have major impacts on the other side of the planet, wise travelers understand the lure of the seas.

In this chapter we explore two bodies of water: the Mediterranean Sea and the Pacific Ocean.

THE MEDITERRANEAN SEA

> All our religion, almost all of our law, almost all our arts, almost all that sets us above savages has come to us from the shores of the Mediterranean.
> — Samuel Johnson[1]

From the earliest times, first in Europe and then in the New World, the Mediterranean has been a traveler's magnet, attracting those who seek the sources of western civilization. Compared to the Atlantic Ocean, the Mediterranean is a small place. Its designation as a sea marks its size. While the Atlantic encompasses 31.8 million square miles, the Mediterranean is less than a million square miles (965,000 square miles). The Med (to use its familiar name) runs about 2,400 miles from west to east. It is 1,000 miles at its widest point and narrows to a mere nine miles at its western end, the Strait of Gibraltar. At its eastern end, it narrows into the Bosphorus Strait in Turkey, and from there it widens into the Black Sea, bringing the commerce of Europe into northern Turkey and southern Russia.

Waters of the Mediterranean Sea wash ashore on three continents: Europe, Africa, and Asia, offering sea-borne commerce to twenty-one countries, plus the two island countries of Cyprus and Malta. Six more large islands and about 3,500 smaller ones dot the Med. Each of the Med's countries has its own culture, history, and language, and almost all give the Mediterranean Sea its own language-derived name. Early Arab cartographers called it the Inner Sea. Ancient Egyptians called it the Great Green Sea. And Homer's Greeks called it the wine-dark sea. As an expression of imperial ambition, the Romans called it Our Sea. By the seventh centu-

[1] James Boswell, *The Life of Samuel Johnson* (New York: Everyman's Library, 1993), 35.

ry, *mare Mediterranean* (late Latin), a wonderfully expressive term, had come into common use: The Middle Earth Sea.

The Middle Earth Sea is especially suited to Mediterranean man's earliest attempts at maritime commerce and exploration. Tides are small. There are rough winds in winter, but summer sailing is smooth. More important, thousands of beaches dot the sea, excellent for dragging a small ship ashore at night or in a storm. And landmarks abound, many of them visible for a hundred miles or more, excellent for those who navigated only from memory.

The countries of the Med range from prosperous (France, Monaco, Italy) to poverty-stricken (Morocco, Albania, Tunis), from democratic (Spain, Israel) to dictatorial (until recently, Libya), and from Roman Catholic (Malta, Croatia) to Orthodox (Serbia /Montenegro) to Muslim (Turkey, Algeria, Tunisia, Albania), and from those who have known peace for more than a half-century to those either currently ravaged by war or balanced on its knife's edge (Algeria, Lebanon, the former Yugoslavia).

The Sea in the Middle of the Earth is the place (Spain, France) where our Cro-Magnon ancestors refined their civilization, living in caves and hunting with flint-chipped arrowheads. Perhaps as early as 35,000 years ago, they celebrated their hunt or perhaps worshipped their animal gods with pictures drawn on the walls of deeply recessed caves. On the southern coast of the Mediterranean Sea, as early as 5000 BCE, the Egyptians farmed, lived their lives around the flooding of the Nile, and believed in an afterworld presided over by gods. By 3000 BCE, they were building great temples and developing an extensive repertoire of medicines. By 2500 BCE, they performed life-saving surgery, made beer, wove linen cloth, invented paper, and wrote on it, leaving extensive records of their history and accomplishments.

MEDITERRANEAN GIFTS

Mediterranean people gave us lasting gifts. High (some would say first) on the list of gifts are monotheism and western civilization's moral compass. Sometime around 1250 BCE Moses led his people out of Egypt's slavery. As he wandered in search of a Promised Land, he received the revelation of monotheism and, at the same time, the gift of a universal moral code governing the behavior of men and women for all times and all circumstances. Then, some 1,200 years later, we have another divine revelation and an expanded moral code from Jesus and His Sermon on the Mount. Centuries rolled on, and in a cave in Mecca (culturally part of the Mediterranean world) in 610 BCE, Mohammed hears the command of the Angel Gabriel summoning him to the worship of Islam's one true God and demanding strict obedience to His demands.

A second great gift of the Mediterranean is a writing system based on the sound of words. Other cultures used writing systems, but most used symbols, one or two for each word or concept. These were and are cumbersome and difficult to master. China uses idea-graphs (ideographs): to read a newspaper requires mastery of 5,000 ideographs, and to read a book requires 50,000. The most important texts of ancient China contain nearly a half-million ideographs. In contrast, the English phonetic alphabet uses only twenty-six letters and sounds. The majority of the world's alphabets use between twenty and thirty symbols based on the number of sounds in each language. Significantly, mastery of a phonetic alphabet opens reading and writing to almost everyone. It democratizes learning and permits almost every person to take part in the printed world of thoughts and ideas.

Wind- and oar-driven ships that traveled long distances over water are another Mediterranean gift. At night or in storms, boats could be drawn up on a nearby shore for safety. As sailing skills and ships improved, open-water sailing became more common. As early as 2000 BCE the Phoenicians, from today's Lebanon, traded on the Mediterranean and later ventured into the Atlantic to Cornwall for tin, an essential ingredient of bronze. The cities they founded, notably Carthage, not only gave safe harbor for their ships; they also helped bind the entire Inner Sea into a single trading area.

Not least important, the Mediterranean gave humankind a secular moral compass. The ancient Greeks were first to ask the great questions of lives lived among one's fellows: Why be good? What is honor? What is truth? What is justice? What is the best form of government? Is it permissible for political leaders to lie?

The roster of gifts from the Mediterranean Sea scrolls on. The Greeks gave us the first epic, the first comedy, and the first tragedy. They invented the arithmetic that makes democracy possible (50 percent plus one equal majority rule). They also gave the world two ways of reasoning that are still the foundations of humankind's analytic thinking: deduction and induction. In deduction, analysis moves from a general idea to a specific conclusion. Thus, if all swans are white, if I see a swan, it is reasonable to conclude (expect) that it, too, will be white. In induction, analysis moves from a specific to a general assertion. If one swan is white, then all swans must be white. Moreover, our very word philosophy comes from the Greek: *philo* (love) and *sophia* (learning). The Romans invented the arch, which makes it possible to span great interior space, and they also invented the dome. They laid walls flat on the ground, building roads that spanned continents.

When Greek and Roman civilization collapsed under the onslaught of invaders from north and east, the Church of Rome and the Church of Constantinople kept learning alive in their monasteries. With the spread of Christianity, maps of the then-known world gave visual meaning to the Sea in the Middle of the Earth. Jerusalem was the place from which all distances were measured, the place around which all geography configured. When Constantinople fell to conquerors from the east in 1453, scholars fleeing the city's Turkish invaders gathered in the city-states of Italy to assist the birth of the Renaissance. When Muslims overran the Near East and closed the Holy Land to Christian pilgrims, Islam's religious curtain set in motion the Crusades. And as the Crusades ended some 200 years after the first Christian invasion of Jerusalem (1099), another chain of events was set in motion: the search for the luxury goods that Muslim sailors carried from the Far East. That search–in 1492 brought Columbus to the New World. Mapmakers no longer regarded Jerusalem as the center of the world. And another era in human history had begun.

The gifts of the Mediterranean continue to affect our lives; they are gifts that continue to astound us.

PACIFIC OVERTURES

> The power that rules the Pacific…rules the world.
> — Senator Albert J. Beveridge, Speech Before Congress, 1900

Of the three great oceans, the Pacific is the largest. It dwarfs the Atlantic Ocean by more than a factor of two. The Atlantic is less than thirty-two million square miles. The Pacific is about seventy million square miles, compared to about twenty-eight million square miles for the Indian Ocean. Surprisingly for its size, the Pacific was the last to be discovered by Europeans.

The discovery was stirred by the same impulses that sent Columbus to the New World: quest for adventure, fame, and riches. Columbus argued that he could reach the Indies, as the Far East was called, by sailing west across the Atlantic. His purpose? To convert the Indies to Christianity. And to find the spices that Europe craved.

During the two centuries of the Crusades, the knightly classes of Europe had delighted in the spices of the Indies. Brought by Muslim traders from mysterious ports, spices commanded exorbitant prices, bestowing extraordinary wealth on those who purveyed them.

Why spices? As stated above, for medicine and flavor. Cinnamon reduced fever. Clove alleviated stomachache and toothache. Cardamom enhanced flavor; nutmeg was thought to ward off the plague. And pepper made bad-smelling meat palatable. Before the 1600s, Europe north of the Alps had no winter fodder. Eighty percent of livestock had to be slaughtered. Salt could preserve the meat, but the stench was strong. Pepper, queen of spices, disguised the odor and enhanced the flavor. Pepper was so valuable that it could be sold for its equivalent weight in gold. Travelers often carried a pouch of peppercorns as portable wealth.

Figure 3.2. Pacific Ocean by Abraham Ortelius, 1589

PEPPER PROPELS THE PORTUGUESE

Tiny Portugal, perched on the Atlantic edge of Europe, led the quest to find a sea route to the Indies. League by league, its ships moved south along the western coast of Africa, returning wealth to Portugal: ivory, gold, and slaves. In 1488 Bartolomeu Dias rounded the Cape of Good Hope; ten years later Vasco da Gamma reached the pepper groves of India. By 1520, the Portuguese had sailed to the Spice Islands, the Moluccas, in today's Indonesia. Pepper from India and spices from the Moluccas now made Portugal exceedingly rich. To crown their success, and not a little influenced by their wealth, Pope Alexander VI awarded Portugal the right to convert (and control) heathen people living to the east of the Portuguese-controlled Azores Islands.

Between Bartolomeu and Vasco, in 1492 Columbus claimed the Caribbean Sea, all islands in it, and all lands surrounding it on behalf of Ferdinand and Isabella, rulers of Aragon and

Castile. To quash the likelihood of competing claims and jurisdictions, the Pope negotiated a pact between the Iberians, the Treaty of Tordesillas (1494). The Pope drew an imaginary line on the globe, from pole to pole. All non-Christian lands 370 leagues west of the Cape Verde Islands belonged to Spain. All non-Christian lands east of the islands fell to Portuguese control.

BALBOA LOOKS WEST

> Then I felt like some watcher of the skies,
> When a new planet swims into his ken;
> Or like stout Cortez when with eagle eyes
> He star'd at the Pacific—and all his men
> Looked at each other with a wild surmise—
> Silent on a peak in Darien
> — John Keats, "On First Looking into Chapman's Homer," (sonnet, 1816)

Vasco de Balboa (mistakenly referred to as Cortez by Keats) was the first European to see the Pacific Ocean. He was in the Isthmus of Panama, on the run from creditors in Hispaniola. In Panama he married a daughter of the local chief, Comaco, who showered Balboa with gold. Generous Balboa shared his wedding gift with other Spaniards living, or really hiding out, in Panama; quarrels erupted as gold was begged, borrowed, and stolen. The chief's son chided the Spanish, telling them that to the west on the shores of a great sea, gold lay thick on the ground.

The Spanish were in a believing frame of mind. They had grown up reading and listening to stories of Amadis de Gaula, a medieval knight who overcomes every challenge, battles terrible beasts, rescues beautiful maidens, and is showered with honors. To the Spanish, the New World *was* Amadis brought to life.

So, 190 men volunteered to go with Balboa to find a Great South Sea. They were attacked by hostile tribes, bitten by poisonous snakes, and confronted by an impenetrable jungle. It took them twenty-five days to cross the Isthmus and four days to climb down the mountain to the water's edge. In full armor, Balboa claimed the sea in the name of the Spanish crown. But there was no gold on the shore, only sand.

Disheartened, the men fought their way back. Only sixty lived to tell of their adventures. While they were away, a governor sent from Hispaniola took charge of their settlement and demanded their gold. And when they remonstrated that none had been found, he ordered Balboa to be put to death! The Pacific had claimed the first of many lives.

Figure 3.3. Vasco de Balboa

ENTER MAGELLAN

Spain had not yet overrun the mainland of South America. The silver of Mexico, the gold of Peru, had not yet been stolen. Spanish monarchs angrily envied their Portuguese neighbors. In 1517, Fernando de Magallanes, a Portuguese nobleman, offered his sword to the king of Spain. Ferdinand Magellan, as he is called in English, proposed to make Spain rich by sailing west across Balboa's sea to an as-yet-undiscovered spice island, thus avoiding the Treaty of Tordesillas. So, in 1519 Magellan sailed from Spain in command of five ships, bound for the glory of spices.

He sailed across the Atlantic to Rio de Janeiro and turned south to find a supposed passage into the Great South Sea. South of Rio, the weather turned increasingly cold. On October 21, 1521, he came to a deep bay-like opening and concluded from its salinity that it was not a river emptying into the sea. It was the strait that now bears his name. The Strait of Magellan runs 334 miles east to west, never more than fifteen miles wide and narrowing to a mere two miles. Fierce winds and strong currents make it treacherous sailing even today. It was a sailor's nightmare. It took thirty-eight days for the passage. Says Daniel Boorstin, "Only Magellan's iron courage and deft mastery of men kept him going."[2]

Emerging at last into the Great South Sea, Magellan gives a prayer of thanks: "We are about to stand in an ocean where no ship has ever sailed before. May the ocean be as calm and benevolent as it is today. In this hope I name it Mar Pacifico."[3] One ship had deserted, while another had been wrecked. With a rapidly diminishing food supply, the small flotilla sailed west into the unknown Pacific. As Antonio Pigafetta, Magellan's devoted follower, writes,

> We were three months and twenty days without getting any kind of fresh food. We ate biscuit which stank strongly of the urine of rats.... We drank yellow water that had been putrid for days. We also ate some of the ox hides that covered the top of the mainyard.... The gums of both the lower and upper teeth swelled, so that they could not eat.... Nineteen died.[4]

Ninety-eight days into that terrible crossing, they landed in Guam. Refreshed by food and water, they continued westward and landed at last in the Philippines. Here, Magellan entered into pacts of friendship with local rulers and converted Filipinos to Christianity. He now felt himself under divine protection and grew careless of his safety. He went into battle with too few men against an enemy of a friendly ruler and was killed.

Disheartened and frightened, his men set sail under the command of Juan Sebastian del Cano. One of the ships was boarded by the Portuguese, and its crew was hanged for piracy. According to the terms of Tordesillas, they had entered Portuguese territory. The last remaining ship sailed west across the Indian Ocean, rounded the Cape of Good Hope, and arrived back in Spain in September 1522. Nineteen men of the original 265 had circumnavigated the world on a voyage of 4,200 miles.

The voyage gave hard evidence that the world is indeed round and, in doing so, introduced to Europe a questioning view of faith-based geography. The Bible says nothing about a vast body of water somewhere to the east. Was it possible that Jerusalem was not the center of the world? How was it possible that, by sailing west, one day of the week should disappear, and the faithful indulge themselves with meat on Friday? Such doubts helped the Middle Ages give way to the Renaissance. That, says a present-day admirer, is the ultimate significance of Magel-

---

[2] Daniel Boorstin, *The Discoverers* (New York: Random House, 1983), 263.

[3] Ian Cameron, *Magellan and the First Circumnavigation of the World* (New York: Saturday Review Press, 1973), 143.

[4] Daniel Boorstin, *The Discoverers*, 265.

lan's journey. And it is fitting that the Magellanic Clouds, companions of the Milky Way, should be named after Magellan. "Like them, his memory shines down on the world his voyage opened, illuminating it from infinity to eternity."[5]

Figure 3.4. Ferdinand Magellan
(1810 Engaving, Library of Congress)

DRAKE'S PASSAGE

"In 1577, an English sailor, Francis Drake, would do what no other privateer had ever attempted: he would lead an expedition through the Straits of Magellan and fall upon the unguarded and unsuspecting Spanish settlements."[6]

Loaded with Spanish loot, he sailed his ship, the Golden Hind, homeward from what is now San Francisco to Plymouth Harbor. The expedition took three years and netted its investors a 4,700 percent profit. Queen Elizabeth, a major investor in the voyage, used her share of the profits to bolster the royal treasury. She also funded and chartered the Levant Company, which in 1600 became the East India Company. Drake's voyage thus helped to underwrite the origins of Britain's Far East Empire. Drake was the first commander to complete a journey

---

[5] William Manchester, *A World Lit Only By Fire: The Medieval Mind and the Renaissance: Portrait of an Age* (Boston: Little, Brown, 1992), 290.

[6] Derek Wilson, *The Circumnavigators* (London: Constable, 1989), 38.

around the world. And his success drew in its wake a string of other captains eager for the Pacific's gold and glory. As they pursued their dreams, they discovered many if not most of the ocean's 70,000 islands and filled in the Pacific's map.

Figure 3.5. Sir Francis Drake (Library of Congress)

JAMES COOK

The greatest of the Pacific's explorers is James Cook (1728-79). An officer in the Royal Navy, Cook commanded three long Pacific voyages of scientific discovery.

Cook solved, almost single-handed, most of the remaining mysteries of the world's largest expanse of water; he added new islands and landmasses to the charts; he familiarized himself with the wind and current patterns of previously untraveled oceans; and he kept his ship free of scurvy and fever throughout months at sea.[7]

Cook began the navy's practice of carrying scientists aboard their ships to measure, catalog, and draw the marvels of newfound lands. On his first voyage, from 1768-71, he circum-

[7] Ibid., 171.

navigated Tahiti and discovered and charted (made maps of) New Zealand. He charted the east coast of Australia and nearly lost his ship on the rocks of the Great Barrier Reef. As the ship began to sink, "Cook reacted swiftly and with characteristic coolness."[8] Temporary repairs to the hull were accomplished at sea, and the ship (The Endeavor) was run up on land and turned on its side for complete repairs. From the top of a hill, Cook charted a likely passage through the coral labyrinth and brought the Endeavor safely home.[9]

Figure 3.6. Engraving of James Cook by Nathaniel Dance[10]

[8] Richard Hough, *Captain James Cook* (W.W. Norton, 1995), 147.

[9] See also William Gray, *Voyages to Paradise: Exploring in the Wake of Captain Cook* (Washington, D.C.: National Geographic Society, 1981) and Grenfell Price, ed., *The Explorations of Captain James Cook in the Pacific: As Told by Selections of His Own Journals* (New York: Dover, 1971), Entry for June 1770.

[10] William Holl, Engraver, Collection: National Portrait Gallery, Canberra, Australia.

His second voyage began in July 1772 and ended in 1775 as a triumph of far-flung discoveries. He circled Antarctica and visited Tahiti, Easter Island, the Melanesian Islands, and the Tonga islands. His third and last voyage (1776) also covered immense distances: from England to Capetown to Tasmania, then to New Zealand, Tahiti, Tonga, Christmas Island, north to Alaska, and west again for his discovery of the Hawaiian Islands. Here, a dispute with the natives over stolen property ended with his death in battle. His obituary in the *London Gazette* lamented the death of so "intrepid, so able, and so intelligent a Sea-Officer." After Cook, lamented another obituary, there would be nothing to discover in the vast Pacific. A present-day sailor, Tony Horwitz, who traveled across the Pacific seeking to follow the routes of Cook's three voyages, pays him an insightful tribute:

> If there was an overriding message in his journals it was that people, the world over, were alike in their essential nature—even if they ate their enemies, made love in public, worshiped idols, or like the Aborigines, cared not for material goods. No matter how strange another society might at first appear, there were almost always grounds for mutual understanding and respect. This was a radical notion in eighteenth-century Europe.[11]

And still another tribute to Cook is Australia. Its first settlers arrived in 1788, following Cook's discovery of the splendid harbor in modern-day Sydney.[12]

---

[11] Tony Horwitz, *Blue Latitudes: Boldly Going Where Captain Cook Has Gone Before* (New York: Henry Holt, 2002), 430.

[12] For more about Cook, see Nicholas Thomas, *The Extraordinary Voyages of Captain Cook* (New York: Walker & Company, 2003) and Peter Aughton, *The Fatal Voyage: Captain Cook's Last Great Journey* (Northampton MA: Interlink Publishing, 2005).

4. Politics and Economics: Two Looking Glasses

Few travelers pay more than passing attention to the formal institutions of government in their host country. They have come to see people and places. But travelers are also concerned with human rights and the quality of life in places they visit. Deformed beggars and families living on the street not only distress the traveler; they are also an instant index of a country's quality of life. In visiting and sightseeing, travelers pay attention to personal safety and to the civility and efficiency of public officials. People most frequently ask if there are hassles at customs or long lines at immigration and whether it is safe to walk the streets. These, too, are quality-of-life indexes. So, too, are cues and clues of freedom and democracy. Dictatorships become visible in ways that complicate the traveler's life. Identity checks can be frequent and frightening. The police may impose on-the-spot fines as thinly disguised shakedowns for violating obscure ordinances. The secret police may keep travelers under surveillance. It can be dangerous for the locals to speak to travelers too freely or for too long. Terrorists and others looking to do harm to foreigners may roam too freely.

In the former Soviet Union, citizens lived under the shadow of a fearful truth: the secret police kept a file on everybody. If the file got too big, the police did not add new pages to it. They just put the file away and did the same to the person. For several years, in Yangon (old name, Rangoon) and in Burma (now Myanmar), there were billboards warning the locals to be careful of visitors who may try to rob them of their freedom. In English, these were stern warnings, not about the reality of strangers' plots but about the dangers of expressing discontent.

Even today, taxi drivers are reluctant to take travelers to see the house where Sui Kyu, a Nobel laureate and the legitimately elected leader of the government in 1990, was kept by the country's military under house arrest off and on from 1990 until November 2010.

Travelers quickly sense the differences between free and unfree people. Before the Berlin Wall came down, travelers instantly knew they had crossed from democratic West Berlin to the dictatorship of East Germany. The streets in West Berlin were noisy and crowded. The streets in East Germany were quiet, pedestrians were few, and the few who were on the street avoided being part of a group. Other unfree societies have their own versions of street-side repression.

Travelers from democratic societies know that freedom is essential to democracy. And they also know that both are in short supply worldwide. Democracy House, a private American foundation, lists countries of the world in three categories, using criteria laid out in the United Nations' *Declaration of Human Rights* (1948): free, part free, or not free. As of 2010 Freedom House gave the palm of free to eighty-seven governments (45 percent of the total), the designation part-free to sixty others (31 percent of the total), and not free to forty-seven countries (24 percent of the total). But several of those designated as free had one or more qualifications ("demerits") attached to that label, such as capital punishment, execution of juveniles, or restrictions on a free press. In many Muslim countries, part-free governments impose restrictions on women's freedom with respect to work, public appearance, and the use of automobiles.

What qualifies a country and its government as democratic? Most agree that open and honest elections in which voters freely choose their leaders is the minimum requirement. Government officials chosen by majority rule are the second requirement, but provision is also made for rule by a significant plurality. To qualify as a democracy, elections must take place in regular sequence. "Majorities in flux" is the desired goal so that a majority, once formed, may not hold office forever. And to keep majorities in motion and transition, citizens must have the freedom to orally express and publish their opinions and to meet with others in an attempt to persuade them of a desired course of action. Majorities may rule, but the most successful democracy is one in which the majority will occasionally give way to a minority that expresses intense concern over an issue. And when a democratic society is split among several groups that burn with an intense passion over the great issues of the day, that society trembles on the abyss of civil strife. Freedom House suggests that in 2010 there were 115 countries that were electoral democracies.

Like most aspects of life, democracy is not an all-or-nothing state of affairs. It has many variations and degrees of perfection. The Preamble to the American Constitution speaks of justice and liberty, but the Constitution also acknowledges the existence of slaves and slavery. Countries with a written Constitution sometimes place rights and freedoms in their Constitution, like the first Ten Amendments to the American Constitution and the Charter of Freedoms and Responsibilities in the Canadian Constitution. Democratic governments also require freedom from government coercion that can close down freedom of electoral choice. These include things like protection from arbitrary imprisonment, the right not to incriminate oneself through trickery or torture, and the right to a fair and open trial. The list of democracy's rights and freedoms usually includes the right to worship (or not) as you choose. Also important is geographic freedom (the right to live and work where you wish); and freedom to choose one's vocation, to marry whom you choose, and to acquire the education that will further your life's goals. The American Declaration of Independence bundles these rights and freedoms in a succinct phrase: "the pursuit of happiness."

DEMOCRACY'S IMPERFECTIONS

> Many forms of government have been tried, and will be tried in this world of sin and woe. No one pretends that democracy is perfect or all wise. Indeed it has been said that democracy is the worst form of Government except for all the other forms that have been tried.
>
> — Winston Churchill, *Speech before House of Commons*, November 1947

Democracy's imperfections are many and, for many, troubling. Democracy depends on majority rule, but there is no assurance that the majority will be wise. Nor is there any assurance that the majority always understands the consequences of the policy it demands. Majorities are also tempted to abuse their authority. When Alexis de Tocqueville surveyed the new American democracy in the 1830s, he was greatly concerned about the "tyranny of the majority," that is, the willingness of the majority to shut down or refuse to listen to challenging opinions.

IDEOLOGIES

The Enlightenment philosopher Montesquieu famously remarked that what is orthodoxy on one side of a mountain may be heresy on the other side. As wise travelers become aware of the variety of values and beliefs around the world, they also become aware of the role that ideology plays in shaping a nation's culture and its dominant values.

Ideology is a word much used and much abused. A simple definition is this: a set of consistent ideas about ourselves, our society, other people and places, and how the world works. The word was coined by Count Destutt de Tracy in the eighteenth century to describe the way people looked at their world, what we might call their world view. Napoleon coined a derived word, ideologues, to heap scorn on those who opposed his policies. And Karl Marx extended the meaning of ideology to explain how economic and political elites impose their views of the world on the working class. Central to all these uses of ideology is an underlying set of ideas: in human affairs, what we see and what we understand is affected by our values, those ideas we hold dear. Most of us remember the cautionary counsel of friends and parents: "Seeing is believing." But the proverb stands cognitive theory on its head (*cognos* is the Greek word meaning to see, hear, and remember). Our values act to *screen* our experiences: we see what we wish to see, what we wish to believe. Our values come partly from our culture, our habits of the heart, and from family and friends.

IDEOLOGY AT WORK

> The test of a first rate intelligence is the ability to hold two opposed ideas in the mind at the same time, and still retain the ability to function.
> — F. Scott Fitzgerald, "The Crackup," *Esquire Magazine*, February, 1936

Fitzgerald's often-quoted remark speaks to the fact that most of us see the world through more than one ideology. *Wikipedia*, the Internet encyclopedia, lists several sets of ideologies in everyday use, such as ideologies emphasizing ethnicity or nationality (including fascism, racism, Black nationalism); class struggle (including Marxism, Stalinism, Maoism); the individual (including market liberalism, capitalism); the social system emphasizing collectivity (including socialism, Peronism); territory (including nationalism); religion (including Christian, Jewish, Hindu, Islam, Zionism); conservatism (including neo-conservatism); others (including federalism, feminism, animal welfare, the natural environment). This list is far from complete, and few, if any of us, embrace all these ideologies. Most of us develop our personal ideologies according to the intensity of the values we hold. And most of us accord highest intensity to the values imparted by family, friends, and schools, an intensity second only to the dominant values of our culture. Of all the values we carry, three tend to claim a privileged place: religion, nationalism, and economics.

WISE TRAVELERS AND POLICY ISSUES

An important part of the wise traveler's education is to understand the policy issues and political choices of other countries. It is important to recognize that in non-democratic countries, effective political choices do not exist. The "president for life" may keep postponing promised elections. Police may break up political meetings and arrest those who attend. Thugs on government payroll may assault people going to vote. And policy issues tend to be cloudy and obtuse. Slogans, not issues, dominate public discourse. In democratic regimes, policy issues and policy choices tend to be transparent and accessible. That, after all, is what freedom of speech and press is all about. Is this issue important or trivial? And if so, why? For the wise traveler, the more important the issue and the more fully it is discussed, the wider the window it opens onto a country's central values.

DEBATE OVER THE WELFARE STATE

In the Cold War years (1945 to the late 1980s), confrontation between the Soviet Union and western democracies took center stage in policymaking. For the Soviet Union and its allies, an important goal was to export Soviet-style communism around the world. The United States and its allies were united by a mirror-image goal: to contain the Soviet Union. For both sets of protagonists, two matching questions were paramount: (1) how to expand our dominion without unleashing a nuclear war and (2) how to contain the other side's expansion.

Foreign policy aside, and especially since the Cold War ended, the major issue for democratic governments in Europe has been the welfare state. What role should government play in making people's lives better? Which services should be provided at taxpayers' expense? How much should the gap between rich and poor be closed? If we presume that the welfare state is to be expanded, which economic policies will best achieve full employment, low inflation, and economic growth? And can a government even continue to provide a comprehensive welfare state in light of global economic uncertainties and challenges?

In most of the world, these questions are part of socialism's legacy. In the United States, these questions are almost never (except pejoratively) identified with their socialist origins. As Americans, our dedication to the ideals of the free market, in spirit if not in practice, requires that we carefully avoid references to socialism. So, when first introduced, Social Security (government-run old-age pensions) was described as a form of social insurance. Even so, all such policy questions are set within a larger frame of reference: What do the rich owe the poor? What is meant by equality? Is it equality of opportunity or equality of outcome? In general, equality of opportunity is taken to mean that each person shall have an equal opportunity to acquire wealth and all that it can buy. The outcome will depend on such things as hard work, intelligence, native ability, and good luck. Equality of outcome is taken to mean that each person is entitled to some reasonable measure of those things that define a good life—some minimum income, medical services, housing, and education.

A related question turns on ideas about equity, generally taken to mean fairness. If, as President John F. Kennedy once said, "Life isn't fair," then what should government do to make life more fair? In the American context there are two general approaches to solving issues of equity: market equity and social equity.[1] Both terms connect ideas about equality.

Market equity generally means that government allows the market to provide fair shares. Each of us can have the quality of life that we can afford. For example, market equity usually determines what kind of housing we have and where we live, in the inner city, an elegant suburb, or somewhere in between. Social equity generally means that government has an obligation to give each of us some agreed-on share of life's goods and services. For example, in housing, social equity can be achieved through government-issued rent vouchers sufficient for settling the poor in the suburbs. If the devil is in the details, political argument turns on what is meant by fair share? Presume, for argument's sake, that we will not permit the poor to starve to death: what, then, shall be their minimum income? And what other assistance do we provide? Housing? Medical treatment? Unemployment benefits? A pension at the end of one's working life? And how much of each of these benefits?[2]

Other democracies frame their issues differently. Words like market equity and equality of opportunity are usually not part of their political debates. Issues are framed in words that acknowledge their socialist heritage, such as socializing risk and socializing cost, meaning to make the entire society responsible for assuming the cost of risks and benefits. An example from the insurance industry is helpful. In most countries, drivers pay different premiums for their insurance. The premium is based on such things as the driver's age, number of previous traffic violations, number of previous accidents, distance traveled daily, and age and make of the car. This is an actuarial form of insurance. In contrast, if all drivers paid the same premium, that would socialize the cost by dividing it equally among all those who participate. Those whose needs are greatest pay the same as those whose needs are minimal. This socializes needs and risk. It is also a form of transfer payment whereby the rich subsidize the poor. To use the example of medical insurance, those with chronic illness and those who are elderly pay the same premium as the healthy and young. That socializes the cost. And it, too, is a transfer payment.

---

[1] See Lawrence J. R. Herson, *The Politics of Ideas: Political Theory and American Public Policy* (Homewood IL: Dorsey Press, 1984).

[2] See Lawrence J. R. Herson, *The Urban Web: Politics, Policy, and Theory* (Chicago: Nelson Hall, 1990), especially pages 222-226.

All or nearly all taxpayers believe taxes are too high. When proposals are made to increase social-welfare programs, questions spew forth: Aren't we paying too much in taxes right now? Can we afford more generous benefits? For Europeans, answers are made even more difficult by related issues. First, in most of Europe (as in North America and Australia), thanks to the miracles of modern medicine and the success of medical assistance programs, the population is aging. And an aging population needs increased medical assistance. Second, Europe is faced with rising unemployment as a result of automation and jobs lost through international competition. In addition, European youth struggle against government policies that provide lifelong jobs for those already working. This means that employers are reluctant to hire entry-level workers, out of concern that they may stay on the payroll for the rest of their lives.

As a consequence, in Europe unemployment benefits command a significant share of government expenses. How, then, do you weigh the taxpayer's cost of unemployment insurance against the possibility that generous unemployment benefits may destroy the incentive to look for work? At this point in the debate, a moral minefield looms. Do we risk harming our society by creating a generation that would rather live on government benefits than work? How do we find a proper balance between incentives and disincentives, between compassion and indolence?

Each country answers social and economic questions within the context of its own history. Germans, for example, tend to be mindful of the devastating inflation and massive unemployment that followed World War I. They see how those social disasters prepared the way for Hitler and the Nazi Party. Many Swedes and Danes view their generous unemployment benefits as historic compensation for workers' suffering during the Great Depression of the 1930s. And for Swedes, their extensive maternity benefits are justified on many grounds, not least that of contributing to the full equality of women. Travelers willing to explore social-welfare issues get more than information. They also receive keys that unlock the door to a traveler's treasure: serious discussion about a country and its culture.

ECONOMICS MATTER

> (...We) look forward to a world founded on four essential freedoms.... The third is freedom from want.
>
> — Franklin Roosevelt, *Address to Congress*, 1941

> Money sets the world in motion.
>
> — Publilius Syrus (100 BC)

Economics is never just about money, any more than government is just about who rules. Politics and economics are two sides of the same coin (hence the term political economy). Most everywhere in the world, governments play a role in the way crops are grown and how goods are made and distributed. Governments play a role in deciding who is employed and under what conditions. Through public money spent on education, governments affect the skills the worker brings to his or her employment—whether neurosurgery or gardening. Governments affect the prices charged for goods and the cost of borrowing money to start a business or buy a house. Even those who demand that government stay out of economic affairs agree that government must make laws to protect private property, enforce private contracts, and provide a judicial system that enforces those laws.

Figure 4.1. From a 1911 Industrial Worker Publication

What is usually referred to as capitalism or marketplace economics is a political economy that gives buyers and sellers great freedom in economic transactions. But as the previous paragraph suggests, that freedom is never absolute. *Laissez-faire* ("let it be") was the dominant economic arrangement in Europe and North America in the nineteenth and early twentieth centuries. But it was also an economic system of "boom and bust"—a system of economic cycles in which prosperous times gave way to economic failure. And it was also a time when workplace conditions were harsh. On-the-job injuries were frequent, wages were determined by supply and demand, and no public benefits existed for the sick, the old, and the unemployed.

In the Great Depression of the 1930s, economic suffering was intense and worldwide. In the United States in 1932, nearly one out of four workers in the nation was jobless. In Pennsylvania, wages were five cents an hour in sawmills and six cents an hour in brick and tile factories. Describing Chicago during the Depression, Edmund Wilson writes, "There is not a garbage dump in Chicago which is not diligently haunted by the hungry. Last summer in the hot weather, when the smell was sickening, there were a hundred people a day coming to one of the dumps, falling on the heaps of refuse...digging in it with sticks and hands."[3]

In Europe and North America, the Great Depression brought voter demands for economic change. Laissez-faire gave way to "Capitalism with a Human Face," and the welfare state was born. In each country, welfare benefits are determined by national wealth and by an ideological balance between social equity and market equity. The balance is tipped, of course, in dictatorial regimes, such as in China, Venezuela, Cuba, and numerous sub-Saharan countries in Africa. What prevails in these places is the regime's own definition of social equity—giving outsized rewards to Party members and the dictator's faithful followers.

---

[3] Edmund Wilson, *The American Earthquake: A Chronicle of the Twenties and Thirties* (Garden City: Doubleday, 1958) 15ff.

ITALY: A WISE TRAVELER'S EARLY DESTINATION

5. From Etruscans and Romans to Modern Times

A man who has not been in Italy is always
conscious of inferiority.
— Samuel Johnson[1]

Do you know the land where the lemon trees bloom?
— Goethe[2]

Italy has a special gift for the wise traveler: journeys through time to the sites and sights of Rome of the Caesars, the Vatican of the Borgias, and Florence of the Medici, not to mention Venice and Urbino of the high Renaissance. Italy also instructs the wise traveler on how geography and religion shape habits of the heart.

ITALY'S GEOGRAPHY

The peninsula of Italy swings south from the Alps for about 700 miles. Consisting of eight distinct regions, including the islands of Sicily and Sardinia, it is covered by mountains and shaped like a high-heeled, eighteenth-century cavalry boot. It extends south from the Germanic Alps to the southern plains and into the Mediterranean, a short sail to Muslim Africa. Geography has given Italy its character and its history.

---

[1] Quoted in James Boswell's *The Life of Samuel Johnson.* (New York: Everyman's Library), 1993.

[2] J.W. von Goethe, *Wilhelm Meister's Apprenticeship*, from The Harvard Classics Shelf of Fiction, 1917.

Italy is the most perfect of peninsulas. The alpine barrier to the north is seamless. The plain of the Po (Valley) forms a rich natural larder. The long, craggy 'leg and toe' shelter a large number of fertile, impregnable valleys with ready access to the sea. Some of these Italian localities have been rich and extravert; one of them, Rome, gave rise to the largest empire of the ancient world. But after Rome's decline, they could so defend their independence that Italy was not united again for 2,000 years.[3]

Figure 5.1. Map of Italy

[3] Norman Davies, *Europe: A History* (Oxford: Oxford University Press, 1996), 61.

The glory that was the Roman Empire shone for half a millennium after the city's legendary founding in 753 BCE, from the imperial conquests around the time of Christ to the sack of Rome by Alaric's Goths in 410 CE. By the time of Charlemagne (800 CE), the fertile valleys of Italy had evolved into feudal kingdoms and city-states. The Catholic Church in Rome and the territory surrounding it (the Papal State) was Italy's most powerful unifying force spiritually, administratively, and militarily. During the Renaissance (1300-1600), Italy's fertile valleys were territories of forceful ducal families and their powerful city-states: the Medici in Florence, the Visconti and Szfora in Milan, the Montefeltro and della Rovere families in Urbino, and the Gonzaga in Mantua. Italy's patchwork of rival territorial states also included the Papal State centered in Rome and the region of the Veneto with Venice as its capital. These political territories fought for dominance and invited French, Spanish, and German rulers to invade Italy to assist in a centuries-long struggle to control the Italian peninsula. It was not until the middle of the nineteenth century that a revolutionary movement and military struggle united all of Italy's states and territories into a single nation-state. Unification began in Piedmont in 1859 and ended with the incorporation of Rome in 1870. The National Monument to Vittorio Emanuele II in the center of Rome celebrates the unification of Italy. Often called the Wedding Cake because it is built of white marble, the monument's size and appearance bestow its nickname. It took twenty-five years to complete.

Indeed, the peninsula's history in brick, stone, canvass, and bronze beckons and educates today's wise traveler. Monuments, churches, statues, sculptures, and ducal and papal art collections in Rome, Florence, and Venice are what wise travelers come to see. And they are joined in their journey by ghosts and memories of those who have walked the roads of Italy for 3,000 years—travelers, traders, soldiers, and pilgrims.

FROM SMALL BEGINNINGS

Italy's recorded history begins with the Etruscans, a people who flourished from about 700 to 100 BCE in today's Tuscany and Umbria. Their legends claimed immigration from somewhere in Asia, and although their written language remains un-deciphered, we know much about them from their statuary and from comments made by those who conquered them, the tribes who dwelled around what is now Rome.

With its seven hills, Rome commanded the strategic crossing points of the Tiber River. Its people spoke Latin, a language shared with nearby cities in the area of Latium. Legend gives Rome a warrior's heroic beginning. Two orphan boys, Romulus and Remus, sons of Mars, the god of war, and descendants of Prince Aeneas (son of the last king of Troy), climb from the waters of the Tiber and are suckled by a she-wolf. Near the spot where they climb ashore, they founded the city of Rome. The legendary date is April 21, 753 BCE, a holiday still celebrated in Italy.[4] Romulus lives to become king, having killed Remus for scorning him. The twins and the wolf are the symbols of Rome.

From small village beginnings, the city of Rome expanded outward, conquering first the entire Italian peninsula and then beyond to control an empire of two million square miles. Its most western provinces were Spain and Portugal. Its eastern provinces were Armenia on the Caspian Sea and Assyria in the Tigris-Euphrates valleys. Its most northern provinces were Britain and the Lowlands. And in the south was the northern shore of the Mediterranean, whose provinces included Egypt, Palestine, and Syria.

HABITS OF THE ROMAN HEART

> He who desires peace should prepare for war.
> — Vegetius

> No sooner said than done.
> — Quintus Ennius

> It is a rough road that leads to greatness.
> — Seneca

"All roads lead to Rome" was one of the empire's mottos. Rome's fighting forces, its legions, could march quickly along more than 50,000 miles of roads to the ends of the empire. They enforced Roman law, demanded civic order, and built smaller versions of mighty Rome. The genius of the Romans, their habits of the heart, was fourfold. They were brilliant military organizers and tacticians. They were also skillful governors and administrators. They created a social system based on clans and family that was cohesive and that engendered a fierce pride in all that Rome accomplished and stood for. And they were brilliant engineers who used concrete and brick to build beautiful and durable buildings.

The Romans contributed to building construction in three ways. They adopted and adapted the work of the Greeks, embellishing their city and empire with temples and other public buildings. They applied the technique of the arch in a wide range of structures. Finally,

---

[4] Romans now use the holiday to complain about the city's pollution, traffic, and the fact that these problems continue to get worse.

they used the four centuries of their empire in the west for vast programs of public works, with which the modern traditions of civil and military engineering might be said to begin.[5]

These habits of the heart created a republic that governed through consultative assemblies. The republic lasted half a millennium, from 500 BCE to 31 CE. And when the republic proved incapable of handling the wealth, the problems of empire, and the restlessness of Roman mobs, the republic gave way to ruthless emperors who gave the empire peace and public order and secured the loyalty of those who lived far from Rome, through an elaborate system of gifts and punishment. Local rulers were left in place, answerable to Rome's mandate to maintain order and contribute money or food to Rome. Roman soldiers were rewarded with land in the areas where they served. Marrying into the local population, their offspring were expected to be faithful to Rome and its habits of the heart. From their soldier-fathers, sons accepted the principal virtues of Roman civic life. And no matter how far distant, rebels and resisters were mercilessly annihilated.

"What sort of thing is Roman Law?" asked Cicero, an important public orator and writer. In principle, it could not be "bent by influence, or broken by power, or spoiled by money."[6] But principle and practice were often far apart. Emperors could be paranoid and evil, like Nero and Caligula. They could be bent by fawning, scheming courtiers. Very few were models of intellect and compassion, such as Marcus Aurelius who was not only an emperor, but also a philosopher and writer. And some ruled Rome and the larger empire with vision and firmness. Augustus, the first of Rome's emperors, could boast that "...he had beautified the city with magnificent buildings...encouraged religion by building temples and shrines; strengthened morality... by imposing strict laws; and established peace which endured through his long reign."[7]

ROMAN GODS

In ancient Roman religion, the "genius" (Latin: the begetter) was the ruling spirit that perpetuated a household or family. It came to mean the guardian spirit of a guild, a place or an individual, which a person might worship on his birthday. After Augustus, the "genius" of an em-

---

[5] T.K. Derry and Trevor Williams, *A Short History of Technology from the Earliest Times to A.D. 1900* (New York: Oxford University Press, 1993), 165.

[6] See Cicero, *The Orations of Marcus Tullius Cicero*, Translated by Charles Duke Yonge (London: H.G. Bohn, 1888).

[7] Moses Hadas, *Imperial Rome* (New York: Time, Inc., 1965), 58.

peror might be worshiped. The spirit of a woman or a goddess was known and worshiped as "Juno."[8]

As might be expected, Rome's religious beliefs and practices changed during the long years of the republic and the empire. Much mythology of ancient Greece was incorporated into Roman belief, and as the empire extended into the Near East, other gods and rituals made their way to Rome. But there is a fairly constant core to Rome's religious beliefs and practices. Today's wise traveler continues to confront them in statues and paintings.

Figure 5.2. Roman Testudo, Military of Ancient Rome

For the protection of the household, Romans continued to honor the gods who dominated the lives of their farmer ancestors. They gave deference to Vesta, the guardian spirit of the fire in the hearth. Lars was guardian of the household, and Janus (*janua*: door), whose two heads look in both directions, was guardian of the household door. Penates (gods of the Greeks) were renamed and given pride of place in the Roman pantheon (*pan*: all; *theos*: god). Thus, Jupiter (or Jove), the equivalent of the Greek Zeus, is the father god and god of the sky. Juno is the mother goddess, akin to the Greek Hera. Ceres is the earth goddess and goddess of fertility. Neptune presides over the seas. Mars is the god of war, while Venus is the goddess of love. Apollo is worshipped as the god of healing, prophecy, and generally as the god of manly beauty

[8] Daniel J. Boorstin, *The Creators* (New York: Random House, 1992), 407.

and light. Diana, the goddess of the moon, is patroness of women and guardian in childbirth. Bacchus is the god of wine, Vulcan is the god of fire, and Minerva is goddess of the arts.

The legions stationed in Egypt adopted gods of the Nile. Osiris is the god of the underworld, a father god who controls the forces of nature. Isis, his wife, symbolizes renewal and regeneration. And their son, Horus, ensures the continuity of generations. Legionnaires in the Near East often converted to the Persian sun god, Mithras, who brings light and goodness to a world that confronts the forces of darkness and evil. A soldiers' prayer venerates this god as "Mithras, God of the morning, our trumpets waken the Wall. Rome is above all nations, but Thou art over all."[9]

Those who worship many gods are usually tolerant of religious variety. That tolerance made Rome an inviting place for settlers from the fringes of the empire. But in the later days of the empire, Christians were the exception to Roman tolerance. Two factors lay behind Roman persecution of Christians. Roman society was organized around clans, family, and hereditary social class, while Christians professed the brotherhood and equality of those who accepted their Savior. More important, Christians insisted that they alone possessed the truth "and that all other religions...were false."[10] They refused, for instance, to observe the ritual acts connected with the emperor, such as burning incense before his statue, because such gestures were considered to be worshiping the emperor as a god.

The persecution of Christians flared intermittently for about 250 years, from the martyrdom of St. Paul in Rome in 68 CE until 313. At the battle of Milvian Bridge (still on the wise traveler's itinerary) in 312, Constantine (according to legend) saw a cross in the sky with these words: "In this sign conquer." Triumphant in battle, Constantine succeeded to the imperial throne, and in 313, the Edict of Milan gave Christians freedom of worship.

A ROMAN FEAST

For Rome's upper classes, feasting and gluttony marked social display and self-indulgence. In modern terms, it was an exercise in conspicuous consumption designed to enhance the social status of the host. The Emperor Augustus attempted to enforce laws prohibiting extravagant menus and buying rare delicacies for a feast, but to little avail.

Guests at a banquet included friends of the host, those who might help him climb the social ladder, and those well connected to the imperial court. Guests seated themselves on couch-

---

[9] Norman Davies, *Europe: A History*, 160.

[10] Moses Hadas, *Imperial Rome*, 128.

es, three to a couch, placed behind a table. They were entertained by jugglers, musicians, dancers, and acrobats. Guests were attended by slaves—some to serve food, others beverages, and still others to look after their comfort—perfuming their bodies, washing their feet, and attending to their sexual urges.

The more lavish the feast, the greater was its intended notoriety. Petronius Arbiter, in his *Satyricon* (first century CE) leaves us an account of one such banquet. Dishes included beef, testicles, kidneys, liver, sowbelly, lobster, geese, sausages, hare, fish, boar, a haunch of bear, bacon, blackbirds baked in a pie, tarts, honey, apples, pears, and pomegranates, plus generous servings of wine.[11] A contemporary writer calculates the cost of the banquet for fifteen guests (excluding servers, perfumes, and entertainers) at 36.8 ounces of gold. In early 2012 the price of gold was $1,612 per ounce. The total cost of this feast was thus more than $57,000.[12]

"WE WHO ARE ABOUT TO DIE"

In a fresco at Pompeii titled "Vulcan's Worship," the god of fire is busy hammering a design into a gladiator's helmet. One day, the gladiator (swordsmen, from the Latin *gladius*: sword) would wear that helmet or one like it in the Colosseum, where he would fight for his life while 50,000 spectators cheered and jeered. When he fell, mortally wounded, as most did, he would throw away his shield, raise a supplicating hand, and appeal for mercy. If he fought well and bravely, the emperor might let him live to fight another day. But if the crowd demanded his life, displaying a mass of down-turned thumbs, the emperor would probably signal to his opponent, "Kill him!"

Gladiator contests were a favorite entertainment in the Colosseum. Gladiators came from Rome's vast number of convicts and prisoners of war. A few volunteers entered the lists, seeking fame and fortune. A gladiator received substantial training over an extended period of time. His health was carefully tended; he dined on strength-building food, and his wounds were well treated. In return, he was expected to entertain the crowd by fighting to the death with bravery, skill, and cunning.[13] The contests began with the parade of the gladiators, each in combat dress, marching around the Colosseum, each pausing before the emperor, extending the traditional salute: "Hail Caesar. We who are about to die salute you."

---

[11] Ann Seranne and John Tebbel, *The Epicure's Companion* (New York: D. McKay, 1962), 8-13.

[12] Deborah Rucillo, "When Gluttony Ruled!" *Archaeology*, (Nov/Dec, 2001).

[13] Peter Quennel, *The Colosseum* (New York: Newsweek, 1971), 50.

Figure 5.3. William T. Walters commissioned this painting in 1863

Gladiators honed their skills by specializing. One group, the *samnites*, worked with the most common Roman weapons: large shield and short sword. Another group used a curved dagger. A third group fought with a net (to entangle the opponent) and killed with a trident. Successful gladiators had devoted fans and appropriate rewards, such as special food and money. And for those who survived repeated battles, their reward was sometimes discharge from the ranks of the gladiators.

History's most famous gladiator was Spartacus, a deserter from Rome's legions. In 73 CE he and seventy companions broke out of their gladiator school and battled their way to freedom, using kitchen knives as weapons. They routed a pursuing Roman army, and Spartacus, a born leader and brilliant tactician, gathered an army of slaves, dirt-poor farmers, and legion-deserters. His plan was to clear a road and escape the country (Italy) by traveling through the Alpine passes. Spartacus's army was successful for three years, defeating nine Roman commanders, but was finally crushed in 72 CE by the massed military power of ten Roman legions. As befitting a commanding general, Spartacus died a warrior's death, sword in hand.

As a grisly warning to those who might be tempted to challenge Rome's authority, 6,000 of Spartacus's followers were crucified, and their bodies hung along 130 miles of the Apian Way. The Howard Fast novel *Spartacus* served as the basis for a 1960 movie of the same name, with superb cast and spectacular battle scenes. The more recent movie *Gladiator*, starring Russell Crowe, is a story of a gladiator's suffering and revenge. It depicts a gladiator's training, his combat, and his ultimate triumph. The realistic swordplay and scenes of a spectator-jammed Colosseum make one believe that he or she is in the middle of the action in ancient Rome's most famous arena.

History has its echoes. In 1916 during World War I, a group of militant German socialists took inspiration from their Roman predecessors. Calling themselves Spartacists, they proclaimed socialist opposition to the oppression of the "capitalists' war" and called on European workers to overthrow their governments and bring an end to the war. In 1919 the Spartacists staged an uprising in Berlin, but government soldiers quelled the uprising and killed its leaders.

ROME DECLINES AND MOVES

Barring some great catastrophe, cities do not disappear outright. Rather, they gradually erode. The capital of the empire was moved to Constantinople in 330 CE: "New building and renovation ceased; the grand buildings were stripped of marble, bronze or gilded ornaments...houses were pulled apart for building materials and disappeared."[14] Generals, administrators, and families of wealth moved to Constantinople. Other important families took up residence at their great agricultural estates in various parts of the empire. "Ten years after the Saracens attacked in AD 846... (the city's population) had fallen to a mere 17,000."[15] And cows grazed in the Imperial Forum. As Catullus lamented, the everlasting night now held sway.

The Roman Empire, for all its faults, accomplished three purposes of effective government: internal peace, good order, and the safety of its citizens. When the empire collapsed, effective government slipped away, and all across the old empire, tribal loyalties asserted a shadowy imitation of effective government.

ROME FALLS

As a political and administrative entity whose power ran from Britain to Persia, Rome's decline and collapse have been subject to much theorizing by historians. Edward Gibbon's *Decline and Fall of the Roman Empire*, first published in 1776, concluded that two forces lay behind the decline and fall: "... an over-commitment to otherworldly Christianity plus an excessive gigantism, the empire outgrowing its communications and transportation network."[16]

---

[14] Peter Hall, *Cities in Civilization* (New York: Pantheon, 1998), 655.

[15] Ibid.

[16] Norman Cantor, *In the Wake of the Plague: The Black Death and the World it Made* (New York: Free Press, 2001), 189.

Other theories speak to the economics of empire: "A society with an agricultural foundation... was impoverished to support a state and an army which could not render the services necessary for maintenance of that society."[17] And behind that impoverished agriculture was a series of epidemics (smallpox, bubonic plague) that caused a shortage of agricultural manpower: "The result was a decline in food supplies...This caused shrinking of an already inadequate tax base, decreasing funds for bureaucracy and defense."[18] Theories spin on. But the net result is in the plaintive elegy of Edgar Allen Poe: "To the glory that was Greece / and the grandeur that was Rome."[19]

THE WISE TRAVELER IN ROME

> Everyone, soon or late, comes round by Rome
>
> — Robert Browning, "The Ring and the Book"[20]

> While stands the Coliseum, Rome shall stand;
> When falls the Coliseum, Rome shall fall;
> And when Rome falls—the world.
>
> — Lord Byron, "Childe Harold's Pilgrimage"[21]

The modern city of Rome sits in, on, and around the streets and buildings of ancient Rome. Today's city has a diameter of almost six miles, with as many as three million inhabitants. But for the traveler, the first—or hundredth—sight of the Colosseum or the Pantheon always delivers a moment of wonder: how did they do it? The answer is simple. They did it with muscle power and mass labor. They did it by using the skills of craftsmen from all over the Roman world. They did it by borrowing the ideas and plans of people they conquered. They did it with their own gift for practical invention. And they did it using the manpower of the Roman legions.

---

[17] Herbert Heaton, *An Economic History of Europe* (New York: Harper, 1948), 61.

[18] Norman Cantor, *In the Wake of the Plague*, 190. See also David Landes, *The Wealth and Poverty of Nations: Why Some Are So Rich and Some So Poor* (New York: W.W. Norton, 1998), a resonance of Adam Smith's *The Wealth of Nations.*

[19] Eager Allan Poe, "To Helen," (Poem), 1845.

[20] Robert Browning, *The Ring and the Book*, V. 296, 1868-69.

[21] Lord Bryum, "Childe Harold's Pilgrimmage," (Poem), 1812-18.

Each of the Roman legions consisted of 5,000 to 6,000 men. And every legion contained a cadre of engineers (like today's U.S. Army Corps of Engineers). Foot soldiers carried, in addition to their weapons, spades that were put to use in building the roads that enabled the legions to move quickly through their assigned territory.

> The Roman engineer who erected public buildings, bridges or roads was titled an *architectus*.... [Ideally] he had to be ...a man of letters, ...draftsman, mathematician...familiar with Stars, astronomy, calculations... The architectus had attached to his staff a surveyor...and a leveller.[22]

One of Rome's great contributions to architecture was the arch; they borrowed the idea from the *tholos* (beehive-shaped Etruscan tomb, influenced by the Greek) to build up monuments with levels. The interiors of Greek buildings were limited in size (and space) by the weight that a lintel could carry between pillars. Extended too far, a long stone will break under its own weight. But an arch pushes the weight of its stones and bricks downward and outward to the supporting walls. The Romans improved the arch by joining two arches (a vault) at right angles and by supporting each vault on massive pillars. Using the arch and vault, Roman engineers could enclose vast interior spaces. Walls could be thin, which allowed windows to be cut, letting in sunlight.

Two of the most spectacular domed-arch buildings in Rome are the Pantheon and the Baths of Caracalla. Arches on high pillars were the basic form of the aqueducts that brought water to the city. When Rome achieved its greatest population late in the first and early second centuries CE, its population stood at more than a million. Eventually, eleven aqueducts served the city and they "carried about 200 million gallons of water daily into Rome."[23]

SEEING ANCIENT ROME

Moviegoers know a lot about ancient Rome. They have seen Caesar strolling and gossiping in the Forum Romanum. They have watched gladiators and Christians die in the Colosseum. They have eavesdropped on Senators in the Baths of Caracalla, gossiping about the emperor and his latest scandal. Of course, most of what appears on movie screens was built on Hollywood sound stages and backlot locations. The real sites of ancient Rome are mostly in ruins

---

[22] Victor Wolfgang Von Hagen, *Roads That Led to Rome* (Cleveland: World Pub Co., 1967), 33-34.

[23] Moses Hadas, *Imperial Rome*, 164.

today. Some were razed during the invasions of the fifth century CE, while others were "mined" to provide marble and granite for Renaissance rulers. And still others simply collapsed from centuries of neglect. Rome's population, which stood at one million in 30 BCE, the beginning of the Augustan Age, dwindled to less than 20,000 in the late Middle Ages (around 1350).

Hollywood selects the style of Roman life that has box office appeal: the brutality of gladiator combat in the Colosseum, intrigue surrounding the emperor, heroic generals, and triumphal parades. But Hollywood and history are often far apart. The Rome of the Republic and the Caesars was, by today's standards, a cruel and unsanitary place. Streets were twisting, narrow, and piled high with garbage. Social classes were rigid and rigidly separated. At the bottom of Roman society were slaves, who worked under brutal conditions in mines and fields to produce the wealth that supported the city. Family life could also be cruel. Though not often invoked, the head of the family, the *pater familias*, was legally empowered to put to death disobedient wives and children. A hereditary elite, the patricians, dominated political and economic life. Commoners, the plebeians, lived in squalid tenements and depended on their aristocratic patrons for favors and food. The wealthy lived lives of elegance and grace. The poor merely scraped by. Unemployment was widespread. To keep unruly mobs in check, the government offered blood-sport entertainment in the Colosseum: fights to the death, humans eaten alive by wild animals, and free food for the unemployed (known as the famous policy of Bread and Circuses).

> Slaves were a visible presence in Rome and all through the empire. Disobedience and mutiny were constant concerns. Death was the usual punishment for either offense.... Drastic laws were passed providing that all slaves in a household, even when they numbered in the hundreds, might be killed if one of them murdered his master.[24]

A MENU OF SITES AND SIGHTS

With time and energy, wise travelers can make their way to over one hundred sites of ancient Rome. Here are several that help convey the spirit of the place.

The Forum Romanum (Imperial Forum)

Its location is important. It lies at the foot of the Capitoline Hill, the highest of the seven hills of Rome and the political center of the republic and empire. The modern monument to the unifi-

---

[24] Ibid., 84.

er of Italy, Vittorio Emmanuelle, is atop the Capitoline—an intentional political symbol. Nearby is an equestrian statue of the emperor-philosopher Marcus Aurelius.

Below the hill, the Imperial Forum is an agglomeration of five forums built over 165 years by Julius Caesar and four successive emperors. From its beginnings, the forum was the site of government buildings, temples, and shops. The Roman Senate was located here. Senators, priests, merchants, and generals made it their business to see and be seen here. This is where Caesar was murdered. And this is the location of the Golden Milestone, from which all roads led and returned to Rome. The forum today is a landscape "littered" with bits and pieces of temples, lonely columns, a crumbling triumphal arch, and uneven marble slabs. But a wise traveler's imagination helps to turn back the centuries.

Figure 5.4. Roman Forum

THE COLOSSEUM

The Colosseum's size makes it Rome's most recognizable site. A huge oval (610 feet long and 510 feet across), it was almost 200 feet high and could hold 50,000 spectators. It is the prototype of all the amphitheaters and football stadiums ever built. Large sections of the arcaded outer walls still stand, along with tiers of seats. The floor of the Colosseum is mostly pulled up. But beneath what was once the floor and in full view is the elaborate subterranean network of passageways, cells, and chambers.

As moviegoers know, the Colosseum was the scene of Rome's most elaborate pageants and gory amusements. Gladiators fought to the death. Wild African animals devoured unarmed prisoners. Women were raped by wild beasts. Odd (and inventive) spectacles were the source of amusement for crowds always seeking an unusual display of death: a woman fighting a dwarf; a sinking boat paddled by a desperate man trying to stave off snapping crocodiles; prisoners being torn apart by wild dogs.

Among the many films that display the spectacle of Rome are *Ben Hur* (1959), with Charlton Heston as a galley slave and Colosseum charioteer; *Gladiator* (2000), as mentioned above; and two versions of Caesar's infatuation with Cleopatra: *Cleopatra* (1934 and 1963).

Figure 5.5. Roman Colosseum

The Pantheon

The Pantheon, which was rebuilt by the Emperor Hadrian around 125 CE, survives as a crowning achievement of Roman architecture. The façade is in the style of a Greek temple with a simple triangular pediment resting on eight soaring Corinthian columns. Behind the pillars, under the portico, is a double doorway, forty feet high and twenty feet wide. The doors open onto a vast circular space (the *cella*) crowned by the largest dome ever built. The dome "has a diameter of just over 142 feet and is coffered in five concentric rings meeting in the center in a large, circular … oculus [eye] 142 feet from the floor... [and] nearly 30 feet across."[25]

---

[25] Doreen Yarwood, *The Architecture of Europe* (New York: Hastings House, 1974), 50-51.

Figure 5.6. Pantheon

The Pantheon was dedicated originally to the gods; hence, its dome represents the firmament. It was rededicated to the Virgin and Christian martyrs in 609 CE. The acoustics of the *cella* are whisper splendid, and the eye of the dome bathes the temple in soft, lovely light. For centuries, travelers have marveled at the Pantheon's interior. Half the interior height is wall; half is the dome. The dome is a vast circle of coffered spaces that seem to grow smaller as they move upward. The floor is marble and is slightly convex so as to fool the eye into seeing it as perfectly level. These harmonious proportions bring to mind transcendent Roman poets:

> Live among men as if God beheld you;
> Speak to God as if men were listening.
>
> — Seneca

> I am a man, and nothing that concerns a man
> Do I deem a matter of indifference to me.
>
> — Terence

> Suns may set and rise again. For us, when once our
> brief day is set, there's the sleep thru' everlasting night.
>
> — Catullus

ORIGINS OF THE RENAISSANCE

> The nations of Europe so describe this unique force which overwhelmed, like a restless tide, the thought and spirit of Medieval man.[26]

The Renaissance began in the early 1400s and slowly extinguished the mind-set of the Middle Ages. The French word *renaissance* means rebirth. The Renaissance meant the rebirth of many things that helped shape the modern mind: the challenge of travel and exploration; learning for learning's sake; freedom of inquiry, especially the freedom of secular inquiry; education using (and rediscovering) Greek and Roman texts; and above all, a return to the classical mind-set that proclaims many important ideas: Man is the measure of all things. Happy is he who knows the cause of things. For every cause, there is an effect.

Every age has machines, architecture, and graphic art that represent its mind-set, its technology, and its way of life. Think of the space shuttle of the late twentieth century and what it embodies: a dazzling technology, a response to the Cold War, and confidence that what humans can imagine, they can achieve. Great cathedrals embody the Middle Ages. Their vast interiors, their soaring spires, their huge colored windows, and the patient way they were built—many were under construction for a century or more—embody society's preoccupation with life after death and lives dedicated to the idea that life on earth is no more than a journey toward the afterlife. In other words, architecture in the Middle Ages was dedicated to the transcendence.

In contrast to the Middle Ages, the art and architecture of the Renaissance reflect a different technology and a different mind-set. At the end of the Middle Ages, man realized that he needed to have a place in culture, and a movement called Humanism was born. During this period, artists went to rediscover Latin and Greek philosophy and out of this came the Renaissance to wake up man. In statues and paintings, the human body is reproduced in lifelike detail. The nude, especially the female nude, is no longer regarded as the repository of sin, but as the celebration of divine intent. Two noteworthy examples include Botticelli's *Birth of Venus* and Michelangelo's *Dawn,* in the tomb of the Medici in Florence. Faces are drawn to reflect character—ambition, cruelty, and smug self-satisfaction. Clothes indicate vocation and social status—churchman, businessman, or military leader. And the body inside the clothes displays movement and pose that give insight into the character and personality of the subject. The ste-

---

[26] Ibid., 308.

reotyped likeness of the Middle Ages is no more; every portrait compels us to look at a singular human being.

To see the difference between the Middle Ages and Renaissance, go to the Brancacci Chapel in Florence. On the wall, you will see two frescos of Adam and Eve. One was painted by Masolino (Middle Ages) and the other by Masaccio (the birth of the Renaissance). Masolino's work is simple representation with beautiful color and composition, while Masaccio's work is emotional participation. In Masaccio's work, Adam and Eve are suffering, moving, not standing still. Art is no longer representation, but interpretation.

Figure 5.7. Adam and Eve frescos in the Brancacci Chapel in Florence.
On the left is the work of Masolino, and on the right is that of Masaccio.

It was during the Renaissance that man started to apply mathematics to architecture, painting, sculpture, medicine, physics, astronomy, etc. This also began with Masaccio, when he applied mathematics to his painting to give perspective. The principles of perspective transformed a flat, two-dimensional canvas into a three-dimensional "reality" that is built around a vanishing point. Renaissance architects used this technique to plan cities so that vistas become real-world vanishing points. The technology of bronze casting also created a three-dimensional "reality." A noteworthy example is Lorenzo Ghiberti's doors for the Baptistery in Florence. Renaissance technology also created soaring domes that cover vast interior spaces. Witness the dome of St. Peter's in Rome and the dome of the Cathedral or Duomo in Florence.

Whereas life in the Middle Ages revolved around feudal lords and their agricultural estates, life in the Renaissance revolved around cities. The feudal castle was replaced by palaces, such as the Strozzi in Florence and the Farnese in Rome. Italy was the center of Renaissance change, and Rome, Florence, Ferrara, Venice, Urbino, Milan, and Mantua were the most powerful and dynamic urban centers. Their princes, dukes, and Popes vied to beautify their cities and used their wealth to hire the best and most imaginative craftsmen of their time. Architects and craftsmen created buildings in a new style that was and is the crowning achievement of Renaissance cities—the Basilica of St. Peter in Rome, the Duomo in Florence, and the urban domiciles of the rich and powerful, such as the Medici Palace in Florence, the Farnese Palace in Rome, and the Vendramini Palace in Venice.

RENAISSANCE STYLES

"Restless" and "profuse" are words that describe the several Renaissance styles. Facades curve, sculptures twist and bend, and rococo is the term applied to the most ornate Renaissance style. The word comes from the French *rocaille*, meaning rock and shell. The style is exuberant: a profusion of rocks, flowers, and shells adorned with angels and *putti*, or cherubs, sleeping, climbing, gazing. Historians sometimes classify Renaissance architecture into time-related styles: early, high, Baroque, and rococo. They also divide the Renaissance into divisions marked by centuries: Duecento (thirteenth century); Trecento (fourteenth century); Quattrocento (fifteenth century); and Cinquecento (sixteenth century). But names and stylistic divisions are less important than the achievements of Renaissance art and architecture, especially in Rome, a city and a state ruled by its Popes.

ROME OF THE RENAISSANCE POPES

A succession of Renaissance Popes endowed Rome with a stunning array of masterpieces, an endowment that would probably not be possible today. The Pope's secular authority is now confined to a small area inside the larger city of Rome. When the war for Italian unification ended in 1870, the new civil government made Rome the national capital. The Papal State was squeezed into its present boundaries: Vatican City, a sovereign state inside the city of Rome and ruled by Europe's last absolute "monarch." The city-state's population is about 1,000. Triangular in shape and lying on the west bank of the Tiber River, the size of this independent country is about 109 acres. It has its own "army," the Swiss Guards, whose bright, striped uniforms were designed by Michelangelo. It issues its own postage stamps and sends its ambassadors to other nations' capitals.

The word Vatican comes from the Latin *vates,* meaning prophet. For the world's nearly one billion Roman Catholics, Vatican City is a place of religious pilgrimage and veneration. For travelers of other faiths, the city inspires awe and wonder evoked by its architecture, its museums, and its role in western history.

For both pilgrims and secular travelers, the city's evocative center is St. Peter's Square and the Basilica of St. Peter. Actually an ellipse, the square is one of the world's largest and is enclosed by two encircling arms, a colonnade designed by Gian Lorenzo Bernini, with 284 Doric columns, each sixty-four feet high. Atop the colonnade are statues of 140 saints. Marking the center of the square is an obelisk, shipped from Egypt by the Emperor Caligula for self-glorification. On either side of the obelisk are two fountains that can produce theatrical water displays several times a day.

The symbolism of the square works on several levels. Saints recall the martyrdom of early Christians. Water signifies the rite of baptism. The cross atop the obelisk proclaims the triumph of Christianity over paganism. And the encircling arms of the colonnade (actually a set of four colonnades) symbolically embrace all who enter. The square invokes the power and the glory of the "universal church" and its more than one billion communicants. The square is more than a dramatic setting for the Basilica of St. Peter. As visitors walk into the square, the colonnade concentrates their gaze on the Basilica at the far end.

ST. PETER'S BASILICA

> The Mother Church of Christendom is dedicated to the apostle who is believed to be the first bishop of Rome and whose successor each Pope, as supreme head of the Roman Catholic Church, feels himself to be. The history of St. Peters reflects the history of the Papacy.[27]

From the central balcony of the portico, the senior member of the College of Cardinals proclaims the election of a new Pope. And from this balcony the Pope addresses the adoring

[27] *Baedeker's Rome,* 3rd edition (New York: Random House, 1999), 148. Baedeker publishes a series of excellent guides, noted for illustration and careful text.

crowds in the square below and sends his blessings and proclamations to *urbi et orbi*—to the city and the world. Five bronze doorways lead to the massive church interior: 610 feet in length, rising to 390 feet directly beneath the dome.

Figure 5.8. St. Peter's Basilica

The church is in the form of a Latin cross. The Papal Altar stands in the center of the arm of the cross (the transept) and is reached by a wide aisle (technically, the nave). Above the Papal Altar is a bronze *baldachino* (canopy) created by Bernini, whose twisting columns are a superb example of Renaissance art and technology, with its emphasis on dynamic movement. Between the portico doors and the Papal Altar are five side aisles, each ending in a chapel. In the right aisle closest to the doors is Michelangelo's *Pieta*, a sorrowing Mary holding her son just taken down from the cross. Like the *baldachino*, the *Pieta* embodies the brilliance of Renaissance artistry.

Adjacent to St. Peter's are a dozen-and-a-half museums, papal apartments, libraries, and chapels containing the Vatican's art and architectural treasures. Four of the most famous are the Sistine Chapel, the apartments of the Borgia Popes, the Vatican Library, and the Pinacoteca

(Picture Gallery). Michelangelo painted the walls and ceiling of the Sistine. One of his frescos has become a global icon: the *Creation of Adam*—God reaching out to touch Adam's finger. The Borgia apartments display several rooms of paintings; the most famous are the frescos in the Raphael Rooms.

PAPAL BUILDERS

The word Pope is from the Latin word for father; pontiff, from the Latin, means pathfinder as well as bridge. Both words help to associate Renaissance Popes with their contributions to the Rome that continues to delight strollers and remind them that the gift of a great city is the opportunity for a chance encounter.

FOUNTAINS, STEPS, AND PARKS

The Trevi Fountain was designed by Nicolo Salvi at the command of Pope Clement XII. More than twenty years in construction (1732-51), it is Rome's largest fountain. Baroque in style, horses rise and plunge, and Neptune commands the fountain flanked by two Tritons. Those who recall the movie *Three Coins in the Fountain* remember that tossing coins into the water makes dreams come true and assures the traveler's return to Rome.

Figure 5.9. Trevi Fountain

The Triton Fountain was built by Bernini for Pope Urban VIII. Five years in construction, the fountain is dominated by dolphins supporting the Pope's coat of arms and by a triton sounding a conch shell.

The Baroque Spanish Steps have been a favorite haunt of tourists for at least 200 years. It has 137 steps punctuated with ramps and leads upward from a fountain to a fifteenth-century twin-tower church. The steps invite walkers to sit, gossip, and bask in the sun in good weather.

The Borghese family bequeathed to Rome a Pope (Paul V), several cardinals, and a lovely villa and gardens set off by artificial lakes and ponds.

Figure 5.10. Spanish Steps

For a trip bridging the past and present, travelers can visit the Piazza Bocca della Verità—literally the Mouth of Truth. Moviegoers may remember *Roman Holiday*, where Audrey Hepburn is challenged to stick her arm into the Bocca to test an old legend. Liars will have that hand bitten off!

MODERN ITALY: THE STRUGGLE FOR UNITY

> Italy is only a geographical expression.
> — Prince Klemens von Metternich
> "Letter to British Foreign Minister", August 6, 1847

In the centuries before and after the Renaissance, Italy was a collection of jealous, sometimes warring sovereignties: kingdoms, dukedoms, and elite-run republics. If, as is sometimes said, a nation is an imagined community of those who share a language, a religion, and a history, then Italy in the nineteenth century was a series of nations but not a unified nation-state. In the south, the Kingdom of Naples ruled the "boot of Italy" and the island of Sicily. The Papal State, whose monarch was the Pope, exercised sovereign control over the center of Italy. Parma, Tuscany, Modena, and Lucca were independent states. In the north, the Kingdom of Piedmont guarded its sovereignty against France and the expansionist designs of Austria, which controlled the province of Lombardy and the Veneto, an Adriatic area once part of the Venetian empire.

But beginning with the American and French revolutions, a new ideology swept across Europe. Its followers proclaimed that devotion to a unified nation-state was far more important than devotion to local rulers. To act on this belief, or even to discuss it, meant running the risk of arrest and torture by the secret police of Italy's many rulers. Those who met in secret called themselves *charbonieri*— charcoal burners, solitary woodsmen who cut trees in the forests and burned them to make charcoal. As the secret societies grew, their movement took a more inclusive name, *Risorgimento*, "rising again": the rising of revolutionaries against foreign domination and against Italian tyrants.

In 1849 revolutionaries dethroned the Pope as Prince of the Papal State and established the Republic of Rome. Tuscany soon followed suit. Then, ten years later, Modena, Parma, and Lucca joined the ranks of republican Italy. But a collection of republics was not yet a nation-state. For that to happen, a transcending leadership was needed. That role was assumed by Victor Emmanuel II, King of Piedmont. Through his chief minister, Count Cavour, Victor Emmanuel established a parliamentary regime and modernized his army. Nationalist patriots flocked to his leadership. None was more important than Giuseppe Garibaldi and his army of 10,000 patriots (the red shirts). In 1860 Garibaldi's army swept through Sicily and routed the forces of the King of Naples. The King and Garibaldi met in Naples and in 1861 proclaimed the Kingdom of Italy, a single nation-state whose writ ran the length of Italy—except for the now-tiny Papal State of Latium and the Austrian-dominated areas on the Adriatic Sea. Ten years later, military campaigns against Austria brought the Adriatic stragglers into the fold. After almost 2,000 years, Italy was once again welded into a single nation-state, its political system a constitutional monarchy.

Figure 5.11. Tribute to Victor Emmanuel

The period of Italian unification is unforgettably portrayed in the 1958 novel *The Leopard*. A young revolutionary offers a memorable summing up of the times: "We live between two worlds: One that is dying; the other not yet born."[28] In the novel the Prince of Lampadusa is ready to accept the new regime but has no illusions about the social and economic changes unleashed by revolution. Strivers and place-seekers displace the old aristocracy; money replaces hereditary privilege and the obligations entailed by that privilege. The Prince's young nephew fights for the new regime and welcomes it. Yet, he, too, is conscious of great changes still to come. If we wish things to stay as they are, we must work to change them, he says.

THE OLD NEW ITALY

After unification, the national capital moved to Rome. The wise traveler in Rome sees the celebratory monument (informally called the Wedding Cake) to Victor Emmanuel atop Capitoline Hill. Its symbolism is unmistakable—the glory of ancient Rome has returned! A professional

---

[28] See Giuseppe Tomasi Di Lampedusa, *The Leopard* (Italy: Feltrinelli, 1958).

bureaucracy minded the details of running the state, and paperwork and corruption both helped and hindered modernization. Northern cities took the lead in bringing modern industry to Italy. Milan and Turin became the country's leading industrial and banking centers. Their factories built automobiles such as Fiat and Lankier. And their railroad yards linked Italy to the rest of Europe.

South of Naples, in the region called the Mezzogiorno ("middle of the morning"), social and economic development moved much more slowly. The Mezzogiorno is the poorest part of Italy, and traditional, folk customs predominate. Here, the mafia operated a secret government that resisted the formal and elected government.

MUSSOLINI STRUTS THE STAGE

> Fascism is...an educator and a promoter of spiritual life. It aims at refashioning...man, his character and his faith... [I]t enforces discipline and uses authority, entering into the soul and ruling with undisputed sway.
>
> — Benito Mussolini, *Fascism*[29]

As befitting a democracy, Italy joined Britain and France in World War I. The Italians carried the war into Austrian territory, most notably into what would later become Yugoslavia.[30] Ten years after the armistice, Italy suffered the ravages of the Great Depression. An old piece of political wisdom says that the times bring forth the man. That may be so, but there is no guarantee that the man will be a force for good, not for evil.

Benito Mussolini (1883-1945) began his political career as a socialist and journalist but cast his socialism aside at the end of World War I. The Italian socialists had argued that Italy should remain neutral during World War I, believing that the only right conflict should be a worker's revolution against capitalism. But Mussolini, growing tired of socialism, argued for armed neutrality and was then expelled from the socialist party and joined the army.

Let's stop and consider the meaning of socialism and its counterpart on the opposite end of the political spectrum, namely fascism. Socialism is a political and economic philosophy of the left that rejects individualism, private ownership and private profits in favor of a system based on economic collectivism and some larger group's (governmental or societal) ownership

---

[29] See Benito Mussolini, *Fascismo* (Enciclopedia Italiana, 1932), 847-51.

[30] The campaign is the setting for Ernest Hemingway's *A Farewell to Arms* (1929). It is often characterized as Hemingway's bleakest novel.

of the means of production and distribution of goods. Communism is an extreme form of socialism where government itself withers away in favor of a worker's society without formal governance. In contrast, philosophies of the right such as fascism accept the importance of central political authority and order in a society. And these goals can best be achieved, those on the right suggest, by accepting that some individuals and groups are better suited and better able to govern, whether it is a certain political party, a certain ethnic group or race, or a certain individual, a *philosopher king* in the words of Plato.

Mussolini had tired of socialism and came to believe that he was destined to be the future leader of Italy, moving his philosophical tendencies from left to right. He threw himself into the politics of discontent at war's end and founded a veterans' movement in Milan in 1919. Nationalistic, anti-socialist, and anti-liberal, the movement took its name fascist (from the Latin *faces:* sticks tied together) from the Roman symbol of unity. Wearing black shirts, the fascists found support in the conservative strata of society: landowners, the Church, the military, the aristocracy, and the king. Mussolini convinced the well-to-do conservative titans of industry and other components of Italian society that he alone was capable of pushing back against those socialists and communists who wanted to undercut the traditional capitalistic society.

Figure 5.12. Benito Mussolini

Invited by the king to form a government in 1922, Mussolini devised a non-parliamentary system of government in which each of the major economic and social groups was given representation in the Parliament—which was characterized by a system of control: informers, secret police, arrests, and torture. And Mussolini ruled as dictator.

Mussolini fanned a virulent nationalism inspired by dreams of a modern Roman Empire. After a brutal war in which tons of gas bombs were dropped on civilians, Italy conquered Ethiopia in 1935-36 and fought in Spain on the side of General Franco (1936-39). Mussolini's admiration for Adolph Hitler joined Italy to Germany in a Pact of Steel (The Rome-Berlin Axis). Linked to the Nazis, Italy promulgated its own program of anti-Semitism.[31] Italian armies fought alongside Germany in Russia, Albania, Greece, and North Africa, always disastrously, always being bailed out by the Germans.

When the Allies invaded Italy, the king dismissed Mussolini as head of government. The Germans installed him in a puppet regime in the north. But in 1945 partisan fighters killed him and hung him upside down alongside his mistress in Milan, as jubilant crowds cheered and jeered.

POST-WAR ITALY

At war's end, a national referendum abolished the monarchy and installed a parliamentary republic. Socialists and Communists, repressed under fascism, re-entered the political arena, drawing strength and support from the industrialized north. Conservative voters coalesced around the Catholic Church, and the political arena became host to multiple parties and factions. In the immediate post-war years, pushed by the Stalinist regime in the Soviet Union, the Communist Party asserted a forceful presence in Italian politics. Even further to the political left were revolutionary brigades whose shadowy branches kidnapped and murdered those in the center and on the right. The far right contained remnants of Mussolini's fascists. In the center of the political spectrum were Christian Democrats who pledged the expansion of the welfare state. To their right, but as an ally, was the strong influence of the Catholic Church.

Since the end of the Cold War, new groups have thickened the political and parliamentary mixture. A large Muslim population is countered by anti-foreign, anti-Islamic agitation. Widespread bureaucratic corruption brings nostalgia for the good old bad days of Mussolini. More

---

[31] It was brought to the cinema as *The Garden of the Finzi-Continis* (1970).

recently, the government was dominated by a president whose personal life was fuel for titillating stories.

To give representation to the many factions and interests in Italian politics, the Parliament has nearly 1,000 members: 630 in the Chamber of Deputies; 315 in the Senate, plus seven Senators appointed for life. The structure of Parliament—the number of members and the number of parties—is designed to prevent any single party or ideology from controlling the government, a safeguard against returning to a dictatorship of either the right or the left. With no party able to command an outright majority, Parliament works by means of coalitions.

Coalitions, by their nature, are shifting and unstable. By one count, in the sixty-plus years since Italy became a parliamentary republic, it has had almost that many changes of government. Prime ministers and their cabinets come and go. But many of the same persons appear and reappear as leaders of government. This is not surprising given the bargaining around which coalitions are built and the need to maintain the support of at least 50 percent of Parliament members.

Coalition government has predictable consequences. Its policies are rarely boldly innovative. As such, they evoke widespread criticism from those who want government to solve long-standing problems: unemployment, corruption (cases in point: kickbacks and theft in government contracts), intimidation and bribery of judges, the disparity in incomes between north and south, and the sharing of responsibility between national and regional governments, which often leads to inaction rather than action (cases in point: the annual flooding of St. Mark's Square in Venice; the power of the mafia in the south).

Despite all this, Italy is a democracy. It boasts a thriving middle class. It is a member of the European Union and uses the euro as national currency. It contributes to the United Nations peacekeeping forces, and it asserts leadership in world markets in the domains of fashion and elegant cars. It is a global center of Christian leadership and influence. It also serves as a beacon and a magnet for wise travelers who seek masterpieces of painting, sculpture, and architecture, and thereby an understanding of the history of western civilization.

6. Venice: The Meeting of East and West

> When the Venetians stroll out in the evening, they do not avoid the Piazza San Marco, where the tourists are... The Venetians go to look at the tourists, and the tourists look back at them. It is all for the ear and eye, this city, but primarily for the eye. Built on water, it is an endless succession of reflections and echoes...
>
> — Mary McCarthy, *Venice Observed*, 1961

Venice! The word immediately conjures up a collage of wonderful images—romance, intrigue, exotic travel, Carnival, a cappuccino or glass of wine at a café in Piazza San Marco while strands of classical music from a nearby quartet float past. Marco Polo, East meets West, narrow and grandiose canals (but not roads), and most of all, gondolas slowly meandering through these waterways, rowed by high-spirited young men dressed in the familiar blue and white uniform of the gondolier. As the wise traveler sets foot in Venice for the first time, all of these images compete for attention, causing the mind to jump from one sensory experience to another. Arthur Symons once remarked that a "realist, in Venice, would become a romantic simply by mere faithfulness to what he saw before him."[1]

No matter how little travelers know of Venice, anyone who has ever contemplated a visit to Italy is aware of how completely different Venice is when compared to other Italian cities

---

[1] Arthur Symons, *Cities* (London: J.M. Dent & Co, 1903), 66. Symons (1865-1945) was a social and literary critic whose essay "Episode of a Night of May" elaborates meaningful visual and social experiences.

and to urban areas across the globe. These differences are defined not only by the city's totally different contemporary visual images but also by its unique past, a past so at variance with all other urban centers that Venice occupies a critically important spot on the list of must-see places in the world. As the noted American author Truman Capote once observed, "Venice is like eating an entire box of chocolate liqueurs in one go."[2]

Figure 6.1. Venice

Water defines Venice like no other city; it is its lifeblood. Robert Benchley, American humorist on a newspaper assignment to Venice, famously cabled his editors, "City under water. Please advise." Every part of Venice can be reached via its narrow streets, lanes, and bridges, but not as the pigeon flies. Detours around canals require intricate maps and helpful advice. Goods, however, must be moved by boats and barges. People who wish to travel in Venice with

[2] Truman Capote, U.S. author quoted in *Observer* (London, November 26, 1961), 25.

the fewest interruptions opt to move around by boat. Hotels transport arriving and departing guests aboard sleek motor launches. Mass transit is accomplished by waterbus, the *vaporetto* (which, despite its name, is no longer powered by steam.)

Simply put, Venice is water contained in canals. There is, of course, only one Venice, but other water-bound cities with far different histories are pretenders to the name. Stockholm, for example, prides itself on being the Venice of the North. St. Petersburg is the Venice of the Baltic. Bangkok advertises itself as the Venice of the East. And when the Florentine Amerigo Vespucci arrived at the northwest coast of South America, he found Indians along its shores, their houses on pilings in the water. Nothing would do but to name the place Little Venice, or Venezuela. While these urban centers claim Venice-like status, there is still only one Venice. And near the top of the reasons for its singular status is its history, or more precisely, the many roles played by Venice over the centuries. The city has dazzled visitors through the centuries. And to experience Venice through a gifted writer, one should visit Jan Morris' *Venice*, acclaimed by many as the finest book on the city.[3] Morris explores, explains and quite simply appreciates Venice through its people, its lagoon and the city itself. As we shall see, Venice's story, at the crossroads between East and West, is like no other.

The symbol of modern Venice is, of course, the gondola. The word has enjoyed (or endured) curious uses in days gone by: an open top railroad car to carry coal, wheat, or cement; a pod suspended beneath a blimp; open display shelves in the supermarket; and thick-hulled submersible globes used to explore deep oceans. But these words are curiosities. The gondola we all know is the graceful, high-prowled boat, rowed while standing upright, the personal transport of Venice. The Venetian gondola has a round bottom, making for easy maneuvering, useful in crowded canals. It sits low in the water, rising gracefully fore and aft, prow (sometimes the stern) clad in iron. The stern is small. The prow curves and rises high as the weight of its iron, *ferro*, helps to balance the gondolier standing off-side at the stern. The *ferro* is ornamented with fretwork, occasionally with spikes. The gondolier's platform (the *forcola*) extends outward from the side of the gondola, giving the boat a distinctive asymmetrical bulge. The

---

[3] See James Morris, *Venice* (New York: Faber and Faber, 1960). *Venice* was first published half a century ago and its most recent edition is 2004. James Morris underwent a gender change and her books are now listed as written by Jan Morris. For the author's reflections on the gender change, see *Conundrum* (New York: NYRB Classics, 2006).

forcola is no simple platform. Curves of its surface give the gondolier a variety of footholds with which to maneuver the boat in busy traffic.

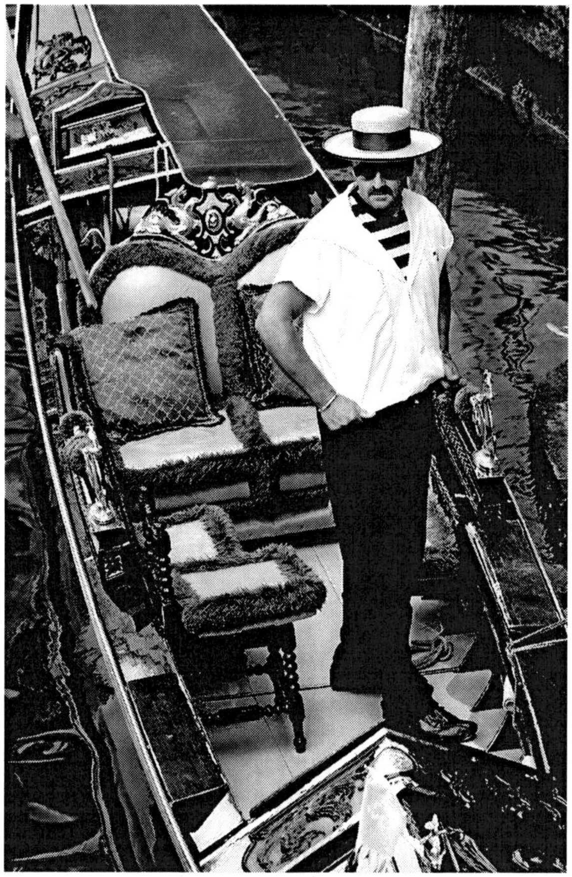

Figure 6.2. Gondolier

The shape of the gondola has remained fairly consistent for at least 400 years. As the personal conveyance of the rich and the powerful, gondoliers were dressed in the livery of their masters, while the gondola itself was ornamented with gold and silver fittings. In the seventeenth century, seeking to dampen conspicuous display, the *doge* (duke) decreed that all gondolas be painted black. It has remained the standard color since.

During that same century, it is estimated that 10,000 gondolas plied the canals. Today there are only about 400 found within the city. For travelers and Venetians alike, few sights in Venice are lovelier or more romantic than a wedding gondola, heaped with flowers, carrying bride and groom to and from their church.

Modernity has come to the ancient craft of the gondolier. They continue to wear their striped shirts and broad straw hats. But visitors may now hire a gondola on the Internet. As the time finally arrives for the big trip, a traveler may wish to carry along Robert Browning's lengthy poem "In a Gondola," a celebration of passionate kisses aboard that craft.

VENICE'S GHETTO

Throughout a significant part of history, Venice stood at the crossroads of the global export trade of the Middle Ages, with goods passing through between east and west. But the city has also exported something that has endured time: words and phrases that have become part of our standard vocabulary. Many Venetian terms have traveled the world, taking on new and sometimes surprising meanings: *gondola*, *lido*, *sequin*, and *Rialto* conjure up thoughts of pleasure. The *arsenale* housed the shipyards on which Venice's maritime power depended. Armed galleys were built in the *arsenale*, along with foundries to cast cannon and whatever else was needed for men of war. Finally, *ghetto*, which originally marked off a neighborhood of iron foundries, has become an international word that signifies isolation, intolerance, and inhumanity.

Jews first came to Venice in 1373, seeking safety from religious persecution. They were permitted to live in an area of foundries, but not without restrictions. At first, their residence was only temporary. The contracts that authorized residence required frequent renewal and frequent payment of fees. But over the centuries, the threat of expulsion was asserted more than it was enacted. Jews were taxed frequently for the privilege of living in the ghetto. Distinctive dress was required of all, and the gates of the two ghettos were locked at night. And only certain occupations were open to Jews: banking, for example, but not the textile trade.

Jews lived and often prospered in Venice. William Shakespeare's *The Merchant of Venice* describes one such individual. The ghetto became synonymous with religious and ethnic segregation as well as the culture within, symbolized, for example, by religious schools and synagogues. When Napoleon's troops entered Venice in 1797, proclaiming the equality of the French Revolution, the ghetto's gates were destroyed.

THE VENETIAN SPIRIT

Aside from a dedication to profitable trade, the Venetians were patrons of theater and music. The San Moise Theater (opened in 1620) entertained a cross-section of Venetian society with comedies and opera. Venetians took special delight in the music of their own Vivaldi (1678-1741). His "Four Seasons" made Venetian music famous throughout Europe, just as it continues to delight listeners today. La Fenice, which opened in 1792 and reopened in 2003, has long been regarded as one of the most beautiful theaters in the world. Its classical facade is a brilliant white, while the centerpiece of its marble lobby is a beautiful staircase. La Fenice burned down in 1996, accidentally at first report. But further investigation revealed that workmen had set the fire deliberately. Repairs had gone slowly, and the contractor, seeking to excuse his delays, ordered electricians to start a small fire to draw attention from the delays. The fire could not be contained, and to the anger and anguish of Venetians, the theater was closed for more than half a decade.

Venetians take pride in the city's elegant and innovative architecture. In the much-admired, much-photographed Baroque church, Santa Maria della Salute, the massive domes and the outward thrust of the walls are brought under aesthetic and structural control by huge stone scrolls on the roof. Wealthy Venetians are remembered as patrons of painters. Masterpieces by Titian, Tintoretto, and Carpaccio adorn churches and palaces. Venetians were masters of industrial technology; warships in the *arsenale* were turned out quickly on production lines. And in pursuit of profitable trade, Venetians, quite literally, traveled to the ends of the earth.

MARCO POLO

Marco Polo, his father, and his uncle are exemplars of the far-traveling Venetians. They set out from Venice in 1271, bound for the court of the Great Khan. Maffeo Polo and Nicolai Polo had accomplished the journey before. Now, seventeen-year-old Marco traveled with them. Their journey was made possible by Mongols from central Asia. Under their leader, Genghis Kahn, they had swept across the Russian steppes in 1228 and had flown their banners of conquest from the Sea of Japan to the borders of Poland, from Siberia to Persia, becoming, as a consequence, the greatest land empire in history.

The Mongols were cruel conquerors but uninterested in religious disputation. Open, safe roads and swift messengers kept the bonds of empire tightly laced. All travelers who obeyed Mongol laws and paid tribute were welcome. The Polos traveled by ship to the Black Sea, and from there they went over land across the ancient Silk Road toward the Mongol capital of Beijing. They were three-and-a-half years on the road, almost dying in the cold, arid mountains of Afghanistan.

The Great Khan, Kublai Khan, grandson of Genghis, welcomed them, taking special interest in twenty-year-old Marco. A keen observer and gifted with languages, Marco became one of Kublai's diplomats, serving the Great Khan on missions across China. In 1292 the emperor entrusted Marco with an important mission: convey a Mongol princess to wed the Khan's Persian vassal. Thus commanded, Marco set out on one of the defining voyages of history. In nominal command of a flotilla of fourteen ships and 600 men, Marco recorded the wonders of his journey. The ships were magnificent—Chinese ships of a size that Europe could not match for at least 300 years, sails that folded like a giant fan instead of being reefed and furled, and three Chinese maritime inventions that would revolutionize European exploration: a compass to guide Marco's ships, watertight compartments, and a stern rudder controlled by ropes and chains.

The route of the flotilla solved one of Europe's great maritime mysteries—how to reach the Far East by sea. Simple, Marco reported. Sail south on the China Sea, traverse the Strait of Malacca, cross the Indian Ocean, head north through the Red Sea, and proceed over land to the Mediterranean. Reverse the route to travel from Europe to China. Marco turned his adventures into a book, *The Million Marvels*, copies of which circulated far and wide. When movable type came to Europe around 1450, Marco's book inspired the Portuguese to seek a sea route to the Indies around Africa. And it inspired Christopher Columbus, who sailed with two books, *The Bible* and Marco's *The Million Marvels*, to seek the Indies by sailing west across the Atlantic. So, in one of history's ironies, it was a son of Venice who inspired sailors from the Iberian peninsula to flood Europe with wealth that would ultimately undo Venice.

AFTER THE FALL OF ROME

Venice's history does not begin with Marco Polo, however. Instead, we must go back 800 years earlier when social organizations were defined primarily in terms of smaller groupings. In eastern Italy, along the mid-to-northern Adriatic coast, the Veneti tribes struggled against invaders, especially the Lombards ("longbeards") who moved west and south from an area along the Danube. Sometime before 400 CE, the Veneti took refuge on islands built from the sediment of rivers that emptied into the sea. The islands were enlarged by dams and channels that diverted river flow, and the Veneti population expanded. Farming, fishing, and coastal trading supported the islanders, their watery moat making them secure against marauders. Gradually the islanders sharpened their skills in naval warfare while also increasingly strengthening their bonds of mutual support. Venice as a social and political entity had emerged.

The city's date of birth is uncertain. The year 421 CE is claimed by the Venetians as their city's founding date. And for the next 800 years, as the brilliant James (Jan) Morris writes, "the

Venetians established their independence, founded their commercial supremacy in the eastern Mediterranean, and evolved their own system of aristocratic Government at home."[4]

As Venice prospered, it became an object of hostile takeovers. Charlemagne took the crown and title of Holy Roman Emperor in 800. Eager to expand the empire's boundaries and coffers, Charlemagne's son, Pepin, mounted an invasion, but the stronghold of islands and their mastery of the sea put an end to Holy Roman ambitions. More important, Venice had a powerful ally, the empire of the Byzantines, whose capital city, Constantinople, was the largest and wealthiest city west of Beijing. Byzantium ruled the eastern Mediterranean, Ravenna was its Italian capital, and the Exarch (a governor with extended authority) of Ravenna exercised Constantinople's authority over Venice.

Venice's eastern trade increased. Trading colonies (and, later, sovereignties) were established across the eastern Mediterranean. By 840, the Byzantine bonds were dissolved, not directly but with characteristic Venetian obliqueness. Without the consent of the Byzantines, the *doge* of Venice made a treaty with Charlemagne's grandson. The treaty now stood as real-world evidence that Venice was free and independent, a republic, one whose architecture carried themes of the great church of Constantinople, Santa Sophia.

VENICE AND THE CRUSADES

In 1095 Pope Urban II called for a Great Crusade to liberate the Holy Land from its Muslim conquerors. Venice now operated three profitable enterprises. The first was the leasing of ships to Crusaders to carry men, arms, horses, military machines, and the lords and ladies who would rule the captured lands. The second was the buying and transporting of treasure taken from such lands. And as a third commercial enterprise, after Jerusalem had been taken by the Crusaders in 1098, Venice organized Europe's very first tourist service: carrying pilgrims to the Holy Land, arranging tours of holy sites, and providing tour guides, housing, and even audiences with powerful and important people.

In 1204, in the Fourth Crusade, Venice schemed to let profit come before virtue. Venice once again agreed (for a handsome profit) to carry Crusaders to the eastern war. But when money was not forthcoming, the *doge* of Venice, Enrico Dandolo, had a plan. Forget the Holy Land; capture Constantinople, throw out Byzantium's emperors, and loot the city! The battle for Constantinople became Christian invader against Christian defender. The conquerors took

---

[4] Ibid., 313.

religious comfort (and the papal blessing) from the fact that the Patriarch of Rome and the Patriarch of Constantinople presided over two rival churches, Catholic and Orthodox.

When Charlemagne's crown had been consecrated by the Pope, the Patriarch of Constantinople took grave offense. Some years later, the Pope excommunicated the Patriarch and all his followers. The Patriarch, in turn, pronounced anathema upon the Pope. It became a breach between Christians of the East and West that remains unhealed today.

The spoils of the Fourth Crusade made Venice even richer in gold, silver, precious jewels, and magnificent works of art. The bronze horses that stand atop the portals of the Church of St. Mark are the most spectacular of Venice's stolen goods (the horses are copies; the originals are stored for safekeeping). *Doge* Dandolo died in Venice. As befitting its ruler, he was buried in the great Church of Santa Sophia, where a plaque marks the place of his crypt. The crypt is now probably empty. When the Byzantine emperor retook his throne, legend has it that Dandolo's remains were thrown to ravenous dogs.

By 1298, the Crusades' glory days were gone. Muslims had captured nearly all of the Crusaders' strongholds. Acre was the last to fall, in 1291. But again, willing to let profit supersede virtue, Venice had few scruples about trading with Islamic cultures. Its merchant fleet now brought to Europe the luxury goods of the East: pepper, spices, silks, and porcelain. Constantinople had been restored as the capital city of Byzantium, but on May 29, 1453, disaster struck again. After years of assault and sieges, the great city was overrun by the Ottoman Turks, who then continued their westward sweep into the Mediterranean. A century after the fall of Constantinople (now renamed Istanbul), the Christian West summoned its fleets for a final assault against Turkish maritime power. The Battle of Lepanto in 1571, the last great battle fought by galleys, brought victory to the West.[5]

THE PEPPER TRADE

With Turkish maritime might weakened, Venice continued to prosper, but new threats to its prosperity were in the making. Driven by national and religious ambitions, the Portuguese sailed around Africa, crossed the Indian Ocean in 1498, and became rich by transporting the spices and gems of the Indies. More important, as a threat to Venetian prosperity, Portuguese

---

[5] This calls to mind a poem by G. K. Chesterton commemorating the battle: "Dim Drums Throbbing in the hills half heard, Where only on a nameless throne a crownless prince has stirred .... Don John of Austria is going to war." "Lepanto" (Poem), 1911.

pepper flooded the market, and the price of pepper plummeted. Even before the Portuguese under the command of Vasco da Gamma landed on India's pepper coast, Columbus had crossed the Atlantic, claiming a New World for Spain. In 1523 the first treasure fleet sailed from the Yucatan to be followed almost yearly by ships carrying the gold and silver of Mexico, Peru, and Bolivia. Spain and Portugal were the new treasure houses of Europe. And the Venetian Republic worried for its future.

THE VENETIAN REPUBLIC

Half a millennium separates the First Crusade from Lepanto. During those years, Venice grew from a city-state to an empire. It dealt with kings and courts as a sovereign power and had colonies in the Adriatic and the Aegean. The city square of beautiful Nauphlion in southern Greece still displays the lion of St. Mark, emblem of its former Venetian overlords. The lion is incised in the stones of Dubrovnik and in several towns north and east of Venice, the region of the Veneto.

As Byron reminds us, "...Venice sate in state, throned on her hundred isles." Venice called itself a republic, but not in the form we consider to be a republic today. All power lay in the city-state, but the city-state was governed by a single ruler, the *doge*, chosen for life by a small, hereditary council of nobles. As centuries passed, the *doge's* power was circumscribed by a still smaller inner council who ruled secretly, killing and murdering those accused by secret informers of working against the interests of the state. The prisons of Venice were notorious for their cruelty, and today's visitors pay attention to a small bridge that links the prison to the *doge's* palace. For centuries, it has been called the Bridge of Sighs.[6]

The business of the Republic was business, and sharp trading was a matter of pride to the merchants of Venice. The Republic called itself *Serenissima* (the Serene One), a singular conceit, part boast and part disguise for the Venetian enterprise. In the year 1000, *Doge* Pietro Orseolo celebrated the enterprise by casting a wedding ring and laurel crown into the sea. He stood aboard his gorgeously gilded state barge, and with pomp and great ceremony intoned, "We wed thee, O sea, in token of true and everlasting dominion."[7] This ceremony (on the Sun-

---

[6] "I stood in Venice on the Bridge of Sighs / A palace and a prison on each hand" from "Childe Harold's Pilgrimage" (Poem) by Lord Byron.

[7] See W. H. Davenport Adams, *The Queen of the Adriatic: Or Venice Past and Present* (Boston: D. Lothrop and Co., 1869.

day after Ascension) still continues, but on a far less lavish scale, and with dreams of tourist wealth now substituted for the wealth of trade.

As for everlasting dominion, in human affairs, everlasting is mostly never lasting. As the wealth of the Indies and the Americas flowed to Europe in Iberian ships, Venice began its slow political decline. It kept on with its trade and expanded its banking enterprises, but

> ...Venice declined in power and virility, her power whittled away in constantly defensive wars against the Turks and by the rise of new commercial rivals in the west. By the 18th Century, her empire was almost gone, and she subsided in carnival and garish excess toward her end as a state.[8]

William Wordsworth summarized Venice's sad decline in his sonnet on the extinction of the Venetian Republic this way: "Once did she hold the gorgeous East in fee, / And was the safeguard of the West."[9]

CARNEVALE IN VENICE

Carnival, as most everyone knows, is the merrymaking in Roman Catholic countries that precedes the austerity of the forty days of Lent. The word's derivation may be from the Latin *carne*, meat, and *vale,* farewell. The Carnival of Venice was thought to have been started to commemorate a military victory in 1162. San Marco Square became the meeting place for dance and merriment. The Carnival soon came to mean letting-go, freedom, festive behavior, and even good-willed madness By the late 1600s, Carnival in Venice had become secularized; for the upper and middle classes it was a year-round series of masquerades. Visitors to Venice noted that women and men wore mysterious and flirtatious disguise even in daylight and that the *domino* (a hooded cape) was common dress.

Why the secular Carnival in Venice? One answer is that Venetians lived under the watchful eyes of secret police and the Inquisition. Disguise was a way of evading those eyes. Sociologists who pay attention to people at play, for example, suggest that Carnival in today's Brazil offers an opportunity to transform desperate lives into fantasies; more important, it is an outlet for social and political unrest.

---

[8] James Morris, *Venice* (New York: Faber and Faber, 1960).

[9] William Wordsworth, "On the Extinction of the Venetian Republic, 1802," *The Poems of William Wordsworth*, New Edition (London: Eward Moxon, 1847), 237.

The archetype of the Venetian libertine is Giovanni Casanova, born in Venice in 1725. His autobiography, no doubt filled with boastful exaggeration, traces the arc of his life. Expelled from seminary because of scandalous conduct, he was a violinist in Venice and an accomplished seducer of women. He was denounced as a magician and sentenced to prison under the roofs of the *doge's* Palace, but he escaped by scrambling "over the leads" and performed diplomatic service for rulers in Prussia, Russia, and Poland. When finally permitted to return to Venice, he arranged dangerous liaisons for wealthy clients, even while working as a spy for the Inquisition. Forced to flee again, he spent his final years (1785-98) as librarian for an aristocrat in Bohemia, his death coinciding with the death of the Venetian Republic.

Figure 6.3. Carnival of Venice, artist Johann Heinrich Ramberg

THE REPUBLIC DIES

In 1797 Napoleon's armies swept into Venice without a shot being fired. The emperor decreed the end of the Venetian Republic. Napoleon then lived briefly in Venice and pronounced St. Mark's Square the finest drawing room in Europe. He traded Venice to Austria the very next year, but in 1806 the French returned to rule the city again. In 1814, with Napoleon temporarily defeated, Austria resumed its rule over Venice. In 1866 Venice joined the newly established Kingdom of Italy and has been one of Italy's provincial capitals ever since. But it is a provincial capital that is also a world treasure.

THE PATRON SAINT OF VENICE

Modern-day Venice is punctuated with statues. One of the most impressive is Bartolomeo Colleoni, a warrior mounted on a massive stallion, the horse's left leg raised in triumphal stance. Colleoni was a commander of mercenaries in the service of Venice. He left his wealth to the Republic on condition that a statue to his glory be placed in front of the Basilica of St. Mark. The rulers of Venice accepted the bequest, but perhaps not wanting to be reminded that their non-naval military power had to be hired, they cleverly circumvented the bequest by placing the statue elsewhere, in front of the School of St. Mark, not the Basilica.

Much more ubiquitous are statues of a lion, the talisman of St. Mark. Venice had long had a patron saint, Theodore of Constantinople. But with freedom from the Byzantines, it seemed fitting that Venice should have another saintly patron, a saint more befitting a rising state. The body of St. Mark, the Evangelist and author of the *Second Gospel*, lay in Alexandria, attended by monks but under the indifferent eyes of their Muslim rulers. Legend has it that two adventurers, commissioned by Venice, stole the body, bribed the Muslim port officials, and for good measure, to keep pursuers and the curious at bay, covered the body with ham and pork (the pig being forbidden to Muslims). The body arrived safely in Venice, to great rejoicing, and statues of Mark's talisman rose across the city. The most prominent is the statue atop a high column in St. Mark's Square. It is a winged lion, a beast assigned to Mark by the *Book of Revelation* in the Bible. Sometimes brandishing a sword, sometimes fiercely rampant, sometimes merely open-jawed, the lion in St. Mark is atop a high column, his wings outstretched, one paw resting on an open book, with this inscription: "*Pax tibi Marce, Evangelista Meus*" ("Peace to you, Mark, My Evangelist").

THE TRAVELER IN VENICE

Almost every traveler will have a personal list of things to see and places to visit. For many it will be Venice's main street, the Grand Canal, two-and-a-half miles long, in the shape of an inverted S.[10] Two high-arching, stone bridges command the traveler's attention, the Scalzi and the Rialto. The Rialto (*rivo alto*, or high bank) was designed by the appropriately named Da Ponte and completed in 1591. Stalls and shops on the bridge date from that same decade. Today the bridge is thronged with gawkers and shoppers.[11]

Figure 6.4. Grand Canal

The palaces (*palazzi*) of Venice testify to bygone wealth. If money is crystallized wealth, palaces are surely crystallized money. One guidebook lists 130 *palazzi* that await the ambitious traveler's attention. Most, however, will settle for a handful of those on the Grand Canal. With

---

[10] The paintings of Francesco Guardi, 1712-93, capture the Canal's colors, the beauties of its riparian palaces, and its lively traffic during the mid-eighteenth century.

[11] Those who bargain for gold jewelry on the bridge may wish to keep in mind the experience of one buyer whose heavy gold ring was later found to owe its weight to an inner core of wax.

an inverse modesty often affected by the super-rich (the "cottages" of Newport, Rhode Island, for example), some palaces are merely "houses." Ca' d'Oro (Golden House) is one of the most celebrated.

Today many *palazzi* are used as business offices. Others house government bureaus. Many remain in private hands, replete with elegant furnishings. Each has a history dating back several centuries, its architectural style reflecting that history. The most attractive palaces are not always the largest. Typically, the palace is crowned with a tile roof and is entered directly from the Grand Canal through a distinctive doorway. Many palaces still have the colors of the livery painted on the mooring post outside the door. In former times, gondolas could be pulled through the doorway and set down on the canal-level floor, the *andron.* Above the *andron* is the *piano nobile,* the sumptuous reception and state rooms of the palace owners. If the architect worked in the Palladian Renaissance style (Andrea Palladio, 1508-80), the facade divides into three stories, the topmost being the most ornate, with tall windows sometimes recessed and fronted by balconies.

Figure 6.5. Rialto Bridge

Visitors wishing to compare architectural styles among the more than one hundred palaces might wish to seek out the Byzantine Fondaco dei Turchi, the Gothic Palazzo Arian, the Renaissance Palazzo, the Ca' d'Oro, and the Baroque Palazzo Treves. And to travel the canals through the camera's eye, one should view *Summertime* (1955) with Catherine Hepburn and Rossano Brazzi (nostalgic romance) and *Don't Look Now* (1973) with Julie Christie and Donald Sutherland (an occult thriller). A more contemporary film is *The Tourist* (2010), starring Angelina Jolie and Johnny Depp.

THE ARCHITECTURE OF PALACES

Although they seem to float on water, palaces were built on a foundation of pilings sunk into the water. Round oak pillars soaked in brackish water were driven into the canal bed at low tide level. Where necessary, a caisson surrounded one or more pilings, water was hauled out in buckets, and when the pilings were leveled, they were sealed with a packing of clay. Afterward, a foundation of planking was laid on top of the pilings to support a base of brick. On the brick, cut stone served as the visible foundation of the palace. Checking the pilings for structural integrity and ensuring that the clay packing remains sealed are most effectively done by draining the canal. The considerable cost tempts palace owners to delay inspection, sometimes endangering the palace. Modern technology offers an alternative to canal draining and piling repair. Where conditions permit, huge screws (augers) can be driven through the ground floor, directly into the canal bed.

CHURCHES

Churches must surely be counted among the splendors of Venice. Sightseers who vow to visit one church every day will spend more than a hundred days redeeming their pledge. Churches display the architectural style and technology of their era and the wealth invested in their construction. Churches built in the Gothic style of the Middle Ages present a tall, three-part facade divided vertically. In the central facade is a rose window high above the center door. Pointed Gothic arches frame doors and windows. Examples include Santa Maria Gloriosa Dei Frai and San Giovani, Bragora. The most admired church in the Palladian style (classical pillars supporting the architrave and statues atop the roof) is San Giorgio Maggiore. Baroque style is displayed in full ornamentation in the Church of the Derelitti. And beneath the Renaissance domes of Santa Maria della Salute is a profusion of neoclassical details and orders. Broad steps carry the visitor from the water's edge to the platform on which the octagonal Basilica stands. The total effect, as Henry James said, is compelling: "Some great lady on the threshold of her salon.... With her domes, and her wide step disposed on the ground like the train of a robe and scrolls, her scalloped buttresses and statues forming a pompous crown."[12] The three most visited and photographed churches of Venice are San Giorgio, the Santa Maria della Salute, and on the square that names it, the Basilica of St. Mark.

ST. MARK'S SQUARE – PIAZZA SAN MARCO

The many squares of Venice are called *campi* (*campo*, singular) from the Latin word for field. Square, or *piazza*, is the word reserved to honor St. Mark, as in *Piazza San Marco*, and its two adjoining smaller *piazzette*. Surrounded on three sides by some of the most elaborate buildings in the world, the vast space of St. Mark's Square throngs with visitors, strollers, gossipers, and vendors, not to mention the ever-present pigeons. Much the same sight greeted Napoleon, prompting him to call the square the drawing room of Europe.

Figure 6.6. St. Mark's Square

---

[12] Henry James, quoted in "Santa Maria della Salute: Part 2," *Love Venice*, Greybeard's blog, August 3, 2006, http://lovevenice.blogspot.it/2006/08/70-santa-maria-della-salute-part-2.html

Artists have long been captivated by Venice and the interplay among its sunlight, its water, and its buildings. J. W. Turner captured Venice at its most mystical. The Impressionist painter Renoir and generations of water colorists also worked at transforming Venetian three dimensions into two. But the master painter of St. Mark's Square is Giovanni Antonio Canaletto (1697-1768). His perspectives are superb, and the details in his paintings are astonishingly faithful. His views of St. Mark's Square are no mere camera snapshots; they are composed and altered by the artist's eye. As one admirer writes, with Canaletto, every carefully detailed brick bursts with sunlight.

The square is punctuated by vertical structures. The *Campanile* (Bell Tower) is 325 feet high. Its spire is topped with a golden weathervane, visible in the sunlight from far out at sea. From its observation galley, *The Logetta*, the viewer sweeps in scenes of the city, the lagoon, and the Adriatic Sea beyond. The *Campanile* collapsed into rubble on July 14, 1902. The tower was faithfully rebuilt, except for the ramp that granted horse and rider an aristocratic ascent to the top. Today's visitor must make do with squeezing into a crowded elevator.

In the *piazzetta*, two tall granite columns stand at what was once the seaside entrance to the city. One carries a statue of St. Theodore; the other is a platform for the winged lion of St. Mark. The space between the columns was used for public executions until the eighteenth century. Today the area is avoided by the superstitious. In the distant north side of the *piazza* is a clock tower with three distinctive facades. One frames a clock, while another displays the winged lion. High atop the building is a huge bell flanked by two bronze figures (Moors), whose hammers strike the bell every hour of the day.

Of the several buildings that frame the square, two are on every traveler's list: the Basilica and the *Doge's* Palace. Vast and overpowering, the Basilica is crowned with five huge domes. It is built on a Byzantine Greek-cross plan. Framing the central doorway is an arch whose intricate carvings celebrate the Labors of the Month. Above the central doorway is a still larger arch, and in front of that arch over the central doorway are the famous four bronze horses. Stolen from Constantinople during the Fourth Crusade, the domes, the facade, and the horses display Venice's early allegiance to Byzantium as well as the city's place as meeting ground between the East and the West. These two themes, sometime vassal of Byzantium and longtime crossroads of East and West, are carried into the church's interior, most notably in its 40,000 square feet of softly gleaming, golden mosaics.

The *Doge's* (Ducal) Palace is the unforgettable secular building of Venice, the place that encapsulates the wealth and power of the Serene Republic. Until the end of the Republic in 1797, the palace was the residence of the *doge*, the meeting hall of the legislature, the central office of administration, and the archive of the Republic. The building's exterior is immediately identifiable, like nothing else in the world. The west facade, fronting the *piazzetta*, has eighteen bays surmounted by thirty-six *loggia* arches, topped by an upper wall with six arched windows and a central door. The upper wall, patterned with lozenges of pink and white marble, seems more tapestry than stone. The *loggia* is framed and punctuated by lancet openings surmounted by large encircled quatrefoils. The encircled quatrefoils are supported by more than three dozen columns. The quatrefoils meet and blend to create delicate Gothic arches that are the signature of the facade.

The palace is adorned with statues, ceremonial staircases, courtyards, marble columns, and vast interior rooms. The Sala del Maggior Consiglio is almost 180 feet in length and, like other rooms in the palace, is sumptuously decorated. This particular room, with its ornate ceilings, is also adorned with paintings by Tintoretto and Veronese. Even among today's throngs of visitors, it is easy to imagine diplomats presenting their credentials here and, as was intended, being overawed by the sumptuous beauty of their surroundings.

IS VENICE DYING?

Like an aging diva who gives a series of farewell tours, Venice has been saying farewell to the world for a very long time. This much is true: Venice has been losing population every year at the rate of 1,500 a year. Today a scant 50,000 make Venice home, a huge drop from its golden age when Venice had about 200,000 inhabitants.

Venice is an expensive place to live. Rents continuously spiral upward. The price of a meal might approach double that of other Italian cities. Noise and pollution abrade the residents' spirits. The canals float litter. Many houses have septic tanks for their toilets. Older living quarters, especially those at water level, flush toilets directly into the canals. Housing and the city's infrastructure resist modernization. For residents, Venice is a make-do place.

Venice sells much but manufactures very little. Decorative glass, tassels for wall hangings, and decorative masks are the chief products of Venice. Most everything else for sale comes from the outside. What does sell is the experience of being in Venice. The city lives on the tourist trade; some seven million tourists arrive every year. The business of Venice is the tourist business and little else, so Venice has become a theme park. Many if not most travelers stay for a single day. Day tourists impose heavy costs on the city's municipal services and its infrastructure. Garbage and sewage disposal are part of the costs, as are feet that wear away floors and arms and hands that rub off precious patina. Above all, tourists in the summer get thirsty, constantly threatening the supply of drinking water.

Two recent days stand as grim warnings of tourist excess. Several years ago, on a single day, 60,000 Czechs poured into the city in 1,200 buses. And on July 15, 1999, 200,000 fans crowded into St. Mark's Square for a Pink Floyd Concert. They camped out in the Square and elsewhere in the city, overwhelmed toilet facilities, climbed pillars for a better view, and chipped away at the stones of Venice as souvenirs of their visit.

Organizations in Italy and abroad are dedicated to saving Venice to protect its treasures for future generations. Protecting Venice by limiting day tourists is a proposal much talked about but not likely to be put into effect. Venice lives on tourist money. But even greater than the tourist threat is the fact that Venice is "losing altitude"; that is, it is sinking into its own canals and lagoon as the sea rises. The buildings of Venice are built on pilings, not directly on solid ground. As the water table is tapped by the city and by mainland industry, the ground beneath the pilings sinks, and the ground floor of many palaces ride in water. Worse yet, for more than a hundred years, Adriatic tides have been rising higher and higher, pushing salty water into the canals and further eroding the brickwork of the palaces along the Grand Canal. The same holds true for buildings on the 177 lesser canals.

St. Mark's Square, a mere thirty-one inches above sea level, is one of the lowest points in the city. From 1900 to 1910, the square flooded fewer than ten times a year. By 1980, the square flooded forty times a year. In the present century, the square floods about sixty times a year. In some inundations, more than 90 percent of the city floods. Worse, in 1996, floodwaters rose so high that precious art was lost or damaged. Worse still, comparable floods are predicted to lie ahead.

Global warming is one explanation for the rising tides. Another is the movement of tectonic plates that cause sea levels to rise. Whatever the explanation, pedestrians in St. Mark's Square cope with constant flooding by putting metal tables around and linking them with sturdy planks. On flood days, tourists are well advised to see Venice by wearing tall rubber boots. Autumn is an especially vulnerable time for travelers.

After years of debate and procrastination, the government of Italy is hard at work on building seventy-eight steel floodgates that will rise in advance of rising tides to keep water out of the lagoon. Environmentalists worry that the project will threaten the wetlands ecology of the lagoon. The floodgates call for dredging sixteen million cubic feet of earth from the lagoon and replacing it with eight million tons of rock and nearly one million tons of concrete. If successful, the floodgates will work much the same way as the floodgates of the River Thames in London, keeping the lagoon from spilling into the streets, *campi*, and *piazze* and preventing sea water from flooding the canals. If unsuccessful, the future of Venice will continue to be problematic.

TODAY'S SHOPPER IN VENICE

Visiting the Venice of today is like taking many steps backward in time. It is an exercise, as the artist Arbit Blatas suggested, like peeling back layer upon layer of a painting, to reveal earlier and earlier iterations of this famous city. But Venice, like every historical urban center of note, also accommodates the modern traveler. The shops of Gucci, Ferragamo, Louis Vuitton, and countless other modern designers adorn the side streets of Venice (along with cheap kiosks whose level of tackiness grows with each passing year). But the hunting grounds for designer purchases of the rich and famous share their valued space with longtime sellers of two traditional products: Murano glass and Carnival masks.

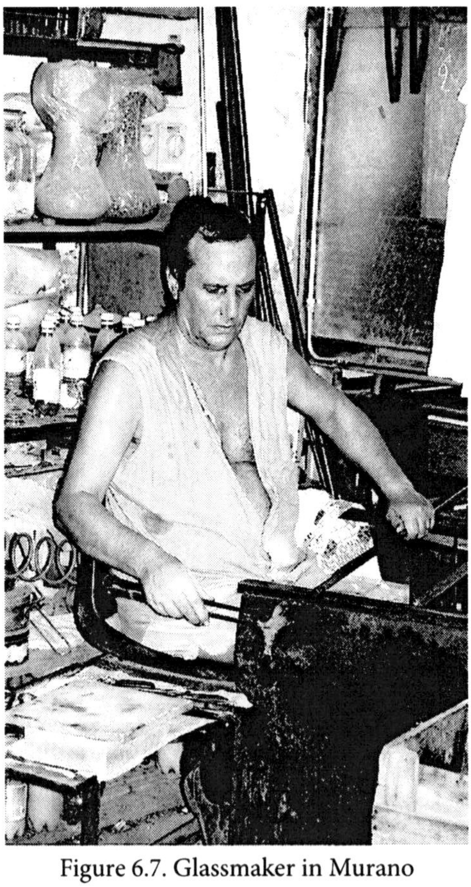

Figure 6.7. Glassmaker in Murano

For centuries only the glassblowers of the Murano foundries could produce such glassware of the highest quality. They were, in fact, the only artisans in Europe who could make glass mirrors. They originally worked within the city limits of Venice, but in 1291 the Venetian Republic ordered the foundries to be moved across the lagoon to the Island of Murano because they posed a fire hazard to the mostly wooden structures of Venice. Although stone eventually replaced wood as the principal building material in the city, the glassblowers remained in Murano. Today travelers who spend more than two days in Venice are likely to take the short boat ride across the water to Murano to watch the artisans at work. But if one is interested simply in purchasing a Murano glass-inspired gift, the shops of Venice will suffice.

Equally available throughout the shopping areas of Venice are Carnival masks. One can buy a simple and relatively inexpensive reproduction, or one can explore higher price ranges, even posing for a one-of-a-kind individualized mask. In the latter scenario, within twenty-four hours an ornate mask with one's likeness is delivered to the hotel. Alternatively, one can purchase a mask of high quality, representing a variety of professions. The one depicting a university professor is especially intriguing, as a large beak protrudes from underneath the processional cap typically worn by professors for formal university occasions.

Venice has something for everyone with an inquisitive mind and a spirit of adventure. But do not delay an effort to visit this most unusual of European cities. While efforts to save the city from sinking into the lagoon move briskly forward, mother nature is hard at work as well, posing a challenge every bit as formidable as those faced by earlier generations of Venetians.

7. The Renaissance: Florence Leads the Way

> In the distant plain lay Florence, pink and gray and brown with the rusty huge dome of the cathedral dominating the center like a captive balloon.... I still think, as I thought in the beginning, that this is the fairest picture on our planet, the most enchanting to look upon, the most satisfying to the eye and the spirit.
>
> — Mark Twain, *Autobiography*, 1892

> [Florence...] still has the sparks of Renaissance genius...
>
> — Peter Nichols, *Italia, Italia,* 1973

Every great city is known for its landmark icons. Paris has its Eiffel Tower, the Arc de Triomphe, and Notre Dame. Rome has its Colosseum, the Pantheon, and the Vatican, with St. Peter's Square and Cathedral. London has its Buckingham Palace, the Tower of London, the Houses of Parliament, and Big Ben. Florence (or *Firenze,* as the Italians call it) also has its landmark icons: the Cathedral (Duomo) and its dome, the Bell Tower that adjoins the cathedral; the covered bridge (Ponte Vecchio), and Michelangelo's statue of David. Every great city also has what the ancient Greeks called *ethos*, the spirit and genius of a place, a collective outlook and a history that explains its landmark icons.

Florence is no exception. The spirit and genius of this great city was the Renaissance—an outlook and an intellectual movement that created the modern age. And more than any other place, the Renaissance was born in Florence.

Renaissance means rebirth. Rediscovery might be a better word, for the Renaissance was a search to rediscover the morality, the ethics, the philosophy, and the learning of ancient Greece and Rome. The Renaissance began sometime in the 1300s and lasted until the late 1500s. It spread from Florence northward to the rest of Italy, and from Italy it spread to France, Germany, and Britain. People living during those years were conscious that their time was a new epoch, a time of cultural separation from what we today call the Middle Ages but what they, however, called the "Dark Ages."

Figure 7.1. Florence

Perhaps the oldest metaphor for human existence is that life is a journey that ends in an afterlife.[1] In the Middle Ages, life was seen as a journey to the grave and beyond the grave, either to Paradise or to Satan's realm. The good life was defined as a life of Christian devotion, prayer, and obedience to tradition and to nature's laws. In the Renaissance, life's journey assumed a new meaning and a new set of goals: to make use of human reason and to use that reason to advance knowledge, to explore the world, to delight in natural wonders, to admire human beauty and the human body, to take pleasure in the infinite variety of human behavior, and to live the good life in accordance with a well-defined code of ethics and morality built on the precepts of Greek and Roman cultures.

Wrapped in and around these goals were new and distinctive achievements in painting and the visual arts, science and medicine, architecture, politics, and exploration and discovery.

[1] In the gravesites of our remotest ancestors are utensils to be used in that afterlife.

In the Middle Ages, artistic creativity was less admired than fidelity to past forms and techniques. Painters were regarded as craftsmen; their modesty (to the point of anonymity) was expected. But the goal of the Renaissance painter was to be recognized for his personal creativity and to be regarded, and celebrated, as an *artist.* In this, as in so many aspects of the Renaissance, Florence led the way.

As distinguished historian Daniel Boorstin says, Giotto di Bondone (1267-1337) was a legend in his own time. He transformed Christian paintings from stylized, "schematic religious symbols" or wooden archetypes into warm living figures. [2] He was accomplished in oils, frescos on walls, and paintings on wooden panels. Giotto embodied what later ages would call the Renaissance Man—master of many skills and talents. As a result, in 1334 the citizens of Florence appointed him architect of the city. "He showed the versatility expected of artists of his age when he began building the bell tower beside the cathedral..."[3]

A FLORENTINE MYSTERY

Other men of genius followed Giotto to the center stage of Florence. The roster of great names who assembled under the civic flag of Florence is remarkable: in poetry, Dante; in prose, Boccaccio; in political analysis, Machiavelli; in painting, Giotto, Masaccio, Uccello, Veroccio, Fra Angelico, Fra Lippo Lippi, Botticelli, and Leonardo da Vinci; in sculpture, Donatello, Luca della Robbia, Ghiberti, Michelangelo, and Cellini; and in architecture, Brunelleschi and Alberti.[4]

In this roster lies one of history's great puzzles. What accounts for this assemblage of genius in one place and in one brief period of time? Perhaps the answer lies in synergy, a word that combines the idea of synthesis and energy, literally a working together so that the whole is greater than the sum of its parts. One possible contributor to the synergy that was Florence is that genius attracts its own kind. To live and work with gifted persons is a powerful stimulus to creativity and achievement.[5] A related component of Florentine synergy is that persons of ac-

---

[2] Daniel J. Boorstin, *The Creators* (New York: Random House, 1992). This book is a lively and readable cultural and artistic history of the West and the men and women who were creators. See pages 380-84.

[3] Ibid., 384. The author also published *The Discoverers* (1985), which chronicles the saga of human discoveries, and *The Seekers* (1998), which tells the story of those who sought and still seek to understand the world in which we live.

[4] This roster follows John R. Hale, *Renaissance: Time Life Great Ages of Man Series: A History of the World's Cultures* (New York: Time-Life Books, 1965), 75. See Chapter 4, "Florence, Intellectual Dynamo."

[5] In our own day, great universities and Silicon Valley are exemplars.

complishment appreciate being rewarded for what they do. Florence in the fourteenth, fifteenth, and sixteenth centuries had wealthy families whose sense of civic duty called them to serve as patrons of the arts. The citizens of Florence were also imbued with civic pride and with education that led to an appreciation of accomplishment. And perhaps as foundation for everything else, Florence was the seat of powerful banking families—the Bardi, Peruzzi, and most important, the Medici. The latter were especially generous patrons of accomplished people.

The great banks of Italy were also Renaissance creators. More than lenders of money and safe places for wealth, Renaissance banks, especially the Florentines, helped to create modern capitalism. They invested in technologies that created national wealth. The Medici invested in mines that produced alum, essential for cleaning the fiber and fixing the dyes in wool, thereby contributing to the success of the Italian wool trade. They invested in the cargoes of ships carrying luxury goods. They invented letters of credit, which facilitated international trade. They coined money, widely accepted for being trustworthy (no falsifying gold content). They kept agents and representatives in foreign capitals to facilitate lending and spending. They underwrote the costs of expeditions of discovery and exploration. Venezuela, for example, was named "little Venice" in part to acknowledge the role of a Venetian bank that underwrote the country's exploration. And most important, they invented the basic tool of modern accounting, double-entry bookkeeping.

AN ARCHITECTURAL WONDER

The citizens of Florence began building a cathedral in 1296, but the 180-foot vertical walls were not ready for a dome until 1418. Architects of Florence tried to rediscover how Rome had built the dome of the Pantheon. But a dome for the Cathedral of Florence was a daunting project. To enclose the roof opening over the apse, a dome would have to span 185.5 feet across. No trees of sufficient size or strength were available to build either a framework to support a dome's weight and size or to follow the ancient Roman technique of building a "formwork" to which brick and stone could be attached. Equally daunting, the weight of a dome pushing down and outward on the cathedral's walls was likely to send the walls crumbling to rubble and dust.

But the problem of the dome gave way to the genius of one of Florence's "Renaissance Men," Filippo Brunelleschi (13771446). Brunelleschi was a painter, a sculptor, a metallurgist who worked in bronze, a mathematician, a designer of complex machines, and an architect. His design for the dome embodied five bold ideas. First, to make the dome's marble and brickwork manageable, he proposed an octagon design. Second, to reduce weight, the roof opening would be covered by two domes, one inside the other, joined by supporting arches and spans. Third, each section of each dome would be secured and given its form by a stone rib, twenty-four in all, rising upward and curving inward to form a small circle held in place by an iron ring. Each rib would be seven feet thick at its base, tapering to five feet at its top. Fourth, the space inside each rib would be built of stone and brick rising upward in horizontal courses to provide structural strength. And fifth, the ribs comprising each dome would be held in place by a horizontal circle of stone and iron.

Figure 7.2. Duomo

To build twin domes that rose upward from 180 feet above the cathedral floor, huge stones would have to be hoisted upward and then moved horizontally to the work site, layer upon layer, upward and upward.

> In all, over a million pounds of stone would need to be raised to the top of the cupola. Since the cathedral was now in use, it was impossible to have a huge hoist at ground level. This meant the hoist had to be manually operated from the working level and, therefore, had to be small in scale—small enough, that is, for several men to operate in the limited space at the top of the dome. Yet it had to be capable of moving marble blocks weighing as much as two tons.[6]

---

[6] Ross King, *Brunelleschi's Dome: How a Renaissance Genius Reinvented Architecture* (New York: Walker and Company, 2000), 144-5.

Again, the genius of Brunelleschi rose to the challenge. He designed massive hoisting and traveling cranes to carry men and materials high in the air and, once there, to move them horizontally to the intended work site. Before the dome was complete, the hoist would raise aloft marble, brick, stone, and mortar weighing an estimated seventy million pounds.

> Cathedral tradition demanded that a lantern (a windowed turret) crown the dome. Several architects submitted plans to the wardens (supervising committee) of the cathedral who consulted widely: masters of theology, doctors of science, masons, goldsmiths, painters, and a mathematician, as well as various influential citizens, including Cosimo de' Medici. Their judgment, in the end, found in favor of Filippo's design.[7]

PERSPECTIVE, SHADOWS, LIGHT

Most everyone who reads these pages takes perspective for granted. We are so used to it in the visual arts that we fail to realize that it is an optical trick—a technique creating an illusion of reality that makes a two-dimensional picture (width and height) appear three-dimensional (width, height, depth). Perspective is a triumph of space. With perspective, a picture on a flat, two-dimensional surface tricks the viewer into thinking that he or she can look into the far distance. Like so much else that we associate with the modern world, perspective is a rediscovery of the Renaissance. And once again, it is Brunelleschi who is given credit (along with his pupil, Alberti) for pioneering the rediscovery. The Greeks and Romans had found ways of conveying distance by foreshortening. In the Middle Ages, figures and buildings "near" to the viewer were made large; those "far" from the viewer were merely made small. And the painting was clearly two-dimensional.

Brunelleschi invented perspective through experiment. In one hand, he held a small mirror. In the other, he held a panel of wood with a small hole in it. Through the hole, he looked at the reflection of a building in the mirror. And then, through memory, he replicated the reflected building on the wood panel. With this picture, he discovered the fundamental principles of perspective—parallel lines and a vanishing point. Over several years, the lines and vanishing point were given mathematical formula. Artists now talked of points, lines, and angles and described their subjects in terms of squares, cubes, and tetragons." And for 500 years, western painting would never again be the same.

Other Florentines also burnished the painter's art. Giotto had turned the artist's eye away from religion to the natural world. To paint the human figure beautifully and realistically be-

---

[7] Ibid., 143.

came the artist's great ambition. Light and illumination were given new use and meaning. In the Middle Ages, light was regarded as a manifestation of God's creation; dark was its opposite. For Florentine painters of the early Renaissance, light is "cool, vernal, bright."[8] Illumination now becomes the "signature" of the great painter. Figures are illuminated by backlight. Some are made to emerge from shadows and stand bathed in light. And others are defined by the merging of shadows and light. In paintings in the Middle Ages, God's grace is signified by light, while saints and celestial beings are uniformly illuminated, bathed equally in the same light. In the Renaissance, the play of light is used for several purposes: to give drama to the subject and to give unity to a scene. And color and light are used to organize the composition of the painting, in order to balance forms and to direct one's eyes along particular lines.

Also outstanding among Florentine artists is Masaccio, the master, some say the inventor, of foreshortening—the technique of enlarging a body part, the hand for example, to bring it fully into the viewer's eye and attention.

SCULPTURE AND SCULPTORS

Renaissance sculpture shared the inspiration of the other arts: to impart a living likeness to images of humans and animals carved of stone and cast in metal. Limbs and muscles must be visible in folds of clothing. And above all, the subject's body must look as if it is about to move or as though it has been captured in movement.

Lorenzo Ghiberti (1378-1455) designed the north and east doors of the Baptistery of the Cathedral of Florence. The most celebrated is the east door. Each of its bronze panels relates a story from the *Old Testament*. Each panel uses lights and darks to shape the scene and employs the principles of perspective to create a three-dimensional reality. And the figures are caught in their movement and the lines of their drapery flow. When Michelangelo first saw the east door, he is said to have exclaimed: "They are so beautiful that they are worthy of standing at the gates of Paradise."

Donatello (circa 1386-1466) was the pioneer of Florentine sculpture. On a study visit to Rome, he and Giotto made drawings of the buildings and estimated heights, seeking to rediscover the techniques used in their construction. His marble statue of St. George portrays a warrior ready to launch himself forward. When Michelangelo saw this sculpture, legend has him shouting, "March!"

---

[8] David Piper, *The Illustrated History of Art* (Vacaville, CA: Bounty Books, 2004), 112.

(H)e created living people out of stone by imparting to them weight and balance and psychological depth of human beings. Most regard *David* as his masterpiece. It dispenses with clothes to become the first life sized free-standing nude since classical antiquity.[9]

Figure 7.3. The David

[9] Robert Coughlan, *The World of Michelangelo: 1475-1564* (New York: Time, 1966), 60.

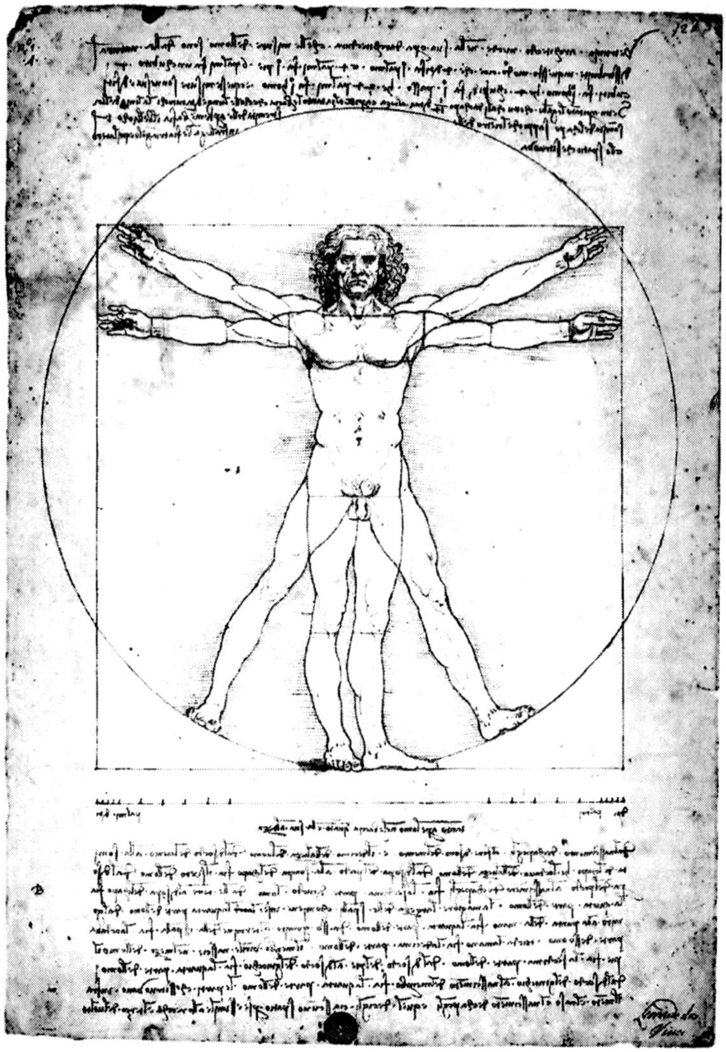

Figure 7.4. Da Vinci's Work, "The Vitruvian Man"

Towering in their accomplishments were Michelangelo Buonarrotti (1475-1564) and Leonardo da Vinci (1452-1519). Michelangelo is a sculptor without peers. His *Pieta* is the face of a beautiful, sorrowing mother cradling a dead son in her arms. His *David* "expresses vibrant power harmoniously contained."[10] And his *Tombs of the Medici* in Florence portray Giuliano and Lorenzo de Medici in calm, majestic death, while beneath them are allegorical images of Night and Day, Dusk and Dawn, that express anguish and sorrow at the death of those "whose

[10] Moses Hadas, *Imperial Rome* (New York: Time, Inc., 1965), 114.

light has been stolen from us."[11] In Rome, Michelangelo's paintings on the ceiling of the Sistine Chapel demonstrate "the scope and power…of his genius."[12]

Leonardo's genius had parallel yet different dimensions. His "curiosity about nature led him deep into anatomy, botany, geology, mechanics and astronomy."[13] He made drawings of flying machines and heavy-duty winches. He dissected the dead and made drawings of the human skeleton, ribcage, and eye. He was a military engineer. And, hardly last, he was a superb painter. His *Mona Lisa* is one of the world's most recognizable paintings, perhaps because his knowledge of perspective gave the figure its air of mystery: He used "two perspectives simultaneously…her figure and her background are constructed on two different vanishing points."[14]

WISE TRAVELERS IN FLORENCE

> Florence is a living arts centre where the people enjoy constant intimacy with masterpieces…. (As the tourist walks)… he will see…the six-balled shields of the Medici, the niches, the flower decked resting places, the altars and sculptures that adorn the facades.[15]

Florence is a city for strollers who delight in palaces, museums, and churches.[16] Cars are barred from the historic city center. The only dangers to the traveler are the pickpockets and the crush of crowds. The city is a "Renaissance museum" studded with palaces, churches, outdoor statues, and three museums—the Pitti, the Bargello, and the Uffizi. All display an embarrassment of riches in paintings and statuary. The historic city is a city on a human scale. All the important places in the city can be reached on foot.

The Piazza del Duomo, with its cathedral, bell tower, and sacristy, is the city's most famous site. The Piazza della Signoria is the political stage of the Renaissance. Dominating the square is the heroic-sized (seventeen foot) Michelangelo's *David* (now a copy—the real one is inside the Academia Museum), whose stance and gaze served as a warning to any lurking goliath that the Republic of Florence is not to be conquered. The Medici Palace begins at street lev-

---

[11] Robert Coughlan, *The World of Michelangelo: 1475-1564*, 142.

[12] Ibid., 114 ff.

[13] Moses Hadas, *Imperial Rome*, 129.

[14] Ibid., 98.

[15] See Michelin, *Italy Green Guide Michelin 2012-13*.

[16] Edgar Allan Poe once wrote of "The Glory that was Greece / And the Grandeur that was Rome." In that spirit, we are tempted to write, "and the legacy and spirit of Florence to inform our world today."

el; the fortress-like first story serves notice that the palace is the center of political power and that it is not easily assaulted. The interior courtyard is graced by a fountain (with a putti by Donatello), lovely murals, and pillars. The courtyard gives entry to (what seem like) endless rooms, beautifully decorated and "peopled" by Renaissance statues. Nearby, the Loggia del Lanzi contains Cellini's triumph, his bronze statue of Perseus holding aloft the head of Medusa.[17] No less famous are statues by Giambologna: *The Rape of the Sabine Women* and *Hercules Slaying the Centaur.*

Everywhere are reminders of those who helped to create western civilization. Buildings are engraved with the twelve balls of the Medici coat of arms. Michelangelo's statues are in the street, in museums, and especially in the Church of San Lorenzo. Dante, the creator of the vernacular Italian language, pined for his Beatrice here and later composed *The Divine Comedy.* Machiavelli worked here, and when he retired from the city, reflecting on what he had learned about power and politics, set down his ideas on rulers and rulership in *The Prince.* Da Vinci worked and experimented here, and Galileo gave lessons in mathematics here. Today scholars remained astonished at how Florence led the way as the Renaissance grew and flourished, despite being "simply" a small city of money lenders and makers of cloth.

[17] In Cellini's Autobiography, he recounts the difficulties of making molten bronze flow to the legs of Perseus.

OTHER EUROPEAN DELIGHTS

8. Germany Rises

Marcel Proust, in *Remembrance of Things Past*, suggests that those who seek the source of a great event must imagine they are following a great river to its source. The river is traced against its flow, but a tributary must also be traced, then another tributary. And still another. Then a stream must be followed. Perhaps a brook. At last, a well in a farmyard is found that feeds the brook. But, no, says its owner. This well is not the source of the brook. This well is fed by an underground spring that rises somewhere else!

And so it is with the origins of Germany. Problems and questions cloud the answer of where and when Germany came into existence. Benedict Anderson famously defines a nation as an imagined community, a vast aggregate of people whose numbers preclude any direct connection, for all but a tiny few. Yet they feel themselves part of a larger whole, part of a community that is usually built on four foundations: a common language, a geographic territory, a religion, and a memory of history's rights and wrongs.

But it is not so in Germany. As to territory, the boundaries of the German state (when it existed) have fluctuated constantly. Germans have never had the psychological security of clearly defined geographic boundaries, particularly on the great lowland of northern Europe. Nor have they possessed an identity based on a distinct language. German is spoken in many areas of central Europe. Beyond the borders of present-day Germany, German is also spoken in

Austria, Liechtenstein, and in areas of Switzerland, Luxembourg, France, and Italy. In Germany as well as beyond its borders, varieties of spoken German create communication difficulties for those speaking different German dialects. As to unity through a shared religion, for more than 500 years, Germans have divided almost equally between Protestants (mostly Lutheran) in the north and Roman Catholics in the south. And as to a history of shared rights and wrongs, Germans suffered the ravages of the Thirty Years' War (1618-1648), as Protestant and Catholic armies crossed and recrossed central Europe, living off the land, plundering food, and leaving peasants to starve, as they mercilessly crushed heretical enemies.

Given Germany's tenuous hold on the four customary foundations of nationhood, Stefan Berger carries the definition of the German nation into Oscar Wilde's territory: "A nation is a group of people united by a common mistake—about their ancestry and a common dislike of their neighbors."[1]

GERMAN ORIGINS

The origin of the name German is lost in the mists of time. So, too, is the origin of the homeland of the first German tribes to enter Europe. Two of these tribes, the West Goths (Ostrogoths) and the East Goths (Visigoths), were settled in the area around the Black Sea by the third century CE. Even earlier, Germanic tribes had established themselves in northern Europe. In 12 BCE Roman legions conquered their territory north of the Alps and east of the Rhine River. But successive revolts of Teutonic (German) tribes cost the legions dearly. In 14 CE a Roman general, Germanicus (who celebrated his victories by appropriating the name of his foes), led three campaigns into the German forests. A hundred years later, under the Emperor Hadrian, Rome secured a triangle that ran from the Rhine to the Danube. Fortifications secured the triangle, but the rest of Germania was beyond Rome's control. Within the boundaries of the triangle (the *limes)* is the city of Trier, on the banks of the Moselle River. Founded by the Romans in 15 BCE, its city gate (the Porta Nigra) served as the entry to Rome's fortified city.

By the beginning of the fifth century CE, the Roman Empire was in severe crisis. As the empire staggered and then collapsed, Germanic invasions grew bolder and more successful. Visigoths and Vandals moved swiftly across frontiers that had been badly overstretched and were rapidly weakening. The fifth century was the time of the wandering Germanic tribes

[1] Stefan Berger, *Germany* (London: Oxford University Press, 2004), xiii.

(*Volkerwanderung*). On the North Sea coast were Jutes, Angles, and Saxons, who flooded what remained of Roman Britain and left an enduring linguistic stamp (and a name, England) on the British Isles. East of the Elbe River were the Swabians, Vandals, Alans, and Goths. In the North were genetic relatives, the Scandinavians. Their descendants were Vikings, who later came crashing into Europe in the eighth century.

Much of what we know about the German tribes comes from the Roman writer Tacitus (56-120 CE). In addition to their territorial restlessness and ferocity as warriors, the tribes were organized in clans, made collective decisions through an assembly of warriors, and worshipped Odin (Wodin), the god of war and protector of heroes who presides over their feasting and roistering in Walhalla. Freyja is goddess of love, wealth, and fertility. Thor is the god of thunder and rain (he assures good crops), but he is also the god of war, using his hammer to crush the skulls of those who oppose him. And among the many other gods is Sigurd, whose magic cloak grants the wearer invisibility.

NATIONAL BEGINNINGS: TRACING THE RIVER OF HISTORY

In the year 9 CE, three Roman legions were annihilated by German warriors in the Teutoburg forest. Rome decided against further incursions into German territory and stabilized its frontier posts on the Rhine and Danube rivers.

In 800 CE Charlemagne was crowned and anointed Holy Roman Emperor by Pope Leo III and laid claim to the inheritance of the now defunct western Roman Empire. He ruled the territory of Roman Gaul (by this time, home of the Franks) and asserted his authority over Bavaria and Saxony. On his death, his kingdom was divided; German lands were inherited by his son, Otto. In 846 CE Clovis, King of the Franks, extended his rule into what is now western Germany.

In 962 CE Otto was crowned Holy Roman Emperor, presiding over an empire that continued until 1806. (Later German rulers will call it the First Reich, or First Empire.) The kingdoms, duchies, baronies, and cities in the empire were sufficiently powerful—and independent of imperial authority—to justify Voltaire's celebrated remark: "The Holy Roman Empire is neither Holy, nor Roman, nor an Empire."

In the thirteenth and fourteenth centuries, seventy north German cities joined in a treaty of support and defense to deal with pirates and to assist in Baltic and North Sea trading. The Hanseatic League was formally organized in 1370. One of its merchant groups, The Easterlings, was given trade privileges in England. Their currency was so trustworthy that it became the standard for British money—the pound, i.e., sterling.

RELIGIOUS WARS

> For where God built a church, there the Devil would also build a chapel.
>
> — Martin Luther, *Table Talk*, 67

> An institution is the lengthened shadow of one man.
>
> — Ralph Waldo Emerson, *Self Reliance*

One of the great (some would say greatest) divisive eras in German history was the period now known as the Protestant Reformation. The opening year was sometime after 1512; the place was Wittenberg in Saxony. Martin Luther, a priest with a doctorate in theology, had been studying the New Testament and came to a conclusion that would stagger Christendom. He had been to Rome and was offended by the luxurious life of those high in the Roman Catholic Church hierarchy. He was even more offended by the Church's view that salvation could be achieved by good works, especially by giving money to the church through the purchase of "indulgences." Indulgences were freely sold in Germany, to the profit of churchmen and secular bankers. By buying an indulgence, the purchaser would be forgiven his or her sins. The indulgence could also be used to grant salvation to and ease the suffering of those already dead.

Contrary to the teachings of the Church, Luther had come to believe that Christians are saved through the gift of God's grace, not through good works. To assert his conclusion and condemn the sale of indulgences, in 1517 Luther nailed ninety-five theses to the Castle Church of Wittenberg. He was excommunicated in 1521 and summoned to the emperor's Diet (council). Commanded to recant, he refused, saying as legend has it (with some disagreement from experts), "Here I stand. I cannot do otherwise. God help me. Amen." With this step, the Protestant Reformation had begun.

Luther's arguments fanned outward. The Scriptures, he argued, not the Pope or papal councils, are the basis of religious authority. Clergy should not be regarded as intermediaries between men and God; and personal understanding is more important than the teachings of clergy. Everyday life is everywhere part of God's work, and accordingly, priests should be permitted to marry (Luther himself took a wife).

The conjoined ideas of freedom from traditional authority and God's will working in everyday life led to widespread revolt by peasants, often led by the clergy seeking to escape the harsh extractions of feudal dues. One estimate reckons that by 1525, around 300,000 peasants, out of a total German population of perhaps sixteen million, were under arms.[2] Nobles mercilessly crushed the revolt, with Luther himself allied to traditional authority.

Figure 8.1. Martin Luther, 1528 by Lucas Cranach the Elder

Thanks to Gutenberg's printing press and Luther's translation of the Bible into German, Luther's ideas and pronouncements spread across Germany and Scandinavia. As a general rule, northern German states, kingdoms, and dukedoms chose to follow Luther's teachings, while southern states remained loyal to Rome. Given the intensity of conviction, war between Lutheran and Catholic domains erupted in a series of battles and campaigns that moved across Europe for thirty years, from 1618 to 1648, with Sweden, Denmark, France, and Austria com-

[2] Mary Fulbrook, *A Concise History of Germany*, 2nd ed. (New York: Cambridge University Press, 2004), 41.

manding the largest armies. The Thirty Years' War was fought mostly in Germany. Castles were besieged, towns and villages laid waste, and peasants starved as crops were stolen and burned. Some districts lost half their population, while others counted themselves lucky if only 20 percent died. After the war, the Peace of Westphalia (1648) treaties ended the Thirty Years' War and formally pushed the Pope out of secular world affairs.

The consequences of the Lutheran challenge to Roman Catholicism were profound. Luther's translation of the Bible created a standard written language all across German-speaking lands, helping to unite those who spoke different German dialects. Prussia emerged as Protestant Germany's leading state and, as will be shortly noted, fought a war to keep Catholic Austria out of the nineteenth century unification of Germany. And when Protestant Prussia invaded Roman Catholic France, French mistrust of German motives became a pivot of international diplomacy for almost a century.

THE RISE OF MODERN GERMANY

> Phoenix: A mythical bird of great beauty. Said to live 500 years, in a nest of spices. Then burns itself on a funeral pyre, and arises again from the ashes in the bloom of youth and lives again through another cycle.[3]

One place to begin tracing the rise of modern Germany is the early victories of Napoleon. By 1806, he had defeated the armies of Austria, Russia, and Prussia. He then reorganized the states of Germany to bring them within the French sphere of influence. As members of his newly formed Confederation of the Rhine, Wurttemberg and Bavaria became kingdoms, and Hesse-Darmstadt, Nassau, and Berg were constituted as dukedoms, with Prussia, Baden, and Hanover given enlarged territories. Even more important, the many dozens of independent cities and baronies were obliterated.

After Napoleon's defeat at Waterloo (1815), the map of Europe was redrawn by the victors at the Congress of Vienna. Germany was reconstituted as a confederation of thirty-nine independent states. Austria was the largest German-speaking state in Europe and was also its most territorially aggressive. Acceding to Austria's demands, the Confederation of the Rhine was dismembered. Its territory reverted to a congeries of independent kingdoms, dukedoms, prin-

---

[3] Adapted from E. Cobham Brewer, *The Dictionary of Phrase and Fable* (Philadelphia: J.B. Lippincott, 1937). 792.

cipalities, and cities—Kleinstaaterei (swarm of little states)—until consolidation began again under Prussian leadership.

Prussia and the North German Confederation

Let us put Germany…in the saddle!
You will see that she can ride.
— Otto von Bismarck, Speech to the Parliament of the North German Confederation, 1867

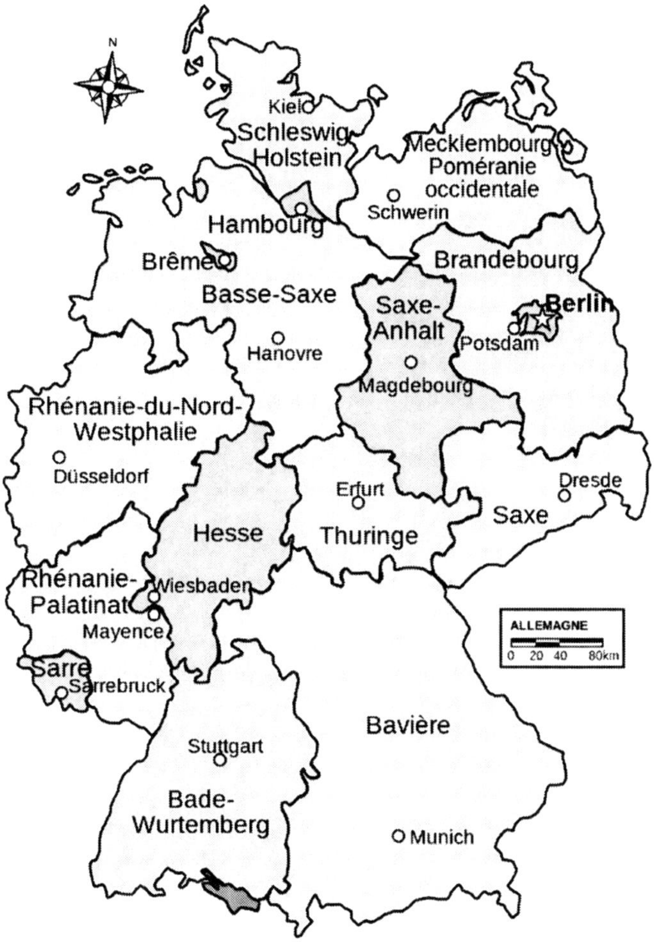

Figure 8.2. Map of Germany

Prussia, as the second largest German-speaking state in Europe, also had territorial ambitions. William I was its king, but its guiding political genius was Prince Otto von Bismarck. In 1866, Bismarck contrived to provoke Austria into war, the Seven Weeks' War. Prussian soldiers were better trained, and its weapons were modern and effective. In a short seven weeks, Austria sued for peace, agreeing to Prussia's plans for a North German Confederation. Under Prussia's leadership, the states of south Germany (excluding Austria) joined the nearly two dozen states of the former Confederation of the Rhine.

THE FRANCO-PRUSSIAN WAR

Four years later, Prussia turned on France. And the Franco-Prussian War of 1870-71 inflicted a stunning defeat on the French. In defeat, the French monarch, Emperor Louis Napoleon, abdicated, and civil war followed. Radical groups seized Paris and withstood a four-month Prussian siege. Outside Paris, a newly formed republican government acceded to Prussia's terms for peace, but the government in Paris (the Commune, or workers' government) refused to lay down arms. Troops of the new Republic bombarded Paris. In the fighting, the Communards set fire to large parts of the city. As soldiers of the Republic took the city, more than 20,000 Communards were killed.

As a reward for victorious leadership, William I, King of Prussia, was declared emperor, or Kaiser, of the newly united German Empire, called The Second Reich. The Kaiser's (and Bismarck's) peace terms were severe: France was forced to surrender two of its historic provinces on its northeast frontier, Alsace and Lorraine. And the seeds of enmity between France and Germany would bear fruit in World War I.

The German Empire would be defeated in the First World War. The same fate would befall its successor in the Second World War, the infamous Third Reich (Third Empire). Out of the carnage of World War II, present-day Europe emerged. And out of war's ashes, the German phoenix rose once again.

WORLD WAR I

> The lamps are going out all over Europe; we shall not see them lit again in our lifetime.
>
> — Viscount Grey, British Foreign Secretary,
> On the eve of war, August 3, 1914

The First World War ushered in what many call history's most violent century. The violence began on June 28, 1914, in Sarajevo, Bosnia (part of the Austro-Hungarian empire) when a Serb nationalist assassinated the heir to the Austrian throne. Austria then declared war on Russia, the protector and patron of Serbian nationalist aspirations. Step by step, the war expanded, pulling in thirty-two countries, arrayed in two grand coalitions. One was known as the Allies and included Great Britain, France, Russia, Italy, and the United States. Its antagonist was called the Central Powers and included Germany, Austria, Bulgaria, and the Ottoman Empire. When it ended on November 11, 1918, more than forty million were dead, and the countries of Europe were bankrupt and exhausted. And the Tsar of Russia as well as all monarchs of the Central Powers had lost their thrones.[4]

THE SOURCES OF WAR

The assassination in Sarajevo was the spark that began the war, but its combustible materials had been laid down long before 1914. One likely antecedent is the Franco-Prussian War of 1870-71. For the French, fear and suspicion of Germany was the centerpiece of its foreign policy. On the German side, victory produced an outpouring of nationalism and patriotism. Germany's new nationalism was also fed by industrialization. The Industrial Revolution had begun in Britain in the eighteenth century and moved eastward. Germany was late in catching up to France, but with unification, German industry moved quickly forward. Mass production of goods is the great achievement of an industrial society. It requires an expanding urban population to work its factories. Mass production also depends on both domestic and foreign markets. And expanding markets require raw materials.

In the nineteenth and early twentieth centuries, Africa offered both markets and material resources, but Germany was a late entry into the colonization of Africa. The recently industrialized Germany, now with the most modern armaments, aggressively demanded its place in the colonial sun. The newly united Germany used its increasing military strength to search for overseas markets and to acquire colonies. In the Franco-Prussian War, its army was led by the king and a general staff charged with strategic planning, which is commonplace today but was an innovation in its time. Equally important, the chief of staff became the prototype of future chiefs, the brilliant strategist, Helmuth Karl Bernhard Graf von Moltke.

---

[4] See C. L. Sulzberger, *The Fall of Eagles* (New York: Crown Publishers, 1977).

Kaiser Wilhelm I also insisted that Germany challenge the British Navy, master of the oceans since the eighteenth century, in both armaments and size. A naval armament race began, with Germany matching Britain gun for gun and battleship for battleship. The race was augmented by Germany's Kiel Canal, completed in 1895, which gave German ships quick and safe passage between the North and Baltic Seas.[5]

As the race for colonies and military domination continued, the countries of Europe bolstered their military strength by looking for sympathetic allies. Germany joined Austria, its German-speaking neighbor, while France and England made common cause. And Russia joined with France, in part remembering an old enemy, the Teutonic knights who were kept from colonizing Russia by the victory of Alexander Nevsky in 1242.

By the first decade of the twentieth century, European statesmen expected and anticipated war. Plans and timetables for general mobilization were in place. It is not surprising, therefore, that the assassination at Sarajevo turned expectation into reality.

ALL "QUIET" ON THE WESTERN FRONT

The "war by timetable" began in early August 1914 amid popular jubilation. It was widely believed that it would demonstrate a nation's military and moral superiority. It would sweep away false values and usher in an era of cultural and moral regeneration. Everyone expected it to be a short, glorious war. In its beginning, the German-Austrian alliance moved on three fronts: the western front, from Belgium into France; the southern front, from Austria into Serbia; and the eastern front, from Germany eastward into Russia. The western front was the key to victory, but it quickly bogged down in stalemate. A line of trenches and dugouts ran from Switzerland to the North Sea. For four terrible years, armies would advance and retreat over the same ten miles. Barbed wire separated the opposing trenches. Artillery and machine guns rained death. The dead and dying were splayed on the barbed wire. The trenches were cesspits of horror: rain and mud, lice and rats, bodies and body parts, and pools of feces and urine. And the cost in lives was staggering. Casualties in the land war were more than thirty-seven million. As just one example, in the first hours of the Battle of the Somme (July 1, 1916), the British suffered 60,000 casualties. The entire Battle of the Somme from July to November cost 400,000 British lives, 200,000 French lives, and 450,000 German lives.

---

[5] See Arthur Herman, *To Rule the Waves: How the British Navy Shaped the Modern World* (New York: Harper Collins, 2004).

As the war dragged toward stalemate, each side vowed a victor's revenge: make the enemy pay dearly in both treasure and blood for the cost of the war!

In the end, it was Germany that gave way. Under the terms of surrender, Germany returned Alsace-Lorraine to France. In all, one-seventh of German territory and one-tenth of its population were lost.

Figure 8.3. The Western Front
Royal Irish Rifles, Somme, July 1916 (Imperial War Museum)

One third of its coal and three quarters of its iron ore resources were gone. It was not going to be a colonial power any more. It was not allowed a strong army and it had to pay massive reparations. On top of all that, the Versailles Treaty [of surrender] declared that Germany was the only guilty party in the outbreak of the war.[6]

Germany was also required "to forfeit large amounts of goods in kind, including timber, steel, and most of her merchant marine and large passenger ships."[7] Small wonder that, as David Frumkin suggests, it was a peace to end all peace!

---

[6] Stefan Berger, *Germany* (London: Oxford University Press, 2004), 121.

[7] Marshall Dill, *Germany: A Modern History* (Ann Arbor: University of Michigan Press, 1961), 273.

The Houses of Hapsburg (Austria), Hohenzollern (Germany), and Romanov (Russia) ruled vast territories, but all three houses and their rulers would be toppled by the end of World War I.[8]

THE WEIMAR REPUBLIC

The war's end was a shock to most Germans. For almost four years, their leaders had lied, telling them that victory was imminent. Anger exploded into violence as competing factions fought to dominate the promised republic. Socialists, workers' alliances, Communists (supported by the new Soviet Regime), army officers, and nationalists took to the streets, weapons at the ready. All through Germany, royal rulers vacated their thrones. Kings, grand dukes, and dukes surrendered power. The kaiser was the last to go, claiming that although no longer kaiser (emperor), he was still King of Prussia. When the Allies talked about bringing him to trial as a war criminal, he petitioned the Queen of Holland for asylum and subsequently took refuge there.[9]

WEIMAR: AN UNCERTAIN DEMOCRACY

> War is nothing more than the continuation of politics by other means.
>
> — Karl Von Clausewitz, *On War*[10]

A democracy, if it is to succeed, needs widespread support that, over time, brings legitimacy, usually defined as widespread loyalty to the regime. At any given time, leaders of the government can be rejected, and the party in power can be viewed as immoral and unworthy. But even so, the system of government (the regime) is deemed worthy of loyalty and support. Alas, for the Weimar Republic, its legitimacy was called into question at the outset.

Even before the end of fighting—the Armistice was November 11, 1918—German military leaders, unwilling to accept responsibility for defeat, claimed that the country had been betrayed. It had been stabbed in the back by enemies within—a conspiracy of socialists, Com-

---

[8] See David Fromkin, *A Peace to End All Peace: The Fall of the Ottoman Empire and the Creation of the Modern Middle East* (New York: Avon Books, 1989) for a discussion of the consequences of World War I.

[9] Martin Kitchen, *The Cambridge Illustrated History of Germany* (Cambridge: Cambridge University Press, 1996), Chapter 10.

[10] Karl Von Clausewitz, *On War*, Edited by Anatol Rapoport (Baltimore: Penguin Books, Inc., 1968). He was a brilliant military theorist and director of The War College in Berlin from 1818 to 1830.

munists, pacifists, alien influences, and those with insufficient patriotism. Belief in the conspiracy was widely accepted, and the violence in German cities at war's end somehow gave greater credence to the conspiracy. Thus, the Weimar Republic (1919-1933) was built on shaky foundations.

> The moderate socialist leaders who had assumed office in the fall of 1918 confronted a nation already under almost unendurable stress due to the external defeat and internal dissension....they decided, once in power, to preserve what remained of the existing social and economic order. Thus, they took it on themselves the thankless task of liquidating the bankrupt ...empire, accepting, on the one hand, the peace settlement...and on the other, the odium of crushing... the radical movement which threatened to engulf Germany in a Communist revolution... [Russian style].[11]

CRISIS YEARS

Weimar was a republic in constant crisis. In March 1920 an anti-republican military force marched on Berlin as a fearful government fled first to Dresden, then to Stuttgart. A general strike in support of the government followed as "The workers left en masse. Life in Germany came to a stop."[12] Finally, the government returned to Berlin. When government authority was restored, the radical left rose. A red army of 50,000 workers from the industrial Ruhr Valley marched on Berlin, while the army stood by. For protection, the government called on the Free Corps, an irregular army of ex-officers and unemployed ex-soldiers—armed freebooters! The Free Corps, a foretaste of the Nazis to come, had its origins in the weeks after the armistice. Bewildered soldiers, without jobs or civilian training, kept their arms and turned their anxiety and anger (*angst*) against those who had stayed at home, while soldier-patriots fought for German glory and German victory. Objects of patriot scorn were the usual suspects—socialists, Jews, and pacifists, "the mealy-mouthed and obsequious."[13] In the fighting that followed, 3,000 died, and to compound the government's misery, French soldiers crossed into Germany, claiming that the Versailles Treaty gave them the "right to oppose resurgent militarism in Germany."[14]

As the government limped along, its members came to fear the spate of political murders. Then the crises of 1923 occurred. The Reparations Committee declared Germany in default on

---

[11] Donald S Detwiler, *Germany: A Short History* (Carbondale: Southern Illinois University Press, 1989), 180.

[12] Marshall Dill, *Germany: A Modern History*, 281.

[13] Ibid., 284.

[14] Ibid., 282.

its delivery of timber and coal. French troops entered the Ruhr industrial region to protect French and Belgian technicians assigned to operate mines and factories for French and Belgian benefit. With mines and factories no longer producing for Germany and with its economy at a standstill, inflation soared. To meet its payrolls and to provide benefits for the needy, in 1923 the government began printing what would soon be worthless money. Stories were told of the elderly who withdrew a lifetime of savings from the bank, and used it to buy a loaf of bread!

> It cost more than a billion marks to send a letter from Germany to the United States. Workers needed wheel barrows to transport their weekly pay. By the end of the year thirteen figures were required to represent the number of marks that equaled one American dollar.[15]

Worse was to come in the worldwide economic Depression of the 1930s. The Weimar Republic completely lost whatever loyalty it had among German voters. Communist turnout rose. More ominously, by 1932 Hitler's National Socialists (The Nazi Party) garnered 37.4 percent of the seats in Parliament (The Reichstag). The President of the Republic appointed Hitler as Chancellor of the Republic in 1933. And the nightmare years began.

> In the nightmare of the dark
> All the dogs of Europe bark,
> And the living nations wait,
> Each sequestered in its hate.
> — W.H. Auden "In Memory of W.B. Yates," 1939

BUILDING THE THIRD REICH

Hitler and his henchmen created their regime of terror on several levels.[16] Foremost was Hitler's messianic conviction that he alone was destined to restore the German people to their former greatness. This conviction was aided by an uncanny ability to evoke adoration from massed crowds and to play their emotions through his oratory.

Equally important were the hard facts of Weimar's political and economic life: a democracy that had been tried and found wanting and an economy incapable of improving the lives of vast numbers of Germans.

---

[15] Ibid., 291.

[16] Two excellent books on the period include Erik Larson, *In the Garden of the Beasts: Love, Terror, and an American Family in Hitler's Berlin* (New York: Crown, 2011) and William L. Shirer, *The Nightmare Years: 1930-1940* (Edinburgh: Birlinn, 2002).

TAKING CONTROL

In 1933 all political parties were banned except for the National Socialist Party (The Nazi Party). Decrees of political and social "coordination" (*Gleichshaltung*) were issued. These included purging from the civil service all Jews and all opponents of Nazism, along with the abolition of independent state and provincial governments. Independent labor unions were abolished; membership was transferred to a government-run German Labor Front. The newly created Ministry of Popular Enlightenment and Entertainment took control of newspapers, radio stations, and film studios. Loyalty and enthusiasm for the regime were demanded of those who enlightened and entertained the public. At universities and in public squares, mass book burnings became a form of public entertainment. Into the flames went books by Jews, Communists, and all deemed unworthy of the new Germany.

In that same year, the first concentration camp was opened in Dachau, near Munich (with enthusiastic support of the press). Homosexuals and opponents of the regime were beaten, tortured, and often killed. "Fear of arrest and fear of informers" led to a "frightened public conformity."[17]

On the death of Weimar's President (General von Hindenburg) in 1934, Hitler added the office of President to his office of Chancellor. He also became supreme commander of the armed forces and imposed on its members an oath "to render unconditional loyalty to the Fuhrer of the German Reich and its people, Adolph Hitler." In his speech to the Parliament on July 13, he declared that the Nazi Party would be the "sole bearer of the political will of the nation."[18] The secret state police, the Gestapo, were placed directly under the Fuhrer's command. It was answerable to no one but its head (Heinrich Himmler) and, through him, Adolph Hitler.

BLOOD AND RACE

In traditional use, the nation-state is defined in terms of geography: authority over persons and things within a set of geographic boundaries. Nazi Germany changed the definition, putting race at its center. Surrounding the definition of race was the idea of the Volksgemeinschaft, a people united by race. Excluded were Gypsies and Jews. One hallmark of the Volksgemeinschaft was "Aryan blood." Historically, Aryan was a term used to mark those who spoke a vari-

---

[17] Mary Fulbrook, *A Concise History of Germany*, 2nd ed. (New York: Cambridge University Press, 2004), 181.

[18] Donald S Detwiler, *Germany: A Short History*, 190.

ant of Indo-European languages. Now it included all those within the Volksgemeinschaft. Aryan was the genetic ideal (tall, blonde, blue eyes) of Nazi Germany.

Figure 8.4. Adolph Hitler

In 1933 signs appeared on the windows of Jewish shops: "Germans defend yourselves. Do not buy from Jews." Jews were "dismissed from all governmental or teaching posts… from the leading professions and important business positions. Jewish owned firms are seized..."[19] In May of that year, mass demonstrations accompanied the burning of books in town squares all across Germany. Into the flames went books by Jews, left-wing authors, and all authors deemed "unGerman."

The 1935 Nuremberg Laws stripped Jews of citizenship and civil rights. They could not vote. Marriage was outlawed between Jews and citizens of German blood. Jews could not employ Aryan domestic servants or take part in the arts. On November 9, 1938, 7,500 Jewish businesses were destroyed, 250 synagogues were burned down, and thousands of Jewish

---

[19] Marshall Dill, *Germany: A Modern History*, 371 ff.

apartments were wrecked. Thousands were thrown into concentration camps. In January 1939, in a speech to the Reichstag, Hitler proclaimed that if war broke out in Europe, its Jews would be destroyed.

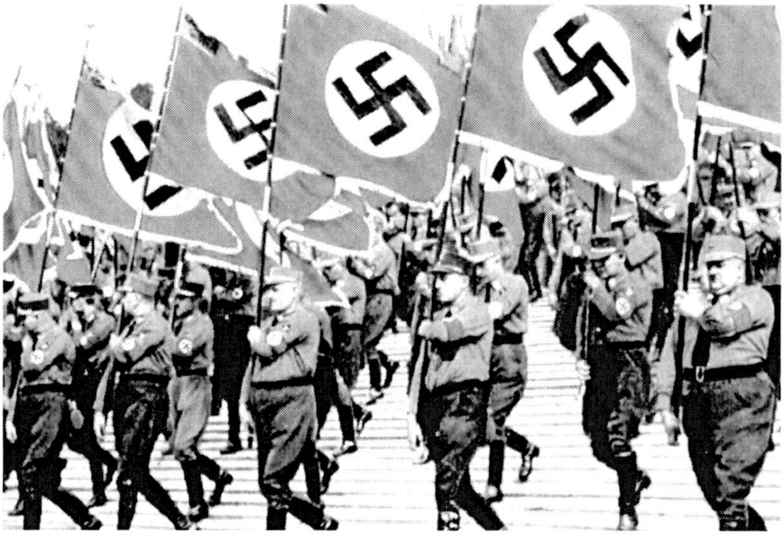

Figure 8.5. Nazi Marching

What was euphemistically called "The Final Solution" began around 1941. In what would later be called the Holocaust, six million Jews and perhaps another million deemed unfit to live would be murdered in Nazi concentration camps. "The most infamous of the camps...was Auschwitz....When all the gas chambers ...were in full operation, it was possible to kill up to 9,000 people within twenty-four hours."[20]

WORLD WAR II

> The sky was good for flying
> Defying the church bells
> And every evil iron
> Siren and what it tells...
> — Louis MacNiece, "Sunlight on the Garden", 1936

---

[20] Mary Fulbrook, *A Concise History of Germany*, 199.

Germany's territorial expansion began in 1936 when, in defiance of the treaties of 1919, German troops took control of former German territory along the Rhine. Some European statesmen were apprehensive, but no military resistance was offered, owing in part to growing recognition that the terms of surrender in the First World War had been overly harsh. In 1938 German troops crossed into Austria, dismantled its government, and in a rally in Vienna, Hitler proclaimed to a rapturous crowd that German-speaking Austria was now a German province. The new province gave Germany an enormous hoard of gold and a half-million workers for Germany's busy armaments factories.

> The regime was immensely popular and was bent on war, and the political economy distorted to the extent that by 1938 52 percent of government expenditure and more than 17 percent of gross national product was being poured into armaments. In the year of Munich [1939] ... Germany was spending more on weapons than Britain, France, and the United States combined.[21]

Germany then demanded annexation of a province in Czechoslovakia whose population was largely German speaking. In September 1939 the British Prime Minister visited Hitler and returned with a promise of "peace in our time"—acceding to German demands without even consulting the Czechs. With the benefit of hindsight, many now claim that Hitler could have been stopped had France and England and the rest of Europe been ready to go to war, first over the Rhine territory and then over Czechoslovakia. But memory of the First World War and fear of losing another generation of young soldiers haunted Europe. A few, Winston Churchill foremost among them, were ready to pay the price of standing up to German aggression, but a fearful public would not be moved.[22]

In March 1939, German armies crushed Czechoslovakia, and on August 31 of that year, Hitler issued orders to attack Poland. France and Britain then declared war on Germany. World War II had begun.

THE PHOENIX DIES AND IS REBORN

At war's outbreak, more than 110 million people had been called to the colors. Once begun, the war in Europe dragged on for almost six terrible years. Only three countries escaped its devas-

---

[21] Paul Kennedy, *The Rise and Fall of the Great Powers: Economic Change and Military Conflict from 1500 to 2000* (New York: Random House, 1987), 304-5.

[22] See A. J. P. Taylor, *The Origins of the Second World War* (New York: Atheneum, 1962) and Roy Jenkins, *Churchill: A Biography* (New York: Farrar, Straus and Giroux, 2001).

tations (Switzerland, Sweden, and Ireland). When the war ended on VE Day (May 8, 1945), civilian and military casualties were comprehensible only to those who had experienced the war firsthand. Millions were homeless. About one-third of a million Brits were dead, as were a half million French; there were more than four million Poles, more than eighteen million Russians, and more than four million German losses.[23]

The victorious Allies considered a plan to permanently destroy Germany's industrial base. Doing so would turn Germany into an agricultural country, leaving it without the means to wage war. Both the British and American governments rejected this draconian solution, and Germany began the slow process of rebuilding a devastated country. One measure of devastation is five billion cubic yards of rubble that was piled high in cities and towns as a result of bombing and shelling. Given Germany's previous intellectual, scientific, and engineering history (its social capital), economic recovery would no doubt have proceeded without aid. But it was given a generous boost by the American Marshall Plan, which contributed $12 billion in post-war aid to Europe to speed economic recovery.

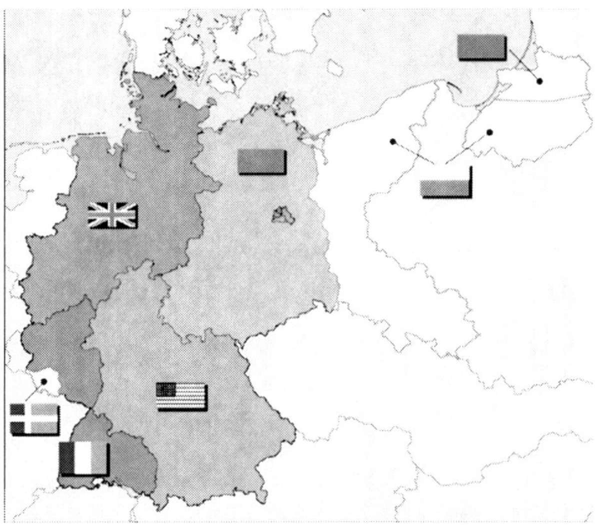

Figure 8.6. Divided Germany 1945

[23] Sources on wartime leaders include Jon Meacham, *Franklin and Winston: An Intimate Portrait of an Epic Friendship* (New York: Random House, 2003); Doris Kearns Goodwin, *No Ordinary Time: Franklin and Eleanor Roosevelt: The Home Front in World War II* (New York: Simon and Schuster, 1994); and David G. McCullough, *Truman* (New York: Simon and Schuster, 1992). See also Geoffrey C. Ward and Ken Burns, *The Roosevelts: An Intimate History* (New York: Knopf, 2014).

TWO GERMANYS: AGAIN, THE PHOENIX

In June 1945, Russian armies swept through Europe. They occupied the eastern portion of Berlin and all of Germany to the east. A Soviet-style dictatorship was installed, complete with secret police and dossiers (and arrests) on those tempted to dissent. Stalinist-style heavy industry produced only a modicum of consumer goods.

To keep East Germans from defecting to the West, borders were sealed, and a wall eventually separated the two Berlins, East and West, in 1961. West Germany prospered, while the standard of living in East Germany spiraled downward. Industrial machinery had been shipped to Russia as war reparations, and rebuilt factories produced shoddy goods.[24] For a decade and a half after the war, meat, butter, and sugar were rationed. Criticism was "construed as treason, minor errors as sabotage."[25]

On November 9, 1989, as the Soviet dictatorship collapsed, the East German government lifted restrictions on travel to West Berlin. Thousands crossed on a visit to the West, returning with souvenirs of "forbidden fruit": bananas, oranges, and chocolate. The Wall collapsed as thousands climbed on it and literally tore it down.

On July 1, 1990, the union of two currencies, the West German and East German marks, went into effect. On October 3 of that year, the two Germanies were united. The phoenix had risen once again.

GERMANY TODAY

German memory is selective. Like most people, Germans remember the good days and suppress the bad. Weapons and memorabilia of the Nazi era are banned, as is membership in any revived Nazi organization. Strict laws control disparaging remarks about non-German ethnic groups. Concentration camps are preserved as memorials to their dead, and a mainstay of German foreign policy is protecting Israel. For half a century after the Second World War, government policy kept German troops out of armed combat. Since then, Germany has served as a mainstay of the United Nations' peacekeeping efforts around the globe.

---

[24] The East German car, the Trabant, was typical: with particle-wood body and an unreliable engine, it belched and staggered to what was often an uncertain destination.

[25] Martin Kitchen, *The Cambridge Illustrated History of Germany* (Cambridge: Cambridge University Press, 1996), 325.

Figure 8.7. Berlin Wall Coming Down

Sites with a prosperous and romantic history are preserved. For example, on Bavaria's "Romantic Road," the town of Rothenburg ob der Tauber is a medieval jewel. Enclosed by fortress walls, its narrow, cobblestone lanes carry the walker to tiny shops, Gothic churches, and a Gothic-Renaissance town hall (Rathus) in Saxony. Dresden is a labor of reconstruction. Firebombed by the Americans and British in 1945 (with civilian casualties of more than 35,000), many of its loveliest old buildings have been meticulously restored, modeled on the work of Italian artist Canaletto (1697-1768). As might be expected, Germany's largest cities also display bold examples of post-war architecture. As much as anything else, the German flag encapsulates history. Its three broad bands of black, red, and gold were the colors of the uniforms of German volunteers during the Napoleonic wars.

Population

Germany's population is close to eighty-three million, compared to France's approximate sixty-five million and Britain's more than sixty-two million. Unlike the former criterion of a nation defined by blood, Germany today is a country of immigrants (einwanderungsland) who arrived after World War II as refugees and migrants from other places in Europe. For most, citizenship is defined by parentage and place of birth. In and among the total population is a sizeable Turkish population, mostly children of guest workers who came for jobs in the post-war period. Mostly Muslim, they have sought to acquire citizenship, which has been a thorny political issue.

Figure 8.8. Section of the Berlin Wall (Author James E. Harf and daughter Marie, Berlin, August 1991)

Economy

Germany's economic strength is reflected in its manufactured products: trucks and automobiles (including some of the world's fastest and most luxurious cars), electronics, steel, machine tools, and ships. In the post-war years, the pace of economic growth, spurred by the Marshall Plan, earned the admiring title *Wirtshaftswunder*. Under the guidance of the Social Democrats, Germany created an extensive network of benefits for workers and the unemployed. Two measures of Germany's economic achievement are membership in the G8 (an association of the world's leading economic powers) and life expectancy, which is one of the world's highest at almost eighty years.

9. Russia: Marx, Lenin, and the Death of an Illusion

Russia is "...a riddle wrapped in a mystery inside an enigma"
— Winston Churchill, BBC Radio Broadcast, 1 October 1939

Figure 9.1. The Kremlin, Seat of Government

EUROPE DISCOVERS THE OLD RUSSIA

In 1553 Sir Richard Chamberlain, English merchant-adventurer, was searching for a northern sea route to China. Beating eastward in the White Sea, storms forced him to land near Archangel. Fishermen, terrified but curious, told him of their king in a far-off city. Chamberlain headed south, endured vicious cold, and eventually arrived in Moscow, the fortress-city of King Ivan. The latter's nobles, bearded, wearing long caftans, disdained the stranger, but after nearly a fortnight's wait, Chamberlain was conducted into the city through massive gates and was staggered by what he heard and saw: an army of 200,000 mounted archers and courtiers dressed in gold. The supreme monarch wore a gold crown, and his symbol of office, a gold scepter, was studded with jewels. Dinner was served on gold plates, attended by servants too numerous to count.

The king was Tsar Ivan IV, and his cruelty and caprice would bestow on him the name Ivan the Terrible. Directly under his command was a secret police force that rode black stallions. They dressed in black, a dog's severed head on the saddle pommel, and they killed and looted on Ivan's orders. They terrified all whom they encountered. Always fearful of rebellion, Ivan was convinced that the city of Novgorod was plotting against him. In 1570 he ordered the entire city of 60,000 put to death. The secret police (*Oprichnina)* were his edict enforcers and intelligence gatherers. They were part of a long line of such men serving a long line of Russia's tyrannical rulers.

WHEN DID THE KINGDOMS OF RUSSIA BEGIN?

The origins of the Russian state began in south Russia, sometime in the seventh century CE. Viking bands from Denmark and Sweden, traveling south along the rivers of Russia (and dragging their long boats on rollers where rivers freeze or run dry) imposed a government on the Rus (a Norse word) in the northern area around Novgorod (new city). Rurik was their leader; his kingdom began in 862. In 882 his successor, Oleg, transferred his capital to Kiev in southern Russia. In 987 Prince Vladimir (whose Viking lineage is Norman-Swedish) married Anna, an Orthodox Christian sister of the Emperor of Byzantium, whose capital city, Constantinople, was a worthy successor to the glories of Imperial Rome. Soon Vladimir converted to Orthodoxy, and Russian rulers would then take the Byzantine title of Caesar (Tsar in Russian, which later became Czar), and future Tsars would adopt the perquisites and style of Byzantine emperors: absolute rule (Tsars styled themselves Tsar and autocrat). The power of the autocrat was undergirded by the Patriarch of Constantinople (and later of Moscow), who claimed for the emperor divine blessing and authority. An aura of mystery cloaked the Byzantine emperor, enhanced by infrequent appearances to adoring crowds who were paid and prompted to shout, sing, and exhibit trance-like hysteria. Much the same mystery cloaked the Russian Tsars. In the twentieth century, Josef Stalin, a dwarfish five feet four inches, made use of the Byzantine mysteries by infrequent public appearances, by an inner circle of doting, fearful attendants, and by larger-than-life photographs and statues that dominated every public place in the Soviet Union. Even in "godless" Soviet Russia, the Church played an important role in preserving Russian culture.

Figure 9.2. Ivan the Terrible (Viktor Vasnetsov painting, 1897)

WHY THE SAYING, "SCRATCH A RUSSIAN, FIND A TARTAR"?

Ivan The Terrible's rule was from 1533 to 1584. All tyrants fear plotters and assassins, but Ivan's fears were also grounded in Russia's history: an invasion from central Asia that began in the early 1200s. The invaders were Mongols (who had conquered and intermarried with Tartars) led by Genghis Khan. Originally called Temujin, his military successes inspired him to take a new name, Genghis Kahn, ruler of the world. Mongol hordes (perhaps the only Tartar word to enter the English language) swept south from Mongolia to install themselves in Peking in 1214. They then rode west with savagery calculated to induce surrender even before their arrival. They traveled (by choice) over frozen ground on wiry Mongolian ponies, two or three tethered behind the rider. Tartars could survive on mare's milk mixed with horse blood. Their chief weapon was a short, bone-reinforced bow, whose deadly range matched the famous English longbow. And before going into battle they put on a silk shirt, woven to enmesh an arrowhead, making it easier to pull the arrow shaft out of a wounded rider's body.

Their first invasion of Russia was in 1223. The second was in 1237, with a massive army that fell on resisters and flayed them alive to drive home the idea that Tartars expected unquestioned obedience. By 1240, the Mongols had moved further west to capture large sections of Hungary and Poland. Then they returned to Russia to rule and consolidate their empire, the largest in the world. The empire's Russian component centered on Moscow, but its full extent ran from the Sea of Japan to Poland and from the Siberian Arctic to the Persian Gulf. Mongols ruled with fist and iron. They took tribute from their subjects but were tolerant of religions and religious disputation. They also opened their empire (twice as large as Rome's at its height) to travelers and traders. And under that dispensation, Marco Polo with his father and uncle traveled for more than three years until they arrived at Peking in 1275, capital of the mighty Kublai Khan. When Marco returned to his native Venice after twenty-five years in the service of the Great Khan, he carried a wondrous secret: a sea route to the fabled Indies lay across the Indian Ocean, a secret that Columbus enfolded in his scheme to reach the East by sailing west.

Mongols dominated Russia for 250 years. During that time, Mongols and Russians intermarried, creating an aristocracy accustomed to deference and obedience. Tsar Boris Godunov was descended from Tartars, and in our own time, Vladimir Nobokov claimed Tartar descent. Scratch a Russian, as the saying goes, and uncover a Tartar. During the murderous dictatorship of Josef Stalin, those seeking to explain his behavior would sometimes whisper, "He comes from Tartar stock." And Leon Trotsky, hounded out of Revolutionary Russia by Stalin, famously described Stalin as Genghis Khan with a telephone. (The murderous arm of the Soviet secret police followed Trotsky to his sanctuary in Mexico City. A hatchet in his skull put an end to his jibes.)

WHY DO THE TARTARS HAUNT RUSSIAN HISTORY?

Altitude, as the saying goes, is attitude. Flat nations lend themselves to tyranny; the ruler's writ can run to the nation's farthest reach. (Consider Ronald Reagan's remark, "You can run but you can't hide!") Conversely, mountains afford places to hide. They make it possible to defy a ruler's writs. They tend to nurture codes of honor that support blood feuds and clan revenge. Above all, they nurture an attitude that demands personal freedom.

Russia, like China, Egypt, and Persia, is a mostly flat place. From ancient times to the present, all four countries have nurtured despotic rulers. The Russian steppes made Mongol conquest easy; and once established as overlords, Mongol rulers deepened Russian obeisance to authority. (An old Russian proverb has it that government is like the weather. It comes from above.) The Mongol conquest put another marker on Russian culture in the form of identity search. Russians have long posed the question, Are we an Asian or European country? A glance at a map shows that far more of Russia lies in Asia than in Europe. The map also displays Russia's geographic reach: Russia extends through eleven times zones; the distance from Moscow to Vladivostok via the Trans-Siberian railroad is more than 6,000 miles. Some Russians insist that Russia is sufficiently insulated from Europe—in language, genetics, alphabet, religions—to establish a Eurasian identity, or if not that, then a culture that is uniquely Russian.

Figure 9.3. Peter the Great

Peter the Great, who ruled from 1682 to 1725, was determined to overcome Russia's Asian identity by dragging it into the West. He built St. Petersburg as his window on the West. And on pain of death, the men of his court were required to shave beards and wear trousers. In the nineteenth century, Russian aristocrats spoke French among themselves; Russian was used only to give orders to serfs. Intellectuals worked, especially in literature, to develop a culture that was Russia's own. And the search for identity continues. The recent novelist Alexander Solzhenitsyn rejected much of western (especially technological) culture. He was a tsarist who distanced himself from political activists such as the *Pamyet* (the word means memory), who insisted that Russia's cultural uniqueness was best preserved by outright hostility to other cultures.

WHAT MAKES A TSAR MEMORABLE?

Peter the Great built a magnificent city, fought a successful war with Sweden to dominate the eastern Baltic, and pulled his country toward the West. Catherine the Great (ruler from 1762 to 1795) was a connoisseur of the arts, carried on a lively correspondence with European intellectuals, built beautiful palaces, and most important, embarked on a successful military campaign to extend Russia's domain south into the Caucasus. Alexander I dealt Napoleon a near-fatal defeat. (Of Napoleon's army of 600,000 who invaded Russia in 1812, only 40,000 lived to return to their homes.) And when the war was done, Alexander stood firm as pivot of the Holy Alliance, dedicated to using the continent's kings to stamp out democratic reforms in Europe.

THE OLD RUSSIA DIES

As the nineteenth century sped to its end, France, England, and Germany became rich through industrialization. Steam power was their great achievement—railroads and steamships for transport, along with factories that raised living standards and brokered the rise of a middle class. Russia remained on the fringes of European prosperity and technology. When war with Japan erupted, Russia suffered a series of stunning defeats. At the battle of the Tsushima Strait in 1904, the Japanese captured and sank eight battleships and nine Russian cruisers, killing 4,000 Russians and capturing more than 7,000 sailors, a prologue to what lay ahead.

Figure 9.4. Czar Nicholas II

The last Czar, Nicholas II, was poorly suited to be an autocrat. His wife Alexandra came under the spell of a mystic monk, Rasputin, whose habits and behavior were less than holy. When the First World War revealed Russia's armies to be miserably equipped, its industrial system incapable of meeting the demands of war, and desperately short of food and supplies, Nicholas took personal command of his armies, leaving the country in the hands of the Czarina and her advisors. Military defeat followed military disaster, and Russia swirled into chaos. Soldiers laid down their arms, surrendered, and deserted. Factory workers stayed at home, and urban mobs shouted for peace and bread. In St. Petersburg, the Czar abdicated and might have slipped safely out of the country but for the arrival of Vladimir Lenin. Lenin, living in Switzerland and plotting a workers' revolution in Russia, leaped at Germany's offer of safe conduct to Russia. He was put in a closed train that thundered east across Europe, arriving at St. Petersburg's Finland Station in time to overthrow Russia's new and moderate parliamentary government. In its place now stood Lenin's Bolshevik Party and Red Army ready to crush all opposition, no matter the cost. The Czar's family was imprisoned, taken to a remote village, Ekaterinburg, and in 1917, the entire family was executed in the cellar of the house that was their prison, their bodies burned, mutilated, and secretly buried in a nearby forest. With their death, the Romanov Czars, rulers of Russia since 1653, came to their bloody end.

Figure 9.5. Vladimir Lenin

WHY CONFLICTING VIEWS OF SOVIET RUSSIA?

Dictatorial regimes are always tempted by the vulgarized version of the Pythagorean dictum: knowledge is power. And none put it to better use than the Soviet Union. Official versions of agricultural and industrial production reflected nothing but glorious achievement. The happiness of Soviet citizens was testimony to a workers' paradise. In Soviet reporting, Karl Marx's predictions of a happy socialist future had become reality.

Of course, we see what we wish to see and hear what we wish to hear. Many outside Russia were captivated by official Soviet reports. The Soviet Union had apparently solved capitalism's worst problem, a boom and bust economy, especially the Great Depression of the 1930s ("I have seen the future and it works," proclaimed American columnist, Lincoln Steffens[1]).

Nothing was further from the truth. The seventy-four years (1917 to 1991) of the Soviet Union are now portrayed by Soviet scholars (and by Russians themselves) as the years of the Soviet Nightmare. Little by little, the truth of Soviet life emerged, a truth presented by such writers as Arthur Koestler's *Darkness at Noon* and *The God That Failed)*, George Orwell's *Animal Farm* and *1984*, and Alexander Solzhenitsyn's *One Day in the Life of Ivan Denisovich* and *The Gulag Archipelago*. Lenin began the nightmare, transforming Russian society, nationalizing factories, farms, and houses, and killing these who opposed him. "All power to the Soviets" was the battle cry. "Property is theft!" was a favorite slogan of nineteenth-century anarchists. And it became a crime to sell or trade anything that one did not make with one's own hands.

STALIN AND THE LONG NIGHTMARE

Following Lenin's death in 1924, all power fell into Josef Stalin's hands, and it remained there until his death in 1953. During Stalin's dictatorship, the Soviet Union became a vast system of forced-labor camps fed by secret trials and the informers of the Secret Police. Stalin presided over a vast killing machine. He is said to have mused that while one death can be a tragedy, a million deaths are a mere statistic. Stalin and his ruling apparatus were responsible for as many as fifty million deaths, perhaps more, excluding deaths attributable to World War II. As ethnic groups and potential rivals for power fell under Stalin's paranoid suspicion, rigged trials sentenced the accused to death (generals, Jews, Communist Party officials.) Whole communities were pulled from their traditional homelands and shipped in railroad cars to distant destina-

[1] http://www.britannica.com, n.d. Steffens first uttered these words in a letter to a friend in 1919 and then repeated variations of the phrase for years in his writings.

tions, many dying en route. Among Stalin's displaced communities in 1943-44 were Muslim Balkars, Chechens, and Ingus suspected of collaborating with Germans—618,000 were put in trucks and railroad cars and shipped east. One-third died en route. In 1944 thousands of Tartars of Crimea were sent en masse to Uzbekistan.

Everyone worked for the state; in principle, all were equal. But, as Orwell famously wrote in *Animal Farm*, "some were more equal than others."[2] In principle, every person was entitled to much the same share of goods and services, but in reality, to make life at best comfortable or at least endurable, principles were set aside to make way for a system of payoffs and illicit bargains. From top to bottom, Soviet society, which proclaimed itself a workers' paradise, became paralyzed with fear and permeated by cynicism and bone-weary resignation. ("They pretend to pay us; we pretend to work".)

Figure 9.6. Josef Stalin (Library of Congress)

[2] George Orwell, *Animal Farm* (Middlesex: Penguin Books, 1951), 114.

The year was 1953. As poetic justice would have it, an aging and perhaps half-mad Stalin died somewhere in the vast halls of the Kremlin, stalked and shot by Lavrenti Beria, his appointed head of the Soviet Secret Police. But, sorry to say, the truth is less poetic. Stalin died comfortably in his own bed.

After Stalin came a succession of Soviet rulers, some short-time servers, some ruthless and efficient. Among them is Nikita Khrushchev, who proclaimed the Soviet right to intervene where socialist regimes are threatened, and sent tanks and troops to crush democratic uprisings in Hungary in 1956 and Czechoslovakia in 1968. Then, in 1988, Mikhail Gorbachev consolidated his power by assuming the position of head of state after having taken control of the Communist Party as Secretary General in 1985. Under his tutelage, in 1991, the Soviet Regime spiraled into final collapse.[3]

THE NEW RUSSIA

Earthshaking political events suggest geologic counterparts. What happens on the earth's surface results from the unseen movement of deep tectonic plates. The Soviet Union's collapse took the world by surprise. Mikhail Gorbachev had slid into authority as the first university-educated leader in Soviet history. Like Martin Luther, he sought to save the institution of which he was part. And like Luther, he ended by creating a new one. Gorbachev's instruments of salvation were glasnost (openness, or speaking aloud), perestroika (economic reconstruction), and democratization (allowing political competition). Once given the opportunity to speak aloud and openly—acts that previously would have brought death, prison, or the lunatic asylum—the dams of resentment broke. The social tectonic plates had collided and collapsed. Grievances flashed from every part of Russian society. People were tired of living two and three generations in a tiny apartment. They were disgusted with the special privileges (clothes, cars, trips abroad, spacious apartments, and special food) for the Soviet Party elite. College graduates seethed at knowing that the best universities were reserved for children of the elite and that a graduate's job and its location were determined by bribes to placement officers. The

---

[3] See David Remnick, *Lenin's Tomb: The Last Days of the Soviet Empire* (New York: Random House, 1994). This Pulitzer Prize bestseller combines history and eyewitness accounts of life in the final days of the Soviet Union, lives lived in fear, with constant recourse to bribery and shortages of shoddy consumer goods (TV sets that exploded when first plugged in, for example). His 1997 book, *Resurrection* (New York: Random House, 1997), chronicles the creation of the new Russian state.

military felt cheated by its failure to match the technology of the West and by the failure of its war to bring Afghanistan into the Soviet fold. And everywhere, everyone was bitter over long lines at food shops, at clothing that came in only one size (the better to fill production quotas), and at the constant shortage of consumer goods. They were angry over television sets that exploded, and above all, they were angry at their government's lies, telling them that they lived better than most everyone else in the world.

Alarmed and desperate, Communist Party plotters attempted to arrest Gorbachev at his Black Sea villa. (Newspaper photos further inflamed public opinion by revealing no ordinary comrade's vacation retreat, but a sumptuous holiday palace, complete with an escalator to carry bathers down to the sea.) Key elements of the military refused to join the coup, however. Boris Yeltsin, a dismissed aide to Gorbachev and who later became President, led street demonstrations against tank units loyal to the old guard. Following this massive defiance, Gorbachev proclaimed the Communist Party dissolved. Shortly thereafter the Soviet Union was declared legally nonexistent. And Russia resumed its traditional name and began a parliamentary regime.

Figure 9.7. Michael Gorbachev

WHAT IS LIFE LIKE IN THE NEW RUSSIA?

When Europe's Communist regimes started to collapse, at least two enormous problems confronted those seeking the regimes' replacement: how to guide an authoritarian society toward democracy and how to replace a command economy with a market economy. Both problems intertwine. Modern market economies (capitalism) operate within an elaborate framework of government controls: contract laws, stock market and banking regulations, laws that protect workers' and consumers' safety and health, and a judicial system that oversees the intricate network of the market's operation. Most important, the judicial system itself is regulated by traditions and laws that embrace the rule of law. All people, no matter what their wealth or social standing, are presumed within the law's control and are presumed equally treated by the law.

Within the traditions of a market economy, each person is reasonably free to buy, sell, enter into contracts, control one's entry or exit from employment, choose one's own vocation, live where one chooses, and marry whomever one chooses. Under this umbrella of freedom, democracies and market societies evolve interactively.

In 1991 the people of Russia had no practical or past experience with democracy. Their history was a millennium of autocratic rule. And for seventy-four years, their economy had staggered and groaned under public ownership of property and centralized government planning. Libraries worldwide contained shelves of books instructing social planners how to achieve the socialist dream of a government-directed economy or perhaps the socialist dream of public ownership of property. But few if any offered instruction on how to move from a government-run economy to a market-run economy.

Great social change greatly disrupts citizens' lives, especially the least autonomous members of society. As part of what was called economic shock therapy, intended to push Russia quickly into a market economy, the Russian ruble was made convertible to other currencies and permitted to float freely, to rise and fall according to what it would bring on the domestic and international markets. The result was ruinous inflation (2,500 percent in 1992) and skyrocketing prices, especially for imported goods. The elderly, subsisting on state pensions, were reduced to abject poverty. Many factory workers, without government-assured sales for their products, went unpaid for months. Some factory managers helped workers to survive by bartering with other factories for useful products. In 1999, 30 to 40 percent of Russians lived below the poverty line (defined as one dollar per day.) And a new economic elite, an oligarchy, emerged. Ten percent of the population is estimated to own 50 percent of the country's wealth. In the former Soviet Union, camouflage attempted to hide the lifestyle differences between rich and poor. In today's Russia, the newly rich flaunt their wealth with mansions, flashy cars, elegant clothes, and membership in exclusive health clubs. Their children attend private schools; many go to universities abroad. Magazines, new to Russian publishing, feature the comings and goings of the rich. Their lives contrast sharply with those of more ordinary citizens, whose average wage in 2007 was $18.17 a day[4] and today is around $25 a day according to most estimates.

HOW DID THE NEW ELITE ACQUIRE ITS WEALTH?

The elite gained wealth mostly by theft and fraud. Russia's road to capitalism began with the government selling at auction its vast property holdings, the greatest transfer from public to private hands in history. Most coveted were income-producing enterprises; apartment buildings, banks, and television stations were bidders' delights. Even more so were oil fields and refineries, natural gas wells, pipelines, gold and diamond mines, and deposits of industrial minerals. Their products could be marketed abroad, and profits could be skimmed for safekeeping in foreign banks. Money for auction purchases was pulled from several sources. High-ranking officials of the former secret police had established secret bank accounts abroad. The same occurred for the former regime's well-organized criminal gangs. These funds were repatriated for the auctions.

But the most brilliant and byzantine scheme played out this way. The Russian government mortgaged its assets to a few well-connected insiders for kopeks on the ruble (pennies on the dollar, as Americans would say). These assets were then mortgaged to banks as security on bank loans. The government invariably failed to pay money due on the mortgaged assets. The same happened for those who (in turn) had mortgaged assets to the banks. The banks then put the assets up for auction, and a bidder's ring used the money *lent by the banks* to buy the assets! An instructive example is Yukos Oil. It was bought by Russia's new oligarchs for $159 million. In 1999 it produced oil worth $18 billion.

But money (as the cliché goes) does not always buy happiness. Because of Russia's legal system (especially business and tax laws), it is difficult to run a large company without breaking some law somewhere on the statute books. Tax collectors and tax police (wearing masks and carrying heavy weapons) stand ready to raid the offices of those who fall out of favor with

---

[4] See Daniel Treisman, *The Return: Russia's Journey from Gorbachev to Medvedev* (New York: Free Press, 2011).

those bearing more political clout. Papers and records are seized; investigations can continue for a year, and a business tied up in tax-police limbo can collapse.

In 2003 the head of Yukos Oil was put in jeopardy when tax officials seized company records and computer discs. Company officials expressed bewilderment, while a knowing public offered at least three explanations for the tax raid. First, because Yukos Oil was one of Russia's largest companies, the raid may have been a warning to other executives that too much independence from government leaders can be a dangerous thing. Second, Yukos had been rumored to be in a merger with American oil companies, which might then have created the world's largest oil company. If so, Russia's political leaders might find their control over the oligarchs in jeopardy. Third, the raid was a struggle between competing groups of oligarchs.

Figure 9.8. Vladimir Putin

Russia's in-and-out President, Vladimir Putin, is a former Soviet KGB agent with extensive work in East Germany. When the Berlin Wall was torn down, he looked to the Kremlin to send tanks to restore the East German regime to power. Wise in the ways of power and secret dealings, Putin is thought to have ordered the tax raids to increase the power of his St. Petersburg cohorts. Equally troubling for Russia's democratic future has been the use of government power to bring independent television under its control. One media tycoon was forced into exile for allowing his television stations to present unbiased coverage of Russia's war in Chechnya. And even in exile, the former oil tycoon was dogged by the Russian government's several attempts to have him extradited to Russia to stand trial for alleged fraud.

AND THE FUTURE?

Prediction in political affairs is always difficult, many times more difficult when a country is moving toward an uncertain future. The new Russia is still struggling to achieve an effectively operating market economy. And it still struggles toward democratic norms. On the negative side, rule of law and transparency in government and corporate dealings are far from achieved. The same is true for impartial judges and a comprehensive framework of civil and contract law. And a number of recent policy moves in the international arena suggest a possible return to Soviet-style Cold War-like behavior on the foreign policy front.

Partly because of difficult economic times and partly because workers' families are uncertain of the future, Russia's population is shrinking. It stood at 143 million in 2010, down by four million since 1989. Life expectancy has also dropped. Hospital treatment is available mostly to the better off. (Something on the order of only one in three hospital beds is occupied.) In 1990 male life expectancy was sixty-four years; in 2010 expectancy had fallen to sixty-three. Significantly, the decline is not attributed to an earlier death at life's end, but to death at middle age, as Russia's men fall prey to alcoholism, industrial accidents, and disease. Children's illness is on the rise; the diet of poor children suffers the constriction of rising prices. And many will also suffer the long-term effects of salt without iodine additives—the cost of additives puts them beyond the family budget. Despair probably falls most heavily on the elderly, as Russia's pension system fails to keep up with inflation. In Soviet days, pensions for retired workers, while far from generous, were at least stable. In 2003 the average retiree collected a pension of 1901 rubles, or $63 per month. Despair feeds on itself. And both inside and outside Russia, this disheartening state of affairs is often described as The Great Devastation[5]. In 2013, the average pension was $285.[6]

On the positive side, private ownership of property is now widespread; citizens live and work in relative freedom. Public opinion polls show that while Russia's older population looks

---

[5] See Michael Specter, "The Devastation," *The New Yorker*, October 11, 2003).

[6] Andrew E. Kramer, "Russia Raises Some Salaries and Pensions for Crimeans," *New York Times*, March 31, 2014, http://www.NYTimes.com.

back with longing on the predictability of their former lives, its younger population is more sanguine about its future.

At the same time, change is afoot in Russia, as the leadership has been showing signs of returning to some old ways associated with the Soviet era. Catherine the Great believed that Russia was so vast and its people so contentious that only a strong ruler would suffice. In the past several years, Vladimir Putin has appeared to take Catherine's words to heart as he has moved toward reestablishing a strong centrally controlled state. He disempowered regional governments and crushed those oligarchs who did not heed his insistence that they stay out of politics. And on the foreign front, he has adopted a very aggressive strategy reminiscent of the Cold War era. Most recently, this assertiveness has led to major interference in Ukraine, taking over the Crimea and using Russian soldiers in disguised uniforms to extinguish Ukraine's attempts to become free of Russian control and join Western Europe through trade agreements and the like. At present and despite protests of the United States and Western European powers, Putin appears to be winning his way.[7]

[7] See David Remnick, "Watching the Eclipse," *The New Yorker*, August 11 and 14, 2014, 52-65.

10. St. Petersburg: What's in a Name?

I love you, Peter's creation, I love your stern
Harmonious look, the Neva's majestic flow,
Her granite banks, the iron tracery
Of your railings, the transparent twilight
And the moonless glitter of your pensive nights...
— Aleksandr Pushkin, "The Bronze Horseman", 1833

St. Petersburg is a royal city, built from the ground up according to a monarch's whim. Like Washington, Brasilia, and Canberra, St. Petersburg is a blueprint set in stone. All four of these cities were designed as national capitals, but only three remain as such. St. Petersburg was knocked from its first-city perch in 1918 after having served as Russia's capital for over 200 years. But as a result of its centuries as Russia's preeminent city, St. Petersburg radiates an imperial grandeur, a style far different from Washington, Brasilia, or Canberra. In the decades of Soviet rule, St. Petersburg became decrepit; but beneath its grime and neglect, a once-beautiful city now stirs back to life.[1]

WHO BUILT ST. PETERSBURG AND WHY?

St. Petersburg was summoned into existence by Tsar Peter (Peter the Great), ruler of Russia from 1682 to 1725. He was a giant of a man: in stature (seven feet tall), in ambition (to trans-

---

[1] See Robert K. Massie, *Peter The Great: His Life and World* (New York: Knopf, 1980); NBC Miniseries, "Peter the Great," with Maximilian Schell, Vanessa Redgrave, and Lawrence Olivier, 1994; and Basil Dmytryshyn, *The Modernization of Russia Under Peter I and Catherine II* (New York: Wiley, 1974).

form insular, backward Russia into a powerful European nation), and in ruthlessness and irascibility. He killed a friend and advisor with blows from the steel-headed staff he always carried; he ordered the death of his son, Alexi, for treason, torturing him with his own hands; not to mention the nameless thousands who died paving the swamp so that a city could be built on the pavement.

Figure 10.1. St. Petersburg

At war with Sweden for twenty-one years (the Great Northern War), Peter's ultimate victory gave Russia huge holdings in what is now Estonia and Latvia and, more important for Peter's imperial ambitions, his "window on the West"—access to the Baltic Sea. To frame that window, a city needed to be built. And in so doing, Peter opened a debate that still continues between Slavophiles and Westernizers, that is, those who wish to keep Russia insulated from western influences and those who seek to unify Russian and western cultures.

Legend has it that in 1703 Peter took his sword (or was it a bayonet?) and sliced two pieces of earth from a marshy island where the Neva River enters the Gulf of Finland. Laying the two pieces crosswise, he commanded that a city be built "here and in this place." Wise (but not wiser) heads counseled that the island was marshy, an unsuitable place for urban development.

But Peter's *diktat* was not to be countermanded, let alone thwarted, and in May 1703 saws and axes began clearing forests. At the end of June (Peter's and Paul's Day), foundations of a church were laid within the fortress that was Peter's new house. Still standing, the oldest "residence" in the city, the house and much else in St. Petersburg are a memorial to Peter's city. Originally built of wood, Peter's house reflects the city's island origins. No stones suitable for building were present on the island. Rich and noble families were commanded to build suitable homes in Peter's city; each was to bring wagonloads of quarried stone. Forty thousand convicts and serfs labored for seven years (1709-1716), digging canals, shoring stream and riverbanks, and constructing the first buildings of St. Petersburg. In 1712, by royal edict, all government ministries and all foreign embassies were commanded to move to the city. In 1714, with docks and warehouses laid out, a royal edict (*ukase*) commanded that every ship and wagon entering the city bring a specified number of building stones. (The edict remained in force until 1779.)

As the city began to rise from the mud flats and swamps of the River Neva, its eye-catching beauty and majesty were assured by edicts that prescribed the height of buildings, their color, the width of city streets, and their periodic cleaning. The city is a monument to its creator, and his presence is manifest in the large bronze statue standing close to the Neva's bank in front of the Imperial Winter Palace, now home to the Hermitage Museum of Art. Commissioned by his successor and admirer, Catherine the Great, Peter surveys his city astride his horse; the horse rears on its great rock plinth, trampling underfoot a great snake that symbolizes Peter's victory over the Swedes.

WHY THE NAME "ST. PETERSBURG?"

Peter came to the throne at age ten, an engine of energy and curiosity about the world and how mechanical things worked. In 1607, he led what would today be called a fact-finding mission of 250 to the West, to bring home to Russia the technical skills of the West, especially in the realms of shipbuilding and the machines of war. Peter traveled not as Great Lord and Tsar but as an improbably disguised (given his height and royal authority) lesser member of the entourage named Peter Mikhailov. The Great Embassy, as it was formally called, concentrated its energies on the two greatest shipbuilding and merchant countries of Europe, England and Holland.

It was Holland that gave Peter his greatest practical education. He bought carpenter's tools and worked as a shipwright. He lodged with a blacksmith's family. He ate in taverns. He took time off from work at the shipyard to visit sawmills, paper mills, and factories. His time in Holland so pleased him that when his new city on the Neva was being built, he named it after the patron saint of Holland, Sankt Peter—and not incidentally, reminding the world that he, too, carried a saint's name.

ST. PETERSBURG: WHAT'S IN A NAME?

Citizens of St. Petersburg pose an unusual conundrum: "My great grandfather was born in St. Petersburg. My grandfather was born in Petrograd. My father and I were born in Leningrad. And my own son was born in St. Petersburg. And yet, our family has never left town." The response, of course, is that St. Petersburg has endured a string of name changes. Peter named St. Petersburg, and its architectural glory reflects that name. Two hundred years on, in the First World War, Russia's enemy was Germany. A German-sounding capital city was deemed unpatriotic, so the name was Russified to Petrograd (*grad*, the Slavic word for city). Petrograd was the first city to fall to the Bolshevik revolutionaries; but as the revolution was being consolidated, Petrograd was deemed too devoted to foreign ideas, too open to invasion from the West. The capital of the new Soviet Union was moved from Petrograd closer to the heartland, to Russia's former capital, Moscow. On Lenin's death in 1924, to honor the father of the Revolution, Petrograd was renamed Leningrad. And after the collapse of the Soviet Union in the early 1990s, the citizens of Leningrad reached back for happier memories and voted to rename their city St. Petersburg.

WHY WAS THE CITY NAMED FOR LENIN?

Lenin was leader of the most successful group (The Bolsheviks) contending for power as the Czarist regime collapsed in 1917. From 1917 until his death in 1924, Lenin was the guiding genius of Communist rule in Russia. Until the collapse of the Soviet Union in 1991, his likeness was everywhere—pictures, plaques, stamps, and medals. His statues were heroic—striding forward, arm outstretched, pointing (it was said) to the future. For seventy years, his memory filled the niche, Father of Communist Russia, and schoolchildren wrote letters to his memory: "Dear Comrade Lenin, Teach us to be Good Communists".

His initial power base was St. Petersburg, and from there, the Communist regime extended outward to all of Czarist Russia. "Like a bacillus sealed in a flask," to use Churchill's famous words, Lenin in 1917 was spirited from his exile in Switzerland and put by the Germans on a sealed train that roared through the Baltic basin until it came to a halt at St. Petersburg's Finland Station. Germany's military motives were simple: to foment revolution in Russia and force it out of the war, thereby relieving the German army from its eastern front, ready to turn for "a final assault" on the West.

WHAT FORCES AND EVENTS FED THE RUSSIAN REVOLUTION?

Russia had a sprawling, poorly organized and equipped army, suffering almost constant defeat and terrible casualties. It had an obsolete industrial system unable to meet military needs and soaring inflation. The Czar, Nicholas II, asserting himself as commander-in-chief, was an incompetent military leader, constantly distracted by family problems (a hemophiliac child) and a wife in thrall to the "healing powers" of a mystical monk, Rasputin.

Figure 10.2. Russian Revolution

The Russian Revolution was a revolution within a revolution within a revolution. Five days in February 1917 decided Russia's fate. The Czar's inner circle plotted against him. The Parliament (The Duma) tried to put his brother on the throne. Most decisively, a spontaneous workers' and soldiers' uprising in Petrograd seized the arsenal and proclaimed a Republic. Into this swirl, Vladimir Lenin stepped from his train and onto the platform of the Finland Station. Seventy-plus years of what would be the tyranny of the Soviet Union had begun.

WHY IS ST. PETERSBURG CALLED THE VENICE OF THE NORTH?

Sited on one hundred islands, cut by the flooding River Neva, the city is drained by a web of canals, over which a profusion of bridges connect the islands. The nineteenth century was a rich period of bridge construction; several are graceful and decorated spans of cast iron. Many of the city's great palaces are on the waterways, and their waterside reflections (in the best of light) give many city views an Impressionist-Venetian aspect. As a Baltic port, the city lies at sixty degrees north. Midsummer, it enjoys nineteen hours of daylight. The long hours of subdued twilight bring "white nights," and the city's soft glow fuses with its shimmering waters.

The city's great size (521 square miles), with a population of more than 4.5 million, demands weeks, even months, for full exploration. Short-term visitors, if they can be coaxed from the centers of tourism, will be rewarded with strolls through the city's parks, sitting on benches and exchanging smiles and greetings with Peter-burgers at ease. Small side streets have their own rewards, giving visitors a glimpse of communal courtyards accessed through tunnel-like entryways.

Figure 10.3. Nevsky Prospekt

The city's longest street (2.5 miles) is Nevsky Prospekt, the site of some of St. Petersburg's most elegant shops. The Singer Sewing Machine building, constructed in 1907, is crowned by a huge dome; inside is the busiest bookstore that a visitor is ever likely to encounter. At the far eastern end of the Nevsky is the monastery dedicated to Alexander of the Neva (Alexander Nevsky), who defeated Teutonic invaders in 1240. (In the monastery lies Nevsky's outsize silver casket.) At number 56 Nevsky Prospekt is a food store whose Art Nouveau interior is a pilgrimage for lovers of a bygone era. At Kazan Square, with a colonnade resembling that of St. Peter's in Rome, is the Cathedral of Our Lady of Kazan. Its classical architecture stands in stark contrast to the nearby Church of the Resurrection (the Church of Our Savior on the Spilled Blood). The Church of the Resurrection is modeled after St. Basil's Cathedral in Moscow, replete with swirling, colored domes, starbursts on the roofs, and an overall profusion of ornament.

Figure 10.4. Church of the Resurrection

In their interiors, both churches introduce the traveler to the architectural and decorative glories of the Orthodox Rite: a profusion of gold mosaics, one or more high vaulting domes (five domes signify Christ and the four apostles), icons, and the *ikonostasis.* Traditional Orthodox icons are embellished with gold leaf, their poses and facial expressions stylized. They offer no perspective. The intent is to convey the immortality and unchanging qualities of their subject. Worshippers stand facing the iconostasis at the nave (there are no pews in Russian churches). Behind the iconostasis is the altar, out of the worshippers' view. The iconostasis is a richly decorated screen with five rows of icons depicting both saints and feasts of the liturgy. Christ presides. The iconostasis has three doors (representing the Trinity); one of them is a central door signifying entry to the Divine Kingdom. In contrast to both Kazan and Spilled Blood, the vast interior spaces of St. Isaac's Cathedral reflect the full power of nineteenth-century European imperial art: malachite columns and pilasters, paintings whose faces portray human emotions, their bodies twisted in mannerist poses. And throughout, the cathedral shines with gold leaf.

ARCHITECTURAL STYLES

Tsar Peter's vision was a western city worthy of a great nation's capital. His first planners and builders were Dutch and German. They planned and built as well as trained Russians in techniques of architecture and engineering. Then came French and Italian master builders (Le Blond and Rastelli) and the elaborate styles and facades of Baroque and rococo. The richest and most powerful families were ordered to build their houses and palaces in the new city. Over the years and centuries, other styles followed: Greek revival, Art Nouveau, and with the revolution, the stolid, severe Soviet style. Many of the city's buildings command worldwide admiration: The Winter Palace (home to the Hermitage Museum), The Admiralty, The Yusupov Palace, St. Isaac's Cathedral, and the Church of the Savior on the Spilled Blood, to name only a small handful.

WHAT WAS THE BATTLE OF LENINGRAD?

Leningrad, as the city was called in the 1940s, withstood the greatest siege of World War II. Soviet dictator Josef Stalin and Nazi dictator Adolph Hitler pledged to a non-aggression pact in 1939. The pact was sealed in cynicism and double-dealing. Stalin used it to buy time to rearm against Russia's hated foe. Germany's time bought opportunity to concentrate military power against France and the Low Countries and to prepare for a final assault on Britain.

German armies wheeled east in 1941, and the siege of Leningrad was underway. German artillery, tanks, planes, and small firearms pounded the city for 900 days. Russian defense was stubborn and heroic. Bitter winter cold and meager supplies of food, clothes, fuel, and electricity all took their toll of more than one million Russian lives; with 900 days lived in grinding, unremitting anguish, 800,000 died of starvation, 17,000 were killed in battle, and 35,000 died of wounds. When the siege was lifted and the German armies retreated, the city emerged in shattered ruins. Its subsequent restoration serves to memorialize the suffering and heroism of the city's defenders and (equally important) the artistic skills and workmanship entailed in restoring public buildings to their former glory.

Figure 10.5. Battle of Leningrad

11. Norway, Denmark, Sweden, and Finland: Three Crowns and a Republic

Strictly speaking, Norway lies outside the Baltic Sea.[1] But its history and culture bind it to Denmark and Sweden. All three countries share much the same genetic inheritance, but to the casual observer, Swedes and Norwegians look most alike. All three countries have languages that evolved from Old Norse. Each country's readers can understand most of what is written in the other two country's languages. Each of the three countries is predominantly Lutheran. Each is a constitutional monarchy. Each has a history shaped by more than three centuries of their Viking forebears' expeditions of war, plunder, and exploration. And each shares a common descriptor: Scandinavian, a term bestowed by Pliny the Elder in the first century CE.

The Danish monarchy is the oldest in Europe, and the Danish flag, the *Dannebrog*, is the oldest in the world. Legend has it that it floated from the sky in 1219 as a sign of Christianity's oncoming victory for the Danish king (Valdemar) in his battle against pagan Estonians. The flag's field is red, displaying a white cross. The vertical arm of the cross is left of center (at the hoist side), and the horizontal arm is longer than the vertical. Norway, Sweden, and Finland use the same design, each with its own color of field and color of cross.

---

[1] For more information on Norway, see Karen Larsen, *A History of Norway* (Princeton: Princeton University Press for the American-Scandinavian Foundation, 1948), and for more insight into Norwegian culture, see the plays of Henrik Ibsen: *Wild Duck, A Doll's House, Hedda Gabler,* and *An Enemy of the People.*

WHAT DEFINES NORWAY?

Geography, as the saying goes, is destiny. Norway is the westernmost Scandinavian country. It thrusts into the North Sea, with a coastline of more than 1,200 miles, but when bays and inlets are counted, the coastline runs to more than 13,000 miles. Norway (literally, the way of the Norse) is glacier country. Some are still extant. Long-gone glaciers formed the landscape: deep valleys, swift rushing streams, waterfalls, and rocky soil (less than 3 percent of the land is arable). And scenically most important, Norway's west coast is cut by fjords, deep glacier-cut valleys into which sea waters have poured. The Sogndal Fjord runs inland for 120 miles. With narrow defiles and depths reaching 4,260 feet, the Sogndal is one of the world's deepest and longest fjords.

With its long north-south site, about one-third of Norway lies within the Arctic Circle. Within that Circle, winter nights last six months, and summer sun shines continuously for the other half of the year. Norway's climate is tempered by the Gulf Stream. Even so, the weather for long periods of time can be damp and bone-chilling. A blackness descends on the spirit (to use the words of a Norwegian writer), and health authorities are on guard to prevent excess consumption of alcohol and lonely lives driven to suicide. Norway does well in its watchfulness. Norwegians consume approximately 4.4 liters of alcohol per person per year, compared to a U.S. figure of 6.7 liters and 8.1 liters in the United Kingdom. Death by suicide in Norway is about 11.9 persons per 100,000, while Austria stands at over 15.0 per 100,000, the U.S. at 11.0, Sweden at 12.7, and Canada at 11.3.

Norway's population is almost 4.9 million, scattered over 125,000 square miles. Its population density is sparse: thirteen persons per square mile (Saudi Arabia's is nine; Germany's is 230). Two-thirds of Norway is mountainous, and the isolation of farmsteads tempts Norwegians to migrate to urban places. About one-quarter of Norway's 4.5 million people live in Oslo's metropolitan area; three-quarters of all Norwegians live in urban settlements. Even so, Norwegians have a strong attachment to their countryside. A simple summer home (a hytte) is the dream (some would say birthright) of every Norwegian. The same can be said for a boat to sail Norway's bays, inlets, and countless lakes. Norwegians invented skiing, a splendid way to travel over snow-covered ground. (The words ski and slalom are Norwegian.)

WHO SAYS OIL AND WATER DON'T MIX?

Until recently, geography consigned Norway to the ranks of the relatively poor. By tradition and necessity, Norwegian farms are small. The countryside's small valleys and rocky hillsides do not lend themselves to farming that achieves an economy of scale. To preserve Norway's farming tradition (and with memory of Norway's wartime need for a food supply), the government gives farmers an income sufficient to match those of city dwellers. Norway's principal exports have been timber from its extensive forests (Norway invented the water-driven power saw) and fish from ocean waters.

Until the middle of the twentieth century, Norway also earned much of its foreign exchange through its fleet of freight-carrying ships. But poverty and lack of economic opportunity sent Norwegians on a nineteenth century exodus. The United States was the principal place for social and economic opportunity, and the state of Illinois was a favorite destination; from about 1830 to 1920 some 750,000 Norwegians emigrated to distant places.

Then, in the late 1960s oil was discovered offshore, and Norway's long history of a cash-strapped government ended. Equally important, the oil and natural gas industries provided thousands of well-paying jobs. With a prudence that other oil-producing countries might envy, Norway invested much of its oil revenues in its infrastructure and long-term social capital. All-weather roads were built to almost all inaccessible hamlets. New schools were built, and universities were handsomely supported, including free tuition. Universal health care was extended, along with generous provision for unemployment insurance, maternity leave, and single-parent support. Anticipating a future drop in oil earnings, successive governments have earmarked a portion of oil revenues for investment and future earnings. As Norwegians are fond of saying, "Oil has made Norway a pleasant place to live," a sentiment confirmed by a recent United Nations index of best places to live. Norway topped the list according to three measures: life expectancy, education, and income.

WHY IS NORWAY ONE OF EUROPE'S OLDEST YET YOUNGEST COUNTRIES?

Nation and country are imprecise terms, but nation is usually used to denote a population bound by a common culture. Country denotes a nation with an organized, effective government. The beginnings of Norway as a nation are lost in the mists of time. Perhaps the receding of an ice age around 10,000 BCE brought hunters and gatherers northward along Norway's coast. The earliest European records of Northmen date from the Viking incursions that began in the late 700s CE. Viking settlements were organized around clans and chieftains, but sometime around 900, Harald Harfagre (Harold Fairhair) established himself as Norway's supreme ruler, its first countrywide king. Scandinavians frequently fought each other and sometimes cooperated during Viking expeditions into Europe and the British Isles.

In 1380 Norway and Denmark became a united kingdom, and on Trinity Sunday 1397 (after an intrigue that spun around Queen Margarethe, the widow of King Haakon of Norway), the three crowns of Norway, Denmark, and Sweden were united. Norway had been previously devastated by the Black Death, and many of its warrior-leaders were dead. Effective power lay first with the Danes and then with the Swedes. (Norwegians now call this the 400 years that Norway slept.) During the Danish hegemony, Norway was "Danicized"; its culture, its government, and its written language became Danish.[2]

Eventually, Danish economic and military power receded, their ebb-tide engineered by Napoleon. Within easy reach of his armies, Denmark, along with its dependent, Norway, was forced to join Napoleon's alliance against Great Britain. Sweden, meanwhile, had offered its throne to one of Napoleon's marshals, Bernadotte. The latter, now styled King Karl Johan, persuaded Britain and its Russian ally to support Sweden's claim to Norway. Norway's crown remained with Sweden until Norway's independence in 1905. To great Norwegian rejoicing, then, the capital city of Swedish-Norway, Christiana, changed its name to Oslo.

DO VIKINGS STILL LIVE?

Ask a Norwegian, and a likely answer will be that the Viking spirit is alive and well in Norway. Norwegians derive deep satisfaction from solitary outdoor adventures—from single-handed sailing and cross-country skiing to hiking over fells. A visitor to a remote farmstead may see a bed with a tall headboard and short mattress pad. When asked, an elderly farmer may boast that he sleeps as his grandfather did: sitting upright, ready to spring up to grapple with intruders.

Norwegians have long claimed a proprietary interest in polar exploration, an interest easy to understand given their far-north location. One of the first modern polar explorers was Norway's Fritjhof Nansen (1861-1930). In 1888 he led a small party across Greenland from east to west, choosing the most difficult and challenging route: settlements are on the west coast; setting out from the east coast meant, in effect, no turning back. In 1893 he proposed to the Norwegian Geographical Society to probe a long-standing puzzle: Does polar ice drift? With sixteen men in a specially constructed ship, The Fram ("Forward"), the ship was locked into a Siberian ice pack and drifted northward for two years. The ship's hull was shaped like an egg, a design that pushed it up onto the ice flow, safe from the crushing ice. Icebound, it drifted safely into Norwegian waters; not a man was lost.

---

[2] In the nineteenth century, literate Norwegians tried to reconcile two languages: "Landsmal" (language of the countryside) and "Bokmal" (the language of literature). Today the dominant language is Bokmal, Norway's inflection of the Danish.

While the Fram was icebound, Nansen and L.H. Johansen traveled north by dogsled and kayak and reached eighty-six degrees fourteen minutes north, the highest latitude yet reached by man. After four months, they reached the Franz Josef Islands, where they wintered over in a hut built of rocks and driftwood, covered with walrus hide. In 1896, with the spring thaw, Nansen and Johansen began their southward journey. During World War I, Nansen devoted himself to humanitarian relief efforts, and for these he was subsequently awarded the Nobel Prize.

Figure 11.1. Roald Amundsen

Roald Amundsen (1872-1928), born near Oslo, was the first to find and sail the Northwest Passage, from the Canadian coast to the Yukon. In 1910, in Nansen's Fram he sailed south, and on December 4, 1911, became the first man to reach the South Pole. (Robert Scott, the English explorer, reached the Pole on January 17, 1912, but tragically and unlike Amundsen, he along with his men perished on the return to base camp.)

WHY IS THOR HEYERDAHL SO FAMOUS?

By far the most renowned of Norway's explorers is Thor Heyerdahl. Building on Nansen's theories of ocean drift and in an attempt to prove that ancient cultures spread by means of ocean currents, Heyerdahl and his crew sailed and drifted on a raft, the Kon-Tiki, from Peru to Polynesia in 1947. In seeking to account for the origins of Mayan pyramids and Aztec myths (from

Egypt, Hyerdahl asserted), he drifted across the Atlantic on a copy of an Egyptian reed boat, The Ra, coming within 600 miles of Central America. Another expedition, intended to fortify his theories of cultural diffusion, took him by raft from the Tigris River to Pakistan and down to the Red Sea. Other expeditions took him to Easter Island and the Maldives Islands. Most anthropologists reject his cultural diffusion theories, a rejection fortified by DNA testing of Polynesians and Amerinds. Even so, his willingness to endure great privation and risk his life in support of his ideas won him worldwide respect and acclaim.

Figure 11.2. Thor Heyerdahl

SHAKESPEARE HAD IT WRONG: WHAT COULD BE ROTTEN IN DENMARK?

Unlike Norway, Viking memories in Denmark are confined almost exclusively to museums. Population density is one way of comparing countries. The more than 5.5 million Danes crowd together in a country roughly the size of Switzerland. Their major population centers are on the Jutland peninsula and on three of their largest islands, Sjaelland, Funen, and Fyn (home to

Copenhagen). Eight-five percent of Danes are urban dwellers. (greater Copenhagen's population is around 1.5 million.) In contrast to Norway, the countryside in Denmark is fertile. Fifty-seven percent of the land is arable, and Danish agriculture is highly productive. Eggs, butter, cream, ham, and bacon are traditional Danish exports, but in recent years Danish farmers have been struggling against the export regulations of their European neighbors. Denmark, meanwhile, has invested in electronics and in household items of striking, modern design. (Ironically for Danes, the design is often referred to as Swedish modern.) The export of Danish design is worldwide; architecturally, its signature piece is probably the opera house in Sydney, Australia. Its huge roof, suggesting sails lofting, is the design of Jorn Utzon.

Perhaps consumption of alcohol is too fanciful a way of comparing countries and probing national outlook. Still, these statistics are suggestive. On average, each Norwegian drinks 4.4 liters of alcohol per year, while Danes consume 10.9 liters.

Like other aspects of beauty, the quality of urban esthetics lies very much in the eyes of the beholder. Again, and if not too fanciful, a stroll through Oslo and Copenhagen offers interesting comparisons. Oslo's great park is the magnificent Frogner, whose statues record the ages and stages of man's life. Their sculptor is Gustav Viegland (1869-1943), who devoted his life to expressing with hammer and chisel the sorrows and joys, the pain and pleasures of living. The beauty of classical proportions governs his statues, but so do the distortions expressing fear, loneliness, *angst*, and anomie. Photographs of Viegland suggest a person in command of himself and satisfied with his command. But his biography suggests a man forever fleeing his childhood. He was, he says, psychologically scarred by a violent father given to explosions of religious guilt. Gustav cannot forget being awakened at night for a beating. It was Good Friday and, as his father shouted, even children were expected to suffer on that day.

Gustav aside, most Norwegians are far from angst-ridden and dour. Their warmth and friendliness to strangers is enviable. And yet, in contemplating Viegland's statues, the viewer is tempted toward the shadow of another Norwegian artist, Edvard Munch, whose painting in 1893, *The Scream*, is widely regarded as the signature of the twentieth century.

The great park in the center of Copenhagen is Tivoli. Opened as a business enterprise in 1843 and still in corporate hands, Tivoli is a vast flowerbed, an amusement center, an assemblage of restaurants, and boasts outdoor concerts, variety shows, and thousands of twinkling lights. Tivoli is summer's enchanted garden. Each year, more than a million visitors (Danes and outlanders) throng the park. Fireworks are part of the nightly spectacle; so, too, is the marching band of boy soldiers, their uniforms straight from the pages of Hans Christian Andersen.

WHAT IS DENMARK'S FAIRY TALE ASPECT?

Denmark's castles and palaces, with steep roofs, turrets, massive carriageways, and sentries in shakos and eighteenth-century uniforms, are also the stuff of fairy tales. Village streets are cobbled; houses are half-timbered.[3] Travelers arriving by ship will see a bronze statue of Hans Christian Andersen's *Little Mermaid* looking dreamily out to sea. The monarch is Queen Margarethe II, head of state in Denmark's parliamentary democracy. A literary monarch and artist, the Queen has designed stage settings for the theater and has translated books into Danish, while her watercolors illustrate the Danish editions of *Lord of the Rings*. Popular with her subjects, the cigar-smoking Queen is a symbol of the Danish paradox: a socialist, welfare monarchy.

Figure 11.3. Little Mermaid

[3] See the stories of Hans Christian Anderson, fairy tales embedded in morality lessons.

The Danes have a strongly egalitarian (redistributive) system of taxation. More than 75 percent of children between three and six attend free nursery schools. Lifelong education is free. A long maternity leave is statutory. Unemployment benefits hover near 90 percent of previous salary. Like other countries whose population is aging, Denmark struggles with increasing demands on its welfare system, and Danes, like people everywhere, resist increases in taxation.

Government transfers have shaped a society of which Danes are very proud: a society of equals. Danes ride bicycles and drive old cars, in part, because import taxes are high but also because a shiny, new car is regarded as an affront to a society of equals. Denmark is also a society that strives toward government by consensus. Danish commitment to personal freedom has made it a pioneer in the open display of pornography. The commitment has also opened the country to third-world immigrants. (Strollers around Copenhagen's railroad station may be pardoned for thinking that the shops are all run by Turks.) And those who circle the streets around the Radhus (city hall) may also be pardoned for exclaiming over the inviting prospect of outdoor cafes and the elegance of goods on sale.

WHY IS SWEDEN A POLITICAL PARADOX?

> Things are seldom what they seem.
> Skim milk masquerades as cream.
> — W.S. Gilbert, *HMS Pinafore*, 1878

Lucky travelers arrive in Stockholm by ship. The city's close to 800,000 inhabitants live on a chain of islands whose buildings seem to float on sparkling, blue water. As if to remind visitors that Stockholm is a city of the north, in summertime, one or two massive icebreakers are berthed alongside passenger ships at Stockholm's Old Town (Gamle Stan). A few steps from the pier, passengers walk Old Town's cobbled streets and beautifully proportioned squares. Across the water from pier-side is royal and imperial Stockholm, with its majestic archways, handsome Parliament, and royal palace, as well as its architecturally exuberant and beautiful Royal Dramatic Theater. And still farther across the water (ten minutes by boat) is the island of Djurgarden, whose name celebrates Stockholm's delight in natural beauty. (Stock is Old Norse for woods, as in stockade; holm, the word for town.) Nature and the environment are important to the Swedes; the Green Party has a strong voice in the Swedish Parliament.

Sweden is an anomaly. In practice and profession, it is an egalitarian society. Yet, there are great disparities of wealth among its over 9.5 million citizens. Like Norway and Denmark, it is a constitutional monarchy, yet Swedes cling tenaciously to inherited titles of aristocracy. To join the ranks of the upper class, many Swedes have changed their patronymic, replacing the name-ending "son" with the Latinate "ilius," as in Sandilius.[4]

Figure 11.4. Stockholm

During World War II, Sweden alone among the Baltic countries maintained its neutrality. Norway had attempted to do so, but Norway and Denmark were quickly overrun by German armies. Norway and Denmark were fierce resistance fighters. Sweden claims (and many historians agree) that it had no choice but to cooperate with Germany, lest it, too, fall under the Nazi heel. Even so, at war's end, Norway and Denmark were economically devastated. Sweden had become prosperous through its armed neutrality and its sale of metals and alloys to Germany.

WHAT IS ARMED NEUTRALITY?

For more than 200 years, Sweden's stance in international dealings has been what Swedes call an armed neutrality: military power sufficient to ward off would-be attackers. The background of that neutrality is three centuries of Swedish military might and wars of conquest. Sweden

[4] And when the Danish author of *Out of Africa* married Swedish Count Blor Blixen, Karen Blixen took on Swedish ways, and for the rest of her life styled herself Countess Blixen.

joined with Denmark and Norway in the Union of Three Crowns in 1397. Denmark was the Union's engine of energy, its arm of control. The resentment of the Swedish nobility (over taxes and other impositions) boiled into revolt in 1434 and again in 1471 when Swedish victory over the Danes paved the pathway to independence. In 1523 Gustav Vasa took the Swedish throne and became the first of a dynasty of military kings.

Two of them, Gustavus Adolphus (1594-1632) and Karl XII (1682-1710), carried the genes of military genius. They fought their wars for glory, territory, and the plunder that came with territory. Their wars were also religious wars, Lutheranism and Protestantism against Roman Catholicism and Russian Orthodoxy. The House of Habsburg was defender of Catholicism, and Sweden was its chief opponent in the Thirty Years War, 1618-48.[5] Peter the Great bested Sweden in the Great Northern War, a war fought for control of the east Baltic. (In St. Petersburg, at the base of Peter's great statue are the words that Russian children learn by heart: "When Russia celebrates another victory over the foe...") But when the last trumpets had sounded and the last war flags furled, Sweden's territory was truncated, and its energies now turned to literature and invention.

At least one memento of imperial arms survives to astound us. Buried deep in the cold waters of the Stockholm archipelago was a ghostly remnant of Sweden's military glory, the warship Vasa. The Vasa was built in the 1620s on orders from Gustavus Adolphus to honor the founder of his line, Gustav Vasa. Launched in 1628, she was a formidable vessel, built of iron and oak and weighing 1,300 tons. As she sailed into the harbor, with gun ports open to fire a royal salute, an unexpected wind forced her to broach. She sank, drowning most of her crew and carrying everything aboard deep into the sea. The ship's position was discovered in 1956; after being brought to the surface and after decades of patient restoration, the ship is now displayed, mast reaching skyward, in the Vasa Museum.

WHAT IS SWEDEN'S MIDDLE WAY?

Among the Three Crowns, Sweden has the most advanced heavy industry in terms of production and in terms of efficiency. In continental western Europe, Germany, France, Italy, and Sweden are the only producers of large automobiles. In western Europe, only France, Germany, and Sweden build jet fighters. Automobiles and airplanes are the most conspicuous exam-

---

[5] Popular history asserts that the soldier-nutcracker that makes its appearance at Christmastime is in memory of Count Johan Tilly, commander of the Catholic Holy League during the Thirty Years' War.

ples of industrial achievement, but Swedish industries produce a wide range of goods and products. Their success is widely envied.

It is a success with many sources. Lutheran insistence that each person read the Bible for himself or herself was a strong impetus to a literate society. Sweden's fertile soil and forests created wealth for investment in fledgling industries. Sweden is rich in iron ore, copper, and other industrial metals. Freedom of inquiry came early to Sweden, and with it science forged ahead. Carl Linnaeus created a universal system of plant and animal taxonomy. Anders Celcius created the hundred-degree thermometer. C. W. Scheele (1742-1786) discovered and added chlorine to the periodic table. Jons Berzilius (1779-1848) is a father of modern chemistry. In the nineteenth century a spate of Swedes invented things of widespread use and need. L.M. Ericsson invented the table telephone. And Albert Nobel held more than 200 patents, including dynamite, the stick that tamed nitroglycerin. Dynamite helped make war more deadly, but Nobel is now best remembered for bequeathing his fortune to prizes on behalf of humanitarian endeavors.

In the 1930s, Sweden, like the rest of the world, ground to an economic halt. Unemployment and poverty devastated the country. In many countries in Europe, Asia, and Latin America, frightened and angry workers demanded a socialist-communist revolution to rout a failed capitalist system. In still other countries, the way was opened for a dictator to take control of the economy and, in so doing, to crush freedom and dissent. As was said of Italy's Mussolini, despite his methods, he made the trains run on time. And Nazi Germany tackled its unemployment by building its *autobahns* (the equivalent of America's interstate highways) and armaments.

Sweden's response to the Great Depression was "Capitalism with a Human Face." In a phrase made memorable by an American writer, Marquis Childs, Sweden created a "Middle Way" between the extremes of political left and right.[6] Private property remained private. Keyensian economic policy was put into play. The government would serve as emergency employer. Public funds would be used to stimulate demand. The major actors in the industrial system—labor unions, owners and managers, political officials, and banks and bankers—entered into agreements that guaranteed employment and contained no-strike clauses so that factory managers could keep production schedules, and most important of all, so that the welfare state would be vastly expanded. An important component of the Middle Way was gov-

---

[6] See Marquis Childs, *Sweden: The Middle Way* (New Haven: Yale University Press, 1936).

ernment's responsibility for industrial well-being. When Swedish shipyards could no longer compete with cheaper labor abroad, shipyards were shut down, and their workers were given government grants for training and education to enable them to enter other employment.

The Middle Way has served Sweden fairly well for over seventy-five years. But like the second generation of its human creators, it, too, shows signs of aging. Sweden operates under all-too-common rules of human behavior. Benefits once given are jealously guarded and held to be sacrosanct. An aging workforce may be insufficient to support the oncoming generation's welfare expectations. Concern for the environment precludes clear-cutting forests or wholesale construction of atomic energy plants. Of course, government needs more money, but few are willing to see their taxes raised. So, the Swedes themselves now talk of finding a new, twenty-first century Middle Way.[7]

WHO ARE THE FINNS?

Bordered by Sweden and Russia, Finns consider themselves to be Scandinavians, despite a centuries-long connection to Russia. Finland's two official languages are Finnish and Swedish. Out of a population of over 5.4 million, about 5 percent of Finns speak Swedish as a family language (down from 7 percent thirty years ago). The Finnish language is assigned by linguists to a very small language family, Ural-Altaic (or variously to Finno-Ugric). And therein lie clues to the geographic origins of Finnish speakers: Ural, from the mountains that join Europe and Asia, and Altaic, from an area even further east.

Finland was conquered by Swedes in the thirteenth century, and ties with Sweden were strengthened by language and Lutheranism. At the end of the Great Northern War (1721), a large chunk of Finland was claimed by Peter the Great, and after Waterloo, Russia claimed the remainder of Finland as its booty. As a Russian grand duchy (the Tsar was its duke) Finns enjoyed far more freedom than Russians. Even so, in 1917 when the tsarist regime collapsed, Finland declared its independence. In 1918, Red Guards, supported by 40,000 Soviet troops, fought to nullify that independence; but led by Marshal Carl Mannerheim, Finland prevailed, and in 1920 the Soviets acceded to Finnish independence.

---

[7] See Gosta Esping-Andersen, *The Three Worlds of Welfare Capitalism* (Princeton: Princeton University Press, 1990). See also the films of Ingmar Bergman, including *Fanny and Alexander*, and those of Lasse Hallstrom, especially *My Life as a Dog*.

WHO IS CARL MANNERHEIM?

Carl Gustaf Emil Mannerheim, the revered Finnish hero, was born near Turku, Finland, in 1867 and served as a Russian officer for nearly thirty years before taking up Finland's fight for independence. When the Czar was murdered by Russian revolutionaries, Mannerheim considered that his officer's oath to the Czar had been severed. The newly formed Finnish Parliament appointed him commander-in-chief of the Finnish army, and his "army of patriots" quashed revolutionary Red Guards and expelled Soviet troops from Finnish terrain.

Figure 11.5. Carl Mannerheim (on left next to Hitler)

DURING WORLD WAR II, WHERE STOOD FINLAND?

Less than two decades later, at the start of World War II, the Russians returned to demand more Finnish territory. The Winter War (1939-40) ended with Finland's surrender of a region adjacent to Russia and with further payment of a cash indemnity. When Germany entered the war in 1941, Finland (led again by Marshall Mannerheim) allied itself with Germany; but as the Nazis' eastern front weakened, Russia forced Finland to turn against its sometime German ally. At war's end, Finland's independence was affirmed, along with a sizeable reparation to Russia and confirmation of territories lost in the Winter War.

A glimpse of Finland's wartime sympathies crushed by the realities of politics can be seen in an exchange between Winston Churchill and Mannerheim in 1941. In a letter, Churchill writes, "I wish I could convince your excellency that we are going to defeat the Nazis.... It would be most painful to the many friends of your country in England if Finland found itself in the dock with the guilty and defeated Nazis." Mannerheim replied to Churchill: "It would be deplorable if these measures, undertaken for the security of Finland, should bring my country into conflict with England, and it would deeply sadden me if England were forced to declare war on Finland." [8] Mannerheim's Helsinki home is now a museum. Its curators work to give the impression that the Field Marshal might, at any moment, step forward to greet his visitors.

HOW TO DESCRIBE HELSINKI?

Since the devastation of World War II, Finland has prospered culturally and economically. Some of the most elegant cruise ships have slid down its shipyards' ways, and its electronics nearly dominate the manufacture of cell phones. Helsinki, the capital city, contains over 600,000 people, 10 percent of the country's population (20 percent if the over one million in the metropolitan area are included). The city is built on a peninsula, and shipboard travelers can stroll from the dock directly into the city. A busy series of markets display fish, fruits, and vegetables along with hats, furs, and handicrafts. Connected to the marketplace is the Esplanade (*Esplanadi)*, a park whose *alle* is filled with mothers, baby carriages, and children at play. The Esplanade invites strollers to linger on benches and to take coffee at one of its quiet, clean cafes across from the park near some of Finland's most famous shops. Further on is the art deco entrance to Finland's oldest department store, Stockman's. And adjacent to Stockman's is Finland's largest bookstore, The Academic (Akateeminen).

Churches, the Parliament, and other government buildings are built of light-colored Finnish granite, giving the city its sobriquet, the white city. After Finland achieved independence, architects found inspiration by intertwining Finland's sagas with a distinctly modernist style. Finlandia Hall combines strong vertical lines and a massive frontality. Perhaps the most distinctive of Helsinki's architectural achievements are the railway station (with massive figures holding great lamp globes) and the Rock Church (The Taivallahti), built deep into solid rock. And resonances of Helsinki's Russian past—shades of St. Petersburg—echo in the red brick spires and onion domes of the Uspensky Cathedral and in the severe classical style of the University Library. Trams (street cars) cross and crisscross the city. City-paid English-speaking

---

[8] Winston Churchill, *The Grand Alliance* (Garden City, New York: Houghton Mifflin Company, 1950), 450-51.

tour guides roam the city, to give directions and put the visitor at ease. Best of all, Helsinki is an easy city for the stroller. Even better, it is relatively crime free.[9]

Figure 11.6. Helsinki

[9] Tove Jansson is the most translated Finnish writer. *The Summer Book* (New York: Pantheon, 1974) is the story of six-year-old Sophia and her aging grandmother spending their summer on a small island in the Gulf of Finland. Their talks distill our eternal preoccupations--life, death, love, and existence. She also writes a series of wry comic books.

THE EASTERN MEDITERRANEAN

12. Searching for Ancient Greece

First-time visitors to Athens are usually disappointed in what they see because they carry expectations formed by schoolroom pictures of the Acropolis and the Parthenon. Frozen in time, these sepia studies usually show an artist's version of the Parthenon high above a small town of quiet streets and outdoor cafes. The real-life Acropolis and the Parthenon are here, but Athens is a huge city. With over three million inhabitants in the greater Athens area, the city is home to around one-third of the population of the entire country. Athens began its growth from small city to metropolis in the years following the First World War. Growth was hurried and unplanned. Greece had lost a war with Turkey in 1922, and many thousands of ethnic Greeks living in Turkey were forced to repatriate. Most were from families that had been living in Turkey for centuries. Athens today is a city with traffic-clogged streets and massive, high-rise buildings, where air pollution takes its toll on people as well as ancient monuments.

Yet, in and around modern Athens, antiquity still shows through. Athens' high plateau, the Acropolis ("high city") is visible from most parts of the city. The Acropolis was the city's military redoubt. And on it sits the glory of ancient Athens, the Parthenon, temple to the patron of the city, Athena, the virgin goddess of wisdom and protector of agriculture (*partheno*, or virgin). The Athens of the Byzantines is well preserved in several of the city's low-domed brick churches. The National Archaeological and the Benaki Museums dazzle the visitor with their antique treasures. And visitors can imagine themselves in Socrates' Athens by walking through the *agora* (the marketplace), whose modern reconstruction is augmented by the *stoa*, a colonnaded building that displays many of the items dug out of the *agora*.

Figure 12.1. The Parthenon

Modern Athens is at its most elegant display in and around Kolonaki Square, with elegant restaurants, shops, and apartment buildings. Reminders of Turkish Athens (the time of the Ottoman conquest: 1460-1832) are found in the Monastiraki area, where at least one former mosque has been converted to a museum. The Athens of national unity and independence is celebrated in Syntagma Square. The Parliament building is here and also the tomb of the Unknown Soldier, guarded by *evzones*, soldiers in flared white kilts and pompom shoes. And Athens' liveliest nightlife area is located in the Plaka. The tired traveler can find shade and a quiet restaurant in daytime Plaka.

Shipboard travelers arrive in Athens' port city, Piraeus, a busy ferry and freight ship harbor. This is the Piraeus of ancient times, when Athens built protective walls from the harbor to the city to ward off enemy attacks. The walls are long gone, and today a railroad connects Piraeus to Athens. If anything, Piraeus's streets are busier than Athens', and many buildings and shops are downright squalid. But a short and inexpensive train ride from Piraeus's central station can bring the visitor within walking distance (or a short taxi ride) to places on the wise traveler's must-see list. But for those who come without the protective cocoon of a guided tour, it is useful to remember that the crush of Athens, with its sights and sounds, can overwhelm the visitor, especially those who have come to find the Greece of antiquity.

WHERE IS THE GREECE OF ANCIENT HISTORY?

Most of the antiquities of Greece lie off the tourist track. The Parthenon in Athens is the conspicuous exception. This temple to Athena invites surprise at its modest size of 220 feet long and raises wonder at its centuries of neglect. Greece was part of the Ottoman Empire until it achieved independence in 1829, and Turkish overlords had little interest in relics of long-dead infidels. From time to time they "quarried" the building for use elsewhere and sometimes ground up pieces of its marble for lime. They used the Parthenon to store gunpowder, and it was badly damaged by Venetian shells during an attack on the city in 1687.

During the eighteenth and nineteenth centuries, the Greeks themselves showed scant regard for the temple. As devout communicants of the Orthodox rite, they saw the temple as a monument to pagan heresy. The most beautiful of the temple's sculptures, its monumental frieze, was a gift to the Earl of Elgin by an indifferent government in Istanbul. Shipped to Britain in 1806, the Elgin Marbles were bought by Parliament in 1816 and have been in the British Museum ever since. The Turkish gift, legal under the conventions of the time, is today contested by the Greek government, which asserts that Turkey had no right to give away Greek treasure; so, the Marbles are, in effect, considered stolen property.

With independence, the Greeks reclaimed their history. Doing so was a way of defining themselves as other than Muslim Turks: a definition politically and culturally important to a new nation, especially because there were large Turkish populations in Greek cities and a large Greek population on the Turkish mainland (the father of modern Turkey, Kemal Atatürk, was born in Thessalonika).

WHAT IS THE GEOGRAPHY OF MODERN GREECE?

Greece today has a land mass of 51,000 square miles. Its population is over 11.3 million, one-third of whom live in Athens. Mountains, islands, sunshine, and water are the traveler's usual description of Greece, and in that description lie travelers' delights: 2,000 islands, with lovely beaches and crystal waters, and on the mainland, remote villages, high winding roads, spectacular views, and deep, forested valleys.

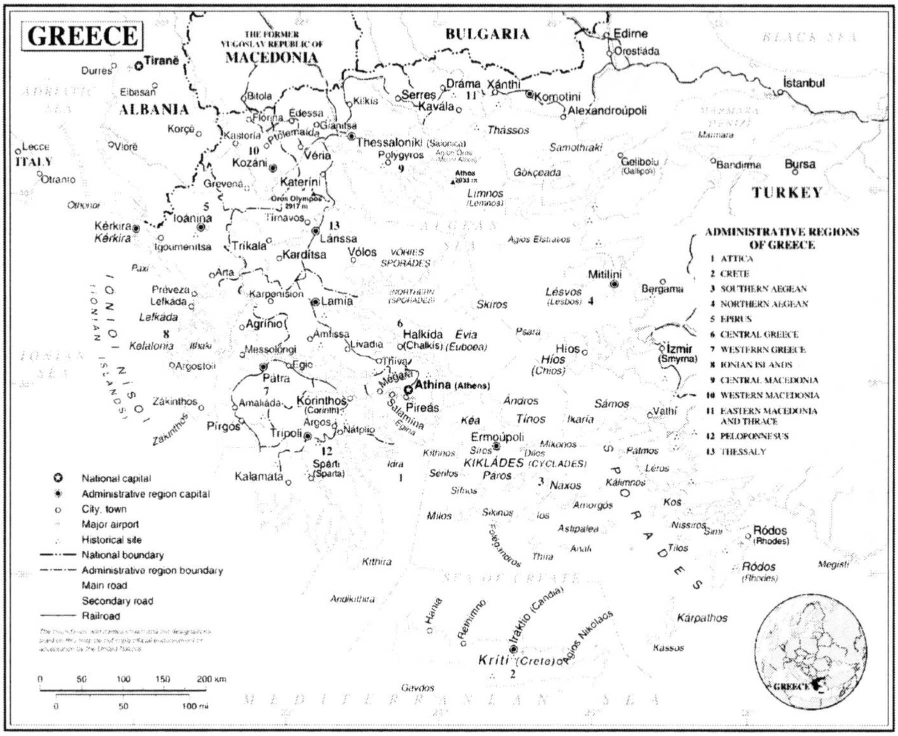

Figure 12.2. Map of Greece

Greece shares borders with Turkey in the northeast, Bulgaria in the north, and the Republics of Macedonia and Albania in the northwest. On Greece's western shores is a branch of the Mediterranean, the Ionian Sea. The Ionian is the "softer" sea, its winds and climate gentle. The Ionian Islands gave their name to a familiar style of Greek architecture. Its seven major islands (Corfu, Paxoi, Lefkada, Kefallonia, Ithaki, Zakynothos, and Kythira) are imprinted on the legends of the Trojan War. Ithaki (Ithaca) was home to Odysseus and his faithful wife, Penelope, who waited twenty years for his return. During the Napoleonic wars, the British Navy took command of Corfu and made it the capital of an Ionian Confederation. Its streets and byways mirror the sunny style of its once Venetian overlords. But a tangled past can sometimes be brought to life with misguided excess. Empress Elizabeth of Austria carried her vision of the Trojan War to a palace built in 1890. Its site is lovely, and the palace is called the Achilleion; its halls, gardens, and statuary glorify the great Achilles (in whom, some say, the empress saw the spirit of a son, Rudolph, who killed himself at an early age).

The seven Ionian Islands became a British protectorate in 1815 and remained so until 1864. Its major naval base was at Corfu. British aristocrats, who administered the islands and built some of its most pleasing piazzas, took pleasure in more than the islands' soft climate. As devoted readers of Homer (they could read the original Greek), they fancied themselves successors to the great Odysseus and the mighty Agamemnon. Odysseus's kingdom was the island of Ithaca. From nearby Mycenae on the Peloponnese mainland, Agamemnon sent one hundred ships to the siege of Troy. It was from a rock on Levkas Island that the poet of love and longing, Sappho, threw herself into the sea. And as readers of Roman history, the British knew that Anthony and Cleopatra had spent a last night ashore on the island of Gaios before sailing out to the fateful battle of Actium.

East and south of Greece lies another branch of the Mediterranean, the Aegean, Homer's "wine-dark sea." The Greeks mixed their wine with water, but it is not likely that, whatever the mixture, the Aegean's color was ever wine dark. The Aegean is the stormier sea. It is dotted with islands whose sunny beaches attract modern-day sun worshippers. One island group, the Cyclades, especially fulfills the search for "picturesque Greece." Houses are whitewashed, shining in the sun, their roofs a deep blue. Their architecture is simple and expressed in cubes and rectangles. Mountains rise straight from the water, and gnarled trees dot the landscape.

Thira (Santorini) is what remains after an ancient earthquake blew much of the island literally sky-high. Ships anchor in a crater, a caldera, that marks the ancient volcano. High above the water, villages can be seen perched precariously on the island's rim (volcanic residue, pumice, is still scooped from the island's walls and center). And it may have been dim memory of Thira's explosion that gave rise to the myth of an island in the ocean, the lost Atlantis.

Crete is the Aegean's largest island. More than 1,000 years old, it was the center of a wealthy trading empire until its mysterious collapse sometime around 1400 BCE. Its ruins were unearthed by a wealthy archaeologist, Sir Arthur Evans, who named it the Minoan Empire after its legendary king, Minos. Evans reconstructed and recreated what he claimed was a royal palace at Knossos; frescos from its walls display a vibrant (some say joyful) culture of comely youth attending fierce bulls. The women of the frescos are elegantly coifed, their eyes accented with kohl.

Crete is the site of one of western mankind's most haunting myths: the Minotaur, half-man and half-bull, forever imprisoned in an underground labyrinth, venting his anguish and rage by demanding human sacrifice. His father, King Minos, ordered that seven young men and seven maidens be sent periodically from Athens as sacrifice to the Minotaur, punishment for killing Minos' favored son. Every age finds its own meaning in the legend of the Minotaur; every age sees its own counterpart in the story of the half-human monster, and every age sees a reflection of its heroic ideal in Theseus of Athens, who volunteers to save his beloved city-state by killing the Minotaur. Theseus's bravery and ingenuity—along with that of his lover, Ariadne—crown him with success. She defies the king and provides the thread that will mark Theseus's way through the labyrinth. He, with courage and ingenuity, will find immortality.

Figure 12.3. Reconstruction of Knossos in Crete

It was master-artificer Daedalus who built the labyrinth for King Minos. And when Minos refused Daedalus's promised reward, Daedalus fashioned wings of wax to carry him and his son, Icarus, to Sicily. But Icarus flew too close to the sun. The wax melted, and Icarus fell into the sea and drowned, perhaps a victim of thoughtless daring, or as the Greeks saw him, a youth afflicted by an unwise and unwelcome character flaw, *hubris.*

The second largest Aegean island is Rhodes, once home to one of the Seven Wonders of the Ancient World, a lighthouse reputed to be one hundred feet high. Its very name, Colossus, enters our language to signify great size. Rhodes is also the sometime home of the Knights of Jerusalem, later of Cyprus, Rhodes, and Malta. Caesar studied oratory in Rhodes, and the castles of the Knights seem to have stepped from the pages of medieval glory. They were, alas, extensively reconstructed to bolster Mussolini's ambitions to be regarded as a modern-day Caesar.

Figure 12.4. Island of Rhodes

In Rhodes, in Crete, everywhere in Greece, street life is made lively by outdoor cafes where (mostly) men sit, smoke, drink wine, gossip, and argue politics—fitting activities for descendants of ancient Greeks, the originators of fiery political argument and outdoor debate.

WHAT IS GREEK FIRE?

The Classical Greeks, led by Athenians, were masters of naval warfare. Their galleys were equipped with bronze ramming prows, and as they closed in on the enemy, deadly fire was sprayed from the prow—most likely a mixture of water and phosphorus (*phos*: fire; *phorus*: to carry, as in Christophorus). Greek fire was difficult to extinguish and burned long after the battle was lost or won. The English writer Oliver Taplin uses the metaphor Greek fire for the never-dying light of Greek ideas—ideas that shape and mold our civilization.[1] But even more important to our Greek inheritance are the questions that ran alongside the ideas—questions and ideas, W. H. Auden says, that are the geology of western civilization.[2]

WHAT GAVE THE GREEKS THEIR SPECIAL QUALITIES OF MIND?

For this question, no single answer will do. An eminent scholar, Maurice Bowra, invokes the familiar theme that altitude is attitude, that geography is destiny.[3] A flat landscape is fertile soil for absolute power. Such were the governments of ancient Egypt and nearby Persia, the ever-encroaching enemy of Greece. In contrast, mountains nurture independence because they afford hiding places from the tyrant; and more important, as his agents attempt to enforce dictatorial power, they meet with resistance made bold by mountain hiding places.

Another scholar, H. D. F. Kitto, offers a variant on geography's contribution.[4] Most of Greece faces southeast. Its clear skies and sunshine encourage outdoor meeting and exchanges. Out in the open, men and women could feel free to talk, argue, and exchange ideas. Personal freedom is corollary to this free exchange. Where the Egyptians and Persians (and, in fact, dictators today) erected statues of themselves to celebrate their power and remind their subjects of that power, the Greeks erected statues to the beauty of their gods. "Let us act like gods, whom we so much resemble," said Aristotle. And the temples to their gods were small, like the palaces of Greek kings. The words of Pericles (495-429 BCE), elected leader of the Athenians, can serve as the Athenian credo:

> ... Our Constitution is called a democracy because power is in the hands not of a minority but of the whole people... And just as our political life is free and open, so is our day to day life in our relations with each other... We are free and tolerant in our private lives, but in public affairs we keep to the law...

---

[1] See Oliver Taplin, *Greek Fire* (New York: Atheneum, 1990).

[2] See Marvin Perry, et al., *Western Civilization: Ideas, Politics and Society*, 10th ed. (Boston: Wadsworth, 2012), 97.

[3] See Leslie Mitchell, *Maurice Bowra: A Life* (Oxford University Press, 2009).

[4] See H.D. Kitto, *The Greeks* (London: Penguin Books, 1951).

> Our love of what is beautiful does not lead to extravagance; our love for things of the mind does not make us soft…[5]

But it is never wise to take a creed at face value. Too much may be hidden in fine words; too many exceptions may mar their beauty. The two great political powers of classical Greece were Athens and Sparta. We remember Athens for its democracy and for the beauty of its art and architecture. But behind those achievements was a social system built on slavery. Athens was a city-state, part urban, part countryside, a polity of about 950 square miles. Athens in its golden age (fifth century BCE) probably used 125,000 slaves: 65,000 in domestic employment, the rest hard at work in fields and mines. The overlords of slaves were about 100,000 Athenians, of whom only 45,000 men were permitted to participate in public life. Women were mostly hidden away, presiding over house and children, rarely seen in public. Athens was the largest of the Greek city-states, with an estimated total population of 275,000. In that population were layers of social classes: aristocrats with inherited land, merchants, bankers, artisans, and slaves. And neither citizen nor slave was a large group of resident aliens, the *metics,* who worked the full range of Athenian occupations (and as many scholars say, they were the engines of enterprise that made Athens prosperous).

For the framers of the American Constitution, Athens was admired for inventing democracy, but its democracy was a warning against permitting all power to rest in a single assembly. The memory still burned of the assembled Athenians putting Socrates to death for his unpopular and unsettling teachings. One consequence of that memory was to help justify the American framers' insistence that political power be shared among three branches of government.

Sparta, Athens' chief rival, is not much admired by democratic societies. It was a political system with tight control over its citizens, a society organized to produce a disciplined army. Like Athens, its economy rested on slavery. But unlike Athens, its women enjoyed great freedom in their personal lives and played important roles in the polity's public life. The rivalry between Athens and Sparta eventually flared into a disastrous conflict. The Peloponnesian War (432-404 BCE) brought ruin to Athens and crippled Sparta's military might. The war ushered unscrupulous leaders into Athenian politics. It shut down the creative energies of Greece's golden age and sent that age spinning to its end.

---

[5] Thucydides, *The Peloponnesian War*, Book II. 34-46, translator Rex Warner (London: Penquin, 1972), 143-51.

For at least a millennium, the West has pondered the meaning of the war. Did it foreshadow World War I and the disastrous consequence of its peace? Does it parallel the Cold War? Was it the West against the Muslim world? If so, should the Peloponnesian War be seen as a warning to the democracies of the West? As a grim fingerpost for the United States?

HOW DO WE REMEMBER THE GREEKS?

We remember the Greeks by their contributions to our own lives. Like the character in the play by Moliere who delights in discovering that he speaks prose[6], we speak Greek words all our lives. Much of our vocabulary of science, love, and literature is Greek or Greek-derived. Cosmos is Greek for order; phobia is fear; telephone and telegraph are combined from Greek words for distance, sound, and sign. "Ologies" of every sort (zoology, sociology) come from the Greek word meaning a branch of learning or body of knowledge. Lyric comes from the Greek harp, the lyre; museum comes from the muses, the nine goddesses, patrons of the arts. Nostalgia comes from two words, home and pain; economy from household management. And theory—the very center of knowledge and understanding—comes by way of theater, meaning to behold. Theory explains; it sets out the connection among events, behaviors, and values. And it can do so because the Greeks saw the world as conforming to rules and patterns, a world that was orderly, that was "cosmos."

Most every person has his or her own list of gifts from the Greeks. Those who live in democratic societies honor Athens as the first democracy (*demos*: the people; *cracy*: to rule). And as the framers of the American Constitution took pains to observe, a wise democracy is more than mere numbers; it also requires a Periclean virtue, protection for the opinions of the minority.

Those with special appreciation for literature know that the Greeks invented both tragedy and comedy. Comedy enables us to laugh at our own foolishness and to accept with grace unhappy turns in our own lives. Tragedy, as many (including Aristotle and Freud) point out, enables us to confront the unthinkable and the unbearable: the death of someone we love, the self-destruction of someone we admire. The Greeks gave us lyric poetry, cries of the heart, its joy and its wounds. The poems of Sappho call across time:

> On the black earth, say some, the thing most lovely
> Is a host of horsemen, or some, foot soldiers,

---

[6] Moliere, *The Bourgeois Gentleman*, 1670.

Others say of ships, but I—whatsoevever
Anyone loveth—[7]

The Greeks did more than give us insight into our lives; they offer us the belief that each of us has a dignity and self-worth that can attain its fullest purpose when put in the service of a great enterprise. Civic obligation is an enduring facet of that enterprise. Here is Pericles's "Speech to the Assembly of Athens," following a military reversal:

> I hold that it is more in the interest of the individual that his country should prosper than that he should flourish while his country falls.... Born as you are, citizens of a great state...you should be ready to face the greatest disasters .... Cease then to grieve for your private afflictions, and address yourselves instead to the safety of the commonwealth.[8]

And in his oration honoring Athenians who have died in battle:

> ... fix your eyes every day on the greatness of Athens.... Reflect that what made her great was men ... who knew their duty....They gave her their lives.[9]

Not all at once, but over the centuries, Greek intellectual leaders rejected the idea that angry and capricious gods are responsible for our suffering, replacing them with ideas of an orderly universe in which every consequence has a cause. "Happy is he," said the poet Hesiod, "who knows the cause of things."[10] With that rejection, the Greeks laid the foundations of modern science (as Einstein said, God does not play dice with the universe). Science rests on the logic of evidence, inference, and conclusion. The Greeks laid out logic's two basic forms, inductive and deductive reasoning.

The Greeks continue to disturb us with their questions, even as they force us to confront the great and small issues of our lives: What is justice? What is honor? What is freedom? What do the rich owe the poor? What does the citizen owe the state, and what does the state owe the citizen? Is it permissible for our leaders to lie? Do women want different things from life than men do? And what do each of us owe to ourselves? Is it true, as Plato said, that it is better to be Socrates dissatisfied than a pig satisfied?

---

[7] C. M. Bowra, translator, *Classical Greece* (New York: Time Life Books, 1965), 18.

[8] W. Julian Korab-Kapowicz, *A History of Philosophy: From Thucydudes to Locke* (eBook, 2012), 8.

[9] Ibid. From Thucydides, *The History of the Peloponnesian War*, published in 431 BC.

[10] Hesiod, *The Theogony of Hesiod*, translated by Hugh G. Evelyn-White (Web), 1914, http://www.sacred-texts.com, accessed 25 August, 2014.

Through their statuary, the Greeks helped to define our sense of human beauty. Sculpture is an Athenian glory, a one-hundred-year struggle to capture in stone the subtleties of face, figure, and clothing. In the 600s BCE, sculpture merely suggested its human subject. Faces were frozen in enigmatic smiles; clothes concealed the form beneath. By 500 BCE, faces were individual and animated by expression; clothing was draped to reveal muscles and movement, and humans and gods were joined in an opalescent beauty.

The symmetry of Greek architecture continues to be a model for public architecture (The U.S. Supreme Court; The Madeline in Paris). Greeks invented the style of classical columns: Doric, Ionic, and Corinthian. And by swelling each column near its center, Greek architects created an illusion of symmetry when columns stand in a row.

WHO WAS HOMER?

The roster of Greek gifts goes on, but of this long list one more will have to suffice. Sometime around 800 BCE, the poet Homer (said to be blind, said to come from the island of Kos) recited gripping tales of war and adventure; his two most famous are now known as the *Illiad* and the *Odyssey.* These two great epics speak of men and events of 1200 BCE, the war between Greeks and their Trojan enemies. The *Illiad* sings of the war's last year, the death of the mighty Achilles, the Greek ruse to capture the city with a "Trojan Horse," and the final destruction of Troy. The English writer George Steiner says that he can never look at a photograph of a burning city, its inhabitants fleeing the horrors of war, without thinking back to burning Troy.[11]

The *Odyssey* recites the adventures of Odysseus during his twenty-year journey to reach his home and faithful wife, Penelope. As modern writers such as Ian Flemming love to confess, the *Odyssey* is the model for every tale of adventure ever written since Homer first spellbound his audience with tales of heroes and their seduction by women with magical powers, larger-than-life villains, and meddling gods, even as he offers penetrating discourse on his heroes' motives and values. Honor and excellence (*arete*) are the codes by which they live. And many of us today, Americans especially, are fascinated by Odysseus's qualities of mind. *Metis* is the word that captures his way of dealing with challenges: improvising with practical behavior and intuiting solutions to difficult and dangerous problems. Homeric dialogues never cease, which is another way of saying that for 3,000 years, Homer's readers have pondered his epics, seeking

---

[11] See George Steiner, *Antigonas* (Barcelona: Gedisa, 2008).

to understand war and its consequences, seeking to understand the ways in which chance, divine intervention, and human motives determine the outcome of war and its aftermath.

Figure 12.5. Homer, British Museum

WHERE IS TROY?

From the Renaissance on (around the mid-1500s), as western scholars learned to read classical Greek, it was generally assumed that Homer's stories were no more than stories, bits and pieces of folklore, told and retold until woven into a seamless narrative by a teller (or perhaps tellers) of tales known by a traditional name, Homer. Traces could be found of Homer's Greek cities. But where was Troy? The answer, as it unfolded, would lie with Heinrich Schliemann.

Schliemann was born in north Germany in 1822. Like one of Homer's heroes, his life was built around improbable events, some of which Schliemann may have fabricated. This much, though, is true. He was a gifted linguist, a highly successful businessman, and an inspired archaeologist. Using these gifts, he turned the myth of Troy into fact and his own life into myth.

Through a series of business ventures (dealings in gunpowder and indigo in Russia, gold dust during the California gold rush), Schliemann retired at age thirty-six from business and set out to find Troy. Self-taught, he read, wrote, and spoke twelve languages, including ancient Greek and Turkish (then written in Arabic script). As he related, he was now ready to fulfill a boyhood dream: to find Troy. Some biographers suggest that the boyhood dream is a later-life invention and that all Schliemann sought was an enterprise that might bring him fame, a fame that would rest on Europe's fascination with ancient Greece. Schliemann advertised for a Greek wife to share his adventures: young, not afraid of hard work, and willing to learn three languages in two years.

Enter the comely Sophia. She was seventeen, he forty-seven. They would have two children, Andromache and Agamemnon. Popular belief then held that the site of Troy lay on the Turkish shore of the Dardanelles. Winds and currents make it a logical place for safe harbor and trade. But Homer tells of drawing Greek ships up on Troy's beach, and no such beach is to be discovered. Schliemann reasoned that the ancient harbor must have silted up and that Troy lay inland. But where? Inland, near present-day Cannakale, are several mounds suggesting ruins deep in the earth. But which one is Troy? Homer does not lie, said Schliemann. One battle scene has Achilles dragging the body of the Trojan hero, Hector, three times around the walls of Troy. Schliemann and his aides repeated the chase at several sites, until a satisfactory match was found. Here, he and Sophia set their Turkish workers to digging. One day, she spied something glinting in the ground. Workmen were sent home on the pretext that it was her husband's birthday. Out of sight of watchful Turkish officials (whom Schliemann had promised the treasure, should it ever be found), 9,000 gold items were smuggled out of Turkey.

Schliemann was correct in his finding the site of Troy, but in his unsystematic and overly enthusiastic archaeology, he dug down past Troy to a pre-Trojan city. It would not be until the 1930s that Carl Blegan of the University of Cincinnati would find the real Troy. In triumph and with a gift for garnering honors and publicity, Schliemann was feted worldwide. His Trojan treasures were given to the city of Berlin, where they would disappear in the waning days of World War II.

To pile triumph on triumph, Schliemann set out to find the legendary treasures of Agamemnon in the city of Mycenae in the Peleponnesus. The Greek government took no chances with a self-confessed, boastful smuggler. Its agents supervised the digs. Once again, intuition triumphed. Schliemann dug fairly far from the large, domed structure that popular lore called Agamemnon's Treasury. Among Schliemman's great discoveries were several death masks in solid gold. Schliemann proclaimed the most beautiful one to be the Mask of Agamemnon.

When doubts surfaced about its identity, an angry Schliemann heaped scorn on his critics by shouting, "Very well, then. This is not the Mask of Agamemnon. It is the mask of my butcher, Herr Shultz!" [12]

Today, the mask is a treasure of Athens' National Museum. But scholarship remains divided over its authenticity. Schliemann is known to have commissioned forgeries passed off as genuine. The Greek government does not permit non-destructive testing of the mask to fix its probable dates. More nagging still is the assertion by some who have studied the mask that it looks strangely modern: eyes half-closed, half-open that seem to follow the viewer around the room, a nineteenth-century fashionable goatee. And most disturbing, the mask bears a curious resemblance to the ruler Schliemann so wished to impress: Kaiser Willhelm of Germany!

Not so much mystery as irony. When the Trojan treasures disappeared from Berlin during World War II, no country claimed or admitted responsibility. Then, many years later Russia admitted to finding and keeping them. The treasures had been found! They were safe in the Hermitage Museum in St. Petersburg!

WHAT IS THE PELOPONNESUS?

The southern peninsula of Greece, the Peloponnesus is named for the mythical Pelops (literally, Pelop's island; *nesos* means island). It is the site of several of the most important kingdoms and city-states of ancient Greece: Sparta, Argos, and Corinth. Its deep valleys and high mountains guarded the independence of those states, and its numerous bays and harbors provided easy access to the sea. Cruise ships make port in the city of Naphlio, first capital of modern Greece, a lovely, well-proportioned city with an elegant town square.

WHAT IS THE VENETIAN IMPRINT ON THE PELOPONNESUS?

Greece was a province of the Ottoman Empire during the 350 years following the Turkish capture of Constantinople in 1453; and as Ottoman power rose and fell, the ambitious Venice—always hungry for trading opportunities and wealth—seized islands in the Ionian Sea, the island of Crete, and ports on the Peloponnesus. Turkish ruins are scattered about Naphlio. And high above the city is the Venetian fortress of Palamidi, built between 1711 and 1714. Palamidi was built to withstand siege and cannon fire; its vast encircling wall encloses a series of small

---

[12] See William M. Calder III, "Is the Mask a Fake?" *Archaeology* (July/August, 1999).

forts to make it possible for defenders to effect strategic retreats without surrendering the fortress itself.

Figure 12.6. The Peloponnesus

WHAT ARE THE GLORIES OF THE PELOPONNESUS?

The traveler can journey from Naphlio to sites that embody many of the glories of ancient Greece. Tyrins, for example, is home to the great Hercules, whose travels and twelve labors are deeply embedded in the myths of the western world. Even today, Arcadia, in the center of the Peloponnese, stands as symbol of rustic peace and beauty. Its deep valleys and high mountains lead the traveler to villages where monasteries and taverna are the centers of village life. Delphi was home to the oracles and the priestess who could divine the future. Mycenea was the kingdom of the mighty Agamemnon, who sent one hundred ships to the siege of Troy out of duty to his brother Menelaus. It was Helen, his unfaithful wife—perhaps kidnapped or perhaps a willing companion of Prince Paris of Troy—who set in motion the Trojan War. And it was in Mycenea that the great tragedy of Agamemnon's dynasty unfolded. His unfaithful wife Clytemnestra welcomed him home from the Trojan War by murdering him and his children, bequeathing to us a timeless story of infidelity and revenge.

Figure 12.7. Theater at Epidaurus

The theater at Epidaurus is a masterpiece of ancient acoustics; audiences wept (and still weep) during the plays of Euripides that tell the story of Agamemnon and his daughter, Medea. Corinth was a thriving market town that survived into Roman times. Its ruins give the visitor a glimpse of columnar majesty. The Apostle Paul visited Corinth, and his Epistle to the Corinthians stands as a warning to all who commit the sins of self-pride and excessive pursuit of worldly goods. And memories of Olympia stir to life every four years in the Olympics, as athletes of modern nations compete for the sake of glory and excellence—the embodiment of the ancient Greek ideals of *arête*.

13. Ancient Egypt: Travels Beyond the Grave

That undiscovered country from whose bourn no traveler returns
— Hamlet

Most travelers venturing to Egypt travel to see memorials to an ancient past. Disappointment descends on those expecting to find some continuity between an ancient past and today, for there is none. On the streets of Cairo cars clog the roadways, pedestrians mill and surge, and dust from collapsed buildings clings to clothes and noses. Against the cacophony generated by a city of over sixteen million comes the piercing cry of a muezzin calling the faithful to prayer. The traveler coming to Egypt, expecting the sights and sounds of long ago made familiar through movies, books, and opera, is shocked to discover an Arab culture dappled with traces of former British overlords, an upper-class fondness for French and Italian styles, and working-class familiarity with American music. But one should not despair, as the scene, while unanticipated, is magical.

The difference between ancient and modern Egypt was made even more pronounced by the uprisings against the government in the winter of 2010-11. Part of what became known as the "Arab Spring," young Muslims and others joined against the government of President Hosni Mubarak, resulting in the latter's banishment from office. Ancient treasures were forgotten by tourists, as they coped with disruptions caused by riots in the street. Today tourism has dwindled to a mere drop in the bucket as the dire aftermath of the Arab Spring continues to plague Cairo and the rest of the country. But wise travelers await the day when both the Egyptian government and people will open their arms once again to tourists from abroad.

Figure 13.1. Cairo

WHAT DEFINES EGYPT TODAY?

Contemporary Egypt struggles with its modernity. More than eighty-one million people live in a country with little by way of industrialization and with only 2.85 percent of its countryside arable land. Infant mortality is an index of its third-world status: 18.6 per 1,000 births (Italy has 3.1 deaths). Half the population is illiterate. One-third of the population is under age fourteen, while two-thirds are under thirty-five, which means that the population will continue to surge upward. As its population grows dramatically, political unrest rises as well. Egypt is a country with a lopsided division of wealth: a small strata of the very rich and layer upon layer of poor. This income gap is yet another cause of the political unrest that was finally unleashed in early 2011.

As unrest rises, political leadership concentrates its power inward. Egypt styles itself a republic, but a republic is not the same as a democracy. In true republics, voters elect their representatives, but in flawed republics like Egypt, the voters are manipulated and deceived by their rulers. Political unrest is controlled by the army, the secret police, and a compliant legal system. These three arms of the government are important in the government's constant struggle to contain the demands of Islamic fundamentalists who seek to expunge from their country western ways and western ideas. Even beyond widespread poverty and the presence of Islamic fundamentalists is still another threat to Egypt's social and political stability. It is the "intellectual proletariat," young men for whom no employment is possible. Egypt awards some 800,000 university degrees each year. Most are in the social sciences and humanities, an education with limited vocational outlets. University graduates make up 90 percent of the unemployed. Newspapers and fiction recount the same story endless times: young men forced to live with their families, despairing of marriage, sitting in front of a government office for weeks and months, hoping to be invited in to sweep floors or run errands, so that sooner or later they may find a place on the lowest rung of a government job.

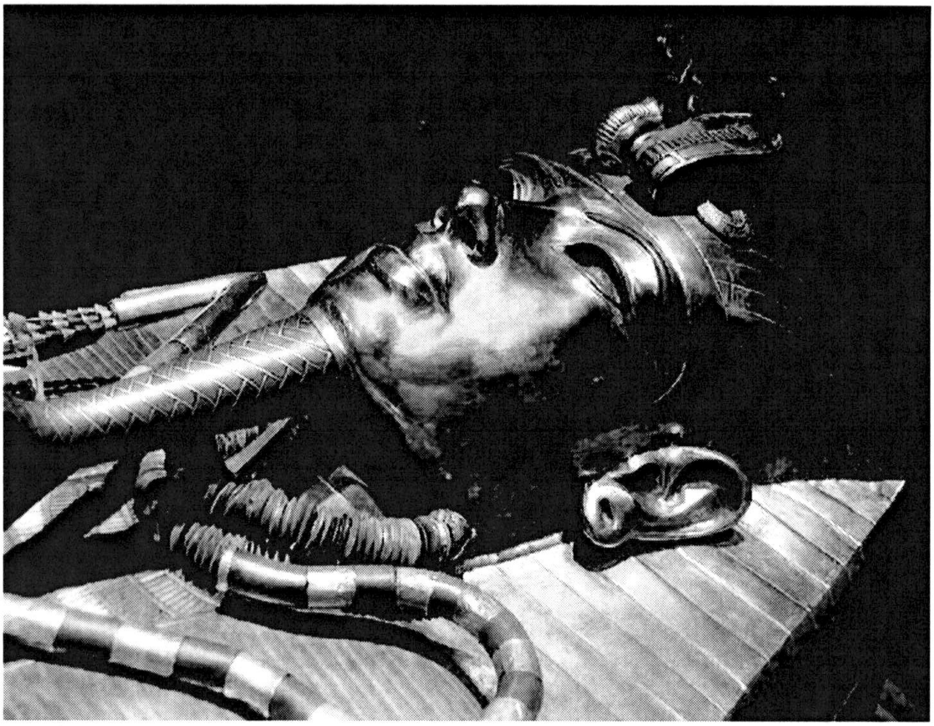

Figure 13.2. King Tutankhamen

WHAT DOES THE WISE TRAVELER SEEK?

Wise travelers, as a rule, do not come to Egypt to involve themselves with the country's contemporary problems. They come, instead, in search of an ancient and glorious past. For those arriving in Cairo, the past begins almost at the city's doorstep. Just outside Cairo rise the great pyramids, sole survivors of what were once called the Seven Wonders of the Ancient World. The Egyptian Museum in Cairo displays the dazzling treasures buried with the young pharaoh, Tutankhamen. Much further south in the Valley of the Kings, travelers can enter tombs built and decorated as final resting places for other mighty kings. And in the Temple of Luxor, travelers stand awed and dwarfed by the vastness of the temple and the size of its pillars.

What most seize the wise traveler's imagination are two things: the architectural and artistic achievements of an ancient civilization and the fact that these achievements sprang from a singular dedication: assuring the most powerful persons in that ancient civilization a happy life after death.

HOW DID THE EGYPTIANS ENVISION LIFE AFTER DEATH?

One of mankind's oldest metaphors proclaims death to be a journey. Now as in the past, every culture ponders the mystery of death, and most take comfort in the belief that death continues the journey of life, but in another realm. As far as is known, every culture provides for the journey to the afterlife—with words, ritual, or gravesite possessions (gifts for the guide who will lead the dead to another realm or implements that will be useful in that realm: a plow, a flail. And some cultures add such personal possessions as a sacrificed dog or slave!). Across history and cultures, prayers and rituals help bind humans and their gods and help assure success for the journey to the afterlife.

But even when the afterlife is a reward for an earthly life well lived, it is not easily entered. Every religion has its own commandments and behaviors that are believed to help the deceased enter into a blessed afterlife. Most of us who live today are reasonably well aware of our own culture's beliefs about achieving the afterlife. But when we become travelers to Egypt, we need to know more. How did the ancient Egyptians ensure an afterlife? What fingerposts would point the dead toward the afterlife? And what instructions did they need to enter a happy eternity?

Almost all who visit the tombs of ancient Egypt today are monotheists, especially Christians and Muslims. None require after-death instruction to reach the promised place. For monotheists, it is before-death behavior that helps to achieve the promised place. In ancient Egypt, a successful journey to the afterlife required both before-death and after-death instruction.

WHO WAS THE FIRST EGYPTIAN TO TRAVEL BEYOND THE GRAVE?

Every religion relates the story of mankind's beginnings and, in so doing, establishes the special relationship between God and the religion's communicants. Jews and Christians take their earliest history largely from the *Old Testament*. Muslims take theirs from the Koran, a history that parallels much that is in the *Old Testament*. For the ancient Egyptians, earliest history is told through the sufferings and resurrection of Osiris. Legend has it that Osiris was an early king of Egypt, ruling over a barbaric land whose people had no knowledge of the arts, agriculture, or law until Osiris brought them knowledge. Osiris was married to his sister Isis and, in that way, kept intact a bloodline that descended from the gods of the earth, suns, and moon. That intact bloodline was preserved through their son, Horus.

Seth, an evil and jealous brother, murders Osiris, castrates him, and scatters his body parts to the most distant parts of the world. But the loving Isis finds the body parts and sews them together, thus restoring Osiris to life. But even before restoration is accomplished, Isis impregnates herself with Osiris's seed, and a son, Horus, is born. Horus pursues Seth and banishes him to the awful chaos of the wasteland, west of the Nile River (the western desert: the metaphor and venue of death). The family is once again complete: the wise ruler, the loving wife, the son waiting to become ruler if and when his father should return to the realm of the dead. When Osiris dies, his burial place becomes sacred ground. Horus succeeds his father as pharaoh, and so unto the generations: each prince-in-waiting is Horus, each queen is Isis, and each pharaoh embodies the numinous powers of Osiris and the ancient gods.

Osiris is the sacred thread that binds Egyptian history from the first historic pharaohs to the last. When Caesar Augustus added Egypt to Rome's empire in 30 BCE, the Roman legions embraced the religion of Osiris and Isis and carried it to the far reaches of the empire. Isis was a comforting mother-god, and Osiris, the father, promised eternal existence through resurrection. The early Christians were discomfited by what they derogated as the "cult" of Osiris. It was a cult of broken parallels to Christianity: an immortal family, a miraculous birth, a father god, a mother goddess, and a son who carried within him the divinity of his father, and through the son and father, the promise of eternal afterlife.

WHAT OTHER GODS DID THE EGYPTIANS WORSHIP?

Unlike the great monotheisms, the religion of Osiris was a generous religion. It welcomed dozens of gods to the pantheon. Owing to its (almost always) annual flooding, the lower reaches of the Nile River, known as the Delta, was an untamed place, home to dangerous animals: lions, hippopotami, crocodiles, and poisonous snakes. What men fear, they often attempt to placate by supplication. So, the animals of Egypt became gods, represented by statues housed in temples, tended by priests who paid homage through prayers and offerings. Wild animals engender fear, but heavenly bodies inspire awe, especially the sun and the moon, whose predictable passage across the sky reassures us of order and continuity in the cosmos and, by implication, order and continuity in human affairs. Sun and moon both provide a temporal calendar of events, but life depends on the sun. So, we may pay homage to the moon, whose calendric cycles give instructions for planting and harvesting. And we must also respect the river god Nile, whose waters irrigate the desert. But overall, it is the life-giving sun that stands as the predominant god of ancient Egypt.

Initially the gods of Egypt were portrayed as animals. Over time, human heads replaced animal heads. And at various times, human-headed animal gods were surmounted by a symbol appropriate to that god. So, Hathor the cow was goddess of fertility and plenty; her head was woman, often surmounted by horns. A golden disc easily and understandably represented the sun. Annubis, with his jackal head, watched over graves and tombs and guarded the entrance to the other world (often depicted as a field of reeds, looking out over rich fields of grain, a happy place presided over by Osiris, king of the dead). Horus, the now and future king, was the far-seeing falcon, forever scanning the horizon for enemies of his kingdom, including the forces of disorder, the chaos that his father Osiris had banished from Egypt and which Horus had also pushed away from human affairs by overpowering the evil Seth. Isis had become Hathor, the cow-goddess of nurturing and fertility, and Osiris merged with Ra, god of the sun, whose daily rebirth gives promise of immortality and resurrection. Toth, the god of wisdom and learning, appears as the sacred Ibis (sometimes as a baboon), while the female hippopotamus signifies fertility and is guardian god of pregnant women. Dozens, if not hundreds, of gods populated the Egyptian pantheon. Even the lowly beetle, the sacred scarab beetle, has a place in the roster of gods: out of beetle eggs, rolled across the desert in a casing of dung, new life emerges, thus reaffirming the miraculous cycle of life and death.

Egypt's plenitude of gods reflects the continuity of Egyptian history: a language-sharing people (the language of Egypt became Arabic in the seventh century, reflecting conquest by the Muslims) bound together for more than 5,000 years by a slowly changing kingship, along with slow changes in other aspects of a common culture—arts, technology, agriculture, and theology. Egypt was and is a geographic entity defined by the Nile: a narrow strip of fertile land on either side of the river, stretching now as in the past about 4,000 miles south to north, with desert and death to the east and west where river water does not flow. The desert was always to be feared. With no fixed human settlement, it was a continuation of the disorder, the chaos that Osiris had banished from the Nile's banks. The western desert was a metaphor for death, the place where the sun went down every night.

WHAT ROLE DID THE GODS PLAY IN EGYPTIAN LIFE?

The gods of Egypt did more than preside over various corners of the cosmos. They were active in the service and disservice of the human realm. Accordingly, they required attention and supplication. Local gods might be venerated directly by common folk (such as barren women seeking to conceive), while national gods required kingly prayers to protect the kingdom from invaders or to ensure that the Nile would rise high in the yearly rain. Gods must be prayed to; the more important the god, the greater his or her temple, and the greater the number of priests in attendance.

The gods were cloaked in mystery. Religion was not congregational. Only priests and occasionally high nobles could enter the temple. Ordinary Egyptians remained outside the temple gates and walls. On certain days devoted to the god, priests, or only the high priest, would break the seal of the temple doors. The god's statue would be washed, anointed, and prayed to. Flowers and food would be laid before the god.

During some eras of Egyptian history, it was taken for granted that the statue was no mere symbol. Once the temple doors had been opened, the god himself would now reside inside his statue. On the highest of holidays, the statue might be taken from the temple and carried in glorious procession to the Nile, where he or she would be placed on a barge to ride the river, thus reassuring the god and all others that he or she was part of the cosmic flow that carried the sun god on his daily journeys. The journey began each dawn as the sun mounted his chariot to ride through the skies; it ended at dusk when the sun dismounted his chariot and stepped into the barge that carried him through the night on an underground river that flowed beneath the mighty Nile.

HOW DID THE JOURNEY TO THE AFTERLIFE CHANGE OVER TIME?

The idea of a journey to an afterlife and the religious beliefs that assured the journey remained constant over pharaonic Egypt's three thousand-year span. At first, it was the royal house that sought immortality by preserving the remains of the king (pharaoh means noble house). Then the quest was extended to aristocratic families, and a thousand or so years into Egyptian culture, the promise of immortality was extended to all ranks of Egyptian society.

Temples in which gods were worshipped were built and rebuilt. Local gods were elevated to the status of gods of the nation, and gods of the nation were sometimes cast into dustbins of disuse. For one brief period, all the old gods were set aside, and a monotheism rose in their place. The sun god was proclaimed singular and supreme.

WHY DID HERODOTUS CALL EGYPT THE GIFT OF THE NILE?

As the world's longest river, the Nile runs more than 4,000 miles. It has two main branches, the White and the Blue Nile. Each has its own schedule of rise and fall. The Blue Nile rises highest in August (an average of twenty feet at Khartoum), while the White Nile begins its rise in

April. High up in the mountains of Ethiopia, 4,000 miles from the Mediterranean Sea, spring rains push the waters of the Nile River on their southward journey. Floodwaters carry nutrient-rich soil, and as they spill over the riverbanks, the desert is irrigated, and the flood plain's nutrient base is renewed.

Figure 13.3. Pyramids

The rich-watered banks of the Nile rewarded the inhabitants of Egypt by making them a people of plenty. Abundance gave rise to a literate and leisure class, allowing for division of labor and task specialization. Specialization, in turn, helped to foster dazzling achievements in art, architecture, and technology. The culture flourished.

To travel the Nile by boat is high on the list of wise travelers' coveted destinations. And to go ashore at various important stopping points to experience the massive architecture of ancient Egypt is unforgettable.[1]

---

[1] See the adventurous traveler, Alan Moorehead, *The White Nile* (New York: Harper & Rowe, 1960) and *The Blue Nile* (New York: Harper & Rowe, 1962). Another fearless traveler was Captain Sir Richard Francis Burton, the peerless Victorian adventurer, who disguised himself as a Muslim to visit Mecca. He defied Muslim warriors in an attempt to find the source of the Nile River, and to the shock of Victorian sensibilities, he translated *Tales from the Arabian Nights*. Three biographies are Edward Rice, *Captain Sir Richard Francis*

WHEN DID ANCIENT EGYPTIAN CULTURE BEGIN?

When Herodotus viewed the Pyramids in the 460s BCE, Egypt was even then unimaginably ancient. Its unrecorded history reaches back to 7000 BCE, and the Egypt of the pharaohs begins sometime around 3000 BCE. Measured against Egypt's history, Homer is a latecomer. He recited his epics sometime around 800 BCE, and his tales describe events in the Age of Heroes, sometime around 1200 BCE.

While Europeans on the northern shores of the Mediterranean hunted and gathered, wore animal skins, and lived in caves, Egyptians perfected an astonishing civilization. The wealthy lived in elaborate villas, sat upon four-legged chairs (an Egyptian invention), and wore finely spun linen. Egyptians doctors practiced surgical interventions and prescribed drugs, herbs, and salves. Cadavers were preserved for a seemingly infinite number of years. Written notation had been perfected, and scribes and other literates wrote complex thoughts and elegant poetry on papyrus (hence our word paper). Agriculture enhanced by irrigation flourished. And Egypt's consequent wealth and leisure helped to create a thriving urban life along with magnificent architecture and the means to assure that the dead would live on through a journey after this life.

That life is a journey is a near-universal human conviction. Also nearly universal is the conviction that the human journey continues after death—in another way, in another realm. For the ancient Egyptians, nothing was more important to the afterlife journey than a well-preserved corpse from which the soul could venture forth into death's realm and, from time to time, return from death's domain to find sanctuary on earth.

To speak of ancient Egypt is to summon a culture that prospered for more than 3,000 years, during which time beliefs and ideas changed and evolved. Even so, the basic idea abides that life after death was a continuation of the journey that begins at birth.

WHAT WAS THE PHARAOH'S ROLE IN ANCIENT EGYPT?

Similar to other oriental despotisms (Persia, Babylon, China), the pharaoh had a god-like status. Like other such despots, the ruler of Egypt presided over rituals that kept the cosmos in order. For Egypt, an orderly cosmos helped assure that the Nile, through its annual flooding, would make the Egyptian desert bloom. Egyptian rulers claimed descent from the sun god, Ra,

---

Burton (New York: Scribner's, 1991); Fawn Brodie, *The Devil Drives: A Life of Sir Richard Burton* (New York: W.W. Norton, 1967); and Frank McLynn, *Burton: Snow Upon the Desert* (London: John Murray, 1990).

who was worshipped continuously all through ancient Egypt's long history—so much so that Pharaoh Amenhotep (about 1350 to 1334 BCE) proclaimed Aton, god of the sun, as omnipotent. And to signify that supremacy, the pharaoh changed his name to Akenaton ("He who is devoted to Aton"). In keeping with his new name and the status of his namesake, Akenaton shifted his capital to a new city built to celebrate Aton as the one true God.

But however supreme, no pharaoh ruled alone. He was supported by a vast organization of nobles, officials, bureaucrats, soldiers, and priests. It has been many times remarked that Egyptian society resembled its pyramids: a tiny ruling family at the peak and below them a small elite: nobles, court officials, great landowners, generals, and priests. Beneath them and greater in number were military leaders and persons of skills and technical accomplishments. And at the very large base was the vast majority of society: tenant farmers, workers, common soldiers, and slaves.

Figure 13.4. Akenaton

Not long after Amenhotep commanded that statues and temples of all other gods be destroyed, the priests who had devoted their lives to the old gods (and had amassed great wealth in doing so) conspired with others of the pharaonic elite to supplant Akenaton by his son-in-law, Tutankhamun. The latter was no more than nine or ten years old when he assumed the throne, presumably easily led by those at the top of the pyramid. But whether forced, led, or merely advised, he restored the old gods, moved his capital back to Thebes, and would someday achieve modern-day fame by the discovery of his tomb in 1922.

TO THE EGYPTIANS, WHAT IS THE HUMAN SOUL?

Although the concept of the soul is freely used in western discourse, such use masks a long history of dispute over its ultimate meaning and significance. What, for example, is the soul's substance? Its purpose? Its origin? Its relationship to the body? Where does it reside? What is its connection to God? What happens to the soul after death? Where stands the soul between life and death (the Psychopannychia controversy)? Is the concept of soul completely equivalent to life force?

No one can now say how closely the words used by the Egyptians to denote "life force" were equivalent to our concept of soul. Nor can we know very much about theological controversies that may have attended their life-force-soul words. We do know, however, that the Egyptians considered these concepts as having not less than three major components: the Ka, the Ba, and the Akt.

The Ka enters the body at birth. It animates the body and derives nourishment from the food ingested by the body. According to some accounts, it is the Ka's need for life's necessities, such as shelter, warmth, rest, food, and comfort, that drives the body to sleep, eat, seek shade, and so on. When the body is asleep and when the sleeper dreams of moving about or traveling, such dreams are the Ka's roaming outside the body.

The Ba also enters the body at birth, and it shapes and defines individual personality. It imparts to the body a style of speaking, observing, and a manner of moving. A restless energy, the Ba flies between the living and the land of the dead, keeping in touch with gods, ancestors, and possibly the future. The Ba is often represented by a great bird with arms outstretched and bearing the face of a lovely woman.

The Akt is the third vital component of the body's soul and spirit. Its mystery is vividly conveyed in texts dealing with the dead and in pictures on tomb walls. The Akt departs the body at the moment of death, never to return. It searches for the land of the reeds, and when it arrives there at Osiris's domain, it may catch sight of ancestors and gods, but entry is denied pending a final trial. Toth, the bird-god of wisdom, presides, along with Anubis, the jackal-god of death. The Akt places the dead person's deeds, sometimes depicted as his or her heart, on a balance scale, weighed against the heft of cosmic order. This anguish-filled moment is often pictured as a goddess, feather in hand, preparing to examine the scale, or perhaps to let the feather tip the balance.

After the weighing, Toth conducts the Akt to a table. On one side of the table sits Osiris. On the other side is a demon-dog. If the weighing of deeds has been favorable to the deceased, the Akt will be presented to Osiris, who will welcome the Akt to the realm of the favored dead. If the weighing has been unfavorable, the demon-dog will carry the Akt to a second death, to be eaten or consumed by demons!

WHY DID THE EGYPTIANS PRESERVE THE BODIES OF THE DEAD?

As death is understood in everyday experience, every corporeal body will someday die, but the Ka has eternal longings. If the body can be physically preserved, the Ka can keep its home; otherwise it will slip into nothingness. The Ba, too, has eternal longings. It seeks to rejoin the Ka by reposing in the preserved body. So, when the body is preserved, the Ka and the Ba can continue their existence, and in this way, these components of the soul-spirit will dwell in eternity even when the Akt has achieved its own eternity in Osiris's pleasant domain.

Ka, Ba, Akt, and the body itself are four components of the soul-spirit. To these, a fifth might be added: the name that the deceased carried in life. The name will help to guide the Ka and Ba to their rightful body-home. For that reason, the preserved corpse usually had its name spelled out on its outermost casket. And as further insurance against the soul-spirit's oblivion, the outermost casket was often adorned with a portrait of the face of the deceased. Done in gold and precious stones, for example, the face of King Tutankhamen is the unforgettable icon of Egypt's royal burials.

WHY AND HOW DID EGYPTIANS BUILD ELABORATE TOMBS?

> Safe bind. Safe find.
>
> — Shakespeare, *The Merchant of Venice*, 1596.

Death is humankind's most democratic institution; it comes to rich and poor, the just and the unjust alike. Even so, initially it was only the pharaoh, as descendant of Osiris, who was deemed worthy of the special preparations that would ensure immortality, including an elaborate tomb and mummification. Gradually, the special preparations were democratized, extending downward through the social pyramid to nobles, to great officials, and to the wealthy. For a long time, the poor continued to make do with what nature had provided: burial in the desert's hot, dry, body-preserving sands.

Egypt's first settled agricultural communities date back to about 7000 BCE. Pharaonic Egypt began sometime around 3000 BCE, and about 500 years later, work was begun on the massive tomb complex of Pharaoh Djoser. Previous royal tombs were built of mud. Djoser's tomb builder was Imhotep—architect, physician, literary scholar, and vizier (high executive officer). Presumably, all four roles and skills were put to work in the service of the royal tomb. The scholar and the vizier understood the importance of interweaving the legend of Osiris with the life of Pharaoh Djoser. The physician understood the skills needed to preserve the royal body against decay. The vizier used his political power to organize the army of skilled and unskilled workers who built the tomb. And as architect, Imhotep set the pattern for ages to come: a tomb built of stone, the royal body protected from thieves by a maze of passageways, with drawings and sculpture celebrating the lineage, virtues, and accomplishments of the pharaoh. Set near ancient Memphis (not far from today's Cairo), Djoser's tomb is a *mastaba* (Arab for bench), a series of bench-like structures set one on another and rising in the form of a vast step pyramid. As pyramid, Djoser's tomb was a forerunner of the mightiest tombs ever built: the three Pyramids of Giza.

WHAT WAS FOUND IN A ROYAL TOMB?

When the renowned English archaeologist Howard Carter first peered into Tutankhamen's tomb, his employer Lord Carnarvon cried, "What do to you see?" And from a dazzled Carter came the answer: "Yes, wonderful things!"[2] The tomb was systematically emptied, and its inventory, now on display in Cairo with bits and pieces of the collection shown in exhibitions in museums around the world, continues to invoke a sense of awe.

Tutankhamen's tomb is unique because it was virtually untouched by grave robbers. Other tombs are celebrated for their frescos depicting the verdant fields in Osiris's domain, the home life of the deceased, his or her worldly possessions, and other significant events of his or her life on earth, not least of which were military victories. Often left untouched by plunderers is mummified food, sustenance in the great beyond, as well as the mummified bodies of animal pets—dogs, cats, and birds who will give pleasure and companionship in the world beyond. Most poignant is the monkey, wrapped in linen and unguents, who sits quietly awaiting for his master to summon him for the great journey.

---

[2] "Remarkable Discovery in Egypt – Rich Relics of Fifteenth Century B.C.," *The London Sunday Post,* December 24, 1922.

Figure 13.5. Howard Carter, Tut's tomb opened

Figure 13.6. King Tutankhamen's Tomb

WHY DO THE PYRAMIDS STILL EXCITE WONDER?

The grandest of the three pyramids is the tomb of Khufu (Cheops in ancient Greek). Built sometime around 2500 BCE, its monumentality challenges comprehension. Measuring 755 feet square at its base, level on all sides to one inch, the pyramid covers thirty-five acres. It is aligned with the four cardinal corners of the compass. It soars almost 500 feet, and its sides are sloped to a near-perfect fifty-two degrees. Something on the order of two million precisely cut blocks of stone, some weighing two-and-a-half tons, set in more than 200 courses, were used in the pyramid's construction. And when finished, the entire surface was covered with smooth-cut limestone. As befits a monument to the king who proclaimed himself a descendant of Ra, it must have dazzled the beholder as its surface shimmered and glowed with the reflected light of the sun high in the cloudless Egyptian sky.

Inside the pyramid is a series of galleries and chambers sloping down and up in precise gradients, designed, it is presumed, to lead intruders astray. The main chamber, known as the king's chamber, is almost twenty feet high, thirty-five feet long, and seventeen feet wide. To keep the massive weight of the pyramid from crushing the interior spaces requires a precise overlay of weight-distributing spaces and massive corbelled blocks. The king's open, granite sarcophagus (Greek: flesh eater) is empty, the preserved royal body presumably carted away by thieves many centuries ago.

Unlike the tomb of Pharaoh Djoser, the Pyramids of Giza were not a prototype for tombs to come. Perhaps their cost in men and materials was too great for the kingdom to sustain. Herodotus estimates that 100,000 men worked to build the pyramids. More recent estimates suggest the figure is closer to 20,000 and that they worked for a quarter-century to build the great pyramid. Its massive stones were quarried from the cliffs at Aswan, levered and sledged to barges, and floated northward on barges down the Nile. At the building site, rising ramps were built along the site of the pyramid, some to go up, and others to go down. Manhandled wood rollers and sleds carried the stone blocks upward. At several places along the river, the several thousand site workers lived, toiled, and were fed on beer, bread, and grain. They were free men, not slaves, and the pyramid project served the economy as a public works project, while its sizable encampments of workers, many poor farm boys from far-off places, promoted a socializing loyalty to king and culture.

The pyramids were tomb and spectacle combined. Before and after the pyramids, royal tombs and those of the elite were hidden from view, dug deep into the desert, their entrances artfully concealed. Never mind that tomb-building villages had been constructed near the tomb; planners trusted their skills of concealment to keep looters away. It was a misplaced and mismanaged trust. The only intact tomb found thus far is the tomb of Tutankhamen. Even so, empty tombs continue to intrigue the tourist and dazzle the traveler. In the desert near present-day Luxor in the Valley of the Kings, visitors will ponder the prodigious effort required to use obsidian and bronze tools to cut passageways and chambers deep below ground in solid rock. They will gaze in awe at tomb murals. Some paintings detail the wealth of the deceased (cattle, servants, furniture, etc.); some depict tributes paid by faraway kings and tribes; and still others are anecdotes that celebrate the life of the deceased.

WERE THE PYRAMIDS BUILT BY SLAVES?

As Hollywood likes to tell it, slaves built the pyramids, sweating beneath the overseers' lash and suffering cruelly in the scorching desert. In truth, those who built the pyramids were volunteers and conscripts who lived in workers' barracks and villages, ate well, roistered, and competed for prizes of beer and beef. Precious pepper sprinkled their food to give them strength and, quite likely, to keep mosquitoes from their skins. Hollywood epics fix our history lessons, however. It pleases modern sensibilities to see pyramid builders as slaves, a view that gives dramatic narrative to the *Old Testament*'s Exodus by conflating Hebrews ("Let my people go") with slaves of the pyramids.

MUMMIES: HOW WERE THE DEAD EMBALMED?

Contrary to a staple of Hollywood horror films (*Pace*, Boris Karloff), mummies did not rise or even walk. The mummy was forever to be a safe haven for the Ka and Ba. Shortly after death, and if the deceased were important and wealthy, the corpse would be given to specialists in the making of a mummy. (Mummy is not an Egyptian word; it comes from the Persian word for ground seepage: the oils and tars used to coat and preserve the body.) Several procedures were used. The body was washed and stretched on a board to prevent rigor mortis from distorting its sleeping position. Viscera were removed and placed in jars guarded by spirit statues. The body cavity was coated with herbs, scents, and preservatives, including natron, a sodium-rich mineral mined in the western desert, and then was packed with linen soaked in natron, tar, and other preservatives. A pick inserted through the nose broke into the skull, and a whisk-like implement drew out the brains, which were also placed in a canopic jar.

Afterward, the entire body was wrapped and rewrapped in linen swathing soaked in unguents and other preservatives. And at last, the wrapped corpse was placed inside a series of caskets, the outermost (depending upon rank and wealth of the deceased) covered with precious jewels, gold, and a likeness of the deceased. Mummy, sarcophagus, and nesting caskets were sealed in the tomb, along with implements and adornments of earthly life that would give aid and comfort in Osiris's land of contented souls. Tombs at present-day Abdos, about 300 miles south of Cairo, contained mummified slabs of beef, mummified birds, and jars of figs, beer, bread, oil, fats, and wine. Among the more than 500 items interred with Tutankhamen were a royal bed, a bronze chariot, a chest with scenes of the king's military victories, and a throne sheathed in gold and precious jewels.

Figure 13.7. Mummy on display, Philadelphia Academy of Natural Sciences

Mummy wrappings have had a long and curious "afterlife." Much prized in the Middle Ages for their medicinal powers, they were ground up or reduced to paste by apothecaries. In the nineteenth century, a reddish-brown mummy paste, made by grinding the whole mummy along with its wrappings, was used by artists for painting shadows. When the steam engine came to a coal-less and mostly treeless Egypt, it was reported, perhaps too luridly, that mummies provided the fires that stoked the steam engines.

WHAT IS THE BOOK OF THE DEAD?

Tomb paintings depict life as the deceased lived it; others serve as picture guides to the afterlife to come: what will be encountered there, what choices lie before the deceased, and how he (and she) is to respond to the challenges of Osiris and the other gods and demons. These were to be spoken responses. The last stage of mummification was the ceremony that opened the mouth. Often done in the presence of the grieving family, with servants and priests in attendance, mouth-opening prepared the dead to eat, drink, and speak in the afterlife. The ceremony proceeded with priests or embalmers reading from a scroll that offered prayers to the gods, information as to where to go for the weighing of the soul, and instruction in proper behavior in the afterlife. This scroll, *The Book of the Dead*, was often included in the furnishings of the tomb, and its words were also inscribed on the chamber that housed the sarcophagus. Two of its most famous passages begin,

> I rise up…out of the Hidden Land. May my mouth be given unto me that I may speak therewith in the presence of the Great God…Homage to thee, Osiris, Lord of Eternity, King of the Gods, whose names are manifold, Whose forms are holy, Thou being of hidden form in the temples, whose Ka is holy…[3]

Thus, with the body mummified, the tomb decorated and filled with provisions for the next world, with readings from the *Book of the Dead* completed, the recently departed is ready for a journey to the afterlife and its promise of eternity in the kingdom of Osiris. The doors to the tomb are sealed. And a curse can now be affixed to the seals:

> Listen all of you! The priest of Hathor will beat twice any one of you who enters this tomb or does harm to it. The gods will confront him because I am honored by his Lord. The gods will not allow anything to happen to me. Anyone who does anything bad to my tomb, then [the] crocodile, [the] Hippopotamus and the lion will eat him.[4]

---

[3] A.E. Wallis Budge translation. *The Book of the Dead* (London: British Museum, 1895), Reprinted (New York: Dover Publications, 1967).

[4] Zahi Hawass, *Archaeology*, January/February, 1997, 23.

14. Istanbul: A City on Two Continents

An institution is the lengthened shadow of one man.
— Ralph Waldo Emerson, "On Self-Reliance"

Istanbul is the only major city that sits on two continents, Europe and Asia. Its waterside location gives it easy access to the world's great trade routes; as a consequence, it has been fought over for 2,500 years. Even without knowing the city's history, the traveler in Istanbul knows it to be a city of eras and epochs, one civilization layered over another, the remnant of one culture nestled alongside and inside the remnants of another. Not so much a patchwork of eras and epochs, the city is more like a fascinating mosaic.

The traveler also encounters a universe of faces, each of which reflects some distant (and not so distant) genetic pool: the tall, blue-eyed Turk whose forebears may have been Viking bodyguards to a Byzantine emperor; the broad, square forehead of a man whose family emigrated from Egypt; the high cheekbones of an Albanian Slav whose family, long ago, converted to Islam; the black skin of a person of Nubian ancestry; the face with almond eyes, whose clan exploded out of Mongolia and onto Anatolia; the woman of delicate beauty whose ancestor was a Circassian slave in a sultan's harem; and the Roman ace whose forebear arrived in 334, when Constantine created the Eastern Roman Empire and built his capital in today's Istanbul. All these and others are Turkish faces whose predecessors came to Istanbul sometime between

600 BCE and yesterday, from empires that once reached from the Caspian Sea to the Atlantic Ocean.

And long before the traveler will have seen Hagia Sophia and its minarets rising against the morning mist, and long before the traveler's ship will have tied up in the Golden Horn, the passenger to Istanbul will travel past some of the most important sites of the ancient world. As the Michelin Guide for Motorists would say, "Worth a journey."

The Ottoman Empire had its beginnings in 1308 when Turkish tribes first entered Europe. In quick conquest they overran Greece, Bulgaria, and Bosnia, and from there, the assault on Constantinople began. Using a huge bronze cannon, the walls of the city were shattered. "A great iron chain was stretched across the Golden Horn" to prevent Christian armies from coming to the relief of the city.[1] In a siege of eight weeks, the city was finally taken on May 29, 1453.

Turkey is an Islamic society.[2] Yet, with the overthrow of the sultanate in 1923, it has honored Islam but has maintained a secular society.[3]

SAILING TO BYZANTIUM?

At the Aegean end of the Mediterranean lies the Strait of Dardanelles, forty miles long and one to four miles wide. The Dardanelles is the place of the disastrous landing at Gallipoli by British and French forces during the First World War. The peninsula of Gallipoli (Gelibolu) lies portside of the entering ship. Three monuments stand ashore: one to the French who died during the attempted landings of April and May 1915, another to the memory of the British and empire troops who perished in the landings, and a third to the Turkish soldiers who died defending the strait. Each side threw nearly a half-million men into a long, murderous battle, and each side lost about a quarter-million men. Each memorial shines with an appropriate sentiment to the fallen, but the Turkish memorial is a plea for reconciliation: "There is no difference between the Johnnies and the Memmets...Where they lie side by side in this country of ours."

---

[1] Norman Davies, *Europe: A History* (Oxford: Oxford University Press, 1996), 448-450.

[2] For information about Islam, see John Esposito, *What Everybody Needs to Know about Islam* (Oxford: Oxford University Press, 2002) and Karen Armstrong, *Islam: A Short History* (New York: Modern Library, 2002). A highly respected scholar, Armstrong publishes widely on religion. An excellent translation of the Koran is N. J. Dawood, *The Koran* (New York: Penguin, 2004).

[3] On Turkey and the Turks, see Bernard Lewis, *The Emergence of Modern Turkey*, 2nd edition (London: Oxford University Press, 1968). Lewis is one of the most widely respected Islamic scholars. Also see Beatrice Bliss, *The Turk* (San Francisco: Georgetown Press, 1976).

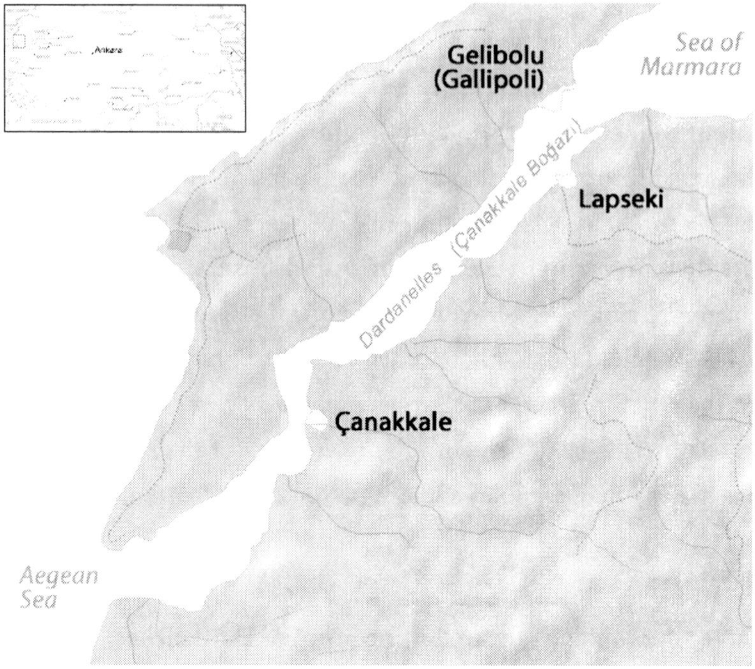

Figure 14.1. Strait of Dardanelles

The Gallipoli campaign was conceived by Winston Churchill as a way of crushing Germany's Turkish ally and as a way of opening a supply line to the faltering Russian army. Had the assault on Gallipoli succeeded, perhaps (but only perhaps) the subsequent history of Russia might have been altered, and Churchill would not have been forced from his post as First Lord of the Admiralty. No less important, the Turkish commander at Gallipoli, Mustafa Kemal (the future Kemal Atatürk), gave the order that would put him on the path to military and political glory: "I do not order you to attack. I am ordering you to die."[4]

The Dardenelles is the Hellespont of Ancient Greece, where Leander drowned as he attempted to swim to his beloved Hero—a crossing of the strait successfully swum by Lord Byron in 1810. Diagonally across from Gallipoli (starboard) is Cannakale, near the site of ancient Troy. The Trojan War is one of the defining myths and memories of western civilization. Fought sometime around 1250 BCE, the war is memorialized in Homer's two great epic poems

[4] http://www.pbs.org/greatwar/historian/hist_tuncoku_01_gallipoli.html.

(composed sometime around 800 BCE), the *Iliad* and the *Odyssey*. The *Iliad* tells the story of the Trojan War and the Greeks' ten-year siege of Troy. Outside its walls Achilles fought his great fight, and it was at the siege of Troy that Odysseus (Ulysses) cunningly contrived to hide warriors inside a great wooden horse, which, when dragged inside the gates of Troy, allowed Greeks concealed in the horse to open Troy's gates to the vengeful besiegers. ("Beware of Greeks bearing false gifts,"[5] cries Cassandra.) And at war's end, Odysseus sets sail for his home on Ithaca, a journey (the Odyssey) that will take twenty years of wisdom, cunning, and mysterious adventure to complete. Homer's tale is the prototype for all the great adventure stories of western literature, replete with villains, improbable beings, bravery in the teeth of great odds, and a quick-thinking, resourceful hero.

Tradition gives blind Homer the honor of creating the *Iliad* and the *Odyssey*; more likely the epics are the product of an ancient minstrel tradition with many singers, each contributing stories and details. Archaeology confirms that several cities and eras are layered one over the other at the site of Troy. Research also suggests that a war pitting besiegers against Trojans was a war between cultures (ancient Greeks versus Hittites from Anatolia) as well as a war to dominate trade in the eastern Mediterranean.

But whatever the precise historical details, both epics, composed almost 3,000 years ago, remind us of the continuity of the human condition and human aspiration: how pride can destroy admirable people; how quick we humans are to blame the gods for personal failings; how stubbornly we cling to our mistakes; how loath we are to admit to making them; and perhaps most important of all, how we compare the most imperfect life in this world with expectations of a glorious life in the next. When Odysseus descends to Hades to speak with the shades of fallen heroes, the great Achilles laments,

> By god I'd rather slave on earth for another man—
> Some dirt-poor tenant farmer who scrapes to keep alive—
> Than rule down here over all the breathless dead.[6]

WHAT IS THE GOLDEN HORN?

The Dardanelles flows into the Sea of Marmara (the Marble Sea), and from there the Sea of Marmara adjoins the Golden Horn, an estuary about five miles long fed by two streams called

[5] This is an English paraphrase of a line originally found in Virgil, *Aeneid*, Book II, 49. 19 BCE.

[6] Robert Fagles, translator, *The Odyssey* (New York: Viking, 1996), 554.

the Sweet Waters of Europe. Just where it joins the Bosphorus, carving and shaping a scimitar-shaped peninsula, the Golden Horn serves as Istanbul's harbor, offering shelter from winds and currents. For mariners both ancient and modern, the Golden Horn is blessed by calm waters and soft winds. It can provide berth for the largest of today's cruise ships. And in ancient times it was the site of (or adjacent to) some of the loveliest and heroic Greek legends. (Jason and his Argonauts sailed from the Golden Horn into the Black Sea in search of the Golden Fleece.)

Near the cruise-ship dock is the Galata Bridge, which spans the Horn. The Galata Bridge unites the two European parts of the city—the medieval port to the north and Constantine's capital to the south, often called Old Stamboul. Fact and fancy frequently merge in Istanbul but rarely collide. The Galata Bridge is said to be the origin of the card game of bridge. Derived from whist, the English residents of Constantinople are reputed to have said, "Let's meet for cards at the bridge."

WHAT IS THE BOSPHORUS?

The Golden Horn joins another of history's great waterways, the Bosphorus Strait. The Bosphorus Strait (from the Greek "ford of the heifer") is the place where the beautiful Io, loved by Zeus, is changed by him into a cow so she might swim to safety across the strait and escape the wrath of the jealous Hera. The Bosphorus is about nineteen miles long and from 0.8 to 2.8 miles wide. Europe begins on its western shore, while Asia begins along its eastern shore. At its northern end is the Black Sea, and while deep-draft ships anchor in the Golden Horn, ferry boats run the Bosphorus, stopping at villages along the strait, carrying locals and travelers to the Black Sea. One of the villages is Terabya, home to ancient warm springs with healing powers so famous that they gave their name to a word that comes down through the centuries: therapy.

WHEN DID ISTANBUL BEGIN?

The legendary founder of the city (sometime around 667 BCE) is the Greek Byzas who was counseled by the oracle at Delphi to build a city "away from the blind." As legend elaborates, Byzas sailed from the Aegean toward the Black Sea and found the oracle's murky counsel fulfilled when he discovered a place on the Bosphorus better suited to defense than an existing village nearby (the nearby village being " blind" to superior defenses). The Roman Emperor Constantine claimed Byzas's city in 324. He won his throne in 311 after defeating a rival at the Battle of Milvian Bridge, near present-day Uskudar. Legend (probably contrived by Constantine himself) states that he achieved victory after heeding a message displaying a Christian cross shining in the sky: *In hoc signo vinces* ("In this sign, conquer").

Following victory, he made good his pledge and established Christianity as the official religion of Rome and its vast empire. What had been a persecuted sect now claimed the imperial throne, but it was a throne threatened by Germanic tribes outside the empire and rocked by dissent within. To govern his empire more effectively, Constantine broke it into two administrative parts, East and West. And in 334 he created a new capital for the eastern component, Constantinople (*polis*, from the Greek, city-state) at the ancient site of Byzas's city, a place where Europe and Asia meet. The line of a divided empire ran through today's former Yugoslavia. East of the line, Christianity evolved toward the Orthodox Communion; the West shifted toward Vatican dominion. (Part of the bitterness today between Serbs and Croatians owes to that long-ago division of empire.)

In the centuries after 334, Constantine's city carried two titles: Capital of New Rome (Rum) and Capital of the Byzantine Empire (Byzantium), whose imperial banner displayed a two-headed eagle: one head facing west (Europe), the other facing east (Asia). The Byzantine Empire lasted more than 1,000 years until 1453, when the city of Constantinople was overrun by the armies of the Turkish-Ottoman Sultan Memmet II. With the pride of the victor, Memmet renamed his city Istanbul.

WHY BYZANTIUM INSTEAD OF NEW ROME?

Long after Constantine, the city continued to be called New Rome, but its culture laced it to classical Greece. Its language was Greek, and its scholars and libraries preserved Greek learning—learning that would someday lay the intellectual foundations of the Renaissance. In the centuries following Constantine's division of empire, the western half came under the jurisdiction of the Patriarch of Rome (the Pope), while the eastern division came under the jurisdiction of other Patriarchs: Antioch, Alexandria, and Constantinople. The relationship between Patriarchs was often contentious, especially over politics linked to theology. The Patriarch of Constantinople took offense at the Pope's crowning and consecrating Charlemagne in 800, an anger that was turned against the Patriarch when in 1204 an army of Crusaders, led by Venice and blessed by the Pope, attacked Constantinople and looted the city. (The great bronze horses that stand in front of St. Mark's Basilica in Venice were part of that loot. The originals are now in a museum; copies take their place.)

It was in the resolution of debates about dogma and liturgy that the Orthodox Communion evolved. And it was in the Orthodox Communion that throne and church reinforced each other. The emperor ruled by divine right and appointed the Patriarch to his sacerdotal seat.

Like Rome, Constantinople was built on seven hills. At its most expansive, Constantinople's empire stretched along the Adriatic, Aegean and Mediterranean Seas. It embraced present-day Greece and parts of the former Yugoslavia, the northern shores of North Africa, the Near East, and portions of the Persian Empire. It was an empire of great wealth, sumptuous display, dazzling architecture, and murderous intrigue. The word "byzantine" comes down to us to describe a way of life and a system of politics that is devious, cunning, opaque, and ruthless. Of the emperors who succeeded Constantine, more than twenty-nine were murdered. Blinding, torture, and mutilation were the fate of many Byzantine rulers. At least one was murdered by his own mother.

WHAT IS THE MEANING OF ISTANBUL?

As a name, Constantinople is self-explanatory: a self-created tribute to its founder. But Istanbul seems to contain no reference or traces to Turkish. One explanation is that Memmet's armies followed the Byzantine-Greek signs to the city (later translated into the Latin alphabet), which read "this way to the city Eis tan pol," which when rendered into Turkic emerges as Istanbul.

HOW DID CONSTANTINE REMAKE BYZAS' CITY?

Constantine's new city had great natural advantages. As a crossroads for trade, it lay on the route to the Silk Road to China and India and on the route to the Red Sea. Access to the Mediterranean carried its galleys to Africa and southern Europe. Its foothold in Europe led to the Balkans and beyond. Blessed with ample drinking water, the city could be defended within walls quarried from local stone. In and around the city lay fertile soil for farming.

Constantine, of course, had imperial ambitions for his New Rome. Among his first projects was building a massive wall to enclose and defend his city, parts of which still stand to overawe the visitor. Joined to what was planned as a racetrack (the hippodrome, built later by Septimius Severus), Constantine laid out a great arena (with a capacity of 100,000) as the secular center of the city. He plundered Egypt for an obelisk of Pharaoh Tutmose and built Bucoleon Palace (now in ruins), celebrated for its golden tree and mechanical singing birds.

> ...a form such as Grecian goldsmiths make
> Of hammered gold and gold enameling
> To keep a drowsy Emperor awake;
> Or set upon a golden bow to sing
> To lords and ladies of Byzantium
>
> — W. B. Yates, "Sailing to Byzantium," 1928

As Christ's secular representative, Constantine convened the great Council of Nicaea, whose deliberations fashioned the *Apostle's Creed* and fixed a date for Easter.

WHAT WAS THE JUSTINIAN'S CONTRIBUTION TO NEW ROME?

Justinian was Emperor of Byzantium from 527 to 565. His legal code is a benchmark of jurisprudence, codifying Roman law to become the basis of later European legal systems. And his architecture still stands. The greatest of his buildings is Hagia Sophia (Sacred Wisdom), an Orthodox church at inception, a mosque for almost 500 years, and a magnificent museum today. Among its glories are its soaring dome (183 feet above floor level), the natural light that floods the building, and the great space of the interior. The once-glorious mosaics that adorned the interior are gone, removed according to the Muslim ban on graven images; but hung from high are magnificent shields displaying Koranic text. A visitor to the gallery will find windows open to observation of the cityscape and, with some hunting, the tomb of Dandolo, the Venetian *Doge* who supervised the looting of Constantinople in 1204. (Legend has it that after the city was recaptured by the Byzantines, Dandolo's bones were fed to ravening dogs; but in Istanbul fact and legend are often conflated.)

Two of the great Adriatic cities, Venice and Ravenna, still carry architectural imprints of their early allegiance to the emperors of Byzantium. St. Mark's Cathedral in Venice, the city's signature in stone, was begun about 828. Its soaring, massive domes pay homage to Constantinople's Hagia Sophia, as does the Church of San Vitale in Ravenna. Built by the Emperor Justinian over the years 526-547, San Vitale's great dome and octagonal core also take inspiration from Hagia Sophia. And reflecting Hagia Sophia adornments before Constantinople's conquest by Muslims, San Vitale displays sacred and secular mosaics (including portraits of Justinian and his empress, Theodora).

Figure 14.2 Hagia Sophia

HOW AND WHY DID BYZANTIUM FALL TO THE OTTOMAN TURKS?

One of history's enduring puzzles is whether the lives of civilizations parallel the lives of those who inhabit them. Do civilizations, like humans, grow from infancy to old age, from youthful strength to a sclerotic death? In its life span of 1,113 years, Byzantium grew, flourished, contracted, and then died. The immediate cause of death was conquest in 1453 by the armies of Memmet II. But it was a death foretold by the conquest of Constantinople in 1204 when a crusade led by Venice and blessed by the Pope looted the city and sent the Byzantine emperors into fifty-seven years of exile. The invasion was inspired by greed but also by the enmity between western and Orthodox Christianity. Whatever the motives of the invaders, Byzantium never recovered its lost strength or its sense of invincibility. The Black Death of 1347 killed almost two-thirds of Constantinople's population, and by 1397, Byzantium encompassed only the city itself and small patches of land north of the city and in the Peloponnesus. Even so, Constantinople did not go down without a fight.

WHO WERE THE OTTOMANS?

Fierce nomadic horsemen, the Turks appeared on the Mongolian fringes of the Chinese Empire sometime around 500 CE. It was the Chinese who named them. Sometime around 900, one of the several Turkish clans, the Seljuks, conquered northeastern Persia; and in 1040, with 16,000 horsemen, they completed the conquest of the Persian (Iranian) Empire and imposed Islam on their subjects. (It was a Seljuk ruler of Jerusalem whose edicts against Christian pilgrims led to the more than 200 years of Crusades and Crusaders.)

By the 1200s, Seljuk power began to wane, and in 1299 a new leader, Osman, began the conquest of the Byzantine territory of Anatolia, the Asian part of today's Turkey. From Osman derives the term Ottoman: "followers of Osman." Ottoman armies moved into south Turkey, conquered today's Izmir, and from there claimed the Gallipoli peninsula. In 1389 at the Battle of Kosovo, they defeated the Serbs, thereby igniting the flames of Serbian anger that lie behind the most recent wars in the country once known as Yugoslavia.

Osman's successor (Murad) annexed Serbia in 1439 and besieged Belgrade in 1440. Murad's son, Mohammed (Memmet) II took the throne in 1451 and began preparations for his assault on Constantinople.

HOW DID MEMMET CAPTURE CONSTANTINOPLE?

Constantinople's walls were formidable. Memmet hired a Hungarian engineer, Urban, to take down the walls. Urban designed huge cannons; the largest had a twenty-six-foot-long barrel and could fire balls of more than one-half ton. Byzantine defenders stood at 7,000; the attackers were an army of 80,000. The Turkish cannon smashed at the walls for six weeks, but the defenders managed to repair the walls after each assault. Then Memmet changed tactics. The weakest sections of the walls were protected by the waters of the Golden Horn. Memmet put seventy ships on wheeled cradles and, using oxen and soldiers, had them hauled overland (the oarsmen pulling rhythmically against the air) and into the waters of the Golden Horn. From there the flotilla's oarsmen rowed the attackers upstream to the city's weakest defenses. And on Tuesday, May 29, Byzantium ceased to exist. To this day, in the Orthodox Communion Tuesday is considered a less-than–auspicious day. The last emperor, Constantine XI Palaeologus, threw himself into the battle and was never seen again. Three days of looting, rape, and killing followed; about 4,000 Byzantines are estimated to have died. And in one of the city's palaces,

Memmet is said to have intoned the words of the Persian poet, Saadi: "The spider weaves the curtain in the palace of the Caesars. / The owl calls the watches in the towers of Afrasiab"[7]

HOW DID THE TURKS CHANGE CONSTANTINOPLE?

With the capture of Constantinople (soon to be named Istanbul), the Ottomans brought to the city the wealth of an expanding empire. At its height in 1653, when their armies besieged Vienna, the Ottomans controlled an enormous territory centered around the Black Sea. In terms of twentieth century geography, in Russia they controlled the Crimea, Georgia, and Armenia. In the Near East they controlled Syria, Arabia, Anatolia (Turkey), The Holy Land, and Egypt. In North Africa they controlled Egypt, Tunisia, Algeria, and Morocco. In Europe they controlled Greece, Yugoslavia, and Hungary. The Ottomans were, in Jason Goodwin's telling book title, "Lords of The Horizon."

Under the Ottomans, Istanbul became a cosmopolitan beehive. Houses and palaces burgeoned. Merchants the world over set up enclaves in the city. Diplomats of the major powers established legations. Religious leaders within the empire had representation in the city (including the Vatican, the Orthodox Communion, and Jews, as well as Shiites and Sunnis). Officials from all over the empire reported to the city. The sultan's wives and concubines (his harem) of many races and ethnic origins lodged within Topkapi Palace. And nearby were the headquarters of an army recruited across the empire.[8]

Topkapi Palace commands Istanbul's magisterial site. It sits at the confluence of the Bosphorus, the Golden Horn, and the Sea of Marmara. In Ottoman times it was a labyrinth of power and the powerful. It was the seat of government; the palace of the Sultan; the rooms of his harem (the seraglio); and the abode of royal family and their servants, slaves, and retainers. Topkapi's reception and throne rooms were faced with exquisite glazed tiles and furnished with divans covered in beautiful silks; and from the gateway of the Sublime Porte (Bab-I-Ali), messengers rode forth to carry imperial rescript to the farthest reaches of empire.

Four areas of Topkapi are especially fascinating to visitors: the sultans' collection of swords, objects of gold, and jewelry; those magnificent emeralds? Rumor has it that they are

---

[7] Jim Bradbury, *The Routledge Companion to Medieval Warfare* (Oxford: Routledge, 2004), 68.

[8] See two books by Jason Goodwin: *Lords of the Horizon: A History of the Ottoman Empire* (New York: H. Holt, 1999); *On Foot to the Golden Horn: A Walk to Istanbul* (New York: Picador, 2003). The latter has an excellent analysis of the lingering problems, particularly Islam vs. Serbs, that beset the Balkans today.

fake and that the real ones were sold off during the last days of the sultanate (or perhaps sooner!).

The harem: Islamic law permits a man to have four wives and as many concubines as he can provide for. The harem's 300 rooms were home to as many as 800 concubines (and their children!) Some concubines were kept for reasons of statecraft and alliance. Most were kept for what eighteenth and nineteenth-century Europeans coyly called "the sultan's pleasure." A bookshelf of harem literature served as a voyeur's delight. So did drawings and paintings of the harem. To keep out unwanted visitors and to assure the purity of the sultan's bloodline, the harem was guarded by a corps of several hundred Nubian eunuchs. The Chief Eunuch and the sultan's mother (the Valide Sultan) looked after the affairs of the harem. It was the Valide Sultan who often chose the women who would become her son's favorites.

The residences of the sultan's siblings: The Ottomans did not follow a system of rule that favored the ruler's first born (primogeniture). The sultan's sons, and they were many, were often given army command or administrative posts in the empire to test their capacity for leadership. Harem politics aside, the best and most promising son might be chosen by the sultan to be his successor. To avoid civil war, the new sultan's surviving siblings were strangled by a silken cord; Ottoman house law forbade the shedding of royal blood. Death by the silken cord ended sometime around 1607; thereafter, the princelings were sequestered in luxury and closely guarded.

The Janissaries: The Ottoman Turks were born of a long tradition of bravery in battle. But bravery alone could not take the place of a large army. All across the empire, the army corps was recruited by persuasion and levy. A levy (a quota: *Devsirme*, a gathering) of healthy, first-born sons was laid on each province or district. These would become slaves of the sultan and members of his army. Families were promised that their sons would be well cared for, trained in the skills of warfare, given an opportunity for promotion and leadership, and assured of honorable careers. These were the Janissaries, the gathered, whose vocation was so respected and envied that fathers would often volunteer their sons for enlistment outside the quota. Intelligence, good physical condition, a willingness to endure hardship, obey orders, and submit to circumcision were the conditions of entry into the Jannisary corps. Each Jannisary unit had its own distinctive dress; each was organized around its soup kitchen (its mess), and in times of stress or rebellion, the great soup caldron would be defiantly overturned.

Ottoman Turkey began its slow decline in the eighteenth century, with Russia as its major opponent. As Christian champions of eastern Europe, especially Orthodox Communion, the Tsars fought a series of wars to push the Turks out of southern Europe. Catherine the Great's foreign policy was aimed at that push. The Crimean War (1853-56) ranged British, French, and Ottoman armies against Russia. Casualties, mostly from disease, were horrific, as many as a quarter million. Bravery, loss, and the incompetence of command are celebrated in Tennyson's poem, "The Charge of the Light Brigade":

> Half a league, half a league,
> Half a league onward,
> All in the valley of Death
> Rode the six hundred
> 'Forward, the Light Brigade
> Charge for the guns,' he said:
> Into the valley of Death
> Rode the six hundred
>
> 'Forward, the Light Brigade!'
> Was there a man dismay'd?
> Someone had blunder'd
> Theirs not to make reply,
> Theirs but to do & die,
> Into the valley of Death
> Rode the six hundred.[9]

WHAT IS ATATÜRK'S LEGACY?

At the end of the First World War, the Treaty of Versailles stripped Germany of its colonies and imposed harsh reparations. The Allies' score with Germany's ally, Turkey, was equally harsh. Under the Treaty of Sevres (1920), the Ottoman Empire was dismembered. Britain and France established protectorates over Lebanon, Palestine, the Arabian peninsula, the Transjordan, and a broad sweep of North Africa.

As the capital of the Ottoman Empire, Istanbul held sway over vast territories from the Near East (Turkey, Arabia, and Palestine), westward to Morocco, and in Europe from Greece and the Balkans to Hungary. It was an empire that lasted almost 600 years, falling to British forces at the end of the First World War. With war's end, the sultanate was abolished, and a

[9] The Crimean War is remembered for Florence Nightingale's heroism and capacity for brilliant administration. From her work, the respected profession of nursing arose. Tennyson's poem was published December 9, 1854, in *The London Examiner*.

new Turkish leader, Mustafa Kemal, moved the capital of the Republic of Turkey from Istanbul to a better-defended place, an ancestral home of the Turks, Ankara.

As herald of a new Turkey, Kemal announced the abolition of the sultanate on November 1, 1922.[10] (The last sultan sailed for Malta on a British warship.) Kemal led the new Republic of Turkey for fifteen years. He secularized the Republic, made education a government enterprise, replaced Arabic script with a Latin alphabet, abolished Islamic law and replaced it with European-based laws, granted women's rights, and forbade the wearing of Ottoman clothes (robes, turban, the fez). He changed the name of the country to Turkiye, Land of the Turks. As his leadership became syndochic for his nation, he was proud to style himself, Atatürk, as Father of the Turks. The officer corps of Turkey's army continues to be inspired by Atatürk's leadership, and over the years, as periodic attempts are made to Islamicize Turkey, the army has intervened to keep the country faithful to Atatürk's vision of Turkey as a secular Republic.

HOW STANDS ISTANBUL TODAY?

Despite the loss of its capital-city status, Istanbul thrives. Its population stands at more than fourteen million and continues to expand. Like all great cities, it is a population pump, pulling people from the countryside to the city's opportunities and the promise of a better life. Much of that pull lies in Istanbul's location: an historic crossroads of trade and commerce. Europe lies at its doorstep, and the Bosphorus waterway is a direct route from the Mediterranean to the Black Sea. By water to the south, the Suez Canal links Istanbul to the Indian Ocean. And by land across to Iran and Iraq, India and China beckon by way of the old Silk Road.

TODAY'S ISTANBUL: WHERE ARE ITS HISTORIC DISTRICTS?

As a thriving, bustling city, Istanbul keeps changing and refashioning itself. The new overlays the old. As the cruise ship makes port on the south side of the Golden Horn (within sight of the Galata Bridge), the traveler enters the stream of contemporary commerce: trams, trains, buses, and ferries are within walking distance of the ship. This is Eminonu, the ancient and modern crossroads of commerce. This peninsula on the south side of the Golden Horn is shaped like a scimitar. On its way to its harbor, the ship will have passed the Sultans' Imperial Palace, Topkapi. On the far southern shore of the peninsula is Constantine's city, Sultanahmet. The site of the hippodrome is now a public park graced by three ancient monuments. The fifteenth-

---

[10] Among the grievances of Muslims today is the abolition of the Sultanate, thus depriving Islam of a single supreme religious leader.

century BCE obelisk was brought by Constantine from Egypt. The base of the obelisk displays Constantine's successor, Theodosius I, and family watching a race. The Serpentine Column was brought by Constantine from the Temple of Apollo at Delphi. And a third monument, thought to date from the 900s, is the Column of Constantine VII.

WHERE IS THE ISTANBUL OF MEMMET AND SULIMAN?

The Galata Bridge beckons; at its southern end lies the Egyptian (spice) Bazaar, and just beyond is the Yeni Cami (the New Mosque). As a Muslim, Memmet transformed many of Istanbul's Byzantine churches into mosques, Hagia Sophia being the most spectacular. Its great dome and four minarets rise tall against the sky, one of Istanbul's most celebrated sights. More than two dozen mosques follow the example of Hagia Sophia. Two of them are especially noteworthy for their size and the beauty of their interiors, the Blue Mosque and the Suleymaniye. The Blue Mosque (officially, the Sultan Ahmet Cami, the Mosque of Sultan Ahment) is graced by numerous domes and surrounded by six soaring minarets. Its interior is suffused with a lovely light, reflecting more than 20,000 blue Iznik tiles and more than 250 stained glass windows. Magnificent carpets evoke the aesthetic unity of the Mosque: walls, windows, and an arabesque ceiling.

Up the Golden Horn (by water taxi, if possible) is the holy village of Eyup. Its mosque is an important pilgrimage shrine, as it is dedicated to Eyub-Al-Ansari, thought to be standard-bearer of the Prophet Mohammed and killed during the Arab siege of Constantinople in 688. The cemetery at Eyup gives the traveler an introduction to Muslim cemeteries (of which there are more than one hundred in Istanbul). Graves are marked by headstones that face Mecca. Men's gravestones are usually topped by a turban (the number of folds indicate the status of the deceased.) A woman's gravestone is often marked by a rose.

WHICH ARE ISTANBUL'S MOST IMPORTANT MOSQUES?

Mosques are the great artistic achievements of Islamic Istanbul. Like the great Gothic cathedrals of Europe, Istanbul's great mosques overawe the visitor with their vast interior space, their softly diffused light, their huge chandeliers, and their beautiful carpets on which the faithful stand and kneel at prayer. Muslim ritual commands that those who come to pray first wash their hands, face, and feet at fountains just outside the mosque. Heads must be covered, and when the forehead touches the floor during prayer, the logic of the brimless cap becomes apparent. Shoes must be left outside the mosque, entrusted to its doorkeepers. Non-Muslim visitors are sometimes welcome to enter between prayer times. They, too, must leave shoes with gatekeepers. (To ensure getting one's own shoes back, an opaque bag discreetly tucked under one's arm, might possibly, just possibly, serve as a shoe repository.)

Minarets are tall towers that flank the mosque. The largest and most important will have four; the Blue Mosque has six. The faithful pray five times each day. They are called to prayer by the muezzin, who climbs the stairs of the minaret to call the faithful to their duty. In times gone by, each muezzin had his own style, his own distinctive voice. Today, alas, at most mosques, the muezzin's voice is tape-recorded, and the stairs are not much used.

The mosque is a place of worship, but a Muslim may pray at any convenient place. The mosque is a meeting place, a place where the prayerful assemble to experience a bodily and spiritual communion with other Muslims and a place where, on the holy day of Friday, those at prayer also hear a sermon.

Istanbul has several hundred mosques. Each usually has a garden, a fountain for ablution, and a cemetery. Flanking each mosque are one or more minarets. Flanked by four minarets, Hagia Sophia was consecrated for Christendom by the Byzantine Emperor Justinian in 537. (Mindful of its great predecessor, the Temple of Solomon in Jerusalem, Justinian supposedly cried, "Ho, Solomon! I have surpassed thee!") In Ottoman times, Hagia Sophia was rededicated as a mosque. And under Atatürk's regime, Hagia Sophia became a museum, open to all.

Figure 14.3 Blue Mosque

By common consent and popular acclaim, the Blue Mosque (framed and lit by 260 windows) and the Suleymaniye (with exquisite glazed tiles and stained glass) are Istanbul's most glorious.

WHAT IS ON SALE IN THE GRAND BAZAAR?

Most visitors to Istanbul make their way sooner or later to the Grand Bazaar in the Beyazit area. In Ottoman times, the merchants in the Grand Bazaar sold the wealth of empire in all its forms and varieties. Today the Bazaar concentrates on four kinds of goods: jewelry, carpets, tiles and other ceramics, and antiques. The Bazaar is a vast labyrinth with passages and cross passages. Home to something on the order of 3,000 shops, the Bazaar's merchants stand outside shops and stalls, trying to lure visitors inside. ("What are you looking for? How can I help you? Come in; just have a look. No charge for looking…"). Dozens and dozens of shops carry much the same merchandise. How, the visitor wonders, can these places support themselves?

Many of the carpet merchants use a clever way of catching the eye and ear of the passers-by. As the visitor approaches a shop, a walker coming in the opposite direction will ask, in a succession of languages, "What time is it?" If and when an answer is volunteered, that language is relayed to the shopkeeper, and when visitors approach they are greeted fulsomely in their own language. Once the visitor enters the shop, rugs are unrolled is quick succession. "Which one do you like?" the shopkeeper keeps asking. If any preference is expressed, the bargaining is now presumed to begin.

"Let the buyer beware" is advice especially suited to the purchase of a carpet. The agony columns of travel magazines are filled with stories of those who have had their rugs shipped home ("Save you the trouble of packing and carrying"), only to discover that the carpet is not the one ordered and paid for in Istanbul. If possible, purchasers should carry the rugs home. And buyers are especially warned of the pitfalls involving silk carpets. Skimmed milk masquerades as cream; in the half-light of the shop, viscose thread takes on the sheen of silk. And as carpets are unrolled, a complimentary service of tea is offered. Tea must be boiled, but the tea-bearers who rush through the Bazaar carrying small cups of tea cannot always be counted on to observe the rules of hygiene, either for themselves or their tea service.

Throughout the Bazaar and most everywhere else, bargaining is the order of business. Visitors shy of bargaining will be encouraged by the invitation, "Just make me an offer." A useful rule to follow is the simplest: No merchant has ever lost money on a transaction, no matter how small the final offer. A less reliable rule is this: Merchants claim they can separate the sincere from the specious bargainer by watching the prospect's eyes. Excitement makes the pupils dilate (remember comic strips and cartoons?). From that claim comes another suggestion: Avoid eye contact with those with whom you bargain! And if you truly want to wander the Grand Bazaar without interrogation, smile, don't speak, and carry a Turkish newspaper conspicuously (but carelessly) displayed.

Figure 14.4. Grand Bazaar

WHAT HAS HAPPENED TO BYZANTINE MOSAICS?

Unlike most pictorial representations, a mosaic does not mix or mingle colors. A mosaic is a picture formed of small colored stones or bits of colored stones. As is often said, the essence of a mosaic is that the bits and pieces of the picture touch but do not mingle. Romans were masters of the mosaic; some were composed of almost microscopic shards. Byzantine churches and public buildings used mosaics, to great and dazzling effects. In the typical Byzantine church, high on the ceiling of the central dome is a mosaic of Christ, the pivot of the universe. Angels, saints, patriarchs, and kings spill across the walls, sometimes against a backdrop of the heavens in their majesty. Portraits in mosaic are stylized. Postures and attitudes are conventional. Their intent is to convey the everlasting, unchanging majesty of their subjects.

During the Byzantine epoch, every church was characterized by its (almost flat) central dome; its interior was a mosaic blaze; its portraits (its icons to be revered and worshipped) were masterpieces of the mosaic art form. After Constantinople surrendered to Islam, mosaics were destroyed or painted over. Islam makes use of parallels, the Code of Moses (the *Mosaic* Code) that forbids graven images. Fortunately, a few of the old churches remain, with their mosaics fairly well preserved. The Church of St. Savior in Chora is probably the paramount mosaic display still *in situ.* The stylized, static icons can help remind the traveler of the enduring qualities of New Rome-Constantinople-Istanbul.[11]

[11] Huston Smith's *The World's Religions* (New York: HarperOne, 1992) contains concise treatments of many faiths. In addition to Islam, there are treatments of Hinduism, Orthodox Communion, Christianity, and Judaism.

OLD AND NEW ASIA

15. God Seekers in Asia

> Oh, East is East, and West is West,
> and never the twain shall meet,
> Till Earth and sky stand presently
> at God's great judgement seat
> — Rudyard Kipling, "The Ballad of East and West," 1895

Scholar Huston Smith tells us, "Every religion is a blend of universal principles and local setting."[1] And the two interact: religion shapes a culture, and culture shapes religion. How and to what extent engender fierce debate among anthropologists and theologians. Most religions also share a set of overlapping components. Some are commands, some are explanations, and still others are promises of rewards and punishment.

First is the metaphysical: Who, or sometimes what, created the universe and all things within it, including humankind? And to what purpose? How does the creator view humankind? Lovingly? Sternly? Inherently good? Prone to evil? Think of Genesis in the *Old Testament.*

Second is what is sometimes called salvation history. Why did the Creator choose to confer divine blessing on a certain group of people?

Third, how shall the chosen worship their creator? What rituals are demanded? Is prayer required as a means of acknowledging the greatness of the creator? Will it also bring divine intercession to those who pray?

---

[1] Huston Smith, *The Religions of Man* (New York: Joanna Cotler Books, 1965), 5.

Fourth is a component common to all religions: The behavior that is demanded (or commended) to all who seek the creator's blessing. Think, for example, of the Ten Commandments and the Sermon on the Mount.

Fifth are questions of end times, eschatology. What happens when we die? What lies beyond the grave? The possibility of becoming one with the divine, an eternity of happiness for those who have fulfilled the moral code? Or an eternity of terrible suffering for those who have violated the code?

The wise traveler can seek an understanding of religions other than his own by asking six straightforward questions: 1) Is this religion based on divine revelation, such as the word of God speaking to or through someone? Examples include the voice in the burning bush, Jesus's Sermon on the Mount, and Mohammed in the cave in Mecca. 2) Is this religion built on the teachings of a wise, moral leader? Examples include the Buddha, Mohammed, and Mahavira of the Jains. 3) Is this a religion of one God or many gods? 4) What is the fundamental text of this religion? Examples include *The Torah, The New Testament, The Koran*, and *The Veda of Hinduism.* 5) What are the major schisms in this religion? Examples in Christianity are Roman Catholics, Protestants, and The Orthodox Communion, while in Islam, we find Sunni and Shiite, and in Buddhism, Theravada and Mahayana. 6) What is the most potent symbol of this religion? Examples include the five-pointed star, the cross, the crescent, and the golden temple (of the Sikhs).

The wise traveler who pursues these questions will apprehend a country and its culture in far richer relief than by visiting a checklist of monuments, churches, and public buildings.[2]

THE BUDDHA AND HIS FOLLOWERS

With a boundless heart
Should one cherish all living beings;
Radiating love over the entire world
Spreading upward to the skies,

---

[2] For additional reading, see Jonathan Clements, *Confucius: A Biography* (Stroud: Sutton, 2004); Karen Armstrong, *A History of God: The 4,000-Year Quest of Judaism, Christianity and Islam* (New York: A.A. Knopf, 1993); Huston Smith, *The World's Religions* (New York: HarperOne, 1992); Ninian Smart, *The World's Religions* (Cambridge: Cambridge University Press, 1998); and James Legge's translations of Confucian Analects, *The Great Learning and the Doctrine of the Mean* (New York: Dover, 1971) and *The Works of Mencius* (New York: Dover, 1970).

And downward to the depths.
— The Buddha, *Words of Love* (The *Metta Sutta*)

THE CONTEXT

Says professor Lucien Stryk, "The Sixth Century B.C. has been called the most remarkable in the spiritual history of mankind…"[3] It produced Mahavira, Lao-Tze, Confucius, Zarathustra, Paramenides, and not least, the Buddha. Extend the time frame from 800 to 200 BCE, and we confront the Axial Age, a period "pivotal to humanity,"[4] because the Axial Age also includes the great Hebrew prophets of the sixth, seventh, and eighth centuries, as well as Socrates and Plato (c. 427-327 BCE):

The Axial Age marks the beginning of humanity as we now know it. During this period, men and women became conscious of their existence, their own nature and their limitations in an unprecedented way. The experience of utter impotence in a cruel world impelled them to seek the highest goal and an absolute reality in the depths of their being. The great sages of the time taught human beings how to cope with the misery of life, transcend their weakness, and live in peace in the midst of this flawed world.[5] This last sentence applies with ringing resonance to the life and teachings of Siddhartha Gautama, who would later be known as the Buddha.

THE BUDDHA: EARLY LIFE

Tradition has it that Siddhartha was born sometime around 560 BCE in northern India, in the Gangetic Plain in an area close to present-day Nepal, about one hundred miles from Benares. His father, of the Gautama line, ruled a small kingdom and claimed his throne as a member of the hereditary warrior class. Hereditary classes, today's caste system, had been imposed on India by conquerors from an area around the Caspian Sea in about 1500 BCE. Calling themselves Aryans ("noble people"), these conquerors descended on India to create a society organized on four hereditary classes. At the apex were Brahmins, the priestly class, guardians of the sacred rituals. Next were Kshatriya, the warrior class, keepers of civil order and defenders of government and political boundaries. Beneath the Kshatriya were Viasya, the caste of farmers and artisans. And near the bottom of the social ladder were Shudra, consigned forever to serve as

---

[3] Lucien Stryk, *The World of the Buddha* (New York: Grove Press, 1994), xxxv.

[4] Karen Armstrong, *Buddha* (New York: Viking, 2001), 10.

[5] Ibid., 11.

peasants and laborers. Siddhartha's rejection of hereditary castes, which forbade intermarriage and precluded social advancement, would become a foundation of his teaching.

SIDDHARTHA'S EARLY YEARS

Great men and women often attract biographers' embellishment. Think of George Washington and the cherry tree. The story is told that Siddhartha's upbringing resulted from a soothsayer's prophecy that the young prince would renounce his throne to become a seeker of wisdom and a social reformer. To foreclose that future, his father distracted Siddhartha by giving him palaces and 40,000 dancing girls. When he left the royal grounds, guards swept the roads clear of the sick, the dying, the crippled, and the aged so that Siddartha would not see the poverty and disease stalking the countryside. "Every year the river flooded the (Ganges) valley, destroying overnight crops wrung from a harsh earth; yearly too the monsoons came, spawning famine and drought and spreading their leavings—dysentery, cholera, and countless other ills."[6]

An early embellishment recounts Siddhartha's visit to his father's harem. There he sees old and aged crones among beautiful women. Why and how, Siddhartha ponders, do we age, and why do we suffer? Siddhartha is now in his twenties, and his life is embellished with the legend of the Four Passing Sights. Despite the best efforts of his guards, the first of the forbidden sights to assault his eyes was an old man "bent in body, leaning on a staff and trembling."[7] On another side, Siddhartha saw a man ravaged by disease, and on a third side, a corpse. On a fourth side, he saw a monk "with shaven head, an ochre robe and (begging) bowl," thus making the prince aware of an alternative lifestyle—withdrawal from everyday pursuits and pleasures.[8] And so his life quest begins to discover the source of suffering and unhappiness. At age twenty-nine, Siddhartha slips away from his lovely young wife and their beautiful child (yes, the king has given him the jewel of the kingdom for a bride). And thus Siddhartha begins his journey toward a life of contemplation, teaching, discovery, and enlightenment.

ENLIGHTENMENT

In the traditional recounting of Siddhartha's road to enlightenment, he spends six years first as a solitary dweller in the forest, then studying with Hindu wise men, then with a band of ascetics who subsist on near-starvation rations and deny themselves adequate sleep and even the

---

[6] Lucien Stryk, *The World of the Buddha*, 23.

[7] Huston Smith, *The Religions of Man*, 124.

[8] Ibid.

pleasure of personal cleanliness—all the while concentrating the mind, seeking to find knowledge that cannot be expressed, knowledge that is ineffable.

Figure 15.1. Buddha

Finally, after sitting under a tree and just when knowledge is about to break forth, an evil spirit, Karma-Matra, the god of love and death, tries to break Siddhartha's concentration. Karma-Matra sends his daughters (Desire, Pining, and Lust) to tempt Siddhartha. But Siddhartha "only moved his hand to touch the ground with his fingertips, and thus bid the… Earth bear witness to his right to be sitting where he was."[9] Enlightenment had arrived, and Siddhartha was now the Buddha (The Enlightened One), and the tree was named the Bo tree (short for Bodhi, enlightened).

THE BUDDHA'S ENLIGHTENMENT: HIS MESSAGE

The gist of the Buddha's message is usually summed up as the Four Noble Truths and the Eightfold Path. The Four Noble Truths are verities: profound but not unique insights. The first truth is that suffering (*dukka*) pervades and informs all of human life. The second truth is that the cause of this suffering is desire (*tannha*). The third truth is Nirvana, "Extinction, blowing out: the extinction of self which brings enlightenment and the liberation from pain (*dukka*)."[10] And the fourth truth is that the way to enlightenment comes from following the Eightfold Path.

The Eightfold Path is signposted with moral precepts and injunctions. Like the Ten Commandments and the Sermon on the Mount, the Eightfold Path serves two purposes. It constrains human behavior and offers humankind the prospect of a safe and orderly existence in which the desires of the individual are subordinated to the welfare of the larger society. And central to Buddhist teaching, it is the path that liberates us from desire.

As elaborated by Buddhist monks and abbots, the Eightfold Path incorporates more than 200 rules for a moral life. But the essence of the path is a set of simple rules, precepts, and aspirations that free us from desire.

Right understanding: Always attempt to see through illusions: for example, the idea that money buys happiness. "Everything we do and say is governed by the mind. The Buddha said that if our mind is defiled and untrained suffering will follow just as the chariot follows the horse."[11] Right knowledge will lead to good thoughts and good deeds.

Right thought and right motives: Always aspire to do good, to respect others, and to lead a moral life.

Right speech: Do not lie; do not slander. Do not gossip. Language is more than a means of communication. Language also conveys good meanings and bad meanings. It signals good in-

---

[9] Joseph Campbell, *The Hero with a Thousand Faces* (Princeton: Princeton University Press, 1968), 32; see also 30-33. Discussing the archetypal hero in world religions, this book was chosen by *Time* magazine as one of the most important issued since the magazine began in 1923.

[10] Karen Armstrong, *Buddha*, 81.

[11] Mary Pat Fisher, *Living Religions*, 2nd ed. (Upper Saddle River, NJ: Prentice-Hall, 1999), 117.

tentions and bad. Thus, use right speech so as not to mislead others, to give them understanding of your good intentions, to encourage them to lead moral lives, to love all things both great and small.

Right behavior: Do not kill. Do not steal. Do not lie. Do not be unchaste. Do not drink intoxicants. Be moderate in consuming food. And do not do to others what you would not want them to do to you.

Right livelihood: If possible, and for even a short time, become a monk; join a religious community. Short of that, do not peddle poisons. Have nothing to do with prostitution. Do not buy, sell, or trade weapons. Do not earn your livelihood through deceitful practices. Engage in nothing that brings suffering or even discomfort to others.

Right effort: "Buddha laid tremendous stress on the will... There are virtues that must be developed, passions to be curbed, and evil mind states to be transcended if love and detachment" are to prevail.[12]

Right mindfulness: Ignorance, not sin, is a major impediment to the virtuous life. Check your mind. Be on your guard. Pull yourself out, as an elephant from the mud.[13] "Better than a hundred years lived in vice without contemplation is one single day lived in virtue and deep contemplation."[14]

Right Meditation: "When the mind is fully stilled, it becomes a quiet pool in which the true nature of everything is clearly reflected."[15]

> Better than a hundred years of not considering how all things arise and pass away is one single day of life if one considers how all things arise and pass away...Better than a hundred years of not seeing the Eightfold Path than a single day of seeing the Path...[16]

THE BUDDHA AS TEACHER

As teacher and preacher, the Buddha was constantly on the road, speaking to crowds, gathering followers, setting up communities of monks. Tradition has him teaching and preaching into his eighth decade. Tradition also describes him as a dynamic teacher, using gestures and

---

[12] Huston Smith, *The Religions of Man*, 162.

[13] Mary Pat Fisher, *Living Religions*, 118.

[14] George N. Marshall, *The Challenge of a Liberal Faith* (Boston: Unitarian Universalist Association, 1988), 90.

[15] Mary Pat Fisher, *Living Religions*, 118-9.

[16] George N. Marshall, *The Challenge of a Liberal Faith*, 91.

signs to help convey his message. These gestures, or *mudras* (of which more presently), are the familiar iconography of Buddhism.

A framework for the Buddha's teaching are ideas and concepts anchored in Hindu cosmology. *Samsara* (literally "keep going") is the endless cycle "of death and rebirth that propels people from one life to the next."[17] *Karma* is the universal law of cause and effect. Good deeds and bad deeds carry into the next existence and affect life lived there in the endless cycle of death and rebirth. *Nirvana* means literally the blowing out of the flame of the self "which brings enlightenment and liberation from pain (dukka)."[18] The end of the cycle of birth and rebirth, the end of suffering and desire, to become one with the universe, as the wheel of existence stops turning.

> No suffering for him
> Who is free from sorrow
> Free from the fetters of life
> Free in everything he does
> He has reached the end of his road...[19]

THE TWO VEHICLES

The story is told that as the Buddha lay dying, his anxious followers crowded around, begging him to transcend mortality and to declare his divinity. They could beg him, as a divine being, to accept their prayers and assist in their salvation. To this the Buddha reportly replied, "Do not look to others for your salvation. Be a lamp unto yourselves." And in keeping with that tradition, novitiates are brought into a temple and told to open the door of a small shrine. When they do, they see a mirror. And in the mirror each sees his or her own face.

This is austere stuff. Perhaps the oldest human metaphor is that life is a journey, that death is a continuation of that journey, and that the afterlife is a happy place. The ancient Chinese and Egyptians filled gravesites with implements that would be useful in that happy place. Egyptians knew that the dead would harvest grain in fields presided over by Osiris. Vikings believed that the afterlife in Valhalla is a place of continuous feasting and roistering. Ancient Native Americans gave ornaments and useful implements for the afterlife to their dead. And,

---

[17] Karen Armstrong, *Buddha*, 204.

[18] Ibid., 203.

[19] Fisher, *Living Religions*, 120.

of course, the pillar of Christianity is that resurrection awaits the godly, who will dwell forever in the house of the Lord.

Buddhists who accept Buddha's Lamp are called Theravada ("tradition of the Elders"). Buddhists who reject Theravada's claims of authenticity call them (pejoratively) Hinayana, the smaller vehicle. Theravada dominates Sri Lanka and Burma. Because Theravada must work out their own salvation, without reliance on "gods or any force beyond themselves," the monk is their ideal. "It is he who shaves his head, puts on the coarse yellow robe, takes up the begging bowl, and goes forth to seek release from life."[20]

As is often remarked, Theravada is a spare religion, but it is not a jealous religion. It does not demand an exclusive dominion, nor does it pursue or punish heresy. Unlike Judaism, Christianity, and Islam, an injunction akin to the First Commandment's "Thou shall have no gods before me" is alien to the Buddhist spirit. So, a belief in folk gods and spirits continues for those who wish to invoke them. Buddhist temples often display statues of benevolent gods and spirits to guard against evil ones. Buddhists often wear amulets containing images of the Buddha to protect them from evil and bad fortune. For the same reason, many also wear a wristlet that has been blessed by a monk.

Even so, or perhaps because of Theravada beliefs, relics of the Buddha are of great importance. Fragments of his bones, clothes, and the Bo tree are venerated and often housed in bell-shaped structures *(stupas)*.

MAHAYANA

Another story of the Buddha's last days inspires the majority of Buddhists: the Mahayana (riders on the "greater vehicle"). In that story, disciples who press him for further knowledge watch as the Enlightened One pulls a branch from a tree. Thus speaks the Buddha: "Just as this tree has many branches, and just as this branch has many leaves, so it is that this leaf has many veins." With this inspiration, those who will call themselves Mahayana use this parable to comfort themselves on their journeys through the cycle of existence. Comfort and help come from two sources. One is the belief that the Buddha was more than a man. He was a divine being come to earth in the form of a man "because he loved humankind" and wished to assist in the journey to salvation.[21]

---

[20] Lewis M. Hopfe, *Religions of the World* (Upper Saddle River: Prentice Hall, 1987), 155.

[21] Ibid., 157.

The second fountain of comfort is the Bodhisattva, an enlightened being who interrupts his or her own salvation to assist others in reaching their salvation. For many Mahayana, Buddha and Bodhisattva may be prayed to, sometimes for intercession in the difficulties of daily living and other times for guidance on the path to salvation and to remove whatever pitfalls may lie on the path. In many temples, a statue of the Buddha is surrounded by dozens of Bodhisattva, usually standing in stiff attendance.

BUDDHISM EXPANDS

Sometime around 250 BCE, the most powerful ruler in India, the Emperor Ashoka, underwent spiritual transformation. He became a fervent Buddhist, sending missionaries across Southeast Asia. He mediated between Theravada and Mahayana, especially with respect to what Westerners would call ontological disputes, with the Theravada insisting that "only present events were real," while Mahayana insisted that "past, present, and future events are all equally real."[22]

For today's wise traveler, one visible remnant of Ashoka's missionaries is their travel northward into territory subdued by Alexander the Great, who crossed into India around 326 BCE. There, Hellenic civilization took root. And statues of the Buddha were carved and molded in the Gandahara style: naturalistic stance, flowing drapery, and realistic facial expression.

Missionaries carried Buddhism into Sri Lanka, China, Korea, Tibet, and Japan. And two of Buddhism's strands wove themselves tightly into Japanese culture.

Amitabha, also called Amida, is a Bodhisattva who uses his powers to save men and women by his grace. He brings them at death to Paradise, seen as the Pure Land of the West. A branch of Mahayana, Amida are permitted to eat meat, marry, and live like laypeople. Communicants gather in meeting halls and seek entry into Paradise by calling out to Amida, intoning his name numerous times day and night.

In contrast to Amida Buddhism, Zen is a contemplative, introspective religion. For its adherents, one cannot look to other persons or institutions for salvation, nor can reason alone bring salvation. Salvation is to be found in a flash of insight. One way to acquire insight is to sit quietly, not a muscle moving or an eyelid blinking, in the presence of a master. The master will attempt to confuse reason by posing riddles, or *koans*, such as, "What is the sound of one hand clapping?" and "Why may a finger slip quietly into water while the palm is resisted?" While the

---

[22] Fisher, *Living Religions*, 278.

novitiate meditates, he hopes that "a flash of enlightenment (*satori*) will come and will lead the initiate to the truth beyond reason."[23]

Simplicity, beauty, and slow, careful movement are the hallmarks of Zen. And they reflect much that the Japanese value: the hiker who climbs Mount Fuji to sit in solitude contemplating its snow-covered peak, the archer who uses intense concentration to make the arrow fly to its mark, the lady who practices graceful movements while following an ancient ritual to pour tea, and the person who finds beauty in a stone garden that displays a rhythmic pattern of rocks laid on carefully swept soil.

THE BUDDHA OBSERVED

Statues of the Buddha come in all shapes and sizes, from fat to skeletal, and from giant figures carved in mountains to tiny heads held in the hand. Heads, hands, and feet veer from the ordinary. The Buddha's head has four distinctive features. The elongated earlobes remind us that he once wore the earrings of a prince. The bump on top of his head signifies the Buddha's enormous capacity for wisdom. And the face is always serene, eyes usually closed in meditation. Centered just above the eyes is a tiny bump, the Third Eye, the center of spiritual insight. By tradition, all fingers and toes are of the same length. Seated, the Buddha is either cross-legged or has one foot bent at the knee, the foot fully on the ground. When both legs are folded at the knee, the left leg is tucked beneath the right, each foot resting on the opposite thigh. This is the lotus position, and the lotus bears iconic meaning: beauty rising out of watery mud.

The devoted often put tiny foils of gold leaf on the Buddha. Placed on the mouth, gold leaf may help the giver to utter only right speech. When the gold leaf is placed on the forehead, the giver may be blessed with wisdom. And when the leaf is placed on the heart, the donor may live a life of kindness and charity to all whom he or she meets.

Mudras are the characteristic postures of the Buddha. When the right hand is raised palm out and the left is touching or pointing to the earth, this is the *Bhumisparsa,* Buddha calling humankind to witness. It is also the calming proclamation; some choose to see it as subduing evil. When walking or standing, with one or both palms facing outward, fingers pointing upward, this is the Buddha dispelling anxiety and fear.

When seated with legs folded and hands in his lap and palms up, the Buddha is meditating *(Samadhi). Vitarka* is when the raised arm is bent at the elbow, palm out, thumb and forefinger

---

[23] Ibid., 163.

touching, which signifies that the Buddha is teaching. When seated with fingers of both hands touching and in obvious motion, the Buddha signifies the wheel of life and existence.

And the most solemn and revered of all is the Buddha lying full length. Sometimes the head rests on folded hands; sometimes the head is slightly raised, resting on a crooked elbow and upturned palm. This is the Buddha slipping away from existence, preparing to achieve Nirvana.

16. China: The Asian Civilization

> China? There lies a sleeping giant. Let him sleep!
> For when he wakes he will move the world.
> — Napoleon

TRADITIONAL CHINA: 2000 BCE TO 1912 CE

China easily overwhelms the wise traveler. Its size is vast, about 3.7 million square miles (third in size, behind Canada and Russia). Its population is the world's largest (over 1.3 billion). Its climate ranges from subtropical to Siberian. Its agricultural zones range from deserts adjoining Pakistan and the Caucasus, to the wheat and barley fields in the north, to the tropical fruits and wet-rice fields in the areas adjacent to the Pacific Ocean.[1] China's two major rivers, the Yellow and the Yangtze, are among the longest in the world, and its mountains in Tibet are among the world's highest.

An eminent student of China has remarked that western civilization has been moving westward for 2,500 years: from Athens to Rome, to western Europe, and to North America. But the center of Asian civilization has stayed in China for the same 2,500 years.[2] China is not only the world's oldest continuing culture, but its written language (still in daily use) is the world's oldest. It is the unusual design of the language that first confronts the wise traveler from the

---

[1] China is among the world's largest producers of rice, tea, peanuts, and sweet potatoes.

[2] See John King Fairbank, *The Great Chinese Revolution: 1800-1985* (New York: Harper Perennial, 1987).

West. China's written language dates back at least 3,500 years. Writings on divination ("oracle") bones used in the Shang Dynasty (1500-100 BCE) can be read and understood today. Of course, the pronunciation of words has changed enormously over the centuries.[3] More important, given China's vast size, the Chinese have always spoken many different languages and dialects. But the written language is remarkably unchanged. In the blink of an eye (and a flick of the brain), literate readers can turn from today's newspapers to the thoughts and musings of Confucius (551-479 BCE).

The reason, but not the accomplishment, is simple. Unlike western languages whose written words convey sounds, Chinese writing is divorced from sound. It uses ideographs (picture symbols) to convey meaning. Accordingly, China's written language mystifies the wise traveler. In tourist centers many signs are transliterated into the western (Roman) alphabet. But even these can be daunting, especially to English speakers. Two late nineteenth-century British scholars, Thomas Wade and Francis Giles, devised a system for "Romanizing" ideographs. Revised by Giles in 1912, Wade-Giles became for most Westerners the standard way of transliterating Chinese characters. But in 1979 the Chinese government, motivated in part by national pride, replaced Wade-Giles with a new transliteration, Pinyin, based on Mandarin (China's official spoken language). In Pinyin, for example, the sounds *ch* and *ch'i* in Wade-Giles are now rendered as *q*; thus the Ch'in Dynasty is now the Qin Dynasty. And in another Pinyin change, Peking is now Beijing.

For the foreigner, merely saying a word (using either Wade-Giles or Pinyin) rarely conveys meaning to a Chinese listener. Chinese is a tonal language. The meaning of a word is determined by its tone and pitch. Chinese words are one syllable. Mandarin has four tones; each tone assigns a different meaning for that one word. For starters, try saying an English word using different tones. Better yet, say the words "Mary," "merry," and "marry," and ask a listener which meaning is conveyed by your pronunciation!

To be literate in Chinese is also daunting. To read a newspaper requires mastery of about 4,000 ideographs. To read, for example, the Confucian texts requires mastery of 50,000, and full mastery of Confucian texts requires an understanding of more than 488,000 ideographs. In Imperial China, literacy and government appointment went hand in glove. The Chinese invented the civil service. Appointment to its lowest ranks required successful completion of a written examination. Further advancement required further examinations. Aspiring bureau-

[3] This is also true of English, which is pronounced very differently today compared to the time of Chaucer, a mere 700 years ago.

crats would spend ten, twenty, and even thirty years preparing to pass their examinations. The scholar-bureaucrat was a symbol and archetype of government authority: stoop-shouldered, nearsighted, and taking pleasure in discourse, painting, and poetry. But it was the combination of literacy and the education for administrative appointment that were the foundations of China's long-lasting system of imperial government, from sometime around the Shang Dynasty (circa 1500 to circa 1000 BCE) to the revolution of 1912.

Figure 16.1. Map of China

China's first emperors are shadowy figures, beginning their reigns as early as 1900 BCE. The historical record begins with the Ch'in Dynasty. Its first emperor, Shih Huang Ti, took the throne in 221 BCE. Remembered for his ruthless rule, he supposedly conscripted 300,000 laborers to extend the Great Wall. His tomb in Xian is now a celebrated tourist site, with its silent army of 7,500 life-sized soldiers (terracotta warriors, a must-see site for wise travelers). And it is from Ch'in Shi Huang Ti that China takes its name. More important (with due allowance for revolutions and rebellions), from the Ch'in dynasty onward, China was governed by a succession of emperors until 1912. One must go back to ancient Egypt to find another system of government that had remained intact for more than 2,000 years. It was a system built on the two Chinese social inventions now used almost everywhere in the world: bureaucrats and a civil service appointed by means of a competitive written examination.[4]

In China's long history, more than a dozen clans held the imperial throne. Some held it for centuries, others for only decades. The emperor's territory and writ varied with his military power and his ability to suppress rebellion. In times of widespread civil unrest, China broke into small kingdoms (e.g., the Three Kingdoms, 220-265 CE; the Five Dynasties and Ten Kingdoms, 907-60 CE). Regimes were overthrown by foreign conquest and by rebellion. China is huge, but land suited to agriculture is small (only 15 percent of the total). Peasant uprising was a frequent aftermath of crop failure and widespread famine.

HORSEMEN FROM THE NORTH

Two of the most powerful dynasties were established by hard-riding conquerors from the north. The Mongol dynasty was founded by Genghis Kahn, whose armies swept through Asia and conquered Russia. His great empire extended east-west from the Sea of Japan to Poland and north-south from Siberia to Persia. His grandson, Kublai, consolidated the empire by toppling the dynasty in 1279, and Kublai established his capital in Peking. He offered safe journey across his empire, particularly on the Great Silk Road. One such journey brought three members of a Venetian family to China to trade: Nicolai, Maffeo, and young Marco Polo. The year was 1271. With a flair for languages, quick-witted Marco served for twenty-five years as messenger and diplomat for the Great Kahn. When he returned to Venice in 1295, he brought with him the "secret" of a sea passage from Europe to the Far East. That knowledge would later car-

[4] See Edward Schafer, *The Great Ages of Man: Ancient China* (New York: Time-Life International, 1967).

ry the Portuguese around Africa to the Far East and would inspire Christopher Columbus to attempt an alternate route to the riches of Asia.[5]

The armies of the Ming Dynasty, who in their turn were deposed by what was to be the last imperial rulers, the Manchus (called in Chinese the *Ch'ing* in Wade-Giles, or in Pinyin, *Qing*). Their ancestral homeland was in the north in Manchuria. Manchu armies conquered China in about 1644. Organized into fighting units, each bearing a distinctive banner, the Manchus attempted to keep themselves separate from their subject people. Chinese men were forced to shave their foreheads and wear a long braid at the neck (called pigtails by Westerners). Manchu women shunned the fashion of Chinese women: they did not bind their feet. The Manchus ruled China for almost 300 years until the revolution of 1912.

The Manchu centuries (1644-1912) were the centuries of China's long slide into humiliation. This mighty country, whose rulers dismissed Westerners as barbarians who had nothing to teach China, was unable to prevent them from setting up European-controlled enclaves in Chinese cities. No less humiliating, after a series of wars with the West, the Chinese were forced to cede control over their customs duties and their ports.

THE OPIUM WARS

Signposts along the Manchu march to oblivion mark a series of wars and rebellions. Like most wars, the First Opium War turned on several issues. The British East India Company, seeking profit in the China trade, did a brisk business in silk, tea, and porcelain. The Chinese had no interest in buying British goods and demanded payment in gold and silver, resulting in a serious trade imbalance. The East India Company reversed the flow of gold and silver by selling opium (grown in Bengal, India) to China. As addiction spiraled, so did the sale of opium. In 1729 about 200 chests of British opium were on sale in China. In 1767 the figure was 1,000 chests, and in 1820 it was more than 10,000. For the Chinese, opium was more than a "recreational drug." It was used by workers to sustain their grueling labor. The word "coolie" means bitter work. As opium money changed hands, Chinese officials became part of the opium network, taking bribes for facilitating opium sales. Worse, opium addiction spread to soldiers in the imperial army.[6]

---

[5] See Daniel Boorstin, *The Discoverers* (New York: Random House, 1983), Chapter 18.

[6] See Lucian Pye, *China: An Introduction* (New York: Little, Brown, 1972).

Attempting to staunch the flow of opium, in 1839 Chinese officials seized a British-owned opium warehouse in Canton. Tempers flared even more when drunken British sailors killed a Chinese person and British authorities refused to hand them over for trial. War broke out, but Chinese guns and warships were no match for British men of war. Temporary peace came with the Treaty of Nanking (1842). Under its terms, China paid a large indemnity (thereby admitting wrongdoing) and gave Britain the right to unrestricted trade in five ports and British citizens the right to be tried in British courts. As further indemnity, the island of Hong Kong was given to Britain. And opium was now a legal substance to be imported and sold without restriction.

The Second Opium War (1856-1860) flared over a series of incidents involving trade, treatment of foreign citizens, and what was now commonly called extra-territoriality—exempting foreigners in designated enclaves from Chinese law. In 1860 Britain and France sent troops into Peking, forced the emperor to flee, and burned the summer palace on the outskirts of the capital.

THE TAIPING REBELLION

As official corruption grew, as lack of import revenue forced the government to cut back on expenditures, and as the literate classes felt the sting of national humiliation, rebellions spread. The most horrific was the Taiping Rebellion (1860-1864). Its leader proclaimed a new era of social justice and heavenly peace, and in the three-way fighting among government troops, mercenaries hired by merchants and landlords, and the Taiping rebels, more than 800 cities were burned, thousands of acres of crops were destroyed, and as many as twenty million were killed (some estimates put the total at forty million).

Taiping's devastation set in motion a chain of events that led to more rebellions, not less than three foreign invasions, and ultimately the final collapse of dynastic rule. In the quarter-century after Taiping, impoverished peasants resisted rapacious landlords by murdering rent collectors and brandishing scythes and axes. Students and intellectuals joined secret societies to plot against corrupt officials and to drive foreigners and their special privileges out of China. And all over China, landlords and peasants, joined by students and mandarins, supported each other in their hatred of Christian missionaries who encouraged their converts to flout traditional marriage ceremonies, denounced concubines and multiple wives, and railed against ancestor worship and worship of traditional gods and spirits.

THE BOXER REBELLION

The Boxer Rebellion of 1900 brought to a boil the widespread fear of foreigners ("foreign devils") and hatred of Chinese converts to Christianity. Railroads (constructed by foreign engineers) snorting steam and rumbling over iron roads were widely believed to unleash evil spirits.[7]

> Telegraph lines were similarly feared. Wind moaning through the high telegraph poles sounded like spirits in torment .... By the end of the 19th Century there were over 700,000 Catholic converts ministered to by more than 850 Nuns and priests. There were also about 85,000 Protestant Chinese.[8]

Figure 16.2. Boxer Rebellion

The Boxer rebels took their name from the stance used in Chinese boxing. Infused with mysticism, the Boxers believed that their raised-fist stance would protect them from western bullets. The climax of rebellion was the Boxer siege of foreign legations in Peking, lifted after nearly two months by the guns of an international force of British, American, Japanese, and Russian troops. To complete its humiliation, China agreed to pay an indemnity, to suspend

[7] The Boxer Rebellion is grippingly portrayed in the movie *55 Days at Peking* (1963), with Charlton Heston, Ava Gardner, and David Niven.

[8] Diana Preston, *The Boxer Rebellion: The Dramatic Story of China's War on Foreigners That Shook the World* (New York: Berkley Books 1990), 27-30.

imperial examinations in towns and cities where foreigners had been harmed or ill-treated, and to permit foreign troops to remain on station in Peking (most remained there until the Second World War).

To its credit and reflecting the long affection of American missionaries for China, the United States used its share of the indemnity for the education of Chinese students. No reliable statistics tally the number of Chinese killed during the rebellion, but photographs and firsthand accounts describe in vivid detail the beheading of several hundred captured Boxer soldiers. The memory of the rebellion has burned deep into Chinese memory (looting by foreign troops, killing of Chinese civilians, the indemnity). When the Communists took over China in 1949, one of their leaders called the Boxer revolt one of the great victories of the Chinese people.

THE SINO-JAPANESE WAR (1894-95)

The Sino-Japanese War was another stab in the heart of national pride. For centuries China had laid a protective arm over Korea. But as Japan "westernized," it emulated the West: modernizing its military forces and aggressively seeking territory, markets, and raw materials. When a Korean religious cult attempted to topple the Korean monarchy, Japan intervened on the pretext of restoring order. The Manchu government also sent troops, but after the revolt ended, Japan refused to withdraw its armies. In a quick war, the Japanese crushed Chinese land and naval forces. In the treaty that followed, China abandoned its protection of Korea (thereby recognizing Japan's predominance) and, worse, paid a large indemnity to Japan.

For centuries, China had executed prisoners by means of a torture called the thousand cuts, literally skinning alive the prisoner bit by tiny bit. After the humiliations imposed by the West and compounded by Japan, many Chinese began to see China and its Manchu overlords as dying the death of a thousand cuts.

As the nineteenth century ended, China was in danger of being carved into colonies by the European powers, much as Africa was. China's staunchest guardian was the United States, whose China policy was shaped by long involvement of American missionaries in China, long-established American schools in China, and American colleges that offered scholarships to young Chinese. In many ways, it was a friendship toward China that rested on an appreciation of Chinese culture, gained through decades of living and working in China. American policy was encapsulated in the slogan of the "open door"—free access to all but colonies for none.

THE EMPEROR AND THE MANDARINS

At the apex of the political system was the emperor, whose power, at least in principle, was absolute. But it was power tempered by the emperor's habits and inclinations. Mostly it was rule through the emperor's chief ministers and their subordinates, the mandarins.[9] The latter entered government service through a competitive written examination. The first step on a very long road was to be certified as a moral person proficient in scholarship. To be certified was roughly the equivalent of a B.A. Three years after certification, if scholarship continued and no moral blemishes were reported, the candidates submitted to three days of continuous writing. Successful passage of this examination was the equivalent of an M.A. degree. It admitted those who were successful to the lower rungs of the administrative ladder. Only about 1 percent of the applicants passed.

> The ultimate imperial examinations were held every three years at the nation's capital.... The candidates were locked into small, isolated cubicles with slits under the door through which food was passed...during the seven days of ... examinations ... Those who passed became Chin-shih or Doctor and were admitted to the higher (civil) service. During the 267 years of the Ming period only 24,874 men became Chin-shih.[10]

Like the English civil service, which was modeled on the Chinese system, mandarins were not specialists; they possessed general knowledge and insight into human affairs derived from Confucian and other classics.[11] The most coveted Mandarin appointments were in the royal court. But given China's vast size, the entire country was subdivided into provinces, each one ruled (in the emperor's name) by his viceroy. Rarely if ever could they administer a province where their family resided, in order to control cronyism and favoring one's own family.[12]

Viceroys and their subordinates, including local magistrates, were expected to live in a style befitting their rank and importance. Every official was expected to support a large number of retainers and servants. Yet the mandarins were poorly paid. The consequence is no surprise: a gigantic pyramid of gifts and bribes. Subordinate officials were expected to favor their supe-

---

[9] Mandarin is not a Chinese word; it was used by the Portuguese, who fashioned it out of the Latin "mandate," meaning to decree. Likewise, the word Pagoda comes from the Portuguese, meaning "noisy."

[10] Lucian Pye, *China: An Introduction* (New York: Little, Brown, 1972), 65.

[11] In contrast to the mandarins, military officers were chosen for specific skills, bravery, and quite often kinship with the emperor.

[12] See Lawrence J. R. Herson, "China's Imperial Bureaucracy," *Public Administration Review* (1967).

riors with gifts, all the way up the Mandarin ladder.[13] Hard times (drought, floods, locusts) did not mean that gift-giving would lessen. Hard times meant that those at the bottom of the economic ladder, farmers with small holdings and tenant farmers, would have to sacrifice their own well-being to make up the shortfall. Hard times increased the suffering of the poor, sowing the seeds of rebellion.

THE EMPEROR AND HIS COURT

Generally, the emperor's first-born son succeeded to the throne; other times it was the son of a favorite wife; sometimes it was a prince of the blood. Murder of a likely candidate was not unknown, especially when family factions struggled for power. In addition to family, military leaders, and mandarins, another set of contenders for power in the imperial court was the eunuchs. With little likelihood of conspiring to place their own sons on the throne, eunuchs served as the emperor's bodyguards and sometimes as his trusted advisors. Often they joined in the struggle for power by entering into alliances with royal factions. The traditional role for the eunuchs was as guardians of the emperor's harem. Sometimes the women in the harem numbered only a few; in some reigns, though, they numbered in the thousands. By tradition, the emperor had a duty to supply dozens, even hundreds, of offspring for posterity. In doing so, he was thought to demonstrate the vigor of his rule. Usually it was the Chief Eunuch who chose the emperor's sexual partner. And that choice gave the eunuchs a special power—providing the emperor with a son and possible heir as well as providing the family of a favorite wife or concubine access to the throne and to the inner circles of political power. In addition to his concubines, the emperor had several wives. The eldest or sometimes his favorite was his consort. She exercised great power over the harem, over the eunuchs, and over the hundreds of household servants. The consort was deeply involved in the politics of succession, attempting to ensure that one of her sons became emperor.

As stated, in principle the emperor's power was absolute. Without any explanation he could order anyone to be seized and tortured to death. The emperor's personal symbol and icon was the five-toed dragon; others might aspire to a dragon with four toes. Thus, his throne was the Dragon Throne. In Manchu times, the emperor would place his symbol, sometimes no more than a vermillion dot, on a royal decree. And appended to that decree were the words "Tremble and Obey." The emperor appointed his chief ministers, each of whom ran one of the

---

[13] Graft in China had parallels to the payoff system of Soviet Russia.

great departments of government. In Manchu times, there were six major ministries, including the Board of Personnel (Civil Appointments), the Board of Finance, the Board of Punishment (courts and sentencing), and the Board of War.

Because the emperor was regarded as the mediator between heaven and earth, many of his most important duties involved performing rituals that bestowed divine blessings on China and its people. The emperor was the son of heaven, and his most important altar was directly below heaven. This central location gave China its familiar name: The Middle Kingdom. The most solemn ritual was the ritual of the winter solstice, during which a young bullock was sacrificed on the altar of heaven to ensure the return of light and warmth to the earth.

> Dressed in an embroidered robe, the emperor climbed to the top of a great stone altar. There, officials called out to royal ancestors and Heaven in a loud, slow monotone, asking for their aid and assuring them of the ruler's devoted support. The ancestors, and deities of the sun, moon, stars, planets, wind, and rain were represented by inscribed tablets. Food was offered before these tablets...[14]

GODS AND SPIRITS IN IMPERIAL CHINA

As might be expected, religious beliefs shifted and changed during the centuries of Chinese history. A popular saying has it that every Chinese is born 3,000 years old. That is, he carries in his mind and in his heart customs and ideas of polytheism and animism that were formed in antiquity. From earliest times, his ancestors would have honored *T'ien* (Heaven), the supreme power that created the universe and all its components. Even today, despite the teaching of the Communist regime, proper respect must be shown to a multitude of gods. Dead heroes can be called on for assistance. Prayers of intercession are offered to *K'wan Yin*, goddess of mercy and bringer of fertility to childless women. Every household had a shrine to the kitchen god, *Tsao Shen*. In Manchu times, each new year, women of the household would put honey and opium on the mouth of *Tsao Shen's* statue to sweeten his report to higher gods and to seal his lips against reporting "family transgressions."[15] Men especially must be mindful of good spirits and wary of evil ones—spirits that emanate from mountains, trees, streams, wind, and water. The cosmos itself is organized around two fundamental life forces, *Yang* (male) and *Yin* (female). Yang is associated with light, warmth, and righteousness. Yin is associated with darkness and

---

[14] Daniel Overmeyer, *Religions of China: The World as a Living System* (Prospect Heights, IL: Waveland Press, 1998), 71.

[15] See the novel by Amy Tan, *The Kitchen God's Wife* (New York: Putnam, 1991).

evil. The organic unity of the Yang-Yin principle is manifest in the familiar symbol—a circle, half dark, half light, each with a small inner circle of the opposing principle.

The most prevalent Chinese beliefs are centered on the family. Prayers along with flowers, incense, and food are offered to the spirit of one's ancestors partly as supplication and partly as prayers for intercession with gods and spirits. Ancestors are guardians of the living family, warding off evil and assisting in its prosperity. Only sons may supplicate and pray to ancestors. A son, when he dies, leaves unbroken the great chain of ancestors and ancestor prayers, thus assuring family longevity and prosperity. This is a cornerstone of the Chinese desire for male children. The son's place in the hierarchy of family values is at the heart of Confucian values and teachings.

Confucius likened the ruler to the polar star, suggesting that all the other stars revolve around it. He further suggested that one should not do to others what one would not want done to them.[16] Kung fu-tse, Master Kung (Latinized as Confucius by the first Jesuits to reach China), is China's greatest teacher. In Hong Kong and Singapore today, schoolchildren in a Confucian temple will light a joss stick in his name and raise clasped hands to honor his portrait.

Confucius was born in the Kung clan sometime around 551 BCE, in what is sometimes called the Axial Age of civilizations' great philosophers.[17] His lifetime coincided with the *Chou* (*Zhu*) era, which saw the breakdown of governmental authority and the rise of plundering wars. He held brief posts as government minister but spent most of his life as a wandering scholar and teacher searching for the principles of a good society, a good life, and the government that would best grant the kingdom peace and prosperity. His teachings were compiled by disciples and come down to us in *The Analects* and in his history of ancient times, *The Spring and Autumn Annals.*

Confucius's concerns were with the world of the living, not life after death. "Do not ask me about the next world," he said. "I have not yet begun to solve the problems of this world." He believed that humans were educable and perfectible—two sides of the same coin. He placed great emphasis on education, stressing the importance of lifetime learning and reflective thought.

---

[16] See James Legge, translator, *Confucian Analects, The Great Learning and the Doctrine of the Mean* (New York: Dover, 1971).

[17] Plato was born about 427 BCE and the Buddha around 563 BCE.

> At 15 I set my heart on learning; at 30 I took my stand; at 40 I had no delusions; at 50 I knew the Mandate of Heaven; at 60 my ear was attuned; at 70 I followed my Heart's desire without going beyond the boundaries of what is right.[18]

Confucius believed that humans should strive to achieve a virtuous life by cultivating two qualities: *Jen,* human-heartedness, a feeling of humanity toward other human beings as well as respect for oneself, and a sense of the dignity of human life,[19] and *Li*, "propriety," the proper way of behaving, whatever the situation, whatever confronts you. *Li* is ritual and something more; it is the golden mean between action and patience and between pride and humility. And most important, *Li* must be observed in the basic relationships that constitute society.

Li is a system of superordinate and subordinate relations. It is the deference of children to their father, the younger son to the older brother, of a younger friend to an older friend, of wife to husband, of father to the emperor. It is the formula for an ordered society. If there is harmony in the family, said Master Kung, there will be harmony in the clan. If there is harmony in the clan, there will be harmony in the village. If there is harmony in the village, there will be harmony in the province. And if there is harmony in the province, there will be harmony in the nation. Confucian values, with their insistence on unequal status, are in marked contrast to present-day western values, with their emphasis on equality between the sexes and among members of society. It is equality that makes democracy possible. Without it, the principle of "one person, one vote" would not prevail.

Li is embodied by deference to ancestors. It inspires the family to achieve success through hard work, thrift, and deferred gratification of marriage and material acquisitions. Many in the West attribute the current prosperity of Singapore, Vietnam, Hong Kong, Japan, and China to the influence of Confucius and his teachings.

WOMEN IN IMPERIAL CHINA

In China women have traditionally been subservient to men. The Yin attributes of cosmology (all things dark and evil) reinforce that subservience. Foot binding was its most painful form. In the tenth century, foot binding was a mark of the aristocracy. Women with tiny, bound feet could not be expected to do hard work or move about quickly. By the fourteenth century, it

---

[18] See Legge, *Confucian Analects*, 2.4.

[19] See Huston Smith, *The Religions of Man*, (New York: Joanna Cotler Books, 1965), Chapter 5.

had spread to other social classes. "It became so widespread that western observers in the nineteenth century found it almost universal, not only among the upper classes but throughout the farming population."[20]

Foot binding began in childhood. The ideal was a foot not longer than three or four inches. Toes were forced under the sole to make the foot narrower. And the foot was made smaller by forcing the big toe and heel closer, "so that the arch rose in a bowed shape."[21] In this way, the arch was broken and the foot could bear no weight. Tiny feet became an object of erotic desire, and girls with normal feet could not expect an advantageous marriage. Marriage itself was far from a matter of mutual love. Marriages were arranged by families and marriage brokers. Often the bride saw her husband for the first time at the wedding ceremony. If she were ugly or deformed and if he could afford it, he was free to take a second wife. If the situation were reversed, as was often the case, and the husband were old, the bride had no such privilege.

Despite women's place in the social order, China's history is also illuminated by rich and powerful women. In the second millennium BCE, one of the wives of the emperor "was an active participant in politics. She had a domain of her own, including a walled town, and could mobilize three thousand warriors at her personal command."[22]

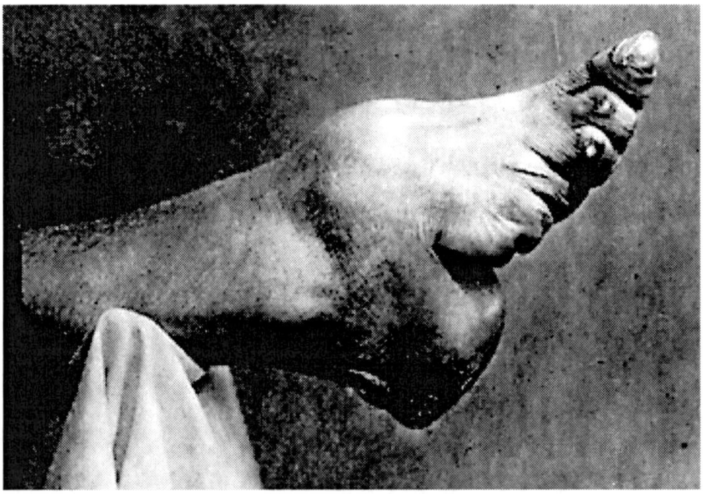

Figure 16.3. Foot Binding

[20] John King Fairbank, *The Great Chinese Revolution: 1800-1985, 1987* (New York: Harper Perennial, 1987), 69.

[21] Ibid., 71.

[22] Felipe Fernadez-Armesto, *Civilizations: Culture, Ambition, and the Transformation of Nature* (New York: Free Press, 2002), 219.

In the waning days of the Manchus, the Dowager Empress was a formidable power. She made national policy, disposed of rival claimants to the throne, secretly sent troops to aid the Boxer rebels, and spent huge sums from the royal treasury (intended to modernize the navy) on a personal pleasure palace. In Communist China, the widow of Mao Tse T'ung, Chiang Ch'ing, headed a small cabal (the Gang of Four) that ruled the country for about a decade.

These, of course, are exceptional women. More usual was the woman who shared the husband's hard work in the fields and, beyond that, bore and raised children, did washing, cooking, sewing, shopping, cleaning house, and provided for the family's comfort.

THE GENIUS OF CHINA

As Robert Temple writes, "Possibly more than half of the basic inventions and discoveries on which the modern world rests come from China."[23] China invented movable type, gunpowder, and the compass—inventions that made it possible for Europeans to conquer and colonize America, Africa, and Asia.[24] China also invented paper (second century BCE), while Europe was still using sheepskin parchment in the late Middle Ages, wheelbarrows (third century BCE; not used in Europe until the thirteenth century), umbrellas, shipboard waterproof compartments, and the post and stern rudder, which made big ships possible.

In the sixth century BCE Chinese farmers were using the iron plow and moldboard to turn over the soil; in the second century BCE the seed drill and rotating winnowing fan, in the fourth century BCE cast iron (which did not reach Europe until the 1300s), and by 100 BCE China was making steel. Porcelain was made in China in the third century CE. It was so much prized by Europe that the search to find the secrets of porcelain spanned several centuries. It eluded Europe until 1709. The list multiplies and includes important discoveries in medicine (circulation of the blood, diabetes and its treatment), hydraulic engineering (the Grand Canal, the longest canal in the world, more than 1,000 miles long, begun in the fourth century BCE), and warfare (the cross bow, artillery, land mines, and grenades).

In architecture, China built spectacular buildings, elaborately decorated inside and out, with rooflines that seem to defy gravity.[25] In humanist pursuits, the Chinese perfected the arts

---

[23] Robert Temple, *The Genius of China: 3,000 Years of Science, Discovery, and Invention* (New York: Simon and Schuster, 1986), 9.

[24] See, for example, Jared Diamond, *Germs, Guns, and Steel: The Fates of Human Societies* (New York: W.W. Norton & Co, 1999).

[25] See Charis Chan, *Imperial China: Architectural Guides for Travelers* (Canada: Penguin, 1991).

of calligraphy and scenic painting. Fiction was published as early as the ninth century, and poetry was prized as early as the Han Dynasty (206 BCE). Poets wrote of friendship, love, sorrow, and longing: thus, a poem by a princess married to a decrepit old man to whom she barely spoke:

> My people have married me
> In a far corner of the earth,
> Sent me away to a strange land....
> Always thinking of my own country
> My heart sad within,
> Would I were a yellow stork,
> And could fly to my old home![26]

THE OLD SYSTEM DIES: FINAL THOUGHTS

By the late nineteenth century, it was obvious to most and painful to those who loved China that the Middle Kingdom desperately needed reform. The once great military power that received tributes from all of Asia and the once great center of invention and culture was now treated with bullying contempt by foreign powers. Where foreign ambassadors seeking audience with the emperor once approached the throne on their knees, foreheads on the floor (the "kow tow"), they now sent armies into Peking. China's continuing humiliation was a significant factor in toppling the dynastic system.

> And the dawn comes up like
> thunder outer China 'crost the Bay!
> — Rudyard Kipling, "Mandalay", 1890

AFTER THE FALL

As a rule, democracies pride themselves on a smooth transition from one set of elected rulers to the next. In the United States, an incoming President sends a transition team to work in the office of the outgoing chief executive. When non-democratic regimes change their system of government, they usually plunge into the maelstrom of factional strife—strife that often brings death and destruction into public life. (Recall Weimar Germany, post-Soviet Russia, and recent

---

[26] Arthur Waley, *Translations from the Chinese* (New York: Alfred A. Knopf, 1941), 18. Among the loveliest of poems are those of Hsi-Chun, the poet of love and longing.

events of the Arab Spring in the Near East and North Africa.) Just so, when the Manchu dynasty fell, China slipped into the maelstrom.

In 1898 the powerful Dowager Empress, Tzu Hsi, died, and the boy emperor climbed up on the Dragon Throne. For centuries Confucian doctrine supported the idea that the emperor ruled by the mandate of heaven. When the ruling house fell through invasions or rebellion, it was asserted that the mandate had been withdrawn. As Mencius, a disciple of Confucius said, "Heaven hears as the people hear."[27] So, it was traditionally expected that in the natural order of things, a new emperor would assume the throne. And the mandate would descend on the new ruler. China had no experience with representative government. Heaven's mandate presumably did not include republican government.

Figure 16.4. Sun Yat-sen

[27] Jiang Qing, *A Confucian Constitutional Order*, translated by Edmund Ryden (Princeton: Princeton University Press, 2013), 184.

When the Manchus fell, four influential groups vied to control events. Several European powers plus Japan were waiting to dismantle China and bring huge areas under their protection (i.e., make them colonies). Only the United States stood firm against colonization. Foreign investors operating mines and railroads, many with huge loans to the imperial government, demanded a Chinese government (or governments) that would honor their investments. Added to the list of contenders for power were local militias dominated by military leaders (war lords). Some worked to keep the status quo and their place in it. Others schemed to put themselves on the Dragon Throne.

Figure 16.5. Chiang K'ai Shek

Students and intellectuals, with help from overseas Chinese, agitated for a republic. Among them was Sun Yat-sen, a guiding spirit of untried republicanism. Born in a village near

Canton, an ex-patriot brother brought him to Hawaii for his education. He later attended western medical schools in Canton and Hong Kong but devoted himself full time to plotting from abroad the overthrow of the Manchus. While Sun was soliciting money and support from the Chinese community in the United States, he was elected Provisional President by the fledgling republican government. Sun hurried to China in time to take the oath of office on January 1, 1912. (October 10, 1911, has been officially celebrated as the birthday of the Republic.)

Events now moved to favor the nascent republican cause. On February 12, the boy emperor abdicated, and 2,000 years of traditional monarchy crumbled into the dustbin of history. The most powerful republican faction was soon to be the National Peoples Party, The Kuomintang, organized in the summer of 1912 (even as the country was sundered into military fiefdoms—the war lords).

In 1918 two new unknowns were added to the algebra of Chinese politics. Sun allied himself to Chiang K'ai shek, a Chinese soldier trained by the Japanese army. In 1923 Sun appointed Chiang military chief of staff of his government. Very quickly Chiang took over leadership of the Kuomintang and would dominate China in good times and bad for the next thirty-five years. In 1918 the Russian revolution also occurred. Shortly thereafter, agents of Soviet Russia began operating in China, working to install a Communist regime.

CIVIL WARS

Nationalists and Communists competed for supremacy. Shanghai was the deadliest confrontation. In 1927 Chiang's troops overran the city and killed the Communist leaders of the workers' unions along with several hundred of the rank and file. Communist uprisings spread to other cities, but these fell to Shanghai's fate.[28] The years 1927 to 1937 were the decade of Chiang's greatest success, even as the Communists under two gifted leaders—Mao Tse-tung (Mao Zedong) and Chou En-lai (Zhou En lai)—were re-grouping in the countryside and taking control of scattered cities. Fighting between the Nationalists and Communists flared sporadically until 1934. A crushing assault by Chiang forced Mao to lead his forces on the historic Long March: a 6,000-mile trek from Kiangsi northward to safety in Yenan in Shensi province. There, the Communists wooed the peasants, redistributed land, created their own version of a Communist state, trained their army, and waited.

[28] A moving account of the Shanghai uprising is told in the fiction of Andre Malraux, *Man's Fate* (New York: Modern Library, 1934).

Figure 16.6. Mao Tse-tung

Figure 16.7. Chou En-lai

JAPAN INVADES CHINA

Manchuria, the ancestral home of the Manchu Dynasty, was Japan's springboard into China. Both Russia and Japan coveted Manchuria's minerals and its ports on the Pacific. Both tried to dominate the province by building railroads, but Japan's ascendancy began after its stunning defeat of Russia in the war of 1904-5 (the Russo-Japanese War). Taking advantage of turmoil in China, in 1932 Japan installed a puppet regime in Manchuria, calling it the country of Manchukuo and, in a diplomatic sleight of hand, installing the last Manchu emperor as its nominal ruler.

Under various pretexts, Japan moved southward and in 1937 began a full-scale invasion of China. Japan was now at war with China, and in December of that year, Japan's anger at China's resistance turned to vengeful hate. The city of Nanking (Nanjing) was put to sword and fire. Best estimates are that in six murderous weeks, 300,000 civilians were killed. Systematic looting, arson, and rape, along with summary execution of civilians were carried out by the Japanese in the Rape of Nanking.[29] Chiang's Nationalist army retreated south and westward to establish a national capital at Chungking, while victorious Japan set about creating its Greater East Asia Co-Prosperity Sphere. After December 7, 1941 (Pearl Harbor), China became an ally of the United States and Great Britain, with the Allies attempting to turn the Japanese flank with men and supplies carried over the Burma Road or flown into Chungking from bases in

---

[29] See Iris Chang's 1997 book by the same name.

India. When the Second World War ended in August 1945, the Nationalists and the Communists resumed their fight for China.

PATH TO COMMUNIST VICTORY

The Communists under Mao had several advantages. One was a disciplined military (the People's Liberation Army), with leaders self-taught in guerilla warfare and an ideology that left no doubt that communism was destined to rule the world. Equally important was the support of the Soviet Union. Soviet Russia entered the war with Japan late. As an ally of Britain and the United States, the Russian army accepted the surrender of the Japanese in Manchuria. And shortly thereafter, Russia rearmed the Chinese Communists with surrendered Japanese weapons.

The Nationalists under Chiang were allies of the United States. During the war, American support of Chiang turned on an overriding objective: defeating Japan. After the war, American foreign policy turned on what was to become a major objective of the Cold War: to contain the spread of communism.

But long before the war ended, Americans fighting in China had become disillusioned and angry over Nationalist graft and corruption and, more important, over Chiang's failure to mount a strong assault on the enemy, presumably to spare manpower for the post-war struggle with the Communists.[30] As the civilian population became fearful of Nationalist looting, rising inflation, and summary execution of suspected Communists, and as battles turned into routs, Chiang and the Nationalist leaders fled mainland China, imposing themselves on Taiwan in late 1949.

In the United States, the Communist victory provoked fierce debate. "Who lost China?" became an accusatory question of American politics. Clouds of suspicion hung over "old China hands" in the State Department, and whispers of "treason" were heard in Congress and in the press. In Peking, on October 1, 1949, a triumphant Mao proclaimed the birth of the Peoples Republic of China.

THE PEOPLE'S REPUBLIC OF CHINA: EARLY YEARS

China's new regime was modeled on Soviet Russia: the Communist Party as master of the state; a hierarchy of rulers with ultimate power in the hands of the Party Chairman (initially, Chair-

---

[30] See Barbara Tuchman, *Stillwell and the American Experience in China* (New York: Macmillan, 1971).

man Mao); the Politburo as the topmost bureaucracy; a rubber stamp People's Congress; secrecy surrounding officialdom; and suppression of dissent. In historic irony, the Communists had replicated Imperial China: all power at the top of a vast pyramid that rested on a base of illiterate peasants.

The new regime began to nationalize all commercial enterprises and all agricultural production. A tight and far-reaching system of social control was achieved by organizing all adults into local work units (the *danwei* system). Controlled by local Party officials but answerable to those above, the *danwei* assigned living units and work. It gave or withheld approval on matters large and small: education of the young, travel requests, marriage arrangements, and permission to change residence. Those denounced as enemies of the people were humiliated in public "struggle sessions," forced to confess to misdeeds and "bad" thoughts. Former landlords, former officials, and "social parasites" (i.e., wealthy families, classical scholars) were "reeducated"—reeducated by hard work in agricultural communes, experiencing firsthand the foundations of China's traditional agriculture: the hoe, wheelbarrow, and the use of human excrement for fertilizer.[31]

> Chairman Mao Reigns
> Obey Orders...Do not
> take a single needle or thread
> from the masses...Speak politely...
> — Chairman Mao, *The Little Red Book*

After a decade as supreme ruler, Mao became impatient with China's economic progress: its rural poverty, its decrepit factories, and its failure to outshine the Soviet Union. The Great Leap Forward (1958-62) was an attempt to catapult industry upward by forcing the rural population to work harder in fields and factories. Farms were collectivized and crop quotas assigned. Communal kitchens were set up to free women for industrial production, most of which was small scale. Farmers melted down pots and pans to make steel in backyard furnaces. To meet quotas, machinery was operated without taking time for repairs, and replacement parts were almost nonexistent. Collectivizing agriculture and shunting workers from farms to factories resulted in crop failure on so wide a scale that as many as twenty (perhaps thirty) mil-

---

[31] See Fox Butterfield, *China: Alive in the Bitter Sea* (New York: Bantam Books, 1982).

lion died of starvation. Unwilling to take responsibility for the disaster, the government blamed it on bad weather. Rulership, said an old proverb, is like the weather. It comes from above.

The Great Proletarian Cultural Revolution (1966-1976) lasted longer than the Great Leap, and its consequences were more disastrous. Mao's purposes were multiple: to demonstrate his grip on leadership, to assure his place in history, to restore the purity of the Party's Communist ideology, and to crush urban resentment (especially among the literate) of the Party's and the state's heavy-handed control over what had once been private lives.

Mao shut down the schools and mobilized the urban young as Red Guards, encouraging them to roam the country and root out Party backsliders and all traces of bourgeois life and thought. Teachers were beaten, and many were killed. Books were burned. Artifacts of middle-class life, such as musical instruments and family keepsakes, were smashed and burned. Traditional monuments and temples, such as Confucian temples, were razed and burned. And children were encouraged to challenge authority and toss aside traditional respect for parents and elders. In the chaos, Red Guard units battled each other for supremacy, killing those deemed unworthy of Mao's leadership. To bring order out of anarchy, the army fought and disarmed the Red Guard.

Figure 16.8. The Great Proletarian Cultural Revolution

The costs of the Cultural Revolution are too numerous to tally, but perhaps the greatest is an entire generation deprived of education and the stability of family life. A deeply moving account of one woman's imprisonment and suffering during the Cultural Revolution is Nen Cheng's 1988 book *Life and Death in Shanghai.* The memoir of a twelve-year-old Red Guard and his subsequent life is *Son of the Revolution*, by Lang Hen and his American wife, Judith Shapiro.[32]

ECONOMIC AND SOCIAL REVOLUTION

Mao died in 1976, and in the hidden struggle for Party leadership, Deng Xioping, with well-honed survivor's skills, took the role of Great Helmsman, as Mao liked to be called. Deng twice survived being purged from Party leadership and had been tagged with the ultimate insult, Capitalist Roader. Deng took power in 1978 and began what was truly a great leap forward. Keeping Communist slogans, Deng introduced free enterprise to China's economy. As he famously said, "It doesn't matter if the cat is black or white, as long as it catches mice."[33] Heralding the change were the Four Modernizations: repairing the country's infrastructure, advancing technology, agriculture, and national defense. In 1980, to slow population growth, the government instituted a one-child policy. Husbands and wives were punished for an unauthorized pregnancy, and forcible abortion could be the consequence of a second pregnancy. Given the importance of male heirs, female infanticide became commonplace, so that since 1949 today's generation of young men face the prospect of never finding wives. One estimate projects that by the year 2020, the surplus of Chinese males will be larger than the entire population of Taiwan. And children, no longer plentiful, are much doted on and spoiled.

TIANANMEN SQUARE

Reform in a complex social system produces unintended consequences. As Deng's market reforms took hold, students and intellectuals hoped that China would follow the Soviet Union. There, *glasnost* (openness) was followed by greater political freedom that led, with breathtaking speed, to the collapse of the Soviet dictatorship. The logic was there for all to see: a free market involves more than buying and selling. It also brings the liberties of everyday life: freedom of information and discussion, freedom to live where one chooses, and freedom to choose one's education and vocation.

The upper ranks of China's Communist Party read history the same way but were resolved to prevent political change. Many still believed in a Communist future; most were determined to keep the privileges of power. And as the pace of economic reforms grew, other consequences

---

[32] Nen Cheng, *Life and Death in Shanghai* (New York: Penguin, 1988); Liang Hen and Judith Shapiro, *Son of the Revolution* (New York: Alfred A. Knopf, 1983).

[33] Speech at Communist Youth League Conference (July 1962).

followed: inflation, unemployment, the drift of rural Chinese to the cities in search of better jobs, the rise of a middle class, and the conspicuous display of China's new breed of millionaires. With little coordinated planning, students, workers, and intellectuals began demanding greater participation in government decisions and an end to government secrecy.

Figure 16.9. Tiananmen Square 1989

In April 1989 students began gathering in Tiananmen Square (named after the Gate of Heavenly Peace in what was once the Forbidden City). In May the government forbade all such gatherings and declared martial law on May 20, ordering that the square be cleared. In silent protest, 50,000 students and workers in the square began a hunger strike, erecting as a symbol of their goals a statue, the "Goddess of Liberty." The numbers soon welled to an estimated 100,000. On June 3 and 4, soldiers and tanks entered the square with orders to use deadly force to clear it. Because of a state visit by Mikhail Gorbachev, television crews were filming in Beijing. As viewers around the world watched, tear gas and bullets crushed the demonstrators. An estimated 2,000 to 3,000 died, and perhaps as many as 7,000 to 10,000 were injured. The "Tiananmen Massacre," as it was dubbed by newsmen, enabled the Communist Party to hold tight the apparatus of political control, while venturing further into a state-controlled market economy.

MAO IN RETROSPECT

Mao's body continues to lie in state in Beijing. His face stares out from the Gate of Heavenly Peace and from every Chinese bank note. The Party continues to rule with a heavy hand, but his economic policies have been repudiated. His death-laden policies (the Great Leap, the Cultural Revolution) are mildly criticized but not repudiated. To do so might subject the Party itself to repudiation.[34]

THE DRAGON AWAKES

By the standards of previous generations, China today is prosperous and prospering. Its economy is now the second largest in the world, second only to the United States. China's economy has been growing by almost 10 percent a year. And its per capita income has been growing by about 8 percent over the last three decades. Hundreds of millions have risen out of poverty, and infant mortality has plummeted. China is a country of millionaires, and where roads in cities used to pulsate with waves of bicycles, automobiles now choke the streets. Young people have thrown away the once-mandatory Mao denim tunic and trousers; they now dress in the latest western fashions, with cell phones as accessories. China's consumption of oil grows to rival that of the United States. Its industries now produce planes and missiles. China is a power to be reckoned with in international affairs. And to the detriment of the environment, China's manufactures flood the world. Wal-Mart, the world's largest retailer, is China's biggest customer. (Go into any Wal-Mart, K Mart, Toys R Us, or Target store; challenge yourself to find a product that is not made in China.)

Dissent remains a major concern for China's leaders. Journalists are monitored, and to keep them within approved boundaries, they are occasionally jailed for revealing "state secrets" (a catch-all category). Even so, as prosperity grows it tends to dampen dissent.

Perhaps the most striking portent of what lies ahead is revision of school textbooks. Communist ideology and recounting the heroic role of the People's Liberation Army have been all but eliminated. Mao is hardly mentioned. What are now stressed in schoolbooks are technology, globalization, and adapting to new ways.[35]

---

[34] See Roderick Macfarquhar and Micheal Scholenhals, *Mao's Last Revolution* (Cambridge: Harvard University Press, 2006).

[35] For additional reading, see Jonathan D. Spence, *The Search for Modern China* (New York: Norton, 1990) and Peter Hessler, *Country Driving: A Chinese Road Trip* (New York: Harper Perennial, 2011).

Figure 16.10. The Great Wall

THE SELECTIVE TRAVELER IN CHINA

China's vast size can easily daunt the traveler. Best to know before you go, and for that, a good guidebook is essential. Two excellent choices are *The Lonely Planet, China* and *Travel Around China*.

As Confucius once said, "The journey of a thousand miles begins with a single step." An excellent first step is Beijing's Tiananmen Square. Its acreage is a symbol of the country's vastness. Its Gate of Heavenly Peace is the site where Mao proclaimed the People's Republic. Mao and the Proclamation are marked by a giant portrait of Mao. The huge palaces of the Forbidden City were home to two dynasties. And the Great Wall of China is easily reached from Beijing.

Shanghai, China's great seaport, was and is the country's most cosmopolitan city. Great colonial buildings of the nineteenth century are on refurbished display, as are new and modern structures that underscore massive government investment. And well-preserved houses, ghosts of colonial glory, remind visitors of China's subservience to Europe in the eighteenth and nineteenth centuries.

Hong Kong is China's great shopping emporium. Crowds throng the streets day and night, and restaurants and hotels abound.

And finally, two wonderful journeys: by ship up the Yangtze to see the beautiful Three Gorges, and by train to Tibet, a journey of incredible mountain beauty.

Figure 16.11. Tiananmen Square

17. Japan: Swords and Butterflies

> The most beautiful sight in Japan...is the distant apparition of Fuji ...
> the most sacred mountain...and to ascend it at least once in a life-time
> is the duty of all who reverence the ancient gods.
> — Lafcadio Hearn, Fuji-No-Yama, 1898

Any number of words comes to mind when talking about Japan: Samurai, Shinto, Emperor, Empire of the Sun, cherry blossoms, Mount Fuji, industrial giant, cultural contradictions, transformation.[1] Japan's history is one of repeated transformations. In 1945 Japan changed from an arrogant military conqueror to a defeated empire ready to accept peaceful democracy. And earlier, in 1868 it changed from an isolated feudal society into a westernized, industrial nation.

Lafcadio Hearn, one of the first Westerners to settle in late 19th-century Japan, saw the contradictions in the Japanese culture wherever he looked. He viewed the esthetic appreciation of cherry blossoms and moonrise alongside the steel-hard outlook of a nation of warriors ready to die for the emperor. During World War II, Ruth Benedict, an anthropologist writing for the American military, made these contradictions the title of her influential book, *The Chrysanthemum and the Sword: Patterns of Japanese Culture.*

---

[1] The chapter is built on the following sources: Lafcadio Hearn's *Glimpses of Unfamiliar Japan* (Boston: Houghton Mifflin & Co., 1894), *Japanese Fairy Tales* (Tokyo: T. Hasegawa, 1898), and *Japan: An Attempt at Interpretation* (New York: Macmillan, 1904). Also see Jonathan Cott, *Wandering Ghost: The Odyssey of Lafcadio Hearn* (New York: Knopf, 1991).

As Hearn wrote, the butterfly is a favorite decoration for a woman's kimono; its soft, shimmering colors symbolize more than happiness. The butterfly also symbolizes two of Japan's oldest religious traditions: Shinto, in which gods inhabit all of nature, and Buddhism, with its promise of the soul released from future anguish after death. In Japan, Hearn said, an encounter with a cloud of butterflies is an encounter with departed souls. The Japanese themselves see the butterfly as a symbol of Japan's capacity for re-inventing itself—from egg to caterpillar to butterfly. Each stage is a metamorphosis, a seamless blending of being and becoming.

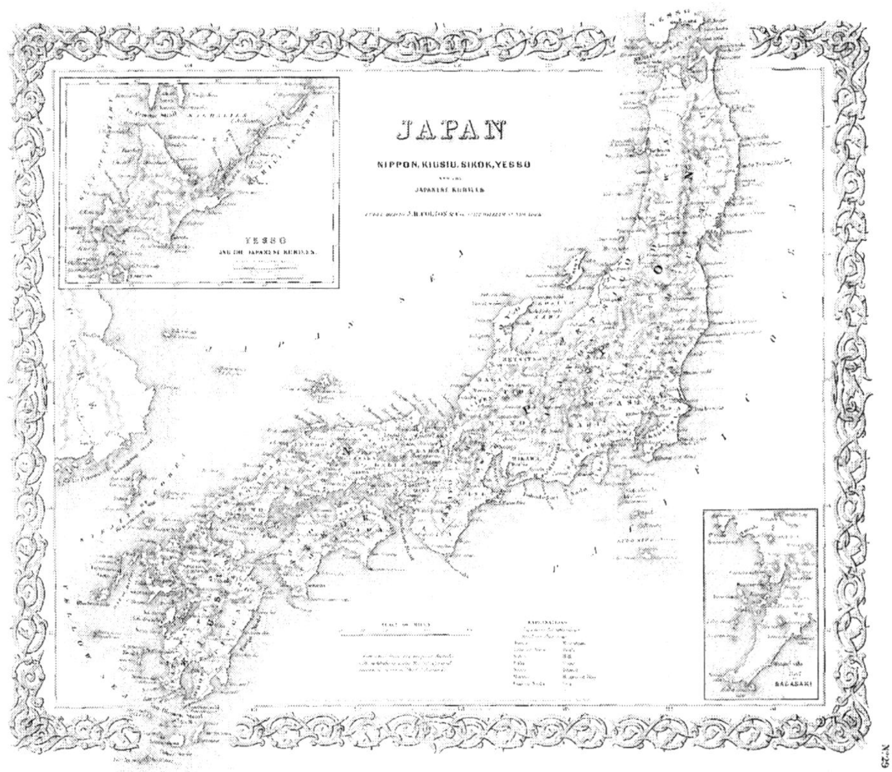

Figure 17.1. 1855 Colton Map of Japan

And what of the sword? It was the weapon of Japan's hereditary warrior class, the samurai. Every samurai carried two swords, one a long curved blade imbued with sacred power and the other a short dagger-like weapon. For the samurai, swords embodied his code of honor, Bushido: the way of the warrior. Two swords were a mark of the samurai. The short sword also carried the disgraced warrior into eternity. He used it for ritual suicide rather than face dishonor.

WHO WAS LAFCADIO HEARN?

Lafcadio Hearn (1850-1904) was himself a person of transformations. Born to an Irish father and Greek mother on the island of Levkos, Hearn was educated in Britain and Switzerland, lived in the West Indies, and became a newspaper reporter in Cincinnati. Sent to Japan on a magazine assignment in 1890, he took a Japanese wife, fathered a Japanese family, taught at Japanese universities, became a Japanese citizen, and changed his name to Yakumo Koizumi. His written and spoken Japanese was clumsy, but his writings about Japan charmed English-reading audiences, especially because he lived in Japan during a time of a political, economic, and social upheaval that began when four American warships entered Tokyo harbor in 1853.

WHAT WAS THE AMERICAN MISSION?

The American battle fleet (two paddle-wheel steamers and two sailing ships) was commanded by Commodore Mathew Perry, who carried a letter from President James Buchanan to the ruler of Japan. Japan had been closed to the outside world since 1638, when its de facto ruler, the Shogun (meaning he who quells barbarians), commanded all foreigners to leave or else be tortured and beheaded. (An exception was made for a limited number of Dutch traders.) The successor Shogun worried that foreign traders and missionaries sooner or later would bring foreign armies, which would ultimately lead Japan to fall under foreign control.

Reasons for worry abounded. Over the course of three centuries, much of the East—the Philippines, Malaysia, Indochina, and China—had been disrupted by European powers. The British fought two wars (the Opium Wars of 1839-42 and 1856-60) against China, aimed at forcing the latter to let the East India Company sell opium there. At the end of the First Opium War, China was forced to cede Hong Kong to Britain and to permit it to establish an extraterritorial enclave in Shanghai. In 1854 England and France were at war with Russia (The Crimean War), and they served notice that Russian ships would not be permitted to find safe harbor in Japan. The industrialized countries of the West were hungry for raw materials and markets. Africa, Asia, the Near East, and the Pacific Ocean islands were stark reminders of western colonization. First came merchants and missionaries. Then came western demands to control a country's trade. This was followed by demands that foreign merchants, missionaries, and sailors be governed by European laws and courts rather than by local laws and judges. Then came western warships and soldiers. And finally, what had once been an independent country was now a colony or, to use a gentler word, a protectorate. Feudal Japan was no match for western military power, and the Shogun and the other great lords feared that invading foreigners would destroy Japan's social structure.[2]

Figure 17.2. Commodore Matthew Perry

In the West, Japan was seen as a convenient refueling place for the China trade. Some claimed that Japan could supply coal for steamships en route to Asia. In a speech in the United States Senate, Daniel Webster declared that Japanese coal was nature's gift to the world and demanded that Japan sell it or trade it! As it happened, Japan had no coal to give or sell. Even so, Perry's black ships arrived in Tokyo harbor in 1853 on a mission to demand open trade.

Perry's message was direct, as armed marines quick-marched ashore, surrounding the message and the messenger, rifles at the ready. "I shall return in one year. If open trade is refused, I shall fire on your ports."[3] In 1854 Perry's fleet returned, and a fearful Japan entered into trade with the West. Nagasaki was the most important port for the new trade. It was the

---

[2] Each person lived an assigned, hereditary role that determined one's livelihood, manner of dress, food consumption, housing, and mode of behavior to one's peers, social superiors, and social inferiors.

[3] Wilber Cross and John B. Hefferman, *Naval Battles and Heros* (New York: Golden Press, 1960), 66-69.

city where traditional Japan confronted the West. And to dramatize that confrontation, it was Nagasaki that Puccini chose as home for his heroine, Cho-cho San, or Madame Butterfly. Visitors today can climb a hill leading from the port to the setting of the opera. They can visit Glover's house, the residence of a British merchant and the supposed setting for Puccini's opera. As visitors climb, loudspeakers sound plangent music from *Madame Butterfly*.

History rarely moves in a tidy circle. But If Nagasaki was one of the first Japanese ports open to the West, it is also the place of another great transformation, the end of the Japanese Empire. On August 9, 1945, a B-52 American bomber dropped an atom bomb on Nagasaki and the Mitsubishi arms factory. Nearly one-and-a-half square miles of the city were vaporized; nearly 74,000 died in the blast, and even more were wounded and disfigured. Ground zero for the bomb blast was the northern part of Nagasaki. It is now the site of the Peace Park. Statues, a fountain, walkways, and bouquets of flowers help with healing and remembering. And the visitor proceeds, conscious of the silence in the park.

HOW DOES GEOGRAPHY SHAPE JAPANESE CULTURE?

The islands of Japan lie one hundred miles from Korea and 450 miles from China. Seen on a map, the islands look like a giant bow, taut and ready to let fly an arrow eastward. Japan is an archipelago (literally, arc in the sea). It comprises more than one hundred islands, of which Kyushu, Shikou, Honshu, and Hokaido are the largest. The total land mass of Japan is about the size of California, but in that geography live more than 127 million people. By comparison, the vast territory of the United States contains more than 316 million. Much of Japan is mountainous, and only 12 percent of the land is arable. But Japan's arable land is intensely cultivated, and much of Japan's culture springs from its soil.[4]

From China, Japan learned to plant and harvest wet rice. Wet rice is labor intensive. Streams must be diverted. Shallow dams must be built around the rice fields. Rice shoots must be drilled by hand into wet earth. And the earth must be flooded during growing season and drained at harvest time. The entire production cycle requires cooperative work by villages and their families. Out of this cooperation have come centuries of deference to village elders and a strict family hierarchy. Villages keep century-long records of labor and obligations. Each person knows his or her place in the family and village hierarchy.

---

[4] Both "culture" and "cultivate" share the same Latin root.

As Ruth Benedict notes, wet-rice cultivation put a special stamp on Japanese culture.[5] In contrast to the West, where the evolution of democracy has been rooted in individual rights (The Magna Carta, The Declaration of Independence), rights in Japan began as group rights. Rights that an individual might have were derived from his or her place in the group. And as Benedict also notes, in the West, individual rights comport handily with a culture of personal responsibility and its companion, personal guilt. Both are tied to a religious and moral code (the Ten Commandments, The Sermon on the Mount, The Epistles of Paul). Breaking the moral code threatens to bring damnation and suffering after death.

Japan is a culture of shame. Group rights go hand in glove with shame. In shame cultures, moral transgressions bring shame and dishonor to one's family, one's clan, and one's associates. "Saving face" greatly matters in a shame culture. Never ask anyone directly if she has passed her examination or if he has been promoted.

In Japan today, even though wet-rice culture is no longer the spine that supports the nation's body, deference to those above you in the hierarchy still prevails. In the great matrix of obligation, it finds expression in the formality of exchanged bows and in modes of speech. The higher the person ranks in relation to you (also in the corporation, in the civil service, in the social structure), the deeper you bow, and the more deferential is the mode of address. The constant exchange of calling cards serves to fix one's place instantly in the social structure.

Giri, a sense of duty and obligation to others, was the fabric of traditional Japan. Since the Second World War, *Giri* has frayed, and the rituals of deference have rubbed away. Social rebels and teenagers often consider themselves exempt from the niceties of deference. But among the elderly and in rural Japan, *Giri* is deeply felt, and the rituals of deference are on fairly full display.

WHAT IS SHINTO?

> Where do they come from
> Those whom we so much dread?
> — W. H. Auden[6]

[5] See Ruth Benedict, *The Chrysamthemum and the Sword*, (Cleveland: Meridian Books, 1946).

[6] See John Haffenden, ed., *W.H. Auden: The Literary Heritage* (London: Routledge), 301-02.

Humans everywhere fear assault from sudden, violent, natural forces. The islands of Japan stand inside geology's Great Ring of Fire: a chain of volcanoes and earthquakes that circle the globe from the southern west coast of South America, northward to California, north again to Alaska and down along the coast of Asia, rushing south into Indonesia and Hawaii. Far beneath the earth's surface, tectonic plates grind and move against each other. Volcanoes erupt, earthquakes explode, typhoons lash the land, and great tidal waves (*tsunami*) rush through the oceans. Sited across the Ring of Fire, about sixty of Japan's 186 volcanoes are active, and earthquakes continue to shake Japan. In 1923 an earthquake killed 60,000 in Tokyo and 40,000 more in the surrounding territory.[7]

The ancient Japanese knew nothing of tectonic plates. To the Japanese, nature was to be placated and worshipped. Trees, mountains, streams, and rocks each had their gods, called *Kami*, and humans were expected to revere nature and worship the gods. Shinto shrines and temples continue to bind the Japanese to the natural world. Worshippers enter the temple grounds beneath a gateway (*Tori*) that separates the sacred from the secular, the finite world from the endless world of the gods. Worshippers rinse mouths and wash hands in rituals of bodily and spiritual cleansing. Shinto priests are the intermediaries between gods and humans, placating and supplicating gods on behalf of the prayerful.[8]

Shinto shrines are dedicated to a specific *Kami*, who responds to prayers and entreaties. On sale at temples and shrines are talismans, often small wooden placards, on which prayers and entreaties can be inscribed. Some speak to profound human aspiration: "May I live a just and honorable life." Others address more worldly concerns: "May I receive good grades on my examinations."

Shintoism does not demand moral absolutes (no Koranic injunctions or Ten Commandments). In their place it offers moral and spiritual pathways: be grateful for the blessings of the gods and the benefits of ancestors; be helpful to others without expecting reward; and pray that the nation may prosper and that others may live in peace.

Shinto priests perform marriage ceremonies, but they do not preside over funerals. Death is an impurity, an affront to eternal longings. There are no Shinto cemeteries. Death is the domain of Buddhists.

---

[7] Frank Lloyd Wright's Imperial Hotel was one of the few buildings to survive the earthquake.

[8] Western visitors to Shinto shrines may be surprised to discover that priests are both men and women.

WHAT IS JAPANESE BUDDHISM?

Sometime around 480 BCE, when Siddhartha Gautama, the Buddha, lay dying, his disciples pressed around him, seeking reassurance, pleading for further enlightenment.[9] "I am not a god," he said. "Find enlightenment within your person. Be a lamp unto yourself." And with those words, he entered the blessed state of Nirvana (literally, blowing out; the blowing out of desire, the source of suffering), the release of the human spirit into the infinite, spared the pain and suffering of the endless cycle of reincarnation. Basic to the Buddha's teachings are two principles: *Kharma* and *Dharma*. *Kharma* is the universal law of cause and effect: every bad deed produces bad consequences. *Dharma* is duty to oneself, to follow such pathways to enlightenment as one can find. As bad deeds multiply, *Kharma* condemns the bad-deed doer to an endless round of reincarnation and suffering. Conversely, it brings the good-deed doer to Nirvana.

Most people seek some form of immortality, some reassurance that there is life after death. Those seeking reassurance find guidance in another version of the Buddha's death. As he lay dying, he is said to have taken a leaf from the tree under which he lay: "Just as this leaf has many veins and the tree from which it comes has many leaves and many branches, so there are other pathways to salvation." Over the centuries, the austere branch of Buddhism has become known as Minhayana, literally the smaller vehicle, appealing to only a few. The Buddhism of many branches is Mahayana, the greater vehicle. Japanese Buddhism is Mahayana, with several branches and sects.

Characteristic of Mahayana is belief in Bodhisattva, an enlightened spirit worthy of salvation who has postponed entry to Nirvana to assist others in their own salvation. Bodhisattvas are themselves objects of prayer; their statues surround those of the Buddha who himself is prayed to as a god. In Japan, several forms of Buddhism proliferate. The Tendai sect (founded in the early 800s) believes the world to be the province of demons in bodily form that must be placated by special prayers and rituals. In contrast, the Pure Land school of Buddhism knows the afterlife to be a paradise of joy. Prayers are offered to Amida, a Bodhisattva who answers prayer by erasing sins and transgressions, thus assuring entry to the Pure Land. An offshoot of Pure Land Buddhism holds to the belief that the simplest prayer suffices, such as merely repeating the word "Amida." Critics call this "salvation on the cheap." A special form of Pure

---

[9] See Karen Armstrong, *Buddha* (New York: Viking, 2001) and Huston Smith, *The Religions of Man* (New York: Joanna Cotler Books, 1965), Part III.

Land Buddhism is Soka Gakkai. Adherents gather in great halls; brass bands play; gymnasts wheel and tumble. And prayers are shouted to ensure admission to the Pure Land.

Zen Buddhism intrigues Europeans and Americans.[10] Zen adherents use no sacred texts but build their search for enlightenment on enlightenment itself. Zen adherents focus their minds in an attempt to receive a transcendent truth. They sit motionless, intensely concentrating on a metaphysical puzzle given by a Zen master. The most famous puzzle is probably, "What is the sound of one hand clapping?" Another poses a similar mystery: "Why does water offer no resistance to the hand held like a blade, but noisily fights the hand brought down flat?" These puzzles, called *Koan,* are sometimes solved in a flash of inspiration, a transcendent moment called *Satori.*

Zen Buddhism had a special appeal for samurai. Battle-hardened soldiers all over the world understand Zen's appeal: total awareness of one's surroundings, unwavering mental concentration, all the while keeping the body in rigid control but ready to spring into action. Zen continues to appeal to samurai descendants and to those convinced that enlightenment must come from within, that enlightenment comes when we are a "lamp unto ourselves."

Zen Buddhism profoundly influences traditional Japanese esthetics, wherein beauty is found in simple forms, in the symmetry and asymmetry of nature, in the evanescent moment, such as, for example, moonrise, fog trailing across Mount Fuji, a rock garden of swept sand dominated by one or two oddly shaped stones, and a single bud bent low in a vase. Zen is closely associated with Japan's traditional tea ceremony, whose tea masters study for years to follow a strictly prescribed set of movements and gestures.

BEING AND BECOMING: WHAT WAS THE MEIJI RESTORATION?

Turmoil erupted in Japan in the aftermath of Commodore Perry's visit. The powerful nobles and their clans confronted difficult choices. They could continue to keep Japan closed to Westerners and face invasion. If they opened Japan to Westerners, on the other hand, Japan's tightly controlled social system and its traditional way of life would end. In either case, the old Japan would die.

Even before Perry's visit, battles were fought to see which powerful lord could topple the Shogun and seize control of the emperor. And added to Japan's sense of vulnerability were British, French, and Russian military campaigns in Asia. In 1839 and in 1856, Britain invaded

[10] See Ninian Smart, *The World's Religions*, 2nd ed. (Cambridge: Cambridge University Press, 1998) for a good discussion of Zen and Buddhism.

China (the Opium Wars) in reprisal for China's closing its ports to opium from India. One consequence of the First Opium War was China's ceding Hong Kong to Britain. From 1853 to 1856, France and Britain were at war with Russia. Even though the war was fought in the Crimea, Britain and France warned Japan against giving safe harbor to the Russian Far Eastern Fleet.

In the face of Perry's threat along with the consequences of the Opium Wars, in 1858 the Shogun signed an agreement with the United States to open six ports to trade and to permit Americans to live in Japan. Other powerful lords seized upon the Shogun's failure to keep barbarians out, and they conspired to seize the person of the emperor and, in his name, to create a new social and political regime organized around him.

According to tradition, lore, and Shinto teachings, the emperor was descended from a god. As such, he was divine. His divinity had been acknowledged and protected for more than 1,000 years, but his political authority had been far less than absolute. Now in 1868, the emperor was restored as divine head of government, surrounded by powerful lords and samurai who ruled with him and through him. Prince Mutusuhito became emperor taking the name Meiji—"Enlightened Rule."[11]

WHAT WERE THE MEIJI REFORMS?

The Meiji reforms remade Japan. Effective government now resided in the imperial court and its ministries. The great lords returned their land registers to the central government and became provincial governors. Samurai were either pensioned off or given posts in the new civil service. Unlike the knights of feudal Europe, samurai were literate, deeply immersed in esthetic pleasure and appreciation. First, of course, they were required to change their hairstyle by lopping off their traditional topknots. More important, they were forbidden to carry their swords. Peasants were required to take surnames and to assume the status of the emperor's subjects rather than serfs forbidden even to look upon lords and samurai.

Of more far-reaching effect, study groups were dispatched around the world to learn how western countries were run. From Prussia, Japan adopted aristocratic titles and forms of address (Baron So and So, not the British use of Lord So and So). Army organization and administration also followed Prussian models. National military conscription began in 1873. Great

---

[11] See Robert A. Rosenstone, *Mirror in the Shrine: American Encounters with Meiji Japan* (Cambridge: Harvard University Press, 1968). See also Ninian Smart, *The World's Religions*, 2nd ed. (Cambridge: Cambridge University Press, 1998) for a discussion of Shinto.

Britain became the model for the new Japanese navy. The Parliament in Westminster was the legislative model. The new legal code was patterned upon the Swiss. Significantly, little if anything was modeled upon the United States—too egalitarian and too populist was the explanation!

WHAT WAS THE NEW SHINTOISM?

A transformed Shinto became an important component of the Meiji transformation. The emperor's divinity was incorporated into Shinto liturgy, and government officials and members of the military swore absolute obedience to their ruler as a person and as a god. This manifested itself in most unusual ways. In 1912, at the emperor's death, an important government official killed himself out of reverence for his ruler, the same reverence that led thousands of Japanese soldiers to die fighting during World War II rather than betray their oath to the emperor by surrendering to the enemy.

WHAT WAS JAPAN'S NEW FOREIGN POLICY?

As Japan industrialized, military campaigns followed. Military leaders saw a stark lesson in world history. War was better than diplomacy. Respect for Japan would come only from the barrel of a gun. In 1904 Japan attacked Russia, defeated its army, and achieved a stunning naval victory at the battle of Tsushima. Japan was now a major world power. In the spoils of victory, Japan took control over the southern half of Sakhalin Island and brought Korea into its sphere of influence. In World War I, Japan joined the enemies of Germany and was rewarded at the Treaty of Versailles with Germany's Pacific Ocean territories—the Caroline and Marshal Islands and all the Marianas except Guam. Another post-Meiji transformation had begun. Japan was no longer just a country; it was now an overseas empire.

In 1931 Japan began an assault on China that once again transformed Japan. Its soldiers now practiced a brutal, terrorizing military strategy. In 1937 the Japanese army overran Nanking, China. Looting, rape, and pillage on a massive scale followed. General Matsui Iwani ordered all resistance brutally crushed. Tens of thousands of women were raped. Somewhere between 100,000 and 300,000 people died. Surrounding towns were leveled and burned.[12]

---

[12] At the end of World War II, General Matsui was executed as a war criminal. See Iris Chang, *The Rape of Nanking* (New York: Basic Books, 1998), for a riveting account.

The last chapter in the Meiji transformation began on December 7, 1941, with the surprise attack on Pearl Harbor in Hawaii. By 1942, the empire was at its apogee. It ran from the Aleutian Islands in a great arc southward to the Solomon Islands, the Philippines, great swatches of north New Guinea, Indonesia, the western-seaboard provinces of China, Indochina, and Burma—up to the very borders of India.

British casualties in the war for the Far East might be said to begin with the loss of Singapore, where 9,000 empire troops were killed or wounded, and 130,000 surrendered to the Japanese. Many died in building the notorious bridge over the River Kwai. American casualties began with the bombing of Pearl Harbor, with about 3,000 deaths. Estimates of lives lost on both sides of the conflict are next to impossible to establish. In China, for example, deaths from disease and military action are thought to run upwards of at least thirty million. The American war against Japan was long and bloody, in places and islands fetid with heat, rain, and disease-carrying insects. In the battle for Guadalcanal, for instance, 60,000 soldiers and marines entered combat, and 1,592 were killed; hundreds more suffered wounds and disease. More than 100,000 Americans took part in the battle for Iwo Jima; U.S. land casualties were 45,000 dead, 300 missing, and almost 16,000 wounded. In total, the United States sent 1.25 million men to the Pacific War. Total casualties were on the order of 171,000, of whom 27,000 are counted as dead or missing.

Millions died in the long years of Japan's war for the Far East. The fulcrum of Japan's surrender was the dropping of the two atom bombs, in which huge sections of Nagasaki and Hiroshima were burned out and vaporized. In Hiroshima on August 6, 1945, between 60,000 and 70,000 died instantly as a consequence of the first bomb. In Nagasaki three days later, the second bomb was dropped in response to the failure of the Japanese government to surrender. There, the instant death toll was about 40,000. In the imperial palace, those opposed to surrender exchanged gunfire with those willing to end the war. As a last act of a dying empire, imperial princes were dispatched to far-flung fighting forces to persuade their officers that the emperor himself wished them to lay down their arms. The formal surrender took place aboard the Battleship Missouri on September 2, 1945. Though they could not then imagine it, the Japanese nation trembled on the brink of another transformation.[13]

---

[13] For a discussion of the role of the Japanese emperor and the American decision to drop the Atomic Bomb, see David G. McCullough, *Truman* (New York: Simon and Schuster, 1992). Other references are David Boyle, *World War II: A Photographic History* (New York: Sterling, 1998) and Rafael Steinberg, *Island Fighting (World War II)* (New York: Time-Life, 1978). Also, see two movies directed by Clint Eastwood: *Letters from*

Figure 17.3. Ruined city of Hiroshima, U. S. National Archives

HOW WAS JAPAN TRANSFORMED?

Surrendered Japan was a burnt-out country. Its cities were devastated, and its industries and transport were smashed. Hunger stalked the land. Added to the country's burdens, more than six million soldiers and civilians were rounded up and dumped back onto the Japanese homeland. The Americans occupied Japan almost without incident. A nation once ready to resist invaders step by step, with pitchforks and scythes if need be, accepted them quiescently. Under the terms of surrender, the emperor renounced his divinity. Great estates were broken up and distributed to those who farmed them. Industrial wealth was dispersed according to the precepts of America's anti-monopoly laws. A new Constitution proclaimed the sovereignty of the people's will. To that purpose, it established universal suffrage and parliamentary governance. Enshrined in the Constitution was a provision whereby Japan renounced war; the country could create a defense and security force, but not an army or navy.

Iwo Jima (2006) and *Flags of Our Fathers* (2006). Finally, see *The Last Samurai* (2003) starring Tom Cruise fighting to protect the last samurai warriors after the Meiji Restoration.

HOW DID THE KOREAN WAR TRANSFORM JAPAN AGAIN?

To use the butterfly metaphor, Japan's transformation was in its chrysalis stage, its poverty painful, its industries weak. Then the Korean War erupted in late June 1950, and the United States made Japan its military provider and military-staging area. Japan's economy thrummed, and a new creature emerged—not a butterfly but an economic giant.

A thousand years of agricultural poverty and the privations of an empire at war had made the Japanese a culture of thrift. In post-war Japan, the savings rate of workers and families was the highest in the world. Liquid capital in banks fueled industrial expansion. Also important to industrial success was the old tradition of loyalty to great lords and to clan and village leaders. This was now transformed into loyalty to employers and companies and willingness to work long and hard to assure corporate success. Loyalty, along with 1,000 years of deference to those in power, enabled the Ministry of International Trade and Industry (MITI) to direct economic growth by offering loans on favorable terms to industries marked for success.

The new Japan was not without its economic problems. In recent years it has struggled against a worldwide economic downturn exacerbated by questionable bank loans. But even so, Japan today compared with Japan in 1945 is an amazing transformation.

WHAT REMAINS OF THE OLD JAPAN?

Visitors to Tokyo see modern Japan in Technicolor splendor: sleek, high-rise buildings and a glaring, insistent profusion of neon signs. Crowds throng the streets; occasionally an older woman will be wearing traditional sandals and a kimono. Beneath the pavement is an efficient subway system that carries so many passengers that, it is said, Norwegians studied its passenger-loading arrangements to improve packing sardines. English signs are everywhere, but they jar the English speaker. Words seem to be either out of context or meaningless in their context. ("Inferno Is Cream; After Shove Shaving Crème"). Layered over and under the new Japan are thought-waves of the old Japan.

Two words capture these thought ways: *uchi* and *soto. Uchi* denotes house, community, the spirit of Japan. The Japanese, it is often observed, are race proud. *Uchi* reflects that pride. *Soto* connotes all things beyond the spirit of Japan. Foreigners (*gai jin*) are *soto,* and foreign things are *soto.* One's forebears may have lived in Japan for a century (Koreans, for example) but one is still *soto.* One's forebears may have lived abroad for a century (the Japanese in Brazil, for example), but the Brazilian Japanese returning to Japan is regarded as *uchi.* Lafcadio Hearn, whom the Japanese called the ghost from the West, would have understood.

HOW IS JAPAN'S HISTORY EMBEDDED IN ITS CITIES?

Japan is a seabound nation dotted with harbors and ports. Country and city are quickly accessible to cruise-ship visitors. For example, Yokahama and Tokyo are embraced by Tokyo Bay. And Kobe, Osaka, and Hiroshima are easily accessible from Kyoto. More important for the visitor is Japan's refusal to let modernity tear down history's treasures. Tokyo, with some of the most valuable real estate in the world, holds tightly to the vast acreage of the Imperial Palace and its surrounding park. The busy port of Nagasaki keeps sacred the site of the city's atomic explosion, as does Hiroshima's Peace Park, the memorial to the approximately 200,000 who ultimately died in August 1945 in both cities. An earlier history is commemorated in Osaka, whose beautiful medieval castle is flanked by boxy, modernist skyscrapers.

And many will argue that the two most beautiful historic sites in Japan are lovingly preserved. One is the shrines and temples of Kyoto, whose quiet gardens, long rooflines (the Heian Shrine), and three-storied temple pagoda evoke a sense of sacred beauty in visitors and supplicants alike. The second is the architectural complexity and beautiful symmetry of Shirasagijo Castle (the White Heron Castle), about twenty-five miles west of Osaka near the city of Himeji. The castle, built in less than a decade (1609-1619) by about 25,000 workers, soars 150 feet skyward, with each of its many roofs rising on top of one another in a graceful upward curve. Its high keep (donjon) is protected from earthquakes by massive pillars that rise up from the ground and give and sway, but do not break, when the ground trembles. The castle is a monument to feudal Japan, and as a tour guide may say, it evokes the ghosts of samurai and their great lords, the Shogun.[14]

A POSTSCRIPT ON JAPANESE WRITING

There are essentially two writing systems in use today. The alphabet-based writing system uses symbols (letters) to represent sounds. A group of letters, when sounded aloud or in the mind, creates words. The great advantage of an alphabet writing system is its simplicity and efficiency. Using only twenty-six letters, the English alphabet gives meaning to the (nearly) half-million words listed and defined in the *Oxford English Dictionary.* In contrast, a picture-based writing system requires thousands of pictographs (symbols) to convey meaning. Chinese is a pictograph system of separate symbols, or characters, for every word. A complicated text, the Confucian Analects for example, uses about 50,000 symbols. Two great advantages of the Chi-

---

[14] See *Great Buildings of the World* (New York: Time Incorporated Specials, 2004).

nese writing system are that it has no connection with the spoken word, and the pictographs have not changed for 2,000 years. As a result, a literate Chinese can read whatever is written down, even though he or she may speak any one of a dozen or so Chinese languages and dialects. And even though a document may be 2,500 years old, literate persons can still understand it.

Written Japanese is based on Chinese pictographs. But written Japanese is more complicated than Chinese. Japanese is a blend of three different systems, one of which is composed of Chinese-like pictorial characters called *kanji* and two alphabets (*hiragana* and k*atakana*), which are really two versions of the same set of sounds. There are over 40,000 *kanji*, but about 2,000 represent 95 percent of characters typically used in written text.[15]

Katakana is often used to denote foreign words, especially proprietary ones (think Wheaties or Coca Cola). Hiragana written in small symbols above the main text reveals to the reader which of the many possible interpretations of the kanji characters is intended. Japan is a country with an astonishing 99 percent literacy rate. Many claim that the intellectual skills and mental dexterity required to achieve that literacy contribute mightily to Japan's technological achievements.

The historian knows that the past informs the present and the present influences the future. As citizens in a society of transformations, the Japanese understand these ideas. And the wise traveler can share that understanding by joining the Japanese in any number of collective experiences: climbing Mount Fuji to watch a sunrise, the solemnity of a visit to the site of the World War II atomic impact, or perhaps the joy and excitement of a kimono shop to admire the beauty of the garment—its shimmering silk adorned with flowers, butterflies, or birds. And if visitors are tempted to invest in that beauty, they may wish to consider Shakespeare's advice: "Costly thy habit as thy purse can buy."[16]

---

[15] http://www.guidetojapanese.org/writingsys.html.

[16] Hamlet, Act 1, Scene 3, Page 3.

18. Vietnam: The Dragon Smiles

For most Americans, Vietnam is a war, not a country. For many others, Vietnam is the country that defeated the United States. It is also a puzzle. How did a society whose farmers still walked behind water buffalo manage to defeat the best-equipped, most technologically advanced army in the world? And for most Vietnamese, the American war was only one war in a long list of foreign invasions.[1]

---

[1] For additional reading, see Frances Fitzgerald, *Fire in the Lake* (Boston: Little, Brown: 1972), an exploration of Vietnamese culture and history set against the context of the American intervention in Vietnam; David Lamb, *Vietnam Now* (New York: Public Affairs, 2002), the story of a reporter returning to Vietnam who examines life and survival after the American war; Stanley Karnow, *Vietnam: A History* (New York: Viking Press, 1983), the definitive work on the Vietnam War; and John R. Jones, *A Guide to Vietnam* (Chalfont St. Peter: Bradt, 1989). Also useful are Larry Berman, *Lyndon Johnson's War: The Road to Stalemate* (New York: Norton, 1989); Chester Cooper, *The Lost Crusade: America in Vietnam* (New York: Dodd, Mead, 1970); David Halberstam, *The Fifties* (New York: Villard Books, 1993), especially Chapter 27; Neil Sheehan, *A Bright, Shining Lie* (New York: Random House, 1988), the account of an American participant in the war who examines the falsehoods of the generals and the American government; and John Laffin, *Brassey's Dictionary of Battles* (London: Brassey's Defence Publishers, 1986). See also the movie *Indo-China* (1992), the story of French rule of Indochina.

Wise travelers to Vietnam are likely to know only of the American war. And if they are American travelers, they may be apprehensive about their welcome (or lack of it) to Vietnam. Not to worry. Travelers will be pleased by the warm welcome and kindness of the people. Vietnam has a population of about eighty-nine million, about two-thirds of whom were born after the American war. Small wonder, then, that more than half of Vietnam has no memory of that war. Travelers will also be pleased by the number of Vietnamese who speak English. (Only the older generation remembers its colonial French.)

Figure 18.1. Map of Vietnam

THE VIEW COMING UPRIVER TO HO CHI MINH CITY

As ships churn up the Mekong, travelers see sights familiar to Joseph Conrad and Somerset Maugham: cargo ships, sampans (with laundry strung on the deck), children scampering on cargo, ferries, fishing boats, tugs—a busy river traffic. Houses and shacks on the riverbank, and closer to the city, church spires and hotel rooftops in the distance. The spell of Conrad is broken, or at least interrupted, by giant signs looming across the water: Toshiba, Sony, and Honda. But at the same time, ships will berth in the city, and the traveler can walk or ride directly to the landmarks of former Saigon.

Traffic is clotted and intense. There are no stoplights or police to punctuate the swarms of motorbikes and cyclos, a bicycle or motorbike welded to a rickshaw. The cautious traveler will do well to cross the street while in the company of locals. The less cautious may follow local advice: walk into traffic slowly, alertly. Those on wheels are accustomed to pedestrians. They will steer around you!

Figure 18.2. Mekong River

All of Vietnam seems to be on wheels, wearing shorts, jeans, ragged clothes, baseball hats, and varnished straw, conical farm hats. A few riders zoom along in elegant display: women riding motorbikes, wearing long cloth gloves, conical straw hat, dressed in an *ao dai*—tight trousers beneath a silk sheath.

SAIGON AND VIETNAM: WHAT'S IN A NAME?

Saigon is the former name of Ho Chi Minh City, a name bestowed on the "Father of Vietnamese Independence," the man who led the war, first against the French and then against the United States. Seen on a map, Vietnam resembles an elongated "S" joined and bisected by two great river systems: The Red River and the Mekong. The country extends north to south about 1,000 miles; it is narrow-waisted, and at Da Nang, where the waist pinches, it is no more than thirty miles wide west to east. China is on the north, Laos and Cambodia to the west. East and southeast is the South China Sea. Mountains and jungle are the usual description of the terrain, but a more precise description might be a low, flat delta in the south and north, highlands in the center, and mountains in the far north and northwest. Climate and weather are tropical, with monsoon rains, typhoons, and humid heat.

Figure 18.3. Saigon/Ho Chi Minh City

Perhaps as early as 5000 BCE, warring ethnic groups were scattered across the mountains and northern deltas of today's Vietnam. The dominant ethnic group called themselves Viet; over time, Viet was conjoined with the Chinese word for south, *nam*. Vietnam is a modern coinage, an elision of the prior name, Viet Nam. Today, the country's formal name is the Socialist Republic of Vietnam, and the socialist in the title salutes the realities of government:

whatever the formal institutions (National Assembly; Prime Minister), power lies with Vietnam's Communist Party and its self-selected and self-contained power elite.

HOW DO OLD AND NEW SAIGON COMPARE?

France made Saigon the capital of its Vietnam holdings. Canals were filled in and replaced by wide boulevards. In architecture, Saigon was a distant mirror of Paris. Hotels and the city hall were and are nineteenth-century *Belle Epoch*. The cathedral is transcribed Gothic. As Saigon prospered, Chinese artisans and merchants brought market economics and prosperity to the southern part of Vietnam.

In 1975, as the last Americans were airlifted from the roof of the American embassy in Saigon, all of Vietnam came under Communist control. Private property was outlawed, and the government controlled buying and selling. Former landlords and middle-class business people were sent to labor camps, where they learned to repent their beliefs and the sins of their former lives. Vietnam's economy then stagnated to the point of being dependent on gifts and loans from Russia and China. Once an exporter of rice, Vietnam now became dependent on rice imports to feed its population.

In the 1980s Vietnam began changing its economic policies. The country's politburo followed the lead of China: keep tight political control but reintroduce marketplace economics—disguised, of course, under proper socialist names. *Doi Moi* is the new economic regime. Under it, Ho Chi Minh City is the engine that carries the country to rising incomes and prosperity. Prosperity, of course, is relative. In 2004 the average per capita income was slightly more than one dollar per day or around $400 per year. But is has risen rather dramatically since, reaching $1,232 per year in 2009 and $1,911 in 2013.[2]

Hundreds of shop stalls line the streets, their owners sitting outside on short-legged chairs. They chat with neighbors and passersby, eating and cooking out on the sidewalk. Gold markets, jade markets, clothes markets, produce markets—each has its geography and its vast, covered enclosure. The Vietnamese are brilliant artisans. They fabricate designer-labeled clothes, oil paintings carrying museum-coveted signatures, newly forged "ancient" samurai swords, fake zippo lighters inscribed with American soldiers' names and—no need for counterfeit labels and signatures—beautiful embroideries. Except for foodstuffs, bargaining for goods is a gentle exchange. Cheerful smiles prevail.

---

[2] The World Bank; data.worldbank.org/indicator/NY.GDP.PCAP.CD.

HOW DO SAIGON AND HANOI COMPARE?

The Vietnamese often say that the North (meaning Hanoi) won the war, but Ho Chi Minh City (meaning Saigon) won the victory. What does this mean? It is simple. While Hanoi stands steadfast as the political capital and stronghold of the Communist Party, it is Saigon that drives the engines of economic success. It is Saigon that makes the country prosperous.

While Saigon is a modern city, laid out by the French sometime after 1859, Hanoi is an ancient capital, built on the banks of the Red River. Legend has it that a king seeking an auspicious place for his capital saw a golden dragon rise out of one of the city's eleven lakes and ascend to the sky. The fortunes of the city rose and fell with successive kings, but in 1882 the French took it over, and today's modern city began.

Figure 18.4. Hanoi

The symbolic center of the city is the vast, grey stone mausoleum of Ho Chi Minh on Ba Dinh Square. The mausoleum is the proud, imposing commemoration of the victorious war for independence, even though it defies Ho's wish to be cremated. Nearby is Ho's simple cottage and work room; many would say a truer expression of his life and work—"I am of no importance; independence is all important." Around the corner from the cottage is a 900-year-old pagoda, which many would also say better reflects the spirit of Ho. The One Pillar Pagoda rises from a single stone pillar to "float" over a Buddhist pond. The pond's lotus flower memorializes the Buddha's search for noble truths.

Buddhism is the religious foundation of Vietnam. Its source is India. The mausoleum symbolizes the modern, secular foundation of Vietnam, a secular foundation that accords with the teachings of Confucius: honor your ancestors. And within walking distance of the mausoleum is the Temple of Literature, representing another Chinese pillar of Vietnam society. In the temple are sanctuaries that celebrate the life and spirit of Confucius with his moral code based on *jen*, right-heartedness (Do not do to others what you would not have them do to you. Give proper respect to ancestors, to ruler, to father, to mother, to siblings, to friends). Until the European intrusions, the rulers of Vietnam ruled through mandarins, officials who obtained their post through success in scholarly examinations. On the grounds of the temple are steles or slabs of stone, celebrating the achievements of the greatest scholars, those whose examinations propelled them into the upper ranks of the mandarins.

HOW DID INDIA AND FRANCE GIVE VIETNAM ITS RELIGIOUS ROOTS?

India's missionaries, dispatched by the Emperor Ashoka (sometime shortly after 260 BCE) carried Buddhism to India. Initially it was an austere Buddhism (Minhayana), in which a righteous life promised no more than an end to the never-ending cycle of reincarnation and the sufferings of earthly existence. Over time, Hinayana Buddhism developed from earlier foundations. With Hinayana, a righteous life would lead to a happier incarnation and, beyond that, to entry into Paradise: the Pure Land Buddhism of eternal pleasures.

Monks and their begging bowls are part of the human landscape in Vietnam, but much more so in the north. In the nineteenth century the French gave protection to Catholic missionaries, and Catholicism began to spread and flourish. In 1954, as Vietnam began dividing into north and south, rumors of impending persecution in the Communist North sent one million Catholics south, seeking the protection of the southern Republic and its Catholic President.

In stark contrast to Christianity, Buddhism is a welcoming, accommodating religion. One can be both a Buddhist and Hindu, for example, or a Buddhist and a Taoist, or a Buddhist and anything other than a monotheist. (Christians, Jews, and Muslims cleave to the wording and spirit of the First Commandment.) As a consequence, eclectic religions proliferate in Vietnam, especially in the more religiously relaxed south. Here, the wise traveler will be dazzled by a Cao

Dai temple whose communicants celebrate both Asian and western religions and whose saints include Napoleon, Sun Yat-Sen, Joan of Arc, and Winston Churchill.[3]

HOW DID CHINA CREATE THE SECULAR CULTURE OF VIETNAM?

Centuries of Chinese rule north of Da Nang laid the foundations of Vietnamese society: family and clan. Most villages have their clan halls that hold clan records and statues to family gods. Ancestors are respectfully invoked in prayer and prayed to but are not worshipped in the western sense. They are asked to mediate between the nuclear family members and gods, demons, spirits, and the forces of nature. The family in Vietnam is bound by the Confucian code of respect and hierarchy. Everyone has a place; everyone knows his or her place. The mother owes respect and obedience to the father. The younger brother owes as much to the older brother. The older brother owes obedience and respect to the father. And the younger friend owes honor and respect to the older friend. The living and the dead of the clan and the village are joined in a network of respect across generations. This is why the American program of relocating families and villages offended the Vietnamese, as relocation severed those ancient ethical and religious ties.

Until the arrival of the French, the Vietnamese used a writing system composed of Chinese ideographs.[4] To achieve literacy in an ideographic language requires years of patient study with revered and respected teachers. And those who mastered the written language were themselves prized and revered. The great achievers in the state-run examinations were honored with memorial tablets, and the very best were co-opted into the mandarinate, the civil service rulers of the state.

HOW HAS THE SEA AFFECTED VIETNAM'S HISTORY?

Without the tropical waters of the Pacific and Indian Oceans, Vietnam would not be awash with monsoon rains, and without monsoon rains, there would be no abundant rice crop: three per year in the South, two per year in the North. Vietnam's coastline, stretching 1,900 miles along the South China Sea, abuts the sea lanes that join the Pacific and Indian Oceans. Ships

---

[3] See Karen Armstrong, *Buddha* (New York: Viking, 2001) and Donald Swearer, *Buddhism and Society in Southeast Asia* (Chambersburg, PA: Anima Books, 1981).

[4] As is the case in China, the meaning of the ideographs is nearly immutable. But the spoken word attached to the ideograph varies with district and dialect.

have coasted Vietnam since ancient times, and its ship-lane location invited the predatory attention of Europe from the sixteenth century on.

The Portuguese came first, then the Dutch, English, and French. In 1861 the French captured Saigon and began extending control west and north. In just over two decades (1881), France had installed itself in three regions and reduced those regions to protectorates and colonies: Tonkin in the north, Anam in the center, and Indochina in the south. French control expanded to include Laos and Cambodia. By 1900, these two countries, along with Tonkin, Anam, and the south of Vietnam (Indochina), had fused into French Indochina.

Long before French incursions, the Vietnamese had been fighting Chinese invasions for more than 1,000 years. Sometime in the second century BCE, a renegade Chinese general created a kingdom in northern Vietnam. In the first century BCE, the armies of the Chinese emperor created a province extending south to today's Da Nang, called the province of Giao Chi.

WORLD WAR II

As noted earlier, the name Vietnam was coined from Viet Nam, and it emerged during the final years of World War II. The French had been cruel colonizers, forcing the Vietnamese to abandon village self-sufficiency and barter (mostly rice) to serve as poorly paid wage workers on French-owned plantations. With wages in hand, workers were forced to pay taxes in support of the colonial government.

When Japanese armies overran Southeast Asia, Japan's alliance with the Vichy government enabled the French to retain administrative control over their colonies. But war brings opportunities as well as dangers. Vietnamese revolutionaries joined the fight against Japan in hopes of establishing a free Vietnam at war's end.

Ho Chi Minh was one such revolutionary. His name, one of many pseudonyms, means "One Who Enlightens." He went abroad in 1911 working on a French liner. During World War I, he may have been one among the thousands of Vietnamese working in French munitions factories. In 1919, during the Paris Peace Conference, he sent a petition to Woodrow Wilson pleading that Vietnam be allowed the "self determination" that Wilson had proclaimed to be the right of all people. When his petition was swallowed by the indifference of the victors, Ho joined the Communist Party, moved to Moscow, and became an agent of world revolution. He returned to Vietnam in 1941, working with American agents in the war against the Japanese. At war's end and with the help of American translators, he spoke at a rally in Hanoi, proclaiming the words of The Declaration of Independence.

Figure 18.5. Ho Chi Minh

But once again, Americans listened with deaf ears. Fear of communism was the new American foreign policy. President Harry Truman supported France in its demands to reclaim its former colonies. American money and supplies went to the French, and the war against Japan was now replaced by the French war against the Vietnamese. The statistics of the war reveal Vietnamese determination. This war lasted from late 1945 to 1954. When it ended, 50,000 French lives were lost and an additional 100,000 wounded. More than $2 billion was spent on the war. When the final battle at Dien Bien Phu was lost, France did not concede defeat but insisted on a division of Vietnam along the seventeenth parallel longitude—Ho's regime in the North and a republican regime in the South. The southern Republic was headed by a President who had been educated by the French. Even at the outset, the new southern Republic was in difficulty. Its President was a Catholic in an overwhelmingly Buddhist country. And the division of Vietnam was to be only temporary. A referendum was promised; the entire country was to vote and thus choose its form of government. But there was a shadow over the future. This shadow was the refusal of the Republic of the South, with its American backers, to permit a referendum. They knew that a referendum would bring the entire country under Communist control.

THE AMERICAN WAR

Americans came to Vietnam in the context of the Cold War and with a conviction ("the domino theory") that if Vietnam succumbed to communism, all of Southeast Asia would follow inexorably. Initially, under President John Kennedy, only supplies and American advisors came to assist the Army of the Republic of Vietnam (ARVN). As the ARVN faltered, more Americans were posted to the Republic of Vietnam. Under President Lyndon Johnson, an alleged and unproven shooting incident in 1964 in the Gulf of Tonkin produced a Congressional Resolution granting war powers to the President, that is, to do what was necessary to win the war.

From that point, there was no turning back. The domino theory stood as one pillar of the American war. The other was a widespread conviction that if the United States failed to crush the Communists of the Hanoi regime, America would forfeit the respect and the allegiance of democratic societies worldwide.

As the war proceeded, opposition grew, especially among draft-age American youth. As the war continued, the presence of American troops in Vietnam escalated. And as the war went forward, American strategy now tried to inflict damage on the North (through bombs, defoliation of forests, and resettlement of villages) sufficient to bring the enemy to the bargaining table. In the end, all such strategy failed. This policy failure is still being debated in America today. Some argue that the war was lost because of domestic opposition. Others suggest that the war was lost because the battlefront had no fixed lines of engagement—the same village had to be recaptured over and over again. Others argue that the loss came from America's failure to understand the culture of Vietnam. One such example was the ill-fated policy to remove villagers to a new location, which disrupted the centuries-long connection between families and their ancestors.

And at the head of this line of argument are three other hard facts. First, the ARVN was not as willing to die for its government as their opponents were willing to die for theirs. Second, as generals of the North (General Giap, supreme leader) repeatedly insisted, if you kill ten of us, ten more will take their place. Third is the old observation that men will die for a dogma, but few will sacrifice for a mere conclusion. The Communists had dogma on their side. The Americans had reasoned conclusion. And as chief architect of the war, U.S. Secretary of Defense Robert McNamara said in retrospect, "We were wrong, terribly wrong." Statistics tell the story. More than 2.5 million Americans fought in Vietnam. More than 58,000 died there. For the Vietnamese, in total, the war cost three million lives.

RESIDUES OF THE AMERICAN WAR

Travelers now see old American army trucks rumbling down the road. They sometimes observe legless men and women hobbling down the street. More than three million land mines continue to mutilate, and more than 38,000 people have been killed since war's end. But they also see young faces, too young to remember war and hardship. Perhaps the most visible reminder of the war are those who escaped to the United States as the war was ending or during its immediate aftermath, where their children and grandchildren now live.

OCEANIA

19. Australia: The Culture of Distance

Without evil, there would be no history,
— Manning Clark[1]

And he sees the vision splendid of the sunlit plains extended,
And at night the wondrous glory of the everlasting stars.
— A.B."Banjo" Patterson[2]

Australia is the world's largest island and the world's smallest continent, less than three million square miles (about the size of the United States). With a population of over twenty-three million, it is also the least populated continent, except, of course, for Antarctica. Eighty-five percent of Australians live on the Boomerang Coast, a narrow arc along the southeastern seaboard that runs from Melbourne to Brisbane. Australia stretches about 2,500 miles west to east and about 2,000 miles south to north. As a result, Perth on the east coast is closer to Singapore and Bali than to cities on the west coast. Those who travel inland from Perth will find a mostly empty continent for about 2,000 miles. Two-thirds of Australia is in the tropics, but only 3 percent of the population lives there.[3]

---

[1] See Manning Clark's *A History of Australia*, (Melbourne University Press, 1993). It was originally published in six volumes between 1962 and 1987.

[2] "Clancy of the Overflow" (Poem), 1889.

[3] Source material for this chapter includes Ross Terrill, *The Australians* (New York: Simon and Schuster, 1987); Robert Hughes, *The Fatal Shore: The Epic of Australia's Founding* (New York: Vintage, 1988); in the words of Arthur Schlesinger "The enthralling account of Australia's tragic origins is history of the highest

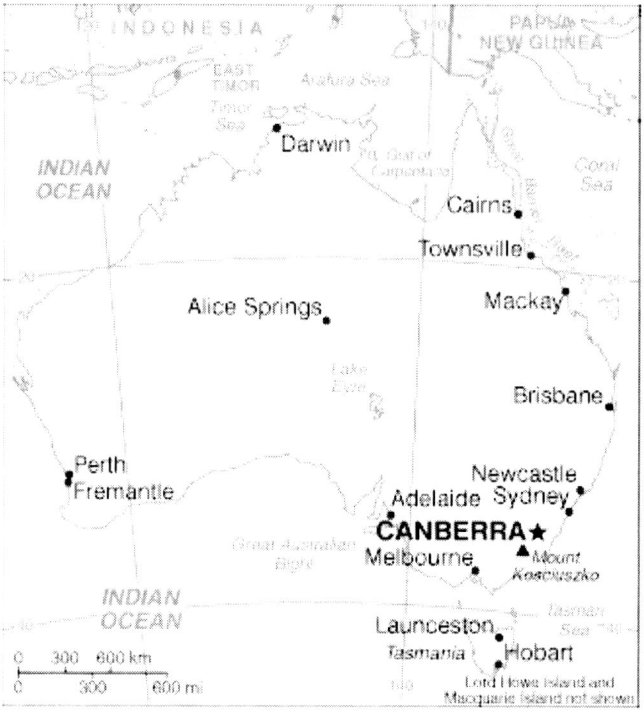

Figure 19.1. Map of Australia

Australians are famous for their breezy, informal manners and their gift for slang: barbie for barbeque, roo for kangaroo, mossie for mosquito, arvo for afternoon, Oz for Australia, and, of course, Aussie for Australian. Australia is also famous for its beliefs and myths. Australia is an urban and suburban nation where white-collar workers outnumber blue-collar. Even so, Australians cherish the idea that theirs is still a frontier society, where hardy folk brave the rigors of the outback and the bush and where, at heart, most every man is the movie hero, Crocodile Dundee.[4]

Everything runs backward in Australia, goes the old saying. The platypus is a mammal that lays eggs. Summer in London is winter in Australia. The white swans of Europe are black in Australia. In most of the world, trees shed their leaves in the autumn; in Australia, trees keep

order…" See also Paul Theroux, *The Happy Isles of Oceana: Paddling the Pacific* (New York: G.P. Putnam's Sons, 1992).

[4] See Donald Horne, *The Lucky Country* (New York: Penguin, 1964), 8. A dour view is found here: "A lucky country run by second-rate people who share its luck."

their leaves but shed their bark. Australia has birds that cannot fly and flowers that have no scent.

Eons ago, Australia was part of a huge land mass that geologists call Gondwanaland. Sometime between 350 and 200 million years ago, the land mass broke up and Australia drifted away, taking along plants and animals found nowhere else in the world: the kangaroo, the wallaby, the platypus, the wombat, and the eucalyptus. Ayers Rock, near Alice Springs, dates from the Gondwanaland epoch. It is the oldest and largest monolith on the planet. Sacred to Australia's first people, the Aborigines, it is also an awesome tourist site. Ayers Rock (returned to native jurisdiction) now carries its original name, Uluru. Uluru rises as tableland to 318 feet above the desert floor and has a circumference of eight kilometers, or almost five miles. A sandstone formation laced with feldspar, Ayers Rock changes colors during the day and in different weather, shifting from blue to glowing red. Seeing the color change makes it easy to understand why native Australians imbued it with sacred powers and status.

AUSTRALIA DISCOVERED

Long before Australia was discovered by Europeans, the idea of a great, unknown continent had been surmised. But for all the wrong reasons! *Terra Australis Incognita* ("unknown land of the south") was presumed to exist in order to balance the weight of continents in the northern hemisphere. Chinese traders may have ventured to the city of Darwin in the early 1400s. Europeans began arriving two centuries later. In 1644 Abel Tasman (whose namesake is Tasmania), flying the flag of the Dutch East India Company, explored the coast of northern Australia, naming it New Holland. But pride of place among the early navigators belongs to James Cook, an extraordinary man. He was born in 1728 to a father who was a foreman on a large estate. At 17, James was apprenticed to a shop owner and taught himself mathematics, navigation, and the running of a sailing ship. He soon qualified as a ship's master. During the French-English War for control of Canada, Cook led an expedition to defeat the French forces. At the war's end, he was given a commission to make charts and navigation almanacs of the Pacific Ocean. He confided in his ship's (called The Endeavor) log: "I intend to go further than any man has gone before."[5] Cook's three long voyages were the great achievements of eighteenth-century discovery: Hawaii, New Zealand, the Cook Islands, Tonga, New Caledonia, and most important, Australia. Cook had been searching to confirm the existence of *Terra Australis Incog-*

[5] In honor of Captain Cook, an Apollo spacecraft flew to the moon as "The Endeavor."

nita. He traveled south to the Antarctic, and while despairing of finding the great southern continent, he found the southern coast of Australia. He charted it northward, claimed it for Britain, and named the new territory New South Wales (1768).[6]

AUSTRALIA'S CONVICT PAST

Few countries have endured as bleak a beginning. The date was January 26, 1788. Eleven English ships dropped anchor first at Botany Bay and then at Port Jackson, today's Sydney. The ships of the First Fleet were former slave and prison ships, not modified for their new cargo. The cargo was 1,030 men, women, and children, sentenced by transportation to a life of prison and exile. The youngest was John Hudson, nine years old. His offense was stealing a suit of clothes. Eleven-year-old James Grace had stolen ten yards of ribbon. And the oldest, seventy-year-old Elizabeth Beckford, had stolen twelve pounds of cheese. Each had been convicted of a crime against property. There were no murderers here (murder was a capital offense) and no prostitutes (prostitution was not an offense deemed worthy of transport). The convict fleet had sailed 15,000 miles and 252 days from Portsmouth. The prisoners were shackled; and in tropical heat and the filth of sailing ship bilge, forty-eight died. The fleet was commanded by Captain Arthur Phillips, who held the power of life and death over his cargo. Soldiers served as guards. Now they would have to survive an unknown land.

THE PURPOSE OF TRANSPORTATION

When the First Fleet arrived, little or nothing was known about the interior of what was to be a vast convict camp. But the convicts and their soldier guards were expected to create a self-sufficient colony, even though almost none had the necessary skills of carpentry, weaving, farming, herding, or masonry equal to their task. Never mind! The lash and the leg iron would be their teachers. The great purpose of the settlement was what Robert Hughes calls "social amputation"—removing from Britain an underclass whose very existence was seen to threaten the established social order. Dickens's *Oliver Twist* tells the story of Britain's urban poor, while *Great Expectations* is the story of a young man befriended by an Australian convict who can never legally return to England.

---

[6] See Nicholas Thomas, *The Extraordinary Voyages of Captain James Cook* (New York: Walker & Company, 2003); Peter Aughton; *The Fatal Voyage: Captain Cook's Last Great Journey* (Northampton MA: Interlink Publishing, 2005); and Tony Horwitz, *Blue Latitudes: Boldly Going Where Captain Cook Has Gone Before* (New York: Henry Holt, 2002).

Overall, about 113,000 convicts came to Australia in the years from 1788 to 1840, the year that transportation ended. Officers in the corps of guards bought or took farmland and sheep pastures from the Aboriginal people. Free settlers (colonists) followed. And as convict sentences ran out or were reduced, convicts and former convicts took jobs with the free settlers. As Robert Hughes notes, Australia became the first open prison to allow contact between prisoners and the free, which led to self-reliance among the former as well as their learning job skills and being rewarded for good conduct.[7] Sydney's early Gothic and Georgian architecture came from the drawing board of Francis Greenway, a convicted forger, pardoned for his work.

SETTLEMENT MOLDS THE AUSTRALIAN OUTLOOK

Convict beginnings are thought to account for two mainstays of the Australian character, or its habits of the heart: a strong insistence on social equality and a mistrust of those striving too hard for success. Strivers are admonished, "Tall poppies get cut down." And social equality finds expression in the usual address, "Good day, mate" (usually spoken as "Goo' dye, mite."), and in everyday behaviors: a lone taxi passenger usually sits with the driver rather than being chauffeured in the back seat.

Convict beginnings also gave Australia its folk heroes. In the United States, the frontier gave America its mythic hero, the cowboy, the moral man, the straight shooter. The escaped convict created Australia's mythic hero, the bushranger, the escapee, the outlaw, the rebel against society. Ned Kelley and Jack Donahue are the most celebrated. Stockmen in Australia were sheepherders (not cowboys), hired hands on vast sheep stations. They worked alongside migratory workers during shearing season. A strong tradition of working-class solidarity (and later, the power of workers' unions) was one result, along with a cult of informality.

Australia's population grew slowly in the decades after the end of transportation. Free colonists were welcome, but passage was expensive. A passage from Liverpool to North America cost five pounds. Passage to Australia cost at least twenty pounds. Then, in 1851 gold was discovered near Melbourne. Prospectors and fossickers from around the world rushed to Australia. And Australia's population soared. More than a million came in the first decade of the gold rush and nearly a million more in the second. The gold rushes were the main factor in raising

[7] See Robert Hughes, *The Fatal Shore: The Epic of Australia's Founding* (New York: Vintage, 1988).

the population from 437,000 in 1851 to 1,700,000 in 1871.[8] Gold was Australia's second beginning.

Gold added to Australia's collective memory. Local authorities required miners to buy a permit to dig. Miners resisted, fought battles with the police, and one incident, the Eureka Stockade Revolt of 1854, became a byword for workers' wariness of an overbearing government. It was a wariness balanced against expectation that government would provide services that offset what Geoffrey Blainey calls the tyranny of distance.[9] The gold rush also brought 40,000 Chinese to the diggings. Racial intolerance flared into anti-Chinese riots. As whites' resentment hardened, Australia began a whites-only immigration policy that lasted until the end of the Second World War.

AUSTRALIA'S ORIGINAL PEOPLE

Australia's indigenous people, the Aborigines, have what is probably the oldest culture in the world: more than 50,000 years. Their likely ancestral home was somewhere in Southeast Asia. Coastal tribes fished, while those in the interior were hunter-gatherers, moving in small bands through a hot, dry, and barren land. They killed with spears and throwing sticks (the boomerang) but did not use bow and arrow. Anthropologists today view them as superb survivors, finding hidden water holes, tracking elusive game, walking the land with only memory and songs to guide them.

The first settlers regarded them as less than human. With dark to black skin, they were seen as fit for slavery. They appeared to have no religion, no hereditary kings, and no settled abode. They also suffered from comparison with the people of Polynesia. Polynesians prayed to gods. They were ruled by kings and queens. They danced and sang. They toasted and feted their European visitors, and they were handsome and sexually forthcoming. When Europe first encountered Polynesia, tales of the South Pacific took on mythic qualities. Surely this was the Eden of the Old Testament. Surely these were nature's noblemen and women, as yet uncorrupted by crass civilization. (Readers of Rousseau saw his "noble savages" in Polynesia.) Tahiti, said a French visitor, is Cythera, the legendary birthplace of Aphrodite.

Australia's Aborigines lived far from Paradise. By European standards, they were not handsome. Too busy just staying alive, they had no time for elaborate displays. They had no

---

8 See *Australian Encyclopedia*, 6th edition (New South Wales, 1996).

9 Geoffrey Blainey, *The Tyranny of Distance: How Distance Shaped Australia's History* (Melbourne: Sun Books, 1966).

gifts for visitors. According to Hughes, the only thing they had to sell was their women. And the offspring of those encounters, trying to live in two worlds, were despised. An old and familiar human trait was at work. Those far down the social scale take comfort in finding and treating with contempt those even further down the scale. The Aborigines made perfect targets for the scorn and hate of convicts and their guards. Scorn was intensified by Aboriginal body adornment. In ritual song and dance, bodies were and still are painted with white clay, mud, and red ochre. Aboriginal body decorations are slathered. Polynesians, on the other hand, display tattoos (a Polynesian word) of intricate design.

Figure 19.2. The Aborigines, The Gliwice Metamorphoses by William Blandowski

WHAT IS DREAMTIME?

What the Australians of the eighteenth, nineteenth, and twentieth centuries did not know were the richness and beauty of the Aboriginal culture. When the Europeans first arrived, the Aborigines spoke as many as 700 languages (today, about 200.) Their gods had different names in different languages, but like the Greek poet Hesiod's account of creation and Kipling's "Just So" stories, the gods of the Original People created the world, its mountains, rivers, rocks, streams, and all living things. And they created the sun, the moon, and all celestial things. Gods and their spirits still live in nature and natural things. Each god has an ancient and contemporary form, and the gods protect the tribes that worship them. Each tribe venerates the totem of its god. To the Original People, death is the return of the spirit to its originating source—to nature and natural things and to the gods who made them. Memory and dreams unite people and gods, and past and present are woven in a seamless web called Dreamtime: what once was and still is.[10]

Dreamtime is a moral code and a wanderer's guide. As the Original People moved across the landscape in an endless quest for food, they sang songs of places and ancestors who walked there. These song-lines (as Bruce Chatwin calls them) helped assure their survival. Aboriginal drawings, especially those that portray totemic gods and Dreamtime journeys, are now made for the tourist trade. Old ones are rare and costly, but even the new ones have a beauty that reveals itself with study and empathetic understanding. The same might be said for the best-known musical instrument of the Aborigines, the didjeridu. A wooden, flute-like instrument, the didjeridu is often made from a stick (about three feet long) that has been hollowed out by termites. It is blown (one deep note) and thumped, and it provides rhythm for singing and dancing.

WHO ARE TODAY'S AUSTRALIANS?

Australians today are predominantly of European descent (91 percent). Until the end of World War II, they were mostly British and Irish. The Irish first came in convict ships, then as free settlers (the Great Potato Famine of the 1840s drove them outward). After the Second World War, Australia opened its doors to eastern and southern Europeans (Italians, Greeks, Poles, Spaniards) and Asians (Chinese, Vietnamese, Filipinos, Malaysians). Two factors pushed the change. If the country was to prosper, it needed more workers. If it was to be secure on the rimland of Asia, it needed cordial relations with its neighbors, especially since it could no longer look to Britain for security or as a trading partner (Britain was about to join the Common Market). The proportion of people residing there who were born in other countries rose from 10 percent in 1947 to 27 percent in 2013.[11] Asians now constitute about 7 percent of the popu-

---

[10] For Dreamtime, see Bruce Chatwin, *The Songlines* (New York: Viking, 1987). Chatwin argues that the Aborigines found their way by using landmarks; the songs also provided their cosmology--how the earth was created and how the Spirit created them.

[11] *Migration, Australia 2011-12 and 2012-13*, Australian Bureau of Statistics, December 18, 2013.

lation. Those from the Near East constitute about 2 percent, and Aborigines (including those from islands in the Torres Strait) constitute about 2 percent.

THE ABORIGINAL PEOPLE TODAY

At the time of the First Fleet, native people numbered about 300,000. Abuse, alcohol, European diseases, and government policy quickly took their toll. As hunter-gatherers, most native people had no fixed abode. Courts held that they did not own their traditional tribal lands, and therefore it could be sold to white settlers. In ways parallel to the treatment of American Indians, native people were forced onto reservations, where they died from diseases spread by indoor living and loss of their traditional way of life. Mixed-race children were taken from the reservation and sent to white schools. White administrators could punish without court trials. The overall aim was to impose a white culture on people of color. At its nadir, the Aboriginal population dropped to a mere 60,000. Then, as white attitudes changed and government policies grew more sympathetic, the population increased to about 407,000 today (about 2 percent of the country's population).

Figure 19.3. Aboriginal dancer on Harmony Day 2013

Even so, the day he is born, the Aborigine's luck runs out. Unemployment is high, alcoholism is high, and Aborigines are in prisons far out of proportion to their numbers in the general population. A good deal of the Aboriginal culture on display for the tourist trade is contrived. However modified, the culture is most freely expressed in the Northern Territory, Australia's least populated area.

WHY AUSTRALIANS BOAST, "WE'RE THE ONES WHO GOT AWAY"

Australia was not the first of Britain's convict dumping grounds. Georgia was the first, and when the American Revolution cut off Georgia as a place for transportation, an even more remote convict camp was needed. Australia was the ideal candidate, across a trackless ocean, with a harsh landscape and few natives to resist white encroachment.

Life for Britain's poor in the eighteenth and nineteenth centuries was cruel and oppressive. Slums were crowded and unsanitary. Those without jobs were sent to workhouses whose overseers made a profit by reducing inmates' food. Jails were worse. Operated as private enterprise, jailers sold privileges for cash, and if prisoners' families could not afford to buy humane treatment for prisoners, they were often chained to floors and walls. Transportation to Australia, however hard, meant a life outdoors and an opportunity for social redemption. When Dickens wrote about a convict who made good, he chose a former Australian convict, Abel Madgewick, as Pip's secret benefactor in *Great Expectations.*

From the First Fleet to the end of transportation (1788-1840), convict guards were mostly English, Scots, and Welsh. Irish convicts were treated with special brutality because of their periodic attempts at rebellion, because many spoke Gaelic, not English, and because of their Catholicism. The Great Potato Famine of the 1840s brought Irish refugees as free settlers on promises of land and a better life. They were striking examples of the poor that got away, or, in another example of Australian humor, "We were sent here by England's finest judges."[12]

AUSTRALIA'S CITIES

With a sparsely settled interior, Australia's major cities are on or near an ocean, which means that visitors have easy access to most of the country's tourist venues. The Boomerang Coast curves south from Adelaide to Melbourne and, from there, north to Sydney and Cairns. In the

---

[12] See Linda Christmas, *The Ribbon and the Ragged Square: An Australian Journey* (New York: Viking, 1988).

far north is Darwin, and on the southwest coast are Perth and Freemantle. Australian hearts may be in the outback, but more than 80 percent of those hearts beat in cities.

Almost all major cities are state capitals with a Parliament, courts, and bureaucracies. Not surprisingly and not just in Australia, the government takes care of itself, which usually means that funds are available for civic improvement, parks, museums, and the like. Australia received its Constitution in 1901; former colonies kept their names but were now states within a federal system. The system has been modified over the years, but like other federal systems, states and the federal government each have assigned powers and powers that are shared. Australia is a constitutional monarchy, and the Queen is head of state. She rules (as titular head, mostly in name) through the will of Australia's federal Parliament. Even so, since 1975 a sizable number of Australians have pushed to make Australia a democracy. But a recent referendum decided for the status quo.

Sydney, the capital of New South Wales, prides itself as Australia's original city, the convict camp of 1788. The site of that camp, a rocky ridge overlooking the harbor, is called the Rocks. The Rocks today are prime real estate, with elegant shops and narrow, dogleg streets. Sydney is the modern, commercial capital of the country. Its high-rise office buildings are sheathed in metal and glass; Sydney Tower, emblem of the city's economic importance, rises to 1,000 feet. And occasional clusters of nineteenth-century terrace houses are reminders of the city's past.

Figure 19.4. Sydney Opera House

Sydney is Australia's largest city, with a population of over 4.5 million. The city and its suburbs fan out into a sprawl covering more than 4,800 square miles. Strung between the Blue Mountains in the west and the Atlantic in the east, Sydney may be approaching the limits of its geographic expansion. And as might be expected, traffic is dense and often snarled. It is a city of neighborhoods and suburbs, but no matter how far inland the city extends, at heart Sydney is a waterside city. Cars and buses carry leisure-time crowds to waterside restaurants and shopping malls, and swimmers and surfboarders to the beach. Bondi Beach (pronounced bon die, in honor of a yachtsman) is almost always crowded with sunbathers and surfers.

For the shipboard traveler, Sydney is defined by two landmarks: Bridge and opera house. Sydney Harbor Bridge connects Rocks and Milson's Point and resembles a quarter-circle lying on its side. Its arch rises to nearly 450 feet. All steel and trusses, the bridge proclaims the technology of its period (it was completed in 1932) and is affectionately called the "Coat Hangar." The opera house is Sydney's architectural masterpiece. Like the Statue of Liberty in New York Harbor and Christ the Redeemer of Rio Harbor, the opera house is Sydney's icon. In profile, it looks like a series of gaping, elongated half-shells. Another description sees it as white sails, lofting and billowing, ready to lift the building beneath off its base and send it floating across the harbor. However described, it is audacious in design and construction. The huge roof shells are sheathed with ceramic tiles and rise to almost 225 feet. Beneath the shells is an enterprise of theaters and concert halls along with restaurants and a recording studio.

The site of the opera house at Bennalong Point is Sydney's reminder to itself of the First Fleet's arrival, and the opera house is a proud symbol of what the city has become in the years since 1788. In 1954 the New South Wales state government announced a competition for an opera house design, and first prize was awarded to a Danish architect, Jorn Utzon, who had never been to Australia and had seen the site only in photographs. Controversy erupted almost immediately. Critics charged that the design was not feasible, that it defied sound engineering. Utzon resigned from the project, and local engineering firms took charge. As construction costs skyrocketed, there was more controversy. "From an original estimate of $7 million, costs soared until the final figure was in excess of $100 million." The opera house was finished in 1973, and as one of the world's great engineering feats, its picture was sent into space so that anyone from another world would know of the Earth's people and their technology.

Melbourne's population is about four million. Sydney is exuberant, say its boosters, while Melbourne is staid. But what can you expect from a city named after the British Prime Minister who taught Victoria how to carry out her duties as Queen? Stories of Melbourne's staid manner and conservative outlook are no doubt exaggerated. But unlike Sydney, where streets cut and turn, Melbourne is laid out as a squared-cornered planner's grid. Its extensive tramway (street car) system is a visitor's delight. The city has a long beachfront. And in 2012, *The Economist* recently rated it as the world's most livable city.[13]

Figure 19.5. Melbourne

Unlike Sydney, which takes pride in its convict beginnings, Melbourne takes pride in the fact that it was established as a colony of free settlers. Sydney has a spacious harbor; Melbourne is reached by traveling inland along the Yarra River. Melbourne's area is about 2,300 square miles. Melbourne has its share of high-rise office buildings, but its central business district is urban-traditional—low-rise buildings of traditional design and building materials. One building, "The Block," is worth the visitor's eye; it is described in a city guide as "exuberantly stuccoed in the Baroque manner." In keeping with tradition, Melbourne has its trams (streetcars) that run on steel rails. In Sydney (or so it is said) money counts, but in Melbourne, it is old money that counts. Perhaps nothing better displays Melbourne's reputation as a city of tradition than the Melbourne Cup. The Cup is run in early November. Like Cecil Beaton's Derby Day tableau in *My Fair Lady,* on Cup Day, the ladies of Melbourne going to the horse races

---

[13] "Australian Gold," *The Economist* (August 14, 2012).

and lunching in the city wear large, elegant hats with dresses and gloves to match. Their gentlemen escorts, some in morning dress, complete the tableau.

On any day, Melbourne is a city to please visitors. Streets are wide and, for pedestrians, easily crossed and navigated. There are ample green spaces and parks where walkers can rest and strike up casual conversations, and the State (of Victoria) National Museum has an excellent display of Aboriginal art.

The city of Hobart has a population of about 214,000 and is the capital of Tasmania, an island-state that lies south of the Australian continent across the Bass Strait. About 140 miles separate Tasmania from the continent, but before steamships, they were hard-won miles. Tasmania sits in the "roaring forties," a belt of strong winds that blow across the globe from forty to fifty degrees south latitude. Like Sydney, Hobart began as a convict colony in 1803. It was the place of second exile, the prison for the hard cases not suitable for Sydney. When free colonists began to challenge Tasmania's Aborigines for land, the small size of the island doomed them to extinction (there was no vast, uncharted outback to shelter them). Extermination hunts were organized, and when those failed, the surviving Aborigines were persuaded to move to offshore islands, where they died of many causes, including smallpox and other European diseases. The last survivor, a woman named Truganini, lived on until 1876.

Today, Tasmania's green and pleasant land of farms and forests belies its harsh history. Hobart, its capital city, rises upwards on the slopes of Mt. Wellington (4,167 feet high). From the top of Mt. Wellington, Mt. Nelson comes into view. It was once a signal station flashing messages from Hobart to the waterfront and inland from Hobart. (Clues to the date of a city's founding can often be found in the names Wellington and Nelson, the two great heroes of Britain's long war against Napoleon.) The waterfront area is a pleasant place for strollers and shoppers. Salamanca Place is distinguished by its Georgian warehouses and Battery Point by its colonial houses.

Adelaide, the capital of southern Australia, with a population of about 1.2 million, is built alongside the Torrens River, about four miles from the coast. It is a city laid out on a right-angled grid. Named after the wife of King William IV (Victoria's predecessor), Adelaide's founders almost came to grief by fixing on a scheme proposed by Edward Wakefield. Wakefield, who was once imprisoned for a crime against property (abducting a fifteen-year-old heiress!), had a plan for colonial prosperity. Under his plan, colonization would best proceed by recognizing that land is usually abundant in far-flung places, but capital and labor are scarce. Therefore, open a new colony to wealthy men with considerable capital, who would then invest in civic improvement and have funds to attract necessary labor. Workmen would be well paid, and those with capital would earn a handsome return on their investment. As has been many times remarked (especially by those who admire Edmund Burke), few things work as well in practice as in theory. And so the Wakefield scheme figured mostly in the planning but not in the realities of Adelaide's early years.

What did contribute to Adelaide's prosperity and attractive cityscape was the availability of a pleasing blue stone for buildings and the original grid pattern that laid out broad streets, including a one-square mile business district and generous parklands. Today's Adelaide has a university, a strikingly modern festival center that is host to the biggest arts festival in Australia, and Rundle Mall, the first enclosed shopping mall in Australia. Above and beyond these attractions, Adelaide is gateway to one of Australia's major wine-producing areas, not to mention the city's proximity to a body of water with a provocative name: The Great Australian Bight.

Perth, the capital of western Australia, with a population of about 1.7 million, receives cruise-ship travelers at its deep-water port of Freemantle, about ten miles from the center of Perth. Both cities lie on the banks of the Swan River, a name that by rights should be called the Black Swan River (the river was discovered in 1677 by the Dutch explorer Willem de Vlamingh and was named for the black swans swimming there). Perth is the biggest city in Australia's west, closer to Singapore and Bali than to Sydney. Until the end of the Second World War and the end of Australia's whites-only policy, Perth turned its back on its neighbors to the east. British settlement began in 1829, but the tyranny of continental distance kept Perth's population small until gold strikes to the north (1890) sent the population spiraling.

Darwin, capital of the state of Northern Territory, with a population of about 1.35 million, is a surprise. By geography, it is Australia's most tropical city, lying on the Torres Strait close to New Guinea. It is also Australia's most modern city, twice destroyed and twice rebuilt. In World War II it was extensively bombed by the Japanese and was rebuilt mostly in its previous incarnation. In 1974 Cyclone Terry destroyed the entire city. Two-thirds of the city's residents were evacuated, 45,000 in all, the largest mass evacuation in Australia's history. In the aftermath of Terry, government funds built a new city of striking modernity.

As the rebuilt and modern capital of The Top End (The Northern Territory), Darwin has a performing arts center, an art gallery (Aboriginal Art) and a flower festival (Bougainvillea), all in sharp contrast to the Northern Territory's frontier spirit and sparse population. Whites mostly live in urban places and Aborigines in rural areas. In the outback, recreation is chiefly bushwalking and exploring in vehicles with four-wheel drive. Bathing in rivers and streams is strongly discouraged. Posted signs and local advice warn against saltwater crocodiles.

Darwin is named for Charles Darwin, whose connection with the city is secondhand. His former ship, the Beagle, explored the area in 1839, and the Darwin name was affixed in 1911. Two other names associated with the Northern Territory tell a livelier story. Rum Jungle is a town about sixty miles south of Darwin, and the name supposedly dates to the gold strikes of the 1870s and the "health insurance" imbibed by miners living in tropical sweat. In the seventeenth and eighteenth centuries, Bugis sailors searched the coast for a Chinese delicacy, sea cucumbers. Their cutthroat stealth remains fixed in the memory of English-speaking children to this day. For it is Bugis who gave us the terrifying admonition, "Be careful or the boogeyman will get you!"

Cairns has a population of about 151,000. Pinch your nostrils and the name comes out almost right: Cans. Cairns once prospered on the sugar industry. Today it prospers on the tourist trade, catering to those keen on deep-sea fishing and exploring the Great Barrier Reef. The latter is the largest coral structure on the planet, stretching for more than about 1,200 miles off the continental coast, with about 350 species of coral, some gorgeously colored, spread across 124,275 miles and 700 islands. "Living polyps extract calcium carbonate from the sea water and so form the coral structure around their bodies."[14] When the coral dies it bleaches white. More than a thousand species of fish swim and dart through the reef.

The reef almost finished off the great Captain Cook. In 1770 Cook sailed west from New Zealand and discovered the Australian coast. On April 20, his ship, The Endeavor, landed at Botany Bay, five miles to the south of what is now Sydney. Even in its day, The Endeavor was not a large ship: ninety-seven feet overall, twenty-nine feet, three inches beam. Sailing north, the ship entered the labyrinth of the reef, and on June 10, disaster struck. The Endeavor hit jagged coral, which sawed open her hull. Small boats put anchors into the reef, and using windlass and ropes, sailors winched the ship into water with a hole in her hull. Cook resorted to a risky maneuver; the hole was plugged by fothering—plugging the leak by draping the hull with a canvass sail reinforced at the end with yarn and oakum.

Pumps, feverishly manned, kept the ship afloat until a passage through the reef could be found. The Endeavor entered a small creek and was hauled ashore. Cook set up a repair camp on its banks: tents, a forge, saws. It was two months of hard work, hunting and foraging for food and keeping sometimes hostile Aborigines at bay. The ship sailed into the reef again, this time through a passage that Cook had found from the vantage of a high shore land point. Once safely out to sea, he came to "a fix'd resolution to keep the Main land on board our rout to the

---

[14] *Australian Encyclopedia.*

northward let the consequence be what it will."[15] It was a bold gamble taken "in order not to miss the hoped-for passage" to the East Indies and the voyage.[16]

AUSTRALIAN ODD BITS

Opals: Australian mines yield more than 90 percent of the world's opals. A unique gemstone, it flashes out a rainbow of colors caused by light moving through its hydrated silica spheres. The town of Coober Peddy owes its existence to the 1911 discovery of opals. Its searing summer heat sent miners and their families to live in underground burrows that are still used today.

Sport: It has been many times remarked and only half in jest that sport is Australia's national religion and that its days of worship are Saturday and Sunday: swimming and surfing, sailing, horse and dog racing, cricket, rugby, Australian football, and the list goes on. Organized competition brings out immense spectator crowds. Australians' love for sport came early in its history, in part because the working class had more free time for leisure. Other observers also suggest that Australians' love of beer owes to that same leisure. Australia leads the world in beer intake per capita.

Waltzing Matilda: As a British colony, Australia took "God Save the King/Queen" as the anthem played or sung on official and patriot occasions. With Commonwealth status in 1901, sentiment grew for an Australian anthem. "Waltzing Matilda" was a popular favorite. In 1974 the government commissioned a public opinion survey, and "Advance Australia Fair" won. Subsequent parliaments issued rulings that "Advance Australia Fair" was the national anthem as long as no royal person was present.

"Waltzing Matilda" is the unofficial anthem. Its words, written by the newspaper man and poet Banjo Patterson in 1895, celebrate a swagman (hobo) who took his belongings (in a rucksack, a "matilda") on a walkabout. The song is a lament; when the swagman steals a sheep and is confronted by police, he leaps into a pond: "You'll never catch me alive said he / And his ghost can be heard as you pass by that billabong / You'll come a waltzing Matilda with me." It is the world's only anthem, says Robert Hughes, that celebrates hard times and death.

---

[15] See James Cook, *The Journals* (London: Penguin Books, 2000) for the story of Cook's three voyages to the Pacific.

[16] Tony Horwitz, "A Week Before the Mast," *The New Yorker*, July 22, 2002, 42. He writes: "The Endeavor was a mirror of the man who commanded it: plain, utilitarian, indomitable."

Australians' favorite name for their country is Oz, a name perhaps inspired by Frank Baum's book, *The Wonderful Wizard of Oz* (1900), where Dorothy gets home by sailing to Australia. Of course, Oz gained new glory by the motion picture.

Figure 19.6. Wizard of Oz movie poster

20. New Zealand: The Long White Cloud

New Zealand prides itself on its remoteness—1,000 miles southeast of Australia and 6,200 southeast of Japan. On the globe it lies almost opposite Greenwich, England; hence the boast that it is the country of the first Pacific sunrise. New Zealand is an island nation that runs about 1,000 miles north to south and less than 300 miles across at its widest point. Its two largest islands are North Island and South Island. Dozens of smaller islands range outward by several hundred miles. North and South Islands and a smaller island, Stewart, are roughly equivalent to the size of Colorado and to the United Kingdom.

New Zealand also boasts that it displays every kind of natural beauty to be found anywhere in the world: mountains, lakes, volcanoes, hot springs, fjords, deep forests, green meadowlands, and scenic harbors. Moviegoers are not surprised by New Zealand's scenic beauty: *The Lord of the Rings* was filmed here. New Zealand sits astride two tectonic plates; their unstable fault lines produce volcanoes, thermal springs, and hot, bubbling mud. The country has 200 mountains that rise to 2,300 meters (7,500 feet). Mount Cook rises to about 12,000 feet. The mountains offer snowfields and glaciers to skiers and outdoor enthusiasts.

Figure 20.1. Map of New Zealand

New Zealand's population is about 4.4 million, 86 percent of whom live in urban places. Human population is dwarfed by sheep flocks, as something on the order of 70 million sheep graze the countryside.

WHEN WAS NEW ZEALAND DISCOVERED?

The country's remoteness had another consequence: it was the last place on earth to be settled. Legend has it that the first visitor was Kupe, a Maori navigator who voyaged in a twin-hulled sailing ship (a catamaran) made stable by parallel outriggers. Maori myth has him arriving around 1000 CE from an ancestral home, Hawaikiki (not Hawaii, but an island somewhere near Tahiti). As his ship approached North Island, his wife, pointing to the far horizon, shouted Aotearota, Long White Cloud. About 300 years later, the first permanent settlers arrived. A Polynesian people, they called themselves Maoris.

Figure 20.2. Milford Sound, New Zealand

WHERE DID POLYNESIANS COME FROM?

Polynesians are thought to have migrated into the Pacific from Southeast Asia. They have a genetic kinship with the people of Indonesia and with the Malagasy of Madagascar (from the Greek, *polys* means many; *nesos*, island.) These people, "Vikings of the sunrise," as Peter Buck calls them, established themselves in a vast triangle from Hawaii to New Zealand, from Tuvalu to Easter Island, an area of ten million square miles.[1] Why they embarked on their hazardous journeys can only be surmised: escape from tribal enemies, a search for food, or perhaps the call of the horizon. Their double-hulled ships moved by sail and could carry as many as 200 people along with food and animals: dogs and a species of rat that when fattened was considered a delicacy. The biggest ships could carry 150,000 pounds. Geneticists suggest that the large girth of many Polynesian women and many of the chiefs is an inheritance of body fat needed to sustain these Pacific argonauts.

---

[1] Peter Buck, *The Vikings of the Sunrise* (Christchurch, New Zealand: Whitcombe and Tombs, 1954). A Maori-European, Buck was a prolific writer who devoted his life to protecting the Maoris.

HOW DID THEY BUILD SHIPS AND NAVIGATE?

The people of Polynesia had no metallurgy, no nails to fasten planks or metal saws to cut them. Bone and stone were used for cutting, and planks were held together with fiber cord and caulked with bark and resin. Long before the compass, Europeans navigated the ocean using time (the sun at noon), with a fixed stellar marker, the North Star (Stella Polaris), being the most used and most reliable. Polynesians took direction from birds flying out at daybreak and returning to their island home at dusk. Trained eyes could spot changing coral colors, and trained ears could identify currents lapping the sides of their canoes. Those emanating from islands make a different sound from those of ocean waves.[2] Polynesian navigators looked for clouds on the horizon, a sign that the sun's heat on land had caused cloud buildup. And they also constructed sky charts out of twigs and bark, using them to follow constellations moving through the night sky. In 1965 Dr. David Lewis sailed with his family from Tahiti to New Zealand, using Polynesian navigation. And in 1976 another catamaran sailor, using Polynesian navigation, made the 2,500-mile passage from Hawaii to Tahiti, thirty-five days at sea.

WHEN WAS NEW ZEALAND REDISCOVERED?

The first European to sight New Zealand was Abel Tasman, scouting for trade opportunities on behalf of the Dutch East Indies Company. Tasman made two important voyages of discovery in 1642 and 1644. His most important discovery was an island that bears his name, Tasmania. Also named for him was a small fierce animal, the Tasmanian Devil, and an extinct animal called the Tasmanian Tiger. In 1642 he anchored at the northern tip of South Island and sent out a boat to reconnoiter, whereupon the natives paddled over and killed four sailors with clubs.[3] Tasman named the bay Murders Bay and fled.[4]

James Cook arrived in The Endeavor in 1769. He had sailed from Tahiti on instruction from the British Admiralty to find the supposed great southern continent. Failing that, his orders read, "you will upon falling in with New Zealand observe the latitude and longitude..." Tasman had been dead for 110 years, but his experience at Murders Bay was known to Cook.

---

[2] See K.R. Howe, *Where the Waves Fall: A New South Seas Island History From First Settlement to Colonial Rule* (Honolulu: University of Hawaii Press, 1988).

[3] Tony Horwitz, *Blue Latitudes: Boldly Going Where Captain Cook Has Gone Before* (New York: Henry Holt, 2002).

[4] See Andrew Sharp, *The Voyages of Abel Janszoon Tasman* (London: Clarendon Press, 1968).

Cook used muskets to put Maori-English dealings into a pattern of mutual caution and, on that basis, charted both islands and claimed them for England.

WHAT WAS MAORI CULTURE IN THE EIGHTEENTH CENTURY?

> Notwithstanding they are cannibals, they are naturally of
> a good disposition and have not a little share of humanity.
> — Journal of Captain Cook

The Maoris shared much with the general Polynesian culture. As elsewhere in the Polynesian Triangle, Maoris lived in a highly stratified tribal society. Chiefs and sub-chiefs commanded, and commoners obeyed. In New Zealand, war between tribes was common, and captives and their children became slaves. Everyone within the tribe lived under a rigid set of rules: who could eat what with whom, including human flesh; who could conduct religious services; how the gods could be appeased; and if human sacrifice was required, whose slaves would be picked. Forbidden things and practices were taboo.

Among the first things Cook discovered about the Maoris was that their weapons were similar to other Polynesians. Polynesians had no metallurgy. Clubs and spears were wood and bone (whale bone for heavy duty.) On other islands, natives stole metal objects, including nails. But Maoris were indifferent to metal weapons and tools. Most Polynesians wore tattoos. (Four Polynesian words have entered English: tattoo, tabu/taboo, mana, which means power/the attribute of power, and ukulele, which in Hawaiian means jumping flea.) The Maori tattoo was special. Sharp stone and bone blades cut the skin, and pigment was inserted beneath the skin. When healed, face, arms, legs, and backs carried designs marked out by ridges. Defiance and anger were displayed by foot stamping, by distorting their mouths, lolling out their tongues and turn… (in) up the whites of their eyes[5].

Wood was plentiful in New Zealand, and Maoris were gifted carvers. They decorated their canoes and meeting houses with intricate designs, often totemic representations of gods and spirits. Chiefs held mana (spiritual power) on behalf of their tribe, and members of the tribe shared that mana. Places of worship, the *marae*, were and are gathering places for sharing mana and other spiritual bonds with members of the tribe. In farming, men dug the ground, and

---

[5] See James Cook, *The Journals* (London: Penguin Books, 2000) for the story of Cook's three voyages to the Pacific.

women planted and harvested. Men hunted and fished; women prepared the food. Fortified compounds protected villagers against frequent enemy attack.

When the Maoris first arrived, they found a surfeit of protein in the moa, a huge, flightless bird up to twelve feet tall, weighing up to 500 pounds. The moa belonged to the same species (ratites) as the ostrich and the emu. The moa had no natural enemies and was soon hunted into extinction.[6] But its present-day "cousin," the tiny Kiwi, lives on as the icon of New Zealand and the nickname of New Zealanders. Its cry (kee whee) accounts for its name.

WHAT IS THE TREATY OF WAITANGI?

By the early 1800s, New Zealand had become lawless. Whaling ships (mostly American) hunted the waters, and men from sealing ships hunted on land. They were joined by escaped convicts and ex-convicts from Sydney, along with gamblers, whores, and thieves. The law of New Zealand was the law of knives and guns. Whites (*paheka*) traded and sold guns to the Maori, and tribal warfare became deadly. Early colonists bought and tricked land from the natives, and white-Maori violence spread.

The British Parliament was reluctant to take on the burdens of formal colonization, but in 1833 James Busby, the first representative of the Crown, was appointed, succeeded in 1840 by Lieutenant Governor William Hobson. Hobson drew up the Waitangi Treaty, designed to settle forever questions of land ownership in New Zealand. Eventually signed by 500 chiefs, the treaty was printed in two versions, English and Maori. And the devil was in that detail.

The Maoris believed that in accepting British sovereignty, they had given Queen Victoria's government control but not ownership of their land. The English version of the treaty is more opaque. It reads, "The chiefs yield to Her Majesty the exclusive right of Preemption over such lands as the proprietors thereof may be disposed to alienate at such prices as may be agreed upon" by the proprietors and Her Majesty's agents.[7] In the end, the English presumed that they were given the right to buy Maori land, while Maoris asserted that land was a tribal possession and that no chief had the right to sell it. A series of wars followed, not to end until the 1870s. And even today, the treaty is resented and contested by many Maoris.[8]

---

[6] See David Quammen, *The Song of the Dodo* (New York: Scribner, 1996), 194-95.

[7] 'Read the Treaty', URL: http://www.nzhistory.net.nz/politics/treaty/read-the-treaty/english-text, (Ministry for Culture and Heritage), updated December 20, 2012.

[8] For tales of adventure and misadventures in a remote colonial outpost, see Lady Barker, *Station Life in New Zealand* (London Macmillan, 1871). It was republished in 2000.

WHO LIVES IN NEW ZEALAND TODAY?

About 80 percent of New Zealand's population today is European-descended. Maoris make up 10 percent; Pacific Islanders, not quite 4 percent; Asians and others, 7.4 percent. In recent decades, Maoris have moved from the countryside to the cities. Today Auckland is their unofficial capital. More than 70,000 Aucklanders have Maori ancestors; their number is augmented by an almost equal number of Polynesians from other Pacific islands. The Cook Islands are an independent nation with historical ties to New Zealand; it is a predominantly Maori nation.

In the past half-century, Maoris have organized politically, demanding redress for the "injustices" of Waitangi. In 1975 the government established a Waitangi Tribunal. The tribunal and later commissions are empowered to adjudicate and redress Maori land claims, fishing rights, and loss of tribal authority. Both Maori and English are New Zealand's official languages (as well as sign language).[9]

WHAT IS THE NEW ZEALAND "OUTLOOK"?

Like most other nations, New Zealanders reflect on the experiences that have shaped their habits of the heart. High on the list is the contrast in geography and history with Australia: a temperate climate, a fertile countryside, and poor to middle-class settlers—no convicts here! New Zealanders tend to see themselves in speech and manners as transplanted English. Loyalty to the Motherland carried New Zealand soldiers into both World Wars. Their losses (along with Australia's) at Gallipoli are mourned every year on Anzac Day, April 25.

New Zealand received complete independence from Britain in 1947. Before then it had become a dominion in 1907, which is celebrated as a national holiday on September 26. It remains a constitutional monarchy, with the Queen as Head of State, represented by a Governor General.

New Zealand has one of the world's most enviable literacy rates, 99 percent, along with an equally enviable life expectancy, 80.3 years, both indicators of a high standard of living. The country is also noted for its history of social legislation: It was the first country to give women the vote (1893), the first country to introduce compulsory arbitration in labor disputes (1894), and the first country to provide old-age pensions (1898). Like the mother country, New Zealand is a parliamentary democracy, but with a difference. Its government has no upper house, no Senate, and no House of Lords. A single, elected chamber, working with its chosen Prime Minister, makes and unmakes New Zealand's law.

---

[9] Human Rights Commission, http://www.hrc.co.nz/diversity (February 2008).

HOW DO CITIES COMPARE?

As an island nation, New Zealand has ports aplenty. Most are renowned for bays and harbors of great beauty. Cruise-ship passengers crowd the railings to capture the views on sail-in and sail-away.

Figure 20.3. The Sky Tower in Auckland

Auckland, on North Island, is the country's largest city, with a metropolitan population of over 1.3 million, covering an area of almost 400 square miles. Harbors and marinas spread across the waterfront. The city boasts that it has more privately owned small ships than any place on the globe.

The city's landmark and symbol befits an island nation: Sky Tower, a 1,000-foot spear probing the sky. Opened in 1997, Sky Tower is the tallest building south of the equator. It serves as a communications tower and tourist attraction. High up are a restaurant and viewing decks that sweep sea and land. Viewing distance is about fifty miles. At night, a lit Sky Tower, Auckland's modern-day lighthouse, is visible far out at sea.

LATIN AMERICA

21. South America: Economics and Politics

All happy families resemble each other.
It is the unhappy families that are different.
— Leo Tolstoy, *Anna Karenina*, 1873-77

An unkind history haunts the twelve countries of South America. Each country in its own way is an unfinished place, a place where democratic instability gives way to military rule and stability, followed again by precarious democracy. Eleven countries were conquered and colonized by Spain; the twelfth, Brazil, was dominated by Portugal. The eleven Spanish-speaking countries fought for independence in the turmoil that followed Napoleon's invasion of Spain in 1807. The struggles for independence continued until 1824, but it was not until the end of the Spanish-American War in 1898 that Latin America was finally rid of Spanish domination.

Brazil was different. It offered its Lisbon rulers refuge from Napoleon and slipped its bonds to the mother country gradually and peacefully. But the democracy that followed the last of its royal rulers (Emperor Dom Pedro II, who abdicated in 1889) has also been part of South America's cycle of military rule and precarious democracy.

Democracy, as Winston Churchill famously said, is the worst form of government—except for all the others.[1] Travelers to South America from western Europe and North America view democracy as a governmental norm rather than as one of history's happiest accidents.

---

[1] "Speech before House of Commons," (November 11, 1947).

With selective memories, they forget what Europe was like before the end of World War II. And they wonder why South America has been so long in coming to lasting democracy. A baker's half-dozen explanations come to hand. Each is plausible. All are creditable. None works alone.

Figure 21.1. Map of South America

WHAT DOES GEOGRAPHY HAVE TO DO WITH ECONOMICS AND POLITICS?

South America is about two-thirds the size of its northern counterpart, with 6.9 million square miles in South America as opposed to 9.5 million square miles in North America. From almost the whole of Bolivia northward, the continent lies within a fervid climate. Ecuador takes its name from the equator, which enters South America at the Amazon River. The south demarcation line of the tropics (Capricorn) enters Brazil near Rio de Janeiro, and the northern demarcation line of the tropics (Cancer) lies far to the north in Mexico. By any rough estimate, more than two-thirds of South America lie in the tropics.

As a general rule, tropical countries do not industrialize. Nor do they readily become democracies.[2] Life in the tropics is hard. Human energy is spent on survival. Time and effort needed to sustain democratic government are better used to stay alive. Insect-borne diseases enervate and kill (think malaria, dengue fever, and yellow fever). Large carnivores and dangerous reptiles lurk in the rivers and forests (think jaguars, crocodiles, pythons, and boa constrictors). Tropical forests do not nurture grazing animals. And even though their plant life is thick and abundant, once cleared for farming, the soil of a tropical rain forest loses its nutrients. Other things being equal (and they rarely are), the more a country lies within a temperate climate zone, the greater its prospects for both industrialization and democracy.

High mountain ranges can be an impediment to foreign invasion (think Switzerland). They can also impede the accumulation of wealth (do not think of Switzerland!). Mountains can sustain goats, sheep, and cattle in upland meadows, but little wealth is achieved above the tree line. Deep valleys can keep human populations isolated. In South America, the Andes are visible on Chile's horizon. They lie just beyond the horizon in Peru and Argentina. Native Americans in those mountain valleys cling to ancestral languages, but it is Spanish language education that will help pull them into the cash economy and prosperity of their country.

Several South American countries are rich in mineral wealth: diamonds, emeralds, and gold in Brazil; silver in Bolivia; emeralds in Colombia; copper and nitrates in Chile; and gold and nitrates in Peru. But mining is labor intensive, and miners are paid poorly for their work, while those who own the land and supply capital for mining machinery and transport capture a large share of mining wealth.

This asymmetrical distribution of wealth can be another impediment to democracy, for democracy requires fairly widespread agreement on the purposes of government, on the idea that voters are sufficiently equal in intelligence to carry the responsibility of voting and that most elected officials can be trusted to carry out the wishes of the majority of those who vote. These broadly shared ideas are the fabric of a democratic culture, a culture that rises most readily where wealth is broadly shared and, more important, when most members of society believe that they have an opportunity for a better life.

---

[2] See Lawrence J. R. Herson, *The Politics of Ideas: Political Theory and American Public Policy* (Long Grove, IL: Waveland Press, 1990) and Jared Diamond, *Germs, Guns, and Steel: The Fates of Human Societies* (New York: W.W. Norton & Co, 1999).

HOW DOES A FEUDAL PAST HAUNT SOUTH AMERICA?

As stated, democracy tends to take root in societies of (more or less) economic equals. More important, it survives best in societies where those at the bottom of the social and economic scale believe they have the opportunity to rise upward in wealth and social status. Societies built on inherited rights and privileges (ascriptive rights) bear the hallmarks of feudal societies, and Latin America from Mexico southward was settled by Iberians who conquered in the name of absolute monarchs, rulers who claimed their throne by divine right. Those who rule by God's grace, accordingly, are supreme in worldly matters. Papal doctrine and the teachings of St. Thomas (asserting that secular law was an extension of natural and divine law) also bolstered absolute government in South America. So, those who carried the arms of Spain and Portugal into the New World also carried grants of feudal privilege. They were entitled to great estates (and patents of nobility) and absolute power over those who lived on their land and worked their great estates.

Power corrupts, as Lord Acton famously said in 1887, to which he added, absolute power corrupts absolutely.[3] Many of the great estates of the Spanish conquerors remain intact after more than 500 years, and they are held by some of the same families. The power of the continent's wealthy citizens and their sense of permanent entitlement owe to South America's feudal past. A sense of entitlement also spreads to officeholders. Provincial governors defy the authority of the central government. Bribery is commonplace in politics. The police expect bribes and often enforce the law by brutal (and sometimes lethal) means. All too frequently, office holders ignore election results or call out armed followers instead of abiding by election results. But when social reform fails to keep up with popular demand, the disaffected threaten revolution, or worse, they resort to guerrilla war. Facing what they perceive as anarchy, the military intervenes to restore public order.

A World Bank study concludes that income distribution in South America is the most unequal in the world.[4] The richest 10 percent of the population get 48 percent of the income; the poorest 10 percent get only 1.6 percent. In Brazil, to take what may be the extreme case, less than 3 percent of the population owns more than two-thirds of the country's arable land, and 8 percent of the population owns about two-thirds of the country's wealth. To state the obvious, a feudal inheritance continues to haunt South America's economy and politics.

---

[3] Lord Acton, *Letter to Bishop Mandell Creighton*, 1887.

[4] World Bank, *Inequality in Latin America and the Carribean: Breaking with History* (Mexico City: 2003).

WHAT DOES RACE HAVE TO DO WITH POLITICS AND ECONOMICS?

Gilberto Fryere, the Brazilian sociologist, once compared the treatment of Native Americans by British and northern Europeans to the treatment of Native Americans by Iberians.[5] The British and North Europeans killed the Indians and drove them westward out of white settlements. Agricultural lands were the great prizes, and the Native Americans stood between settlers and their prize. In contrast, the Iberians had come to impose themselves on the natives (in at least two meanings of the word "impose"). Or as Freyere puts it sardonically, the British and North Europeans killed the natives, but the Iberians opened their arms and hearts and took them to their beds. They created a new race, the *mestizos* (Spanish for mixed). And in so doing, they bred the servants who would tend their livestock, farm their farms, work their mines, and serve as servants in their great houses.

Each country in South America has its own percentage of *mestizos*. (Again, Brazil stands apart. Its servant class has been the mulatto: an admixture of whites and African slaves.) And if there is a rough connection between race and wealth in South America, it is this: the greater the percentage of *mestizos*, mulattoes, and Native Americans in a country's population, the greater the likelihood that wealth will be concentrated in the fewest hands. Again, the greater the concentration of wealth, the less the likelihood of free, open, and contested elections. And still again, the greater the concentration of wealth, the more likely the threat of political violence. Or as Ortega y Gasset puts it, "Violence is none other than reason exasperated."[6]

The "southern crescent" of the Andes makes the point. In that region Peru, Ecuador, and Bolivia are flashpoints of violence. In 2004 an angry mob in a small city in Bolivia's high plains lynched the mayor and set his body on fire for allegedly misusing public funds. The same fate befell the mayor of a small town in the Peruvian highland.[7]

Peru's indigenous population "has long suffered exclusion and profound social injustice." The Peruvian Commission on Truth and Injustice estimates that from 1980 to 2000, 75 percent

---

[5] See Gilberto Fryere, *The Masters and the Slaves* (New York: Alfred A. Knopf, 1967). See also his *The Mansions and the Shanties* (New York: Alfred A. Knopf, 1963). The author was a cultural anthropologist with a special interest in Brazil: "Every Brazilian, even the light skinned fair haired one, carries about him on his soul and body alike, the shadow or at least the birthmarks of the aborigine or the negro, in our affections, our Catholicism, which so delights the senses, our music, our gait, our speech, our cradle so songs, everything that is sincere." *The Masters and Slaves*, 286.

[6] José Ortega y Gasset, *The Revolt of the Masses* (New York: W.W. Norton, 1932), 80-82.

[7] See Michael Sifter, "Breakdown in the Andes," *Foreign Affairs* (September/October, 2004). http://www.foreignaffairs.com/articles/60103/michael-shifter/breakdown-in-the-andes.

of 69,000 victims were of indigenous descent, "most of them from Peru's poorest regions." The racial and economic divisions in South America are captured in the remarks of a beauty pageant contestant in Bolivia: "I'm from the other side of the country, and we are tall, and we are white people, and we know English."[8]

WHO WERE THE MEN ON HORSEBACK?

South America's wars for independence began along the Atlantic coast in 1807 in today's Argentina and Uruguay. Proclaiming the ideals of the French Revolution—liberty, equality, and fraternity—Napoleon marched into Spain and, with cynical attention to ideals, placed his brother Joseph on the Spanish throne. The administrative web that bound Spanish colonies to Spain was severed. The viceroys appointed by the former royal court continued to claim power, but rival claimants to authority were on the ground and at the ready.

Spain in the New World was a cauldron of rival claimants to power and boiling animosities: the church and great landowners versus merchants in the port cities, military officers born in Spain *(peninsulares)* given power by birthright versus officers born in the New World *(criollas)* and denied power and promotion by their birth. Two military forces were in New World contention: American-born militias versus loyalist troops dispatched from Spain. Each was commanded by both *peninsulares* and *criollas.* Also in the cauldron was an ambitious Great Britain seeking to extend its empire. It invaded Buenos Aires in 1806-07 and was expelled by the Argentines not long thereafter. And last were claimants to power organized along fault lines of ideology: liberals—mostly young, educated, and middle class—who pledged themselves to fight for democracy versus conservatives seeking to preserve their privileges by upholding the status quo.

The opening shots of revolution were fired in Argentina in 1810. Armies fought in Peru, Chile, Bolivia, and Argentina, sometimes scaling the Andean heights as they moved across those countries. Whether great men compel events or great events bring forth the man cannot be answered in South American history. What can be asserted is that three great military leaders secured independence for Spanish South America. Their equestrian statues are seen everywhere, horses rearing, the general's hat lifted in salute, his arm high in triumphal glory.

Every large city and many small cities have their Plaza de Armas, their Independence Square, and a statue honoring their Simon Bolivar (liberator of the country named in his hon-

---

[8] Ibid.

or), their Bernardo O'Higgins, or their Jose San Martin. San Martin disputed with his counterpart liberators and voluntarily went into exile. Bolivar and O'Higgins stayed on as military leaders long after independence was won. They helped establish a tradition that is both the glory and the curse of South America, the *caudillo*, the general who will not relinquish power or the general who stands ready to return to power whenever he and his followers are convinced that the country is threatened by groups or factions that they oppose. *Caudillos* were also motivated by less generous concerns. After the wars for independence, armies were large, and many military leaders had no alternative employment. To remain in power was their most attractive livelihood.

Another series of wars followed the wars for independence. These were fought by the newly independent countries to extend their territories, particularly to capture seaports, grazing lands, and mineral wealth. On the Atlantic coast, Argentina and Brazil fought to incorporate Uruguay into their domains. And on the Pacific coast, in the War of the Pacific (1879-83), Chile, Peru, and Bolivia fought for territories of nitrate, copper, and silver. Understandably, these wars also put civilian governments in bondage to military regimes.

WHAT IS THE LEGACY OF THE CONQUISTADORES?

Spain has had an uneasy relationship with Islam for almost 1,500 years. Mohammed, Islam's founder, died in Mecca in 632. Less than a century after his death, Islam held sway from the Pyrenees to Persia. In 711 an army of Arabs and Berbers crossed the Straits of Gibraltar and raced northward across Spain to the Pyrenees. They were turned back by Charles Martel (grandfather of Charlemagne) at the battle of Poitiers/Tours in 732, and for almost 800 years, Islamic Emirates controlled large swaths of Iberia.

In Portugal, Faro became the last Muslim stronghold to surrender to Portuguese Christian armies. In 1492 the last Muslim stronghold, Cordoba, surrendered to the armies of Ferdinand and Isabella, rulers of Aragon and Castile.

The Spaniards fought under the gonfalons of St. James, whose body had been miraculously transported (or so it was believed) from the Holy Land to northern Spain, coming to rest in a field surmounted by stars, Campostella. Resistance to Islam in Spain was a love-hate affair. Muslim armies rarely brought women from their homelands, and in southern Spain especially, intermarriage created skin tones darkened by more than the sun's rays. Islam also brought to Spain a richness of cultural achievement: architecture—think of the bell tower in Seville, the Cathedral in Cordoba; science—Arabs named and may have invented algebra; consider what the state of science might be without Arabic numerals and the concept of zero; and philosophy—consider what the world gained through the Arabs' having preserved the writings of classical Greece. Recall the words of science that incorporate the Arab word for "al" meaning "the": algebra, alchemy, altitude, algorithm, and alkali. Think, too, of that most characteristic Spanish cry of joy and approval: *ole*, derived from the Arabic word for God, Allah.

The Arab and Berber armies also brought to Spain secrets of superb metallurgy. All through the Middle Ages, the great challenge of sword makers was to forge a sword both strong and sharp. Strong swords were dull and resisted sharpening. Sharp swords were brittle. But sword makers in Damascus had perfected the technique of working iron at different temperatures to produce swords and daggers both sharp and strong. Along with Damascus steel (which the Spanish renamed the Toledo blade), Arabs rode to Spain on desert-bred horses, superb in strength and endurance. Both Arab horses and Damascus steel (along with guns and gunpowder) were the Spanish implements of conquest in the New World. Add to it the fighting skills honed during the reconquest (*the Reconquista*) of Spain from Muslim overlords and the determination to make Christianity the paramount religion of the world.

The Portuguese were the first Europeans to reach the Far East. They sailed to their conquests south along Africa and then across the Indian Ocean, impelled by a craving for riches but also by a passion to outflank Islam. The Spaniards sailed west for these same purposes, and when Columbus claimed for Spain the lands of the Western Sea, Spanish intent was the same as Portugal's: to outflank Islam, to bring souls to Christ, and to get rich. Whether they achieved their first purpose is open to debate. But there is no doubting their success in the second and third purposes.

NEW WORLD CONQUISTADORES

The most successful and most ruthless of New World *conquistadores* came from a sun-baked, poverty-struck Spanish area, Estremadura. As several have remarked, they had much to gain by conquest and relatively little to lose. Herman Cortes, born in 1485 in Medellin, Estremadura, joined in the conquest of Cuba in 1511 and, in 1519, commanded an expedition to subjugate the newly discovered Mexico. With 600 men, some twenty horses, and ten small cannons, he captured the Indian settlement of Tabasco and took as his slave and mistress Malinche, who was to serve as his interpreter and his advisor on both Indian psychology and the resentment of tribes exploited by the Aztecs of central Mexico. Even more important, she instructed Cortes on the weaknesses of Montezuma, emperor of the Aztecs.

Myth, magic, and legend determined the outcome of the conquest. Legend had warned Montezuma to fear a god from across the sea: a tall, bearded, fair-skinned man who would seek his throne. To no avail, Montezuma sent word attempting to dissuade the god from across the sea from marching further inland. In counter-legend, the imaginations of Cortes and his men were inflamed by one of the first books ever printed in Spain, twenty volumes of the exploits of Amadis de Gaula, a fifteenth century James Bond-Superman-Odysseus, who overcame his foes by bravery and treachery, a hero who rampaged through strange lands where beautiful women welcomed, dragons stalked, priests wore feathered headdresses, and sacrifice to the gods was the fate of those captured in battle.

Figure 21.2. Herman Cortes

In Mexico, Cortes and his men were transformed into Amadis de Gaula. Indian women were compliant; iguanas were the storied dragons; the Aztec priests wore elaborate feathered headdresses; and human sacrifice also occurred. After a recent Aztec victory in the Aztec capital (near today's Mexico City), 10,000 prisoners of war had been drugged and pushed to the top of a pyramid, where priests cut out the prisoners' hearts and pushed bloody corpses down the pyramid steps to a bloody ground.

In the Aztec capital, Montezuma was captured, but even as Cortes's men roamed the city, word reached Cortes that an expedition had arrived on the coast to relieve him of command and take him captive. Cortes returned to the coast, leaving his lieutenant in charge. Cortes captured the leader of the expedition and returned to the Aztec capital to find that an Aztec uprising was underway. Montezuma was stoned and killed by the Aztecs, and Cortes and his men fled for their lives on June 30, 1520, "the Night of Sorrow." Resolute, Cortes regrouped on the coast and marched inland once again. After a three-month siege, he stormed the Aztec capital and killed the new emperor.

The Aztec treasure that he shipped to Spain was worthy of Amadis de Gaula: 700 pounds of freshwater pearls and several hundred pounds of gold dust and gold ingots. The story of Cortes as conquistador was now part of Latin America's culture and, some would say, its outlook on life. The house that Cortes shared with Malinche still stands at 57 Higuera Street, Mexico City. Even today the house evokes strong emotions among Mexicans. Feminists protest its presence as a symbol of Mexican masculine expectations: that men may be unfaithful while women are expected to serve their husbands with unwavering, complete fidelity. Octavia Paz, the Mexican writer and Nobel laureate, sees Cortes and Malinche as symbols (and progenitors) of gendered behavior in Mexico: the swaggering male, quick to take offense, and the submissive woman, patiently sitting in the shadow of a dominant man.

WHAT WAS THE ENCOUNTER AT CAJAMARCA?

Cortes was the first of mainland Latin America's conquerors. His success ignited an explosion of other invasions and rampages. Francisco Pizarro was born sometime around 1476 in Trujillo, a town in the midst of rocky, impoverished farmland. Pizarro's poverty (and illiteracy) spurred him to adventure in the Americas. In 1513 he fought alongside Balboa on the disastrous expedition across Panama and the discovery of the Pacific Ocean (190 had set out, but only sixty returned.) And he watched Balboa's execution on charges that he had failed to bring back gold.

But in Panama Pizarro had heard of a place on the Pacific coast rich in gold, said to be worshipped by Indians as "Tears of the Sun." Pizarro led two expeditions down the Pacific coast in search of the Golden Tears and returned to Spain to seek permission to conquer and govern those lands of gold. In 1531, with the king's warrant, four half-brothers, and an army of sixty-two cavalrymen and 106 foot soldiers, Pizarro's army wound its way into northern Peru. By torturing Indian captives, Pizarro learned that the Inca Emperor would be making his way to the warm springs of Cajamarca. And it was at Cajamarca that Pizarro crushed an Inca army of 80,000 without a single Spanish death.

The Inca Emperor had earlier been told of the strange visitors. He had, in fact, arranged to meet with them at Cajamarca for a peaceful encounter. Pizarro, of course, had other plans. He arrived early at Cajamarca and hid his soldiers and horses in houses around the town square. While the Inca (the emperor who ruled by divine descent) listened, a Spanish priest read aloud in Spanish and Latin a Proclamation that was required prior to any conquest.

Figure 21.3. Francisco Pizarro

The Proclamation (*The Requerimiento*) was distilled from arguments at the Spanish court: Did the Spanish have a moral right to make war and conquer those who had done them no harm? The conquest of Moors received church sanction; after all, they were enemies of Christ. But innocent people who had never heard of Christ? Conquest was permissible so long as they were given the opportunity to submit to the Church of Rome, to the Savior, and to the king who was His earthly servant. So, at Cajamarca, on November 16, 1532, a priest stepped forward and in Spanish began the long Proclamation outlining the history of a world awaiting the Messiah, the special place of the Church and the Spanish monarchs in that world, and calling on all those who heard the Proclamation to willingly and freely accept Christ, the obligations of Christianity, and obedience to the Spanish throne: "…But if you do not do this, and maliciously make delay... we shall powerfully enter your country and make war against you in all ways... and subject you to the yoke and obedience of the church and of their Highnesses..."[9]

It is not likely that the Inca or his followers understood the Proclamation, but no matter. At a signal, guns began to bark, and soldiers rushed out in flashing armor, swinging swords to deadly effect. Thousands of Indians were killed, and the emperor was a prisoner of Pizarro. The soldiers of the Inca did not dare to counter-attack for fear of killing the Emperor Atahualpa. An army of less than 200 now held for ransom an empire of more than eight million.[10]

Pizarro promised freedom to the emperor provided that a room seventeen by twenty-two feet (approximately eight feet high) be filled once with gold and twice with silver. Messengers carried the ransom across a network of 10,000 miles of roads. When the room was filled with treasure as ordered, the emperor was given a choice: accept the terms of the Proclamation and be strangled. Reject Christianity and burn at the stake. Atahualpa chose to be strangled. His afterlife depended on a bodily journey.

Even by today's standards, the treasure collected at Cajamarca was astounding. Each of Pizarro's men received twenty-four pounds of gold and ninety pounds of silver. A standard coinage in the sixteenth century was the Florentine ducat. Each of Pizarro's soldiers received the equivalent of 3,000 Florentine ducats. By way of measure and comparison, in Spain, the richest man in the kingdom, the Marquis of Villena, had a yearly income of 100,000 ducats. Workers on his vast estates earned one ducat per year. In these terms, each one of Pizarro's men received gold ducats equivalent to almost 3,000 years of an agricultural worker's pay.

WHAT WERE THE CONSEQUENCES OF CAJAMARCA?

The vast fortune shipped to Spain from Peru induced Europe's first inflation: too much wealth chasing too few goods. Added to Peruvian bullion were the output of silver from Mexico and Bolivia, which poured into Spain continuously in large quantities. Best estimates suggest that between 1550 and 1650, nearly one million pounds of gold made their way to Spain along with thirty-five million pounds of silver. The Spanish treasure fleet was fair game for pirates who did their utmost to "liberate" Spanish treasure. Among the most celebrated pirates was Sir

---

[9] Juan Lopez de Palacious Rubios, 1513, encyclopediavirginia.org/El_Requerimiento_by_Juan_Lopez_de_Palacio_1.

[10] See Lauren McIntire, *The Incredible Incas and Their Timeless Land* (Washington: National Geographic Society, 1975), a superb study of the Incas and their empire. McIntire is also a traveling companion of one of this book's authors, Lawrence Herson.

Francis Drake. As imports from outside the Spanish empire slipped into Spain (despite royal policy attempting to hoard precious metals), commerce and trade in Europe began to quicken. Estimates suggest that silver in circulation in Europe increased by 300 percent and gold by 20 percent.

Spain was now the richest nation in Europe (if not the world), and in 1570 it appended the kingdom of Portugal to Spain, along with its mighty seaport river, the Tagus. From here the king of Spain (formerly the Holy Roman Emperor, Charles V) dispatched the greatest fleet yet assembled, the mighty Armada of 1588: 130 warships to carry 30,000 men intent on crushing the troublesome and heretical kingdom of England's Queen Elizabeth. Wind, weather, and faulty planning—along with the courageous battle tactics of the English—put the Armada to flight. Less than half the fleet returned to home base. England, almost without an army, was saved from conquest. And now spared the threat of the Spanish fleet, England, Holland, and France embarked on their own race for empire. The Caribbean islands were detached from Spain. Canada was colonized by the French, and the east coast of North America stood open to English settlers.

The incredible fortune assigned to each of Pizarro's men inspired a string of expeditions in search of more wealth. No rumor was beyond belief. El Dorado, the man of gold, was said to live somewhere north of Peru. His was the tale of a chief covered with gold dust every night by worshipful followers. After his dusting, El Dorado would enter a lake to cleanse himself, and as time passed, the lake had become muddy with gold. When Spanish torture failed to produce directions to El Dorado, the myth was changed. Now El Dorado, in the Spanish imagination, was a city with buildings made of gold. And still later, the city of gold had become a tale of Cibola, the seven cities of gold.[11]

The search for El Dorado pushed the Spaniards north of the Rio Grande and into the first European exploration of what is now the American southwest. And equally important, it led another explorer, Francisco de Orellana, to travel the mightiest river of South America, from the mountains to the sea. As his hapless expedition tried to outrun hostile Indians, Orellana claimed to have been beset by fierce women warriors—the Amazons of Greek mythology. But perhaps the most enduring consequence of Cajamarca was the belief instilled in the Spanish that theirs was a divine destiny in which a handful of Spanish overlords had been chosen to rule a continent.

---

[11] See Jared Diamond, *Germs, Guns, and Steel: The Fates of Human Societies* (New York: W.W. Norton & Co, 1999).

WHAT WAS THE SECRET OF SPANISH SUCCESS?

Over and above daring and confidence, the Spanish came to the New World with 800 years' experience fighting Islam. The Spanish had weapons and armor of steel; the Indians had no metallurgy except for fashioning gold and silver ornaments. Until the use of motor vehicles in the twentieth century, the most formidable and flexible weapon of war was the cavalry. The Spanish had horses, while the Indians had none. In fact, and except for the llamas of South America's far south, neither North nor South America had any animals useful for war or transportation. The first encounter with mounted riders terrified the Indians. They thought that horse and rider were a single creature—huge, aggressive demons. The natives of South America were non-literate. The Incas could keep records with knotted strings, not an alphabet but a memory jogger understood only by a few initiates. As possessors of books and writing, the Spanish could draw on the history of warfare reaching back 2,000 years. They could send messages in writing, precise and concise. The Indians could take counsel, but messages and tactics were at the mercy of those who carried the words.

But it may be that the strongest advantage of the Europeans lay in something that none could see: germs and viruses. Indians had lived in viral isolation for some 30,000 to 40,000 years. They had no immunity to European diseases. When Europeans arrived carrying measles, mumps, whooping cough, and above all, smallpox, the Indians died—by the millions. It is estimated that when Columbus landed in the Caribbean, its islands had a population of somewhere between a half and three-quarters of a million. Fifty years later that population was less than 500. When Cortes came ashore, the population of Mexico is estimated to have been sixteen million. In less than one hundred years, only one million remained. Overall it is estimated that more than 90 percent of Native Americans died in the first century of their initial encounter with the people and diseases of Europe. Wasted and weakened by disease, they were easily defeated by the people from across the sea. As Jared Diamond recounts and as the title of his admirable book succinctly states, germs, guns, and steel were the keys to the Spanish conquest of the New World.

22. Sweet-Tooth Politics: African in the Caribbean

We do sugar o'er
The devil himself
— Hamlet, Act 3, Scene 1, Page 3

Visitors to the Caribbean and the Atlantic Bahamas take their mostly black populations for granted. In terms of race and much of their culture, the Caribbean is an outpost of Africa. To ask why is to unravel a tangled web of greed, cruelty, national ambition, and humankind's oldest addiction. At the center of this ancient web is sugar.

WHY SUGAR?

Sugar may well be humankind's oldest addiction. It is a complex carbohydrate whose simplest and most familiar forms are fructose and glucose. In Biblical times, the chief source of sugar was honey, transformed by the bee from sucrose into fructose and glucose. But until the discovery of the Americas, sugar was always in short supply. Sugar's scarcity and desirability before the Spanish came to America are reflected in the yearnings of the Book of Exodus, which speaks of a Promised Land "flowing with milk and honey." And scarcity made it expensive. Unlike salt, a life-giving necessity for grain-eating societies and a preservative for fish and meat, sugar was an indulgence, a luxury reserved for the wealthy. When Henry VIII hosted a sumptuous banquet in 1526, the royal household had difficulty in finding three pounds of sugar to serve to the king and his noble guests.

WHERE DID SUGAR ORIGINATE?

Legend and history state that sugarcane was first found growing on the banks of the Indus River by soldiers of the Persian king Darius in 510 BCE. Genetic research traces the origins of sugarcane to the island of New Guinea, from which it made its way to China and India. The first written references to sugar describe it as Indian salt. Our English word for sugar is even more telling: it derives from Sanskrit, *sarkara*. From the Far East, sugarcane traveled west. An early scenario has Alexander the Great introducing sugarcane to the eastern Mediterranean, from which it spread to Cyprus, Sicily, and Andalusia.

Another scenario puts sugarcane aboard Arab dhows (sailboats), sailing the monsoon and entering the Mediterranean by way of the Muslim Near East sometime around 800 CE. This scenario helps account for the English word candy: the *Oxford English Dictionary* asserts that the word candy is Arabic in origin, *quandx,* associated with the practice of chewing on pieces of sugarcane. A more intriguing derivation connects the word to *Kandia*, the Arabic name for Heraklion in Crete. Perhaps *Kandia* derives from the Cretan hard candy (boiled sweets) that is the forerunner to modern-day confections.

HOW DID SUGAR COME TO THE NEW WORLD?

The first westward leap of sugarcane was to Madeira. In 1418-1420 Joao Zocaro and Tristao Tiexier claimed the Madeiras for Portugal, and settlement began shortly thereafter under the authority of Prince Henry the Navigator. Located about 350 miles off the coast of Morocco, the Madeiras are verdant tropical islands, washed with abundant rain. They are ideal for sugarcane cultivation. And so, too, are several of the Canary Islands, first claimed by Spain in 1402. Both groups of islands served their masters as rehearsal halls for the conquest of the New World. Madeira was uninhabited when the Portuguese flag was first unfurled. In Brazil, the Portuguese followed Madeira's precedent, settling their new colony by awarding crown favorites vast tracts of land extending inland from the Atlantic coast. The Canaries were sparsely inhabited when the Spanish arrived and were thus open to conquest. Germs, guns, horses, and steel subdued the natives of the Canaries. The same implements proved equally effective in conquering the Spanish New World.

Madeira and the Canaries were important to their Iberian masters in another way. Both places gave their conquerors experience in cultivating sugarcane in the tropics and turning its liquid into sugar crystals. So, when the Canaries and the Madeiras added their sugar to Europe's supply, it was far from enough to satisfy demand, but it convinced Portugal and Spain that New World sugar would find a ready market in Europe.

WHAT DOES SUGAR NEED TO FLOURISH?

Cultivating sugarcane requires hot sun and abundant rain, along with strong arms and strong backs to cut and carry the cane. Equally important, cultivation requires equipment to squeeze and crush the cane stalks. Once crushed, the cane gives up a liquid that can then be boiled off or, more likely in the early history of sugar, left to evaporate in the sun. The resulting residue requires a further treatment to begin its transformation into sugar crystals. In the early history of sugar-making, transformation began by adding previously created crystals to the liquid, perhaps in the fashion of mother vinegar in the acetic process or perhaps something akin to the starter dollop in making yogurt.

WHO FIRST BROUGHT SUGAR TO THE CARIBBEAN?

Any number of Caribbean islands offers an excellent environment for cultivating sugarcane: tropical sun, a long growing season, abundant rainfall, fertile soil, and flat terrain. Columbus noted these facts during his first voyage of discovery, and on his second voyage in 1493 he carried sugarcane to the New World. The Spanish did not come to be planters. They had come to find the silks, spices, gemstones, and precious metals of the Far East, not to till the soil. Every Spaniard presumed himself to rise in social rank upon setting feet in the (as yet unnamed) New World. Farming was beneath the dignity of a Spanish gentleman.

WHAT HAPPENED TO CARIBBEAN INDIANS?

The year 1492 was history's hinge of conquest.[1] As Eric Williams notes, when the Spanish landed in the New World, they fell first on their knees in prayerful thanks. Then they fell upon the Indians. Slavery was an established institution in the Old World. As Columbus suggested to his monarchs, the Indians of the Caribbean were a sweet, gentle, people who would make excellent servants.

Very quickly the Indians were forced into servitude: searching for gold, tending crops, and building shelter for their Spanish masters. Abuse, overwork, punishment, and mutilation came with the Spanish overlords. And so, too, did viral visitations. Smallpox, diphtheria, measles, and mumps quickly took their grisly toll. The Caribbean Indians vanished, but like the Chesh-

---

[1] See Eric Williams, *Capitalism and Slavery* (New York: Russell & Russell, 1944). Oxford educated, Williams was the first Prime Minister of Trinidad and Tobago and was widely regarded as the Father of the nation. See also David Richardson, "The British Empire and the Atlantic Slave Trade" (Oxford Scholarship Online, 1988).

ire cat who vanished, leaving nothing but a smile, the Indians left us a smile of words: canoe, hammock, hurricane, cannibal, cacique, cassava, and tobacco.

Use, misuse, and abuse of the Indians became so scandalous that the Spanish crowns interceded. A Dominican Friar, Bartolemé de las Casas, was appointed Indian Protector, but his devotion to his Indian charges was not matched by a comparable devotion to another preyed-upon people, African blacks. The protecting friar was pleased to let African slaves take the place of New World Indians.

WHY AFRICAN SLAVES?

The origins of slavery are lost in the mists of time. Pharaonic Egypt, ancient Greece, and Republican Rome relied on slaves, not only as overworked toilers on public works and in mines but as tutors for their children, as household servants, and as concubines. Until the fifteenth century, most European slaves were chattel by right of war and conquest. Then, as Portuguese explorers ventured into the Atlantic and down the coast of Africa, sometime around 1450, African black slaves entered the maws of European commerce. Destined for the Spanish New World, traffic in slaves started slowly (in 1505, seventeen slaves were imported into Hispaniola for work in the island's copper mines), and then it increased to a swift flood. By the time the trans-Atlantic slave trade ended in the mid-nineteenth century, upwards of ten million blacks (perhaps as many as fifteen million) had come from Africa to the New World. Prior to the twentieth century, it was history's greatest mass migration. Employment varied for those transported, but no job was more destructive of health and life than the sugar trade.

WHY DID DEATH AND SUGARCANE GO HAND IN HAND?

Sugar cultivation was labor intensive. Agronomists estimate that in the American South, one slave could work from thirty to forty acres of corn, five to ten acres of cotton, but only two acres of sugarcane. The conditions of work in the sugar trade were horrendous. From sun up to sun down, there were hard cutting and heavy hauling of the six-foot stalks. And when the cane arrived at the processing site, it was fed into crushing-stones and rollers (mills) to extract its liquid. The first crushing mills were little more than stones pulled by slaves. The liquid drawn off from the mills was then hauled to boiling sheds where the ambient temperature rose upward toward the liquid's boiling point. Added to these miseries were slaves' inadequate diet and the overseers' lash. Little wonder, then, at the short lifespan of slaves in the sugar trade. One estimate suggests eight years for field hands; another estimate reduces their lives to a scant three years. Dead slaves required constant replenishing, and the Atlantic slave trade flourished.

One estimate reckons that by the mid-1600s, Jamaica was importing 10,000 slaves per year, and Barbados 5,000. Overall the Caribbean had become a long string of slave-holding islands.

WHAT CONNECTS SUGARCANE TO POLITICS AND WAR?

By the 1600s, sugar was an immense source of wealth and national pride. Adam Smith in his *Wealth of Nations* (1776) asserts that profits from West Indian sugar were greater than elsewhere in the world. Sugar riches helped to reverse an ancient equation. Historically, it was almost always the case that political power brought economic power. Now, with increasing frequency in Europe and America, wealth would be used to buy political power. In 1661 Charles II created the first of Britain's sugar barons, as thirteen baronets were bestowed on the richest planters in the English Caribbean.

The relationship of sugar wealth to political power was not lost on the Dutch. Taking advantage of a decline in Portugal's sea power, the Dutch seized the easternmost area of Brazil, Pernambuco, an ideal location for sugarcane. The Dutch held Pernambuco from 1630 to 1654. Slaves were imported by the shipload, so many that Pernambuco today is the most African part of Brazil in terms of skin pigmentation, dress, cuisine, music, and religious practices. The Dutch also carried an advanced technology to Brazil. They installed there the world's most efficient machinery for crushing sugar cane. And as sugar wealth flowed back to Holland, Dutch investors quite literally bet their national future on sugarcane cultivation. The Dutch were trading across the farthest reaches of the globe. Dutch trading had brought the Lowlands into armed conflict with their seafaring rival, England. When an Anglo-Dutch war was ended by the Treaty of Breda (1667), the Dutch willingly traded their North American colony of New Amsterdam for possession of England's claims to its sugar colony of Surinam on the northern coast of South America!

WHAT WAS THE TRIANGULAR TRADE?

> Molasses to Rum to Slaves
> — *1776*, (Musical), Sherman Edwards, 1969.

British North America was, of course, unsuited for cultivating sugarcane, but British North America was deeply enmeshed in the sugar trade. One of the first by-products to emerge from the crushing of sugarcane is the brown, viscous, sweet liquid known as molasses. By itself, molasses can be used for such sweetening chores as baking and for diluting the unpleasant taste of medicine. But its most income-generating use was in the distillation and manufacture of rum.

On the eve of the American Revolution, the sugar and molasses trade was brisk and financially rewarding.

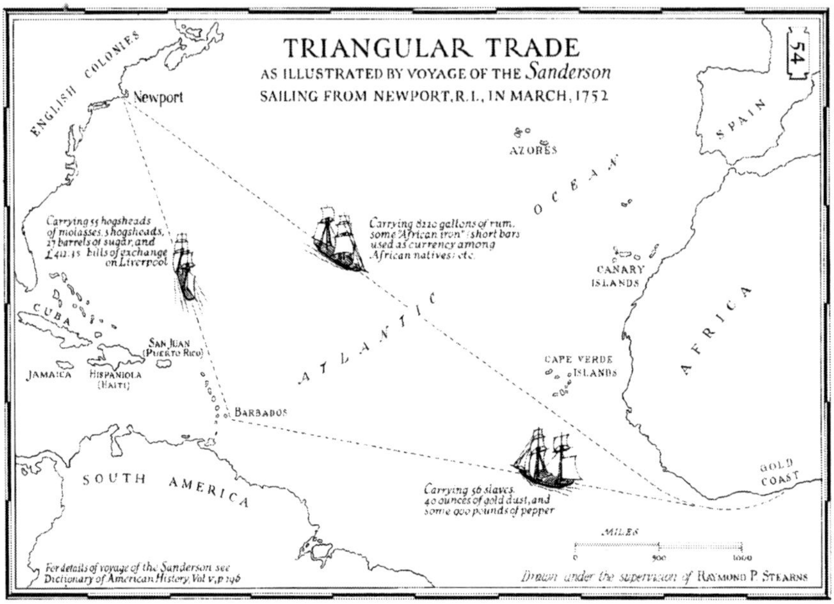

Figure 22.1. Triangular Trade

In fact, sugar, molasses, and rum constituted indispensable components of the infamous triangular trade that held the British Empire together. Molasses and sugar from the West Indies were distilled into rum in the American colonies. Rum was then exported to Britain for sale there and throughout the world. Money from the sale of rum helped to outfit slave ships setting out from Liverpool. These slave ships carried gold, guns, and goods to Africa, where they could be exchanged for black gold, slaves, who were then carried across the Atlantic to the New World. So lucrative for England's North American colonies was the molasses-slave trade that in 1770 Rhode Island alone had more than thirty rum distilleries. And respectable clergy gave thanks to the Lord for making the molasses-slave trade a sizable foundation of wealth in the American colonies. "From molasses to rum to slaves" says the popular song from the musical, *1776*.

HOW DID THE SUGAR TRADE CONTRIBUTE TO THE AMERICAN REVOLUTION?

Distilling rum was not the only American involvement with the sugar trade. Parliament attempted a mercantilist economic policy, seeking to keep gold and silver locked inside the British Empire. Taxes were levied on goods imported from outside the empire to raise revenue and discourage foreign imports. The resulting Sugar Act (1764) and Molasses Act (1783) set in motion a long train of unanticipated consequences. To avoid paying duties on French West Indian sugar and molasses, many American sea captains practiced smugglers' wiles. Royal customs agents responded with unaccustomed vigor, and colonial anger turned violent. A royal revenue cutter, The Gaspée, harrying smugglers, ran aground in Providence Harbor. An angry band of Rhode Islanders boarded the cutter, thrashed the crew, and set her afire. In Boston, with resentment rising against other taxes and import duties, angry colonials took to the streets with shouts of "No taxation without representation." The Boston Tea Party followed. And the War for Independence soon ascended.

WHAT ROLE DID SUGAR PLAY IN THE NAPOLEONIC WARS?

The connection between sugar and war reasserted itself during the long struggle between Britain and Napoleon. Following Nelson's victory at Trafalgar in 1805, British sea power was sufficiently strong (and confident) to blockade the principal ports of Europe. Sugar was now in extremely short supply. A new source of sugar was needed to assuage mankind's oldest addiction. It came from Prussia; in 1747 a Berlin experimenter obtained sugar crystals from sugar beet. A half-century of improving the sugar beet and sugar-crystal refining led Napoleon (1811) to set aside 80,000 acres for sugar beet planting, to establish six sugar beet schools, and to build ten sugar beet factories. The sugar shortage was alleviated. Sugar plant cultivation was now established in temperate climates. And, significantly for the future, state-sponsored science had been given a powerful boost.

HOW DID THE EAST INDIANS COME TO THE AMERICAS?

Two decades after Waterloo, the British Navy effected one of the most important and long-lasting interventions in sugarcane politics. Slavery was outlawed in all units of the British Empire in 1834, and not long after, the British Navy was given orders to suppress the slave trade. Slave ships of every flag were brought under the navy's guns, but quite often slave ships were faster than men of war. If the slave ship flew another country's flag or the flag of a country where slavery was legal (the United States, for example), the British "invasion" of a slave ship created problems of international diplomacy, sometimes resulting in the British captain being sued for loss of legal cargo. But if and when slave cargo was seized, slaves were set ashore as free persons in the nearest, most suitable port. In the Indian Ocean these ports included those on the islands of Madagascar, the Seychelles, Reunion, and Mauritius, thereby swelling their slave-descended African populations. On the coast of western Africa, the British took the area of Sierra Leone under crown protection and established the appropriately named Freetown as a home for newly freed slaves.

HOW DID BRITISH SUGAR PLANTATIONS GENERATE WEALTH AFTER THE END OF SLAVERY?

The answer was contract labor and indentured servitude. From where would they come? Whose poverty might induce them to take up the hard work of sugarcane cultivation? One obvious source was China. The very word coolie hints at explanation: coolie means "bitter work." But the Manchu mandarins frequently closed their ports to emigration. Who else might be willing to emigrate to find bitter work? The answer lay within the British Empire: India.

Hindu and Muslim laborers fanned out across the empire's sugar plantations. Many came to the Durban area of South Africa; and when whites-only laws became oppressive, the Indian colony brought a promising young lawyer to plead their cause in South Africa's courts. In 1894 Mohandas Gandhi challenged South Africa's oppressive laws, and when that failed to improve the lot of Indian workers, he taught his fellow Indians the non-violent protest embodied in the doctrine of *Satyagraha*. That doctrine later became the basis for Gandhi's civil disobedience campaign against the British in India, and in 1964 it made its way across the Atlantic to the Birmingham jail where Martin Luther King, Jr. adapted civil disobedience as a tactic against American discrimination. Its own time and leaders shaped the American civil rights movement of the 1960s. Its genesis lay in many places, and not least among them was the shadow of the sugarcane.

AFTER 1834, HOW DID FRENCH, SPANISH, AND DANISH COLONIES GET SUGAR WORKERS?

Slave smugglers continued to evade British patrols, including those exported from the United States. Slave colonies produced their own crop of slave babies. But as the nineteenth century moved forward, each of the Caribbean colonies created its own schedule for manumission (emancipation from slavery). White plantation owners and their white overseers had always been only a tiny portion of their island's population. And by the time slave importing and slavery ended, each island had become Africa in exile.

HOW HAS THE SUGARCANE AFFECTED POLITICS IN TODAY'S BLACK CARIBBEAN?

The Caribbean Sea extends over 750,000 square miles, nestled between Central and South America and the southeastern United States. In its water lie more than 7,000 islands, ranging in size from the Great Antilles (Cuba, Puerto Rico, Hispaniola, Jamaica) to scores of tiny isles and islets. Languages spoken on these islands are those spoken by their former colonial masters: French in Martinique, Dutch in the former Dutch West Indies, Spanish in Cuba and Puerto Rico, English in Jamaica, and so forth.

As the price of sugar has fallen worldwide, the Caribbean islands look to tourism to support their economies. But tourism can be a fickle economic mainstay. Tourists demand beaches, calm waters, and a seemingly unlimited supply of fresh water. Fashions and fads move tourists to new locations. English-speaking islands draw Americans and Canadians, but tourist wealth often goes to resort developers and not to those whose services cater to tourists. As a result, a triple economy (tourists, developers, service providers) can engender local resentment and civil unrest.

Some islands, however, have found a rewarding substitute for sugar. The English-speaking Cayman Islands have a population of only 37,000, but thanks to offshore banking, the island registers more than 40,000 companies, has 600 banks, with assets exceeding $500 billion. Prosperity and law and order go hand in glove, and in a good tourist year (such as 2006) more than 2.1 million visitors flock to the Caymans. (In 2011, 1.7 million tourists visited the Cayman Islands.)

As another example of the Caribbean's varied mix, the Spanish-speaking Dominican Republic continues as an agricultural exporter (sugar, coffee), but tourism also thrives. The pattern of economic and social cleavages laid down centuries ago continues, with 10 percent of the population owning more than 40 percent of the national income. Jamaica, another English-speaking island, has a population of over 2.7 million. Its heavy dependence on tourism results in two social and economic landscapes: the lush tourist resorts and the out-of-sight slums.

Each of the Caribbean islands has its own economy and its own social structure. But the sugar industry of long ago remains a palimpsest on which the modern age continues to write.

HOW HAS SUGAR SERVED AS PALIMPSEST FOR THE "INDIAN CARIBBEAN"?

In some places transported Indians worked alongside former slaves. In other places they supplanted them. But whatever the conditions of work, imported East Indians gave rise to what might be called a politics of resentment: the struggle for political control among Indians, former black slaves, and the indigenous population.

The politics of sugarcane resentment take different forms that vary with the local mix of races, ethnic groups, religion, economic affluence, and the brutality formerly visited on slaves by their overlords. Brazilian sociologist Gilberto Fryere shows how that brutality has created the foundations of Brazil's present culture, a master-slave relationship characterized by deference to one's social superiors and resigned acceptance of Brazil's vast disparities of wealth.[2]

In the former British colony of Guyana, a per capita income of about $3,750 is the backdrop to the country's politics. The population includes blacks (35 percent), East Indians (51 percent), and Amerinds. Blacks and Amerinds are primarily Christian; the Southeast Asians, however, are Muslim (10 percent of the Asians) and Hindu (40 percent). Muslim and Hindu have cooperated in a successful attempt to wrest control of government from the once-politically dominant blacks. But poverty in tandem with religious and race rivalries can make a troubled polity. Before and since independence (1966), Guyana has been beset by periodic waves of rioting and racial violence.

Unlike Guyana, the Republic of Trinidad and Tobago is a haven of considerable political stability. As its name asserts, it is a Republic of two islands, with Hindus clustered on Trinidad. The Republic has a racially mixed population. Indians arrived after the abolition of slavery in 1833, joined by Madeirans seeking jobs, freedom of religion, and political dissent. Religious dissenters from Britain and France contributed to the white population, so that today the population of the country's two islands is something on the order of 1.34 million, with 40 percent East Indians, 40 percent racially mixed, and perhaps one-half of one percent is white.

Several explanations are offered to account for the country's stability. Some writers ascribe stability to the country's delicate ethnic balance, as no one group is large enough to tilt the scale downward with the weight of their numbers. Other writers see stability in the country's Hindu heritage with its emphasis on *Kharma*—a divine law of action and consequences—which Christians can easily assimilate to the Biblical injunction, "As ye sow, so shall ye reap." Another explanation also lies with religion. Blacks and those of mixed ancestry are nominally Christian, but many also profess Orisha, an African religion brought by slaves. Orishans identify African gods with Christian saints; in doing so, they lessen the likelihood of a country beset by the intolerance often associated with Christian fundamentalism. And still others (including the Trinidad-English writer, V.S. Naipaul) argue that Trinidad's multiple cultural roots are so intertwined that the country's culture can only be derivative and imitative. Happily for stability, goes the argument, derivative and imitative translate into British justice and fair play. Whatever the truer explanation, Trinidad and Tobago's political stability suggests that the shadow of the sugarcane reflects the many skin tones of those who worked the cane fields.

---

[2] See Gilberto Fryere, *The Masters and the Slaves* (New York: Alfred A. Knopf, 1967).

More practically, the stability is self-rewarding. It helps make the Republic attractive to tourists and offshore investors.

Ralph Waldo Emerson once remarked that every credit has its debit side.[3] Sugarcane brought much wealth and pleasure to people and places across the globe. It also brought misery and suffering to many of those same places. Sugarcane set in motion great changes in the economics, the politics, and the lives of those most involved in the sugar trade. Sugarcane underscores the truth of Thomas Jefferson's remark that there is no greater gift to mankind than the discovery of a new food. It also underscores the pertinence of historian Manning Clark's remark that without evil, there would be no history. And yet, the history of sugarcane also underscores another truth about humans and their gifts: It is the spirit-warming human capacity for transcending unspeakable hardship to build new and productive lives in far-off, alien places.

---

[3] Ralph Waldo Emerson, *Compensation*, 1841.

23. Remarkable Argentina

Yes! Please Cry for Me, Argentina

By any measure, Argentina is a remarkable country. With a population of more than 41 million, it is the largest Spanish-speaking country in South America. More than 97 percent of its adult population is literate, and more than 97 percent is of European descent. The highest peak on the continent, Aconcagua, rises on its western border, and in Tierra del Fuego is Ushuia, the southernmost city in South America. Argentina's capital city, Buenos Aires, is often described as the Paris of South America: a city of wide boulevards, lively sidewalks and café life, elegant shops, and smartly dressed strollers. Tree-lined streets and a wide variety of neighborhoods (from shabby, working-class warrens to elegant apartment houses) reinforce the idea that Buenos Aires is the Paris of South America. Its opera house, the Teatro Colon, begun in 1895 and finished in 1898, reflects France's *Belle Epoch*: six balconies decorated in gold leaf and a lobby that calls to mind the Hall of Mirrors at Versailles. The city's pedestrian street, Calle Florida, overflows with shoppers, business people, sidewalk entertainers, gypsy mothers soliciting coins on behalf of their infants, and store clerks standing in front of their shops, competing for tourist attention. (A useful strategy for those seeking to avoid solicitation is to carry a folded local newspaper in hand and in plain sight.) Self-referential is the term often used to describe *Portenos*, the people of Buenos Aires. More psychiatrists and plastic surgeons practice here than in all the rest of South America combined. And the country's icons are famous around the world: tango, *gaucho*, Juan and Evita Peron.

Figure 23.1. Map of Argentina

WHO ARE THE ARGENTINES?

In contrast to the rest of Latin America, Argentina's population is descended from European immigrants (only 3 percent of Argentina is Indian or *mestizo*). They are mostly Italian, Spanish, and German. A popular joke has it that Argentines are Italians who speak Spanish, furnish their homes in the style of Louis XIV, dress like the English, and work like the Germans. If, as has been said many times, geography is destiny, the work ethic and energy of Argentines owe much to Argentina's temperate climate. Its furthest north is subtropical and its furthest south (Tierra del Fuego) is sub-Antarctic. The southern 25 percent of Argentina (south of the Rio Colorado) is Patagonia, a land of dry plateaus that step down from the Andes to the Atlantic.

Buenos Aires has a magnificent harbor that historically has connected Argentina to Europe. The grasslands of Argentina's central region, the *pampas*, are a rich alluvial plain whose topsoil (several yards deep) gave the country its original wealth—abundant crops of wheat and vast grazing grounds for cattle. Throughout South America, *vaqueros* (cowboys) are folk heroes and national icons. And as cattle ranching moved northward to what is now the American West, the language of the vaqueros slipped into English (and, of course, Hollywood movies): lasso, chaps, rodeo, corral, sombrero, and desperado. The cowboy has become the legendary American icon; in Argentina the legendary icon is the *gaucho*—fiercely independent, daring, brave, and capable of enduring hardship, a magnificent horseman. In the nineteenth century, the *gauchos* fought for independence and also fought for a decentralized Argentina under the leadership of General Rosas, the first in a long line of Argentina's strong-man generals.[1]

Argentine hides were first shipped to Europe in the 1500s. For more than 400 years, leather was the all-purpose material of everyday life: shoes, clothes, laces, door hinges, body armor, carriage springs, saddles, ropes, and horsewhips. To bring wheat and cattle from the *pampas* to Buenos Aires for shipment to Europe, foreign investors (mostly British) built railroads and laid down railroad lines. (The British did not come themselves, but their bonds and engineers did.) The same investors built what was long the chief industry of Argentina: slaughterhouses. Other foreigners (Americans, English) built steel mills for rails, bridges, and barbed-wire factories to fence the plains. In 1871 the first steam-powered refrigerator ship sailed from Buenos Aires, bringing Argentine beef to Europe. Under-populated Argentina soon beckoned to Europe's ambitious poor as the land of hope and opportunity. (That and the *pampas* frontier helped to create another Argentine comparison: the United States of South America.) In 1869 Argenti-

---

[1] The great epics of *The Gaucho* are *Martin Fierro* and its sequel, *The Return of Martin Fierro*, by Jose Hernandez (1834-86), Argentine soldier and poet.

na's population was a scant two million. By 1914 it was fourteen million, and more than one-third were foreign-born.

"OUR HISTORY IS WRITTEN IN BLOOD AND FAILED EXPECTATIONS"

The first European to land in Argentina was Juan De Solis. The year was 1516. As shipmates watched in horror from the safety of their ship, de Solis was dismembered and eaten by his Indian hosts. (As the old joke of questionable taste has it, his last words were, "This cruise has cost me an arm and a leg!") In 1535 the Spanish explorer Pedro de Mendoza came ashore to found Buenos Aires. It was a splendid site, a harbor on the shores of a huge estuary, the Rio de la Plata, so named because legend has it that silver here was thick on the ground (*plata*, Spanish for silver; *argentum*, Latin for silver). No such mineral wealth has ever been found, but the fine harbor and its reassuring winds signaled the name, Santa Maria de los Buenos Aires, Our Sainted Lady of Good Air.

The nation that would become Argentina stirred to life in 1806 when a British fleet attacked Buenos Aires and occupied the city. An aroused citizenry drove them out, but in 1807 the British returned, and local resistance and patriotism increased. In 1808 Napoleon invaded Spain and put his brother on its throne. A citizen militia of Buenos Aires declared independence, while the great landlords of the La Plata hinterland and the rich merchants of the city raised royalist banners. Fifteen years of civil war followed (1810-1824): soldiers, colonials, and churchmen loyal to Spain versus soldiers and colonials fighting for independence. In 1814 the wars for independence found their great leader, Jose de San Martin (liberator of Argentina, Chile, and Peru), but just as the war was grinding to its close, Argentina was caught up in a wider war with Brazil (1825-27) over the Rio de la Plata territory that is now Uruguay.

From that war, a ruthless general pushed to power, Juan Manuel de la Rosa (he controlled Argentina from 1829-1852). General de la Rosa crushed Buenos Aires's drive for autonomy, and more important for the future of Argentina, he waged war on the Indians of Patagonia. In today's terms, it was a war of ethnic extermination. Another general seized power in 1852, and now the pattern of Argentine politics was set. In times of political unrest, economic breakdown, and when the civilian government seems to have lost its way, generals and the army take power. This is the pattern shared by all the countries of South America. It is the pattern of the *caudillo*: the military leader who leads a revolution, who saves his country from chaos, and when the revolution is won and peace and order return, the *caudillo* clings to power, proclaiming himself and his army essential to the well-being of the nation.

HOW DID JUAN PERON RISE TO POWER?

Juan Peron was only one in a long line of Argentina's military rulers. But his rule was exceptional. It fused military force with passionate popular support. He dominated Argentine politics for almost a quarter of a century, and even today, *Peronistas* are a pivot (some say the pivot) of Argentine politics. One of the oldest puzzles of history is expressed in an opposing pair of questions: Do the times make the man? Or does the man make the times? This is the great-man theory of history ("The history of the world is but the biography of great men," said Thomas Carlyle[2]) versus the play of time and circumstance ("events call forth the man"). Juan Peron and his wife, Eva, were loved by the masses, but their rise to power calls to mind one explanation of success offered by a big city boss in the United States: "I seen my opportunities and I took 'em."

Figure 23.2. Juan Peron

[2] See Thomas Carlyle, *Heros, Hero Worship and the Heroic in History* (Boston: Adams, 1841).

WHAT WERE PERON'S OPPORTUNITIES?

Juan Domingo Peron was born in 1895 to a family of Italian and French forebears. The Argentina of his childhood was a country of knife-sharp inequality: rich cattle and wheat barons whose estates encompassed hundreds of square miles aligned with rich merchants and industrialists in the cities. Like many ambitious young men without family wealth, Peron found opportunities in the military. He became an army cadet at sixteen; his brains and physical prowess marked him for success. He was six feet tall, winning medals as a skier and boxer and as fencing champion of the army. Unlike most other military officers of his generation, he had a serious interest in politics and sociology and wrote books on social and political affairs.

Posted to Italy in the 1930s as a military attaché, Peron observed Mussolini's reordering of Italian society. Fascism was Mussolini's formula for Italy's regeneration: a society controlled by a political and military party obedient to its leader (*duce*), supported by popular acclaim. Argentina was officially neutral in World War II, but its military admired Hitler and Mussolini. With popular support, a military coup in 1943 overthrew a civilian government that had failed to solve Argentina's wartime social and economic problems. As the colonels and generals scrambled to control government ministries, Colonel Juan Peron claimed a seemingly unimportant office, Minister of Labor and Social Welfare. By 1945, as a result of skillful bureaucratic infighting, he had risen to become Vice President and Minister of War. Late in 1945 he helped to maneuver Argentina into declaring war on Germany, thus assuring friendly relations with the victorious Allies. Most important, he built a base of popular support among the working poor.

The working poor of Argentina's cities (especially in the slaughterhouses and on the docks) were immigrants and children of immigrants nurtured by Europe's socialism, communism, and anarchism. He answered their dreams of social justice by improving workers' lives (holidays, pensions, and severance pay). Equally important were his themes of populism and equality. (Why should the rich bulls occupy the greenest pastures, while the cows are forced to stand outside?) Peron became the hero of the *descamisados*, the shirtless ones, and the army, anticipating danger from a populist uprising, joined with civilian constitutionalists to order Peron's arrest. It is at this critical moment that his mistress, Eva Duarte, changed Argentine history.

WHO WAS EVA DUARTE?

Eva Duarte, Evita as she was later known, was one of five illegitimate children born to the mistress of Juan Duarte, a rural landowner and political boss. After Duarte's death, when her mother accepted the protection of another man, Eva made her way to Buenos Aires. The year was 1934. She was fifteen years old, a woman-child of steely resolve. A succession of lovers and protectors carried her upwards to money, social standing, and a career as radio actor. By 1944, Eva had achieved an enviable place in the world, but for Eva enough was not enough. She contrived to meet Juan Peron.[3]

It was January 22, 1944. Eva was on stage (or possibly in the wings) at a fundraiser for earthquake victims. She walked over to Peron (or did he walk toward her?). As one version tells it, Eva said, "Colonel Peron?" "Yes, my child," he answered. "Thank you for existing."

Figure 23.3. Eva Peron

He was forty-eight; she was twenty-four. Later, when Peron was placed under arrest, it was Eva, together with allies in the labor movement, who flashed word to the *descamisados* to rally in support of the imprisoned Peron. The military backed down. Peron was released from confinement on October 17, 1945, and from the balcony of the Presidential Palace, with Eva at his

[3] See the memorable essay by Alma Guillermoprieto in *The New Yorker*, December 2, 1996.

side, he addressed a cheering crowd of 300,000, calling them to support his bid to become President of Argentina.

Eva and Juan campaigned together, now as husband and wife. Evita had found her destiny, and as she was often to shout to adoring crowds, "my life for Peron." Peron was elected President in 1946, and Evita established her own charitable foundation. The foundation grew rich on money extracted from the rich and (or so it is alleged) skimmed from public coffers. It was charity on a personal and flamboyant scale. Seated behind an imposing desk, aides at her side, Evita would hear petitions: "My mother needs false teeth"; "Our child needs a life-preserving operation"; "We wish to marry but cannot afford a place to live." Evita would hear out the petitioners and, with maximum theatrical effect, would proclaim, "Done!" Her minions would escort the favored petitioners out to be given promissory notes and orders signed by Evita herself.

After her marriage to Juan, Eva traveled to Europe, only to be snubbed by Grand Society. She returned home, a humiliated provincial, vowing to remake herself an image of fashion and elegance. And now the legend of Evita took final form. She engaged dress designers to flatter her petite figure, hairdressers to provide a distinctive coiffeur—hair pulled back, shimmering in halo gold, and jewelers to adorn her dresses with restrained elegance. "They want to see me look beautiful," she said of her adoring crowds. And as a more detached observer put it, the rich were not amused, but the poor found vicarious fulfillment in Evita.

Juan campaigned for a second term. But Evita was mortally ill with uterine cancer. Her life might have been saved with appropriate surgery, but she said she had no time for the hospital. Too weak to stand or comfortably sit, she rode to Juan's inauguration encased, most agree, in plaster of paris covered by a fur coat. When news of her fatal illness reached the streets, thousands knelt in prayer. And when she died, eight people also died, and more than 2,000 were injured in the crush of crowds attempting to pay their respects to Evita. (The opening scene of Andrew Lloyd Weber's *Evita* catches the spirit of the moment. And the entire operetta captures the drama of Evita's life.)

AFTER EVITA, WHAT?

After Evita's death, Peron lost his sure political touch, and without Evita, his rapport with his followers, the *Peronistas*, began to slip away. Democratically inclined officers threatened to bring guns and tanks into the streets. Peron resigned, took refuge in Paraguay (September 19, 1955), and sailed to exile in Madrid. Had Evita lived, would she have counseled defiance? Fearing that Evita's body might become a symbol of martyrdom and opposition, the military hid her body in Milan, Italy. It lay there, a closely guarded secret, until it was returned in 1963 to Spain to the exiled Peron, by now remarried to a third wife, Isabelle. The latter reportedly slept on Evita's casket, hoping to acquire some of her magic.

Eventually, Evita's body was returned to Argentina and now lies in an elaborate mausoleum in the cemetery of the Recoletta Fathers. (The cemetery is a city of the dead, with imposing statues of grief, of resurrection, of the physical and spiritual beauty of those entombed in adjacent castles and palaces of the dead.) Evita is entombed in the Duarte mausoleum, but at his express wishes, Juan is buried elsewhere. As a macabre footnote to Juan's story, in 1987 vandals broke into his tomb and sawed off his hands, attempting to hold them for a ransom never paid. Evita's tomb is much visited. The curious are there in constant flow. But Argentines also come, bringing flowers and lamentations for the woman they still call Saint Evita.

Even in exile, Peron's followers, the *Peronistas*, continued to agitate Argentine politics. In 1973 *Peronista* candidates won the presidency and a majority in the legislature. And in a special election (1974), Peron once again became President of Argentina. His politics swung rightward, and when he died in 1974, his widow Isabel (now Vice President) stepped into the presidency, but increasing turmoil (terrorism and political violence) between radical and conservative factions of the *Peronistas* pushed the military to intervene. In 1976 the military once again took control of the country.

AFTER PERON: WHAT MADNESS? WHAT CRUELTY?

Determined to expunge from public life radicals, socialists, labor union leaders, and all those demanding populist reforms, the military now began the "dirty war" to hunt down, imprison, torture, and kill those susceptible to left-wing politics. University students and their professors were high on the list of the suspected. As many as 30,000 people were "killed or disappeared…from 1976 to 1983, part of a policy to wipe out opposition to military dictatorship. Many were tortured, drugged and thrown from aircraft into the River Plate or the Atlantic Ocean, or buried in mass graves."[4] The cruelty of the regime and the uncertainty of life during the years of the generals come vividly to life on the movie screen in *Missing; Death and the Maiden;* and *House of the Spirits.* In these films, Hollywood spoke of more than Argentina. The films are also an indictment of other South American military regimes of those times, especially Chile and Brazil. Those other military regimes shared with Argentina murder and torture,

---

[4] *New York Times*, June 30, 2003.

but surely the nadir of Argentine military depravity was the practice of invading hospitals (and sometimes murdering new mothers) to steal babies to be given to wives of childless military officers.

Mute remembrance of those terrible times takes place once a week outside the Presidential Palace in the Plaza de Mayo as mothers and grandmothers of the "missing" stand silently on the pavement, holding photographs of their long-lost children. As the years go by, their ranks grow smaller. Soon there will be none left to mourn.

HOW DID THE MILITARY LOSE POWER?

Using patriotic distraction to damp down rising opposition (shades of Machiavelli!), the military invaded in 1982 the British-held Falkland Islands, long claimed by Argentina. And when the Falkland War collapsed in defeat, the generals and admirals moved aside. The leader of the *Peronistas*, Carlos Menem, was elected President. And Argentina moved again into democracy's ranks. The tango rhythms of Argentine politics and economics had returned.

Like other South American countries, Argentina rides the roller coaster of a boom-and-bust economy. In some countries, boom and bust has been a consequence of reliance on the world prices for commodities (rubber and coffee in Brazil, nitrates and copper in Chile, and nitrates in Peru). Argentina has suffered for its historic reliance on wheat and beef exports. Its economy has also been whipsawed by Argentina's laundry-list of long-standing political problems: dictatorial strong men taking money in exchange for business favors, politicians and their followers who profit from the cycle of nationalizing and privatizing railroads, banks, and public utilities, and a decentralized federal system in which the governors of Argentina's twenty-three (nearly autonomous) provinces create standing "armies" of loyal civil servants who "oversee" businesses in their province.

In 2001 Argentina "suffered its worst economic collapse in more than a century."[5] Presidents came and went, with three in one week. Protestors took to the streets. But the military did not intervene, and a civilian President, with assistance from the international community, began the process of rebuilding the country's economy. For Argentina's democracy it was a close call, but a reassuring one. And for those concerned with Argentine culture, we offer this fascinating insight: during the worst of the economic crisis, with banks closed and savings ac-

---

[5] *The Economist*, June 5, 2004.

counts frozen, when more than one-fifth of the population was out of work and desperate, tango bars and halls thrived as Argentines found solace in the dance.

HOW TO DANCE THE TANGO?

To say that the tango is merely a dance is like saying that opera is merely a stage full of singers. One quip has it that the tango is the vertical expression of horizontal desire. True, there is a sexual undercurrent to the tango, but there is also the soulful expression of loss. The rhythms of the tango are insistent; the beat is unmistakable—slow, slow, quick, quick, slow. The sounds of the band are defined by the bandoneon, a small accordion that delivers both rhythm and melody. A stringed instrument—violin, cello, or bass viol—complements the melodic theme. And sometimes a piano provides all three: melody, theme, and rhythm. The music celebrates "urban themes of betrayal, poverty, and misery," but also "sweet tunes that uplift..."[6] The dancer's steps are sinuous: stance is a close hold; chest, stomach, and thighs touch, and legs flash and wrap themselves around one's partner with dazzling speed. Dance exhibitions in tango cabarets offer a wonderful tourist experience. The more adventurous and more competent tourist dancer may, with caution, find a partner in one of the tango venues scattered mostly around working-class neighborhoods. In the tango, as Guillermoprieto suggests, the soul of Argentina is on display.

---

[6] Alma Guillermoprieto, *National Geographic*, December, 2003.

AFRICA

24. The Dark Continent

Africa is mystic; it is wild; it is a sweltering inferno; it is a photographer's paradise, a hunter's Valhalla, an escapist's Utopia. It is what you will, and it withstands all interpretations. It is the last vestige of a dead world or the cradle of a shiny new one. To a lot of people, as to myself, it is just 'home'."

— Beryl Markham, *West with the Night*

As the popular story suggests, repeated millions of times to European and American school children for well over 100 years, Henry Morton Stanley, a reporter sent by the *New York Herald* newspaper to search for a missing Protestant missionary in the wilds of Africa, suddenly cast his eyes for the first time on Dr. David Livingstone in summer 1872, whereupon he uttered in a rather calm voice, "Doctor Livingstone, I presume?" To which the western man in front of him replied, "Yes, that is my name."

At least that is how the initial encounter between Stanley and Livingstone was reported in the *Herald* under the heading, "A Historic Meeting."[1] And what well may have been the first example in human history of a story quickly going viral in the nineteenth-century version of today's social media, newspapers throughout America and, thanks to a copper telegraph cable recently laid across the floor of the Atlantic Ocean, Europe quickly picked up the story and soon the "civilized" world would share the "deepest emotions of pride and pleasure" of Stanley and his discovery.

---

[1] Rubery, Matthew, "On Henry Morton Stanley's Search for Dr. Livingstone, 1871-72," *BRANCH: Britain, Representation and Nineteenth-Century History*, Ed. Dino Franco Felluga, *Extension of Romanticism and Victorianism on the Net*, accessed November 24, 2014, http://www.branchcollective.org.

LEGACY OF STANLEY AND LIVINGSTON

Whether Stanley actually uttered these now famous words or whether it was simply a newspaper's hype to sell more copies is a matter of conjecture, no matter. As newspapers on both sides of the Atlantic followed the story of this encounter in the unknown African continent throughout the summer of 1872, tens of thousands of their readers were learning for the first time about what was soon to be called the "dark continent."[2] When the nineteenth century had begun seven decades earlier, few Europeans and fewer Americans knew anything about the vast African continent and far fewer still had visited it. Yet a scant thirty years after Stanley's pen opened the African continent to western eyes, virtually all of the continent with the exception of present-day Ethiopia and Liberia had been colonized by seven European powers: Great Britain, France, Spain, Belgium, Germany, Italy, and Portugal. For the most part, the resultant structures created by extensive colonization throughout the continent have prevented or at least severely retarded political, economic, and social development since then.

The colonial state system imposed throughout Africa by these seven European powers can be characterized by overwhelming colonial control and exploitation, with an overbearing bureaucracy composed of civil servants and military officers who ruled in an extremely authoritarian fashion with heavy undertones of racism and classism. What differences existed among the seven colonial powers were a matter of degree, not of kind. As one author has stated, "they were alien, authoritarian, and bureaucratic, and distorted African political and social organizations and undermined their moral authority and political legitimacy as governing structures."[3]

LAND OF 10,000 DISTINCT GROUPS

> "There is almost no country in Africa where it is not essential to know to which tribe, or which subgroup of which tribe, the president belongs. From this single piece of information you can trace the lines of patronage and allegiance that define the state."
>
> — Christopher Hitchens

---

[2] See Henry M. Stanley, *Through the Dark Continent* (London: Sampson Low, Marston, Seale & Revington, 2 vols, 1878). It is assumed that the first use of the phrase "dark continent' is to be found in the title of this book.

[3] Ehiedu E. G. Iweriebor, "The Colonization of Africa," Schomburg Center for Research in Black Culture, accessed November 24, 2014. http://exhibitions.nypl.org/africanaage/essay-colonization-of-africa.html.

As with all countries and regions of the globe, Africa and its fifty-five countries that now comprise the continent are a product of their history and traditions, their habits of the heart. In this case, however, the habits of the heart of these varied groups of people, who trace their ancestry to those who lived on land we now call Africa, for one or more millennia were confronted by a colonial rule that sought to ignore, exploit, and even destroy those cultural traditions that had evolved over hundreds if not thousands of years. Before colonial rule, there were as many as 10,000 distinct groupings of people, organized from small social units to large-scale distinct political organizations called states.

It is not surprising that still now there are estimated to be between 1,500 and 2,000 recognized languages spoken on the continent. The most popular languages represent both native tongues (or at least those of conquerors of a bygone era) and those imported by nineteenth-century colonial powers. Arabic leads the way with 170 million speakers, followed by Swahili (140 million), English (130 million), French (115 million), Berber (50 million), Hausa (50 million), Portuguese (20 million), and Spanish (10 million).

AFRICAN RICHES

But the colonial powers of the late nineteenth century were not the first to seek the riches that awaited those who set foot on the African continent. Martin Meredith chronicles the long history of African exploitation in his recently published *The Fortunes of Africa.*[4] In the very first sentence of this wonderful volume, Meredith traces the history of outsiders coveting African riches back to the time of the Egyptian pharaohs. Precious stones and gold were early prizes then (think King Solomon's mines), a quest that was repeated several times over the centuries. Meredith also describes the hunt for arable land, as first Romans and then Arab invaders crossed into the continent in search of bounty from the rich soil. Africa produced still another commodity, ivory, valued by the newly emerging nineteenth-century countries of the Industrial Revolution, which joined existing willing buyers from the Near and Far East.

Probably Africa's most compelling export, slaves, changed the course of history not only on the continent but throughout the receiving countries, first those in what is now the heartland of the Middle East and subsequently those in the western hemisphere. "From molasses to rum to slaves," the chilling story told in song in the musical *1776*, reveals the tragic links among the second wave of slave traders.

---

[4]This section draws heavily from Martin Meredith, *The Fortunes of Africa: A 5000-Year History of Wealth, Greed, and Endeavour* (New York: Public Affairs, 2014).

Perhaps the story of African riches and foreigners' greed and treachery in pursuit of them is best summed up in the following passage:

> As the seemingly well-intentioned French journalist spoke about Africa's *scarcity* and its *limited resources*, Nine smiled to himself almost condescendingly. He considered such statements an absolute joke. Africa did not, nor did it ever have, *limited resources*.
>
> Nine knew something the journalist obviously didn't: Africa was the most abundantly resourced continent on the planet bar none. Like the despots who ruled much of the region, and the foreign governments who propped them up, he knew there was more than enough wealth in Africa's mineral resources such as gold, diamonds and oil – not to mention the land that nurtured these resources – for every man, woman and child.
>
> He thought it unfortunate Africa had never been able to compete on a level playing field. The continent's almost unlimited resources were the very reason foreigners had meddled in African affairs for the past century or more. Nine knew it was Omega's plan, and that of other greedy organizations, to siphon as much wealth as they could out of vulnerable Third World countries, especially in Africa.
>
> The same organizations had the formula down pat: they indirectly started civil wars in mineral-rich regions by providing arms to opposing local factions, and sometimes even helped to create famines, in order to destabilize African countries. This made the targeted countries highly vulnerable to international control. Once the outside organizations had divided and conquered, they were then able to plunder the country's resources.[5]

EARLY EXPLORERS

The first two-thirds of the nineteenth century witnessed a dramatic increase in the exploration (as opposed to exploitation) of the African continent. In addition to Stanley and Livingstone's exploration of southern and central Africa, men like Richard Burton (not the actor), John Speke and James Grant ventured into the great lakes region in the center of Africa and to the source of the Nile, adding much knowledge of the continent and building upon that gained earlier of northwestern Africa. And by the end of the nineteenth century, most major river systems had been fully explored and the huge varied resource base of the continent fully uncovered and charted.

By two-thirds through the nineteenth century only ten percent of Africa was under the control of foreign colonial powers. Portugal, Britain and France had made, by later compari-

---

[5] James Corcan and Lance Corcan, *The Ninth Orphan* (Bay of Plenty, New Zealand: Sterling Gate Books, 2011), 123.

son, modest forays into the continent and had seized the equivalent of five present-day countries. It was about to change, however, so that by the beginning of World War I all of Africa except for Ethiopia and Liberia were under European colonial control. The global thirst for African riches drove the European colonial powers into competition, their thirst wetted by triumphs in other parts of the world.

CAPITALISM AND IMPERIALISM

Figure 24.1. Flag map of European Colonies in 1913

This sudden upswing in European colonialism can be traced to two overarching reasons, one internal and the other external. The former related to how capitalism was thought to grow and thrive in newly industrialized Europe. At some point in the evolution of domestic capitalism, as its theorists (as well as its detractors such as Lenin in his *Imperialism: The Highest Stage of Capitalism*) suggest, capitalism will stop growing unless it expands beyond its national borders in search of both raw materials for use in the manufacturing stage, and new markets for its finished products. Africa was the most suitable place (along with the Far East) for turning trade deficits into trade surpluses. And the continent possessed substantial raw materials not found in Europe but that were now eagerly sought after by European industry and European consumers. At the start of this interest in Africa, the search for faraway ports of call controlled by the European powers was not high on the colonial agenda, unlike the United States, where President Theodore Roosevelt understood how both global trade and global military force projection, on the one hand, and foreign ports of call on the other, went hand in glove. But that would soon change.

COLONIES AS SYMBOLS OF MILITARY STATUS

The second reason why Africa was so coveted by the European colonial powers was external. It related to political and military rivalries that had begun to dramatically increase around the middle of the nineteenth century. It was a century that had begun in war and the threat of global (think European) domination, as France under the leadership of Napoleon Bonaparte had sought to conquer the world under the guise of exporting the democratic ideals of the French Revolution to the rest of the world. Napoleon had been stopped, barely, by a coalition of European powers, and out of the ashes of the Napoleonic War came a new commitment to global peace. In Vienna in 1815, the victorious powers, intent on finding a suitable mechanism for ensuring world peace, had crafted a new solution. They would tweak the current arrangement, what was known as the classical balance of power system, whereby no single country was allowed to acquire a preponderance of power, defined as more power than that of the rest of the major national powers combined. This tweaking involved adding two new dimensions to the strategies then currently employed under the balance of power. First, global peace would become the special responsibility of the larger national powers, in this case the Big Five of Great Britain, France, Russia, Prussia, and Austria-Hungary, rather than giving all nations, large and small, equal responsibility for peace. And second, all national governments would engage in pro-active, formalized and regularized diplomacy so as to forestall any emerging international problem from evolving into a fully blown crisis and even military hostilities (think both the underlying and immediate set of events that resulted in World War I).

This reconfigured and revitalized balance of power system worked fairly well for almost half a century. But by mid-nineteenth century, a new political surge swept across Europe. It was the wave of democratic change, influenced by the two great movements of the late eighteenth century, the American Revolution and the French Revolution. Now the great monarchs of Europe were under attack from within, domestic revolutionaries bent on overthrowing the monarchical system and replacing it with something more akin to majority or at least more democratic rule. The result was a withdrawal of focus on the pro-active cooperative diplomatic ventures designed to prevent international conflict that had characterized the early post-Napoleonic era, replaced by a new emphasis on combating domestic turmoil.

This, in turn, was accompanied by another phenomenon. The Industrial Revolution was beginning to find its way into the military sector of society. And this had a dramatic effect on the comparative power rankings of European countries. No longer was a nation restricted to increasing its military power by adding more local foot soldiers or by finding new military allies and adding their foot soldiers to the mix. Now a country could quickly increase its military capability by applying the fruits of the Industrial Revolution to the military sector, and thus developing larger, more menacing and greater numbers of weaponry and by also increasing the speed by which this expanded arsenal and its men could be transported across greater and greater distances. This required overseas military land and naval bases, which, in turn, could be filled by colonies throughout the globe. Local natives in these colonies could also serve as a source of new military recruits, and at a far lower price than the colonial powers' own citizenry. And what was the last great landmass left to be conquered? The answer was easy—Africa.

DRIVE FOR COLONIZATION OF AFRICA

The watershed event was the Berlin Conference of 1884. Here the European colonial powers arrogantly agreed on the rules of the game for the conquest and partitioning of the African continent. From then until the outback of World War I in 1914, European powers were in a race with one another for as large a piece of Africa as possible. Overarching this struggle was another competition, a series of military arms races to see who would be the greatest military power on the European continent. Both the arms races and the series of crises created by the push for larger and larger empires finally reached a breaking point, in August 1914, when an assassination of an Austrian archduke by a Serbian national earlier in the summer resulted in the European countries finding themselves in a long drawn-out war, which would last four years and would change the landscape of Europe and its colonial empires. The first crack in the system of European imperialism had appeared but it would pale in comparison to the next crack created by another great war, World War II.

SOME BENEFITS OF COLONIAL RULE

> "No other continent has endured such an unspeakably bizarre combination of foreign thievery and foreign goodwill."
> — Barbara Kingsolver, *The Poisonwood Bible*

Colonial rule did produce some benefits. Martin Meredith suggested three important ones: a system of schools, medical services, and a transportation infrastructure. But the extent to which these positive steps impacted large numbers of the local populations is very problematic. Social indicators throughout the continent suggest that the extent to which these benefits reached a significant percentage of people fell far short of what might have been expected by the colonial powers or local leaders. To cite one example, transportation routes focused on moving raw materials from their original sources to coastal ports for shipment to the colonial power, not on a system of intra-country roads that connected the far corners of the country. And almost all economic activity remained tightly controlled by and in the hands of foreign corporations with their own foreign nationals in charge.

END OF POLITICAL COLONIALISM

The colonial era, which had arrived quickly throughout the African continent in a matter of decades, did not last long. It could not survive World War II nor could it survive the call for national self-determination at war's end. As the war dragged on, colonial powers were forced to divert their attention and resources from overseeing their colonial empires toward the war effort on the continent of Europe. They could not afford to continue the iron grip that had allowed them to exploit their colonies, most especially those colonies far removed from the battlefields, so control was loosened dramatically. At the war's end, two phenomena were at work simultaneously. Together they had the effect of ushering in a new era characterized by the collapse of the global colonial system throughout the world, and most especially in Africa.

As the war came to a conclusion, colonial powers were intent on restoring their empires to pre-war levels. But a newly emerging theme would undercut this goal. It was the push for national self-determination. Not only was the push coming from those within exploited areas of the globe, but it had a new supporter. The recently created United Nations made national self-determination one of its leading causes as it began its work in the final days of World War II.

The call for this new global value was taking place in the context of the expanded mandate for the new global organization. Its predecessor had been simply tasked with preventing war but the UN had a larger responsibility. Not only was it charged with preventing war and stopping military conflicts should they break out, it was also tasked with addressing those underlying causes that lead to war. Among the latter was the existing colonial system that suppressed political, economic and social development for a large segment of the world's population. The international community was now on record for the first time, in the form of inclusion in the UN Charter, as wanting to eradicate colonialism through national self-determination. It was now obvious that colonialism was doomed, although most colonial powers were reluctant to admit it at first. And some took police and military action to prevent the inevitable. But they were ultimately unsuccessful.

The early 1950s ushered in the major push for national self-determination. This push would continue for several decades until the African continent (as well as many other parts of the globe) were rid of foreign domination. It was not an easy struggle, however. Political independence came fairly easy to some places, while others had to endure significant military and political hurdles before independence was achieved. And once won, the battle was not over. During the struggle for independence, local groups that usually competed with one another joined forces in the common struggle against the external enemy. But once this battle was over, the ability of local groups to work together to form their own national government was greatly diminished. Civil war was the result (think Sudan, Chad, Ethiopia, and Nigeria, among others) and some proved to be far bloodier than the former struggle against the colonial power.

The typical end result of this intra-country civil strife was one-party or one-person rule. Originally advanced as the best way to achieve political order and economic growth, this emerging cult of the individual or of the party soon became the vehicle for authoritarian governance with the clear intent to maintain control and suppress any internal political opposition. Across most of Africa, dictators emerged and then proceeded to focus on staying in power and increasing their own personal wealth, rather than advancing political participation and economic development. Ruthlessness became the norm and violence became commonplace, in many cases greater than that experienced during the colonial era. Most dictators were from the military, and the latter became the instrument by which the autocratic leaders remained in power. Meredith relates that over one extended period, only six of 150 rulers voluntarily left office.[6]

---

[6] Martin Meredith, *The Fortunes of Africa*, 623-24.

ECONOMIC IMPERIALISM

Economic development took a back seat in favor of self-serving political maneuvering in the early post-colonial era. And the economic development problem was complicated by the residue of colonialism, which had left countries with no competent national economic infrastructure and ruling class, with little or no local ownership of industry and other businesses, and with a heavy dependence on the former colonial power for international trade and investment.

EARLY 1970S PROBLEMS

Then came the travails of the early 1970s. Already underway in Africa was a rising population growth rate, brought on by a sharp decline in death rates because of declines in infant mortality rates (a consequence of well-intentioned intervention by global governmental and non-governmental organizations).[7] Birth rates in the developing world had always taken into account that a high percentage (by comparison to the west) would counteract a high death rate as life was tough throughout Africa. But when death rates declined dramatically without a corresponding drop in birth rates, population grew fast, creating a much higher than usual group of young people who were not ready to contribute economically to society. They had to be fed, housed, educated, and rid of disease before they were ready to enter the economic marketplace. This took badly needed government capital, which, if it existed at all, had to be diverted from projects to increase a country's GDP through economic investment of some kind. The end result was that economic growth did not keep pace with population growth, resulting in economic stagnation or even a fall backward on the economic growth scale.

At the same time food production fell because of two major reasons. First, African weather, which had been rather conducive to food production, took a turn for the worse in the early 1970s. Add to this was the dramatic rise in the cost of energy at the same time, the consequence of OPEC's increasing the cost of oil by 400 percent in response to the west's support of Israel in the Arab-Israeli wars of 1967 and 1973. Decreased rainfall meant an increased need for agricultural inputs like irrigated water as well as energy-based fertilizer. Again, badly needed capital had to be diverted from fueling the economy to simply trying to keep pace with increased costs without any impact on economic growth. As a consequence, for a time food production did not keep pace with people production, the only region in the world to experience this phenom-

---

[7] See James E. Harf and B. Tomas Trout, *The Politics of Global Resources: Population, Food, Energy and Environment* (Durham, NC: Duke University Press, 1986).

enon at that time. And a decade later, the continent would be hit with the AIDS epidemic, taking a severe toll among a significant percentage of able bodied workers.

THE SPECIAL CASE OF SOUTH AFRICA

If ordinary westerners could identify anything about the African continent, among the items on their very short lists would be the idea of apartheid in South Africa and its connection to Nelson Mandela (although most would likely not be able to recall the specific role the latter played in ending apartheid). South Africa had been part of the British empire but had enjoyed home rule since early in the twentieth century. Within the country, there was a racial divide, which led to much contention beginning in the 1940s. As non-whites increased their demands for greater freedom, whites continued their hardened stance, even as racial injustice was being successfully fought elsewhere in the world. Nelson Mandela became part of the fight against apartheid in the 1940s, subsequently emerging as a leader of the non-white opposition, and was imprisoned in the early 1960s for almost three decades. Released in part because of worldwide pressure, he later served as the country's president, after the whites-only government finally gave into worldwide pressure and ended apartheid. Mandela received the Nobel peace prize in 1993. His presidency was marked by reconciliation between whites and non-whites.

A HOPEFUL CONTINENT TODAY

This section takes its title from an article in *The Economist*.[8] Its thesis is simple: the lives of common Africans have greatly improved in the last ten years and we can expect the next decade to be even better. Here are the reasons outlined in the article. First, while Africans struggle with the trails of daily life, most do not fear their lives coming to a violent and premature end. This feeling is supported by social indicators, as secondary-school enrollment has grown dramatically (48 percent) over a recent eight-year period. Malaria-related deaths and HIV infections have declined by 30 percent and 74 percent respectively, while life expectancy is up 10 percent with child mortality sharply down.

The reason: a booming economy claims Oliver August of *The Economist* who crisscrossed the continent to check the current pulse of Africa. Real income has increased over 10 percent in the past decade (compared to a large decline in the previous decade), the fastest of any continent. GDP is expected to rise by 6 percent per year and foreign direct investment has almost

[8] The section draws heavily on "A Hopeful Continent," *The Economist* (March 2, 2014).

tripled in the last decade. Previously scarce goods and services are becoming easily available, as witnessed by the projected fivefold increase in television ownership in a decade.

Political development, measured in terms of movement toward democracy, has also made significant strides. *The Economist* reports that while at the end of the cold war only three out of the then fifty-three countries of Africa could be considered democracies, today the number is twenty-five countries, with twenty-two more moving in that direction as evidenced by "imperfect but worthwhile" elections. Almost all have multi-party constitutions, armies and their corresponding military rulers "mostly stay in the barracks."

And most have stopped shooting at one another, as civil strife has become less frequent and less deadly. Evidence of increased civic engagement can be found everywhere. And socialist economic models are becoming rarer as economic activity has taken on a much more visible capitalist look. As importantly, many of the fruits of recent infrastructure building fueled by both the public and private sector are about to start yielding results.

CAUSE FOR CONCERN

While many share these views and are optimistic about Africa's economic future, there is one cautionary tale to be told. One disquieting force at work, particularly in sub-Saharan Africa, is the continuing presence of high birth rates. As with most developing societies, Africa's demographic history has been one of high birth rates and high death rates. Life was hard and people died young, and so it was important that fertility keep pace with mortality; otherwise a society could disappear. But the post-World War II intervention by the developed world of more modern health practices, particularly programs designed to address high infant and child mortality, had the effect of lowering death rates without a corresponding decrease in birth rates. The result was ballooning growth rates. These, in turn, have placed impediments to solid and sustained economic growth, as the services demanded of the newly born tax government resources. At present the birth rate is over 5 percent per year in sub-Saharan Africa and 4.8 percent for the entire continent, far greater than the current rate of 2.3 percent elsewhere in the world. At this rate Africa's population could nearly triple by mid-century, meaning that one out of every three births in the world would take place in Africa.

Added to the problems associated with having a much larger percentage of the population fourteen years of age or younger because of high birth rates is the likelihood that much of this growth will occur in cities, whose current infrastructures are unable now to cope with population increases of the recent past. As have been observed in China for some time, rapid urbanization results not only in a higher number of cities growing rapidly, it also leads to an emerging group of cities that have taken on mega-city status, with population levels unthinkable a hundred years ago. This mega-city phenomenon has given China an entirely new list of challenges, a fate that is about to confront the emerging mega-cities of Africa. Lagos, Nigeria, for example, is expected to reach 40 million people within a few decades, and many other large cities in Africa will join Lagos as mega-cities.

Prospects for declining growth rates in Africa are dim. For that to happen, two challenges must be met. The first is that incentives for declining births must be present and second, the capacity for birth control must be available. History has taught us that the best contraceptive is economic development. All western societies developed lower birth rates once economic development was set in motion. There were many reasons for this but an important one was that development brought lower mortality rates, including infant mortality, so couples did not have to have as many children in order to ensure that two or three would live to adulthood. Death rates in Africa have declined much faster than the birth rates, in part because of vaccination programs aimed at the young, not because of economic development. So the capital for caring for the young before they can contribute to a country's economy is much more difficult to obtain in Africa when compared to the history of western societies. It is a two-edged sword as high birth rates impede economic development, yet the latter is a major cause of lowered growth.

The good news is that Africa can look to Asia as a success story. Massive birth population control programs led to declining birth rates, which in turn, resulted in economic development, again leading to incentives for lowered births. This is the second challenge in Africa. The easy availability of contraceptives is much less there than in the rest of the developed world, not to mention the developed sector. While contraception is widely available in the west and 60 percent of the rest of the developing world has access to contraception, in Africa access is limited to 20 percent of the population.

GEOGRAPHY OF A VAST CONTINENT

> "The continent is too large to describe. It is a veritable ocean, a separate planet, a varied, immensely rich cosmos. Only with the greatest simplification, for the sake of convenience, can we say 'Africa'. In reality, except as a geographical appellation, Africa does not exist."
>
> — Ryszard Kapuściński, *The Cobra's Heart*

Africa is the second largest continent after Asia.[9] Containing fifty-five countries and eight other territories, it is 11,725,385 square miles, more than three times that of the continental United States. Its population in 2013 was 1.11 billion. Its five largest countries are Nigeria (around 182.3 million in 2015), Ethiopia (about 90.1 million in 2015), Egypt (about 87.5 million in 2015), the Democratic Republic of Congo (about 74 million in 2015), and South Africa (about 54.4 million in 2015). Africa covers 25 percent of the world's landmass and about 15 percent of its population. At current growth rates, Africa's percentage of the global population could rise to 40 percent by the end of the century. Yet its population density is less than half that of Europe and about one-third that of Asia. Its highest mountain is Mount Kilimanjaro in Tanzania at 19,341 feet. Its longest river is the Nile at 4,258 miles and its largest river basin is the Congo at 1,440,051 square miles. Lake Victoria at 26,000 square miles is the largest lake on the continent. The average elevation above sea level is about 2,000 feet, not unlike that of North America. Differences in elevation levels are not pronounced. Plateaus or tablelands tend to be only moderately high, with the more pronounced ones found in the eastern and southern part of the continent.

The equator bisects the continent in half with most of it falling in the tropics. Only the most northern and southern parts of the continent are in temperate zones. The desert regions of the north and the lower plains are quite hot, with contrasting day and night temperatures. Rainfall levels vary considerably with the highest amount found near Mount Cameroon at over an inch a day (390 inches a year), while the lowest at 0.1 inch per year occurs somewhere in Sudan.

AFRICAN NATURAL AND HUMAN-MADE WONDERS

Everything about Africa is massive and diverse. The wise traveler's senses are dazzled with visions of expansive deserts, heavy rain forests, rolling grasslands, snow-covered mountain peaks, huge lakes, and never-ending rivers. From Table Mountain in the south to the river delta of the Nile in the north, to the sand dunes of Namibia and Morocco as well as those in the heart of the Sahara Desert, to the plateau of Nyika Plateau National Park in Malawi, to the Makgadikgadi Pans of Botswana, to the Spitzkoppe in Namibia, to Mount Mulanje in Malawi, to Mount Kilimanjaro, and to Victoria Falls in Zambia and Zimbabwe, physical wonders

[9] For an interesting interpretation of geography and Africa, see James Delehanry, "Africa: A Geographic Frame," in Maris Grosz-Ngaté, John H. Hanson, and Patrick O'Meara, *Africa*, Fourth Edition (Bloomington, Indiana: Indiana University Press, 2014).

abound. Add to it the year-long great migrations of animals in Tanzania and Kenya, and the wonderful parks where a myriad of animals roam, and one's senses have never been so tested.

Humans have also contributed to the beauty of Africa. We must begin with the pyramids and sphinx of Egypt mentioned earlier in this volume. One of this volume's co-authors, James E. Harf, experienced the good fortune of a climb deep inside the Great Pyramid of Cheops until he reached the middle where the sarcophagus containing the body of the pharaoh once stood. Travel further upstream on the Nile and endless temples make their appearance. The many marketplaces or souks in places like Marrakesh and Fez, Morocco, and Cairo give testimony to human's ability to create interesting physical structures, as do European influences in South Africa, Senegal, Kenya, Mozambique, and ancient sites in Ethiopia. One must not forget that the Romans, who left architectural evidence behind everywhere they set foot, included Africa in this dynamic, as found in Tunisia, Morocco Libya, and Algeria. Evidence of ancient African civilizations can also be found in Zimbabwe, Uganda, Gabon, Burkina Faso, and Benin. Living traditional landscapes now considered African Heritage sites are found in Senegal, Zimbabwe, Togo, South Africa, Nigeria, and Mali. And it goes on and on and on.

VIGNETTES FOR THE SOUL

We close this chapter about the great continent of Africa with a series of vignettes written by one of the co-authors of this book, Lawrence J.R. Herson, who has set foot on the continent numerous times. Each conveys part of a personal story experienced over many decades.

Introductory Vingnette

"I have been to Africa more than a dozen times—often with my wife, Libby. The name itself is something of a mystery. Perhaps it comes from the Greek, meaning 'without cold,' but however the origin of its name, it was Herodotus who framed our experience of Africa. Out of Africa, he said there is always something new and much to appreciate, enjoy, and cherish: its animals, its forests, its plant life, and the unforgettable memories such as the time we slept under the stars in one of its deserts. As the old saying goes, geography is destiny. And Africa's destiny owes to the fact that much of it is equatorial. The people of Equatorial lands are poor, most with limited education. Countries are generally without industries and manufactures to generate wealth that lifts a population out of poverty. Reasons abound; tropical people are subject to diseases bourn by insects (think malaria), diseases carried by rivers and streams, and those carried by the earth (think ringworm).

"From the safety of our Land Rover we watch the lioness hunt. As male and female devour their prey; buzzards fly above and slathering jackals wait their turn for what is left.

Egypt

"Set in the eastern corner of Africa, Egypt (as Herodotus also said) is the gift of the Nile. It is an oasis set in the desert, with fertile lands and abundant crops. From the apartment lent by friends, we could look down on Cairo's thronging streets with its eight million plus population. Young men are everywhere to be seen, looking for jobs, still living with their parents, unable to marry without employment. Many sit at the doors of government agencies, hoping to get inside, and thus to begin a humble job that will eventually move them upward. Unfortunately for them, their university degrees are not practical for employment. Gentlemen, they are told, do not work with their hands and rather than studying, say engineering, their degrees are in the liberal arts! Shoddy builders substitute cement; and all too often, buildings collapse in the streets, injuring many and sending most to the protection of other streets.

Kenya

"Most travelers have their favorite country. Ours is Kenya. We go and visit old friends. We admire the tall stately Masai warriors, who shout and shake their spears as in days gone by when they could still hunt lions, and the Zulus, fierce warriors whose tactics were much in the style of Alexander of Macedonia. Let the enemy penetrate your ranks, and when he thinks he has triumphed, attack him from the rear and finish him off. Zulus were the implacable enemies of the British whose soldiers admired their tactics and bravery. Their stories are told in movies: *Zulu* (1964) with Michael Caine and Richard Burton, and *Zulu Dawn* (1979), which tells the story of bull-headed and downright stupid British commanders.

"Most of all, we are fascinated by the big game: lions, giraffes, water buffalo, and elephants. From the safety of our Land Rover, we watch a lioness kill a deer. As lion and lioness devour their prize, buzzards circle, and jackals cringe and slather. We rise early to go to the water hole to watch the animals drink. And our guide takes us to the foot of Mount Kilamanjoro. We climb part way; then return and sit in our camp chairs to watch the clouds encircle the mountain.

"Nairobi is the center of urban life. As we exit a bank after changing money, the bank guard warns us, those men with clubs are watching and waiting to rob you. The guard, gun in hand, delivers us to an Indian shop where earlier we had bought souvenirs. The shopkeepers understood and bundled us into their car, followed by a second car as escorts.

"Our friends and saviors had come to Kenya a generation earlier to help build a railroad. Its trackage spanned rivers, hills, and swamps. Thus was born what Kenyans called the Lunatic Express. Within a few years it would link with other railroads, thus completing a generation's dream, by train from Cairo to South Africa.

Sudan

"Bordering Egypt in the south is the Sudan, a territory that forms part of the British protectorate. It is 1898 and the Sudan is in turmoil and rebellion. Led by a holy man, The Mahdhi, it makes war on the British. And Britain reacts swiftly. It sends gunboats on the Nile; its soldiers equipped with rifles and Gatling Guns, forerunner of the machine gun. Battles are fierce. Hundreds of British solders die; thousands of the Mahdi's followers do as well. The British have formed in hollow squares; the Mahdi's men swarm forward.

"And two remarkable men are part of the British forces: Charles 'Chinese' Gordon and Winston Churchill. Gordon will die defending the fortress-palace at Khartoum. And Churchill will charge forward in one of the last cavalry charges against warriors wearing medieval chain mail.

South Africa

"We came to South Africa, officially the Republic of South Africa, at the invitation of shipboard friends. We had heard and read much about its stormy and cruel race relations—whites dominating and abusing Blacks, Indians, and those of mixed races. And of, course, its almost saintly leader, the long imprisoned Nelson Mandela, kept for years in solitary confinement for his demands for Black and White equality. Located at the southernmost tip of Africa, its seas roil with winds and the meeting of the Atlantic and Indian Oceans. First ships to land or round the Cape on the way to India were often shipwrecked or damaged, almost unable to proceed.

"We were warned by our hosts to take care while walking or even driving. Crime, sometimes violent, abounds. Rape is common and frequent. And as we saw as guests, the White middle class lives in gated communities enclosed with barbed wire.

"The country was born in war. Among its first settlers were Dutch farmers who named themselves Boers. When Britain claimed the Cape, the Boers trekked inward to escape having their culture and their government controlled by the British. But the discovery of diamonds and gold put an end to their isolation. Outsiders from around the world poured in to 'get rich.' And to uphold law and order, the British went to war, called the Boer War. The British withstood at siege in Natal at a place called Ladysmith and the British public were aroused in anger. Parliament dispatched more troops to lift the siege. And among the first to attempt to lift the seige was Winston Churchill, who marched to capture the Boer capital of Pretoria. The war was fought from 1889 to 1902.

"Winston Churchill wrote a series of dispatches about the war and returned home to find himself a hero.

Botswana: The Happy Country

"I lectured about Botswana aboard a ship of the Holland America Line, whose next port of call was Botswana. It is a country of two million, one of the world's least populated countries. Its largest city is Gaborone, its capital. By African standards it is a wealthy country with a per capita income of more than $16,000, most derived from its diamond mines and its flourishing herds of cattle.

"Much of my lecture was based on the novels of Alexander McCall Smith whose novels are built around two women detectives, Mma Ramotswe and Mma Makutsi. Crime is their business. Tracking down criminals and errant husbands, locating missing persons, and keeping close watch on would-be wrong-doers. A light-hearted touch is provided by Mms Ramotswe's husband, Mr. J.L.B. Matekoni, an auto mechanic who diagnoses problems by speaking to ailing cars, and by his two apprentices who spend their time planning love affairs that somehow always go astray. Our favorite novel is *Double Comfort Safari Club*. The detectives' mission is to recover a large sum of money belonging to a guest at the club.

"Botswana's desert offered an opportunity for another of our outdoors pleasures, sleeping under the stars, snug in our sleeping bags. And as always, far from city lights, the heavens are bright with stars.

Madagascar (Now The Malagasy Republic)

"On our visit to Madagascar, the world's fourth largest island, we were pleasantly surprised to find French as one of its two official languages. We made port on an offshore island, Nose Be, and later took a small launch to the island itself.

"The natives are an admixture of Black and Indonesian, and exceedingly courteous and friendly, helped no doubt by our speaking French. Places and people have mellifluous names: Radima and Ranalova. With guide and jeep we climbed to its high plateau, 9,000 feet, where breathing was difficult for those long at sea. Our guide lamented the fact that this once heavily forested island was now barren, the trees cut down for firewood. We ate the local food, something of a mash built around peanuts. And for souvenirs there were T-shirts.

Zanzibar

"Zanzibar is an archipelago of low lying islands in the Indian Ocean. We forewent our usual pleasure of wading in the sea: sharp coral! We were given an audience with the ruling sultan after I identified myself as a professor who writes about democratic regimes. As a new treasured souvenir, we now display on the wall of our apartment an antique print of the sea front of Zanzibar, a single-masted sailing ship, customs house in the background.

"Cloves are one of the major exports of Zanzibar and the air is heavy with its fragrance. As we took our jar of cloves back to the ship, my wife recalled that in Egypt during pyramid construction, cloves were part of the diet of the workers, to keep them healthy and to give them strength!

The Comoros Islands

"We landed on one of its lovely islands and attended Sunday church services. Black ladies dressed in large hats and white gloves were singing. We joined in to welcoming smiles. Afterwards, one of the lovely smiling ladies asked us how we had learned the tune. We said it was a family favorite, not revealing that it was the song, *Danny Boy*!

Sailing the Indian Ocean

"Our ship took us past the Skeleton Coast where we anchored to gaze at shipwrecks along the shore, smashed sailing ships and rusting steel hulls, all victims to storms and near cyclonic winds, and then ashore on present-day Namibia, once German Southwest Africa. Evidence and mementos abound of its years as a German colony. Shops still carry German goods and German names like Backerl and Metzgeri. And streets still carry German names, for example, a grandfather of Nazi Marshal Göring, Shultz, Dr. Stahl. Churches also carry German names, such as Christuskirche, as well as statues like Sudwest Reiter.

"Prosperity came from diamond and copper mining. Germans as directors and engineers; the Herero and Nama the hard labor. To assert German control, the Shutztruppe was used to compel obedience.

"But our days were pleasant, no reminders of past conflict. The Black natives were friendly. Our rusty German was tolerated and we dined on wonderful German cuisine: dumplings, 'mit' pork and the like. Our ship was our hotel and we said farewells to our restaurateurs.

Morocco

"We have spent many a happy summer living in Morocco, fascinated by its thronging life. From a balcony above its central square, Jemaa el Fna (The Square of the Dead), we delighted in the passing show: jugglers, tumblers, story tellers, snake charmers. In an act of boldness, I asked to sound the flute. Slowly, head weaving from side to side, the cobra appears, flicks his tongue and hisses! We watched the blind, tied together on long ropes, cross the square around noon every day. And we flinched as a dentist pulled teeth with pliers and a chisel.

"I solved the mystery of the Oriental rope trick, where a rope is thrown in the air with no visible means of support, and the thrower climbs upward. The trick? The audience faces the sun, unable to see the hook that holds the rope to a nearby balcony!

"Poverty in Morocco is endemic. An English friend told us that a few coins of charity cannot make a dent in poverty. Instead, give a few coins to a beggar. I chose a boy leading a blind father, and Libby chose a begging nursing mother. The next day they were waiting for us outside our hotel!

"Through a friend teaching at a local college, I was invited to lecture at the University of Marrakesh. The language of the educated was French, and mine was passable. As a combat meteorologist in World War II, I was sent by the American Air Force to help train others in the French-speaking colony of New Caledonia. To my great surprise, my students were reading about democratic development, using the French edition of my book on American democracy. Winston Churchill was nearby, painting, at the Hotel Momoumia. At the great market or souk, I bought some Cuban cigars and sent them over to the great man. He raised his hat and waved 'thank you'."

AMERICA'S NEIGHBORHOOD

25. Canada: America's Neighbor to the North

Two common explanations for human affairs invoke destiny's imperatives: geography is destiny, and demography is destiny. Both ideas spring into sharp relief when contrasting Canada with its nearest neighbor, the United States. As President Kennedy said of the two countries, geography made us neighbors, but history made us friends. More wryly, and perhaps more truthfully, Canada's former Prime Minister, Pierre Trudeau, said that living border to border with the United States is like sleeping with an elephant: no matter how kindly and well disposed the elephant, when he sneezes, we catch cold. And if he were to roll over, we would be dead![1]

GEOGRAPHICALLY HOW DO THE TWO COUNTRIES COMPARE?

Canada and the United States share the world's longest unfortified border, more than 5,500 miles. But the two countries share more than just borders. Their borders separate thirteen American states (twelve of the lower forty-eight plus Alaska), seven Canadian provinces, and the Yukon Territory. They also share four of the five Great Lakes (Michigan lies solely in the U.S.) and the most spectacular waterfall in North America, Niagara Falls. Both countries are

---

[1] For additional reading, see Derek Hayes, *Canada: An Illustrated History* (Madeira Park, British Columbia: Douglas & McIntyre, 2008) and R. D. Francis et al., *Journeys: A History of Canada* (Vancouver: Nelson College Indigenous, 2009). Farley Mowat is the author of almost two dozen books, many of which deal with Canada. Two highly regarded Canadian novelists are Joyce Carol Oates and Margaret Atwood.

continental, that is, each extends from the Atlantic to the Pacific. And each shares a high mountain range, the Rockies.

In terms of territory, the lower forty-eight states of the U.S. comprise approximately three million square miles, while Canada's geographic reach is approximately 3.8 million square miles. North to south, Canada extends more than 2,900 miles; east to west it stretches 3,400 miles.

The United States' climate extends from temperate to subtropical, while Canada's extends from temperate to sub-Arctic to Arctic. As a consequence of Canada's northward reach (and its harsh winters), some 90 percent of the population live within 200 miles of its southern border, and 75 percent live within one hundred miles of that border. The United States has a population density of seventy-three persons per square mile, while Canada has eight (Saudi Arabia has six). Equally important to the distribution of Canada's population is the Canadian Shield, centered on Hudson Bay. The Shield is 1,000 miles of rocks and eroded mountains scraped and shaped by ancient glaciers, running across six provinces. The Canadian Shield stands as a wall between east and west Canada and deprives Canada of the rich farmlands that constitute America's Midwest.

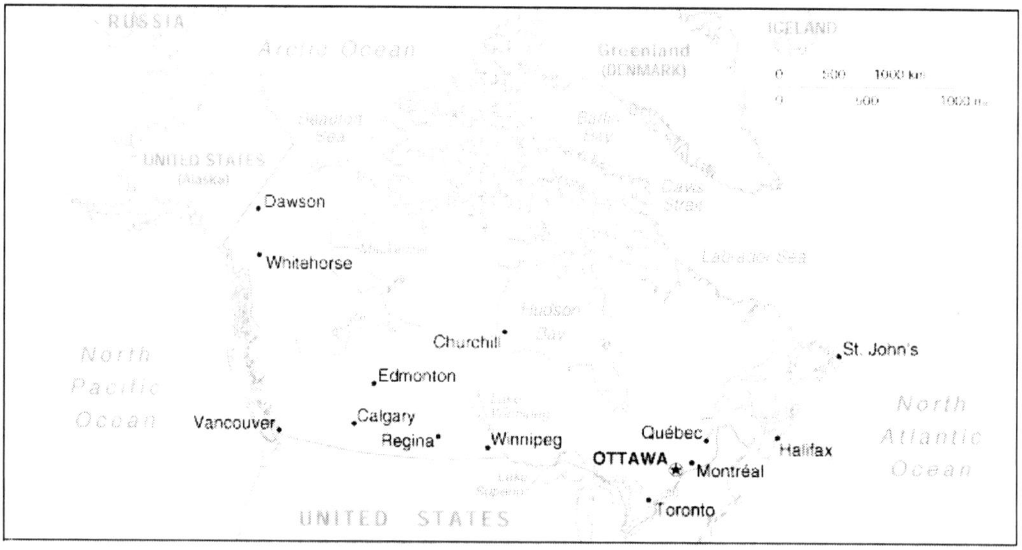

Figure 25.1. Map of Canada

Overall, Canada has only 5 percent arable land, in contrast to about 20 percent in the United States, but it does contain valuable minerals, such as cobalt, nickel, zinc, timber, and copper. The shield has forests and is a refuge for waterfowl. Canada has vast tracts of timber covering about 27 percent of the country and is estimated to have a million lakes and rivers. Canada has 30 percent of the world's freshwater—an increasingly scarce and precious resource on a globe whose fresh water is constantly diminished.

Canada's two largest rivers are the St. Lawrence, which runs 800 miles from Lake Ontario eastward to the Atlantic Ocean at the Gulf of St. Lawrence, and the much longer Mackenzie, which runs northward more than 2,600 miles.

People, goods, and services constantly cross the American and Canadian borders, as Canada is the U.S.'s largest trading partner. And Canada, like the United States, is a member of the G8, the eight nations that lead the world in advanced technology and manufactures.

HOW DOES CANADA'S POPULATION COMPARE WITH THAT OF THE UNITED STATES?

In terms of population, Canada is moon to the American sun. Canada's population is over thirty-five million, while the United States is above 316 million. Canada is as thinly populated as Saudi Arabia. Both countries have proud and sizable immigrant communities, but each has a very different ethnic profile.

Canada's profile demonstrates the idea that demography is destiny. The two largest ethnic groups in Canada are of British descent (about 28 percent of the total population) and French descent (about 23 percent). Officially Canada is a bilingual nation. All public documents and trade labels are written in both English and French. Most of the French-speaking Canadians live in the province of Quebec, where they comprise about 80 percent of the population. Canada (like the United States) also has sizable segments of Asian- and Near East-descended citizens. About 57 percent of Canadians speak English as a first (and family) language, while about 21 percent speak French, and the rest speak one or more of over a dozen other languages, including Chinese (Canada's third most common language).

Blacks account for about 13 percent of the population of the United States, but their number in Canada is relatively small. The differences trace to geography and climate as well as to the use of slaves in the rice and cotton plantations of the American South. Great Britain outlawed slavery in its empire in 1834, thereby making Canada a refuge for runaway American slaves. Canadians pride themselves on continuing their tradition of opening their doors to those seeking refuge and asylum. This tradition came into generous play during the Vietnam War, when hundreds of Americans took Canadian residence to protest the war and to escape military service.

Native Americans (including Inuit) make up 3 percent of Canada's population. They are widely and thinly spread among tribes, languages, and settlements. In recognition of their Native Americans, Canada has recently created a province carved from the Northwest Territory that gives its 25,000 Inuit inhabitants a considerable measure of self-governance and control over land and mineral rights.

WHY IS THE YUKON TERRITORY SO FIRMLY FIXED IN SONG AND STORY?

The Yukon Territory covers 207,000 square miles, more than twice the size of Great Britain, and has a total population of about 36,000. It abuts Alaska to the west, British Columbia to the south, and the Northeast Territory to the east. Its Klondike River is forever bound to memories of the great gold rush (1896-1904), when more than 80,000 fortune seekers endured Arctic hardship, glaciers, mountains, and frozen wilderness to stake claims in the Yukon gold fields. During the gold rush, more than $100 million was hacked and dug from the Yukon. Author Jack London found no gold, but his stories of the gold rush endure: *Son of the Wolf* and *The Call of the Wild.* Robert Service, poet of the Yukon, tells of how he was drawn to "its big dizzy mountains, to its deep deathlike valleys, the cussedest place" he knew, with a human comedy of fierce, larger-than-life characters (see "The Shooting of Dan McGrew" and "The Cremation of Sam McGee").

WHY A MELTING POT FOR AMERICANS AND A MOSAIC FOR CANADIANS?

Americans see their country as a melting pot, but Canadians views theirs as a mosaic. Why the difference? The metaphor of melting pot reflects the motto emblazoned on the Great Seal of the United States, *E Pluribus Unum*, "one from the many"; in effect, out of diverse national origins, religions, and cultures emerge one nation. The metaphor of the mosaic reflects the reality of a picture made of small multi-colored stones. The pieces touch but do not interpenetrate. The two largest Canadian "pieces" are the French-speaking and the English-speaking communities. The French were the first European settlers of Canada. When Canada passed to British control following the battles for Quebec (1759 and 1760), the British victors gave the French guarantees of religious, educational, and linguistic freedoms, as well as recognition of their land titles and patterns of settlement. That, says a distinguished historian, was the most generous and enlightened colonial policy every promulgated.

These two metaphors, melting pot and mosaic, underscore a profound difference in national outlook and national aspiration. The metaphor of the melting pot is manifest in the American Constitution. The rights laid down in the first Ten Amendments (the Bill of Rights) are given to each person individually. The metaphor of the mosaic, manifest in the Quebec Act of 1774, gives rights and liberties to members of an entire group, the former subjects of the King of France.

WHY "JE ME SOUVIENS" ("I REMEMBER") ON QUEBEC LICENSE PLATES?

The slogan comes from a popular song: "I was born under the lily (the fleur-de-lis—the emblem of the kings of France); I live now under the rose (the Rose of the Tudor kings of England)." In that slogan, the province of Quebec laments more than 200 years of history. In the decade following Columbus' first landing in the New World, both France and England tried to find what Columbus had failed to find: a sea route to Asia. John Cabot sailed in 1497 under the English flag of Henry VII and touched the North American coast. His son, Sebastian, also seeking the "Northwest Passage," landed in 1509 at what was later to be called Hudson Bay. French claims to Canada began with the voyages of Jacques Cartier, who traveled the St. Lawrence River in 1535 as far west as the Iroquois town of Hochelaga, the present site of Montreal.

In the 263 years that followed Cabot's first landing, England and France fought a series of wars to settle rival claims to the empire. The Hudson Bay Company was chartered by the British crown in 1670, inaugurating territorial rivalry between Britain and France. In Europe, the War of the Grand Alliance (1688-97) preceded the War of Spanish Succession (1701-14), which, in turn, made way for the War of Austrian Succession (1740-48). In Asia, British and French struggles over India ended with British victory at the Battle of Plassey (1757). In North America a series of British and French wars effectively ended with the English General James Wolfe's victory over General Louis de Montcalm on the Plains of Abraham adjacent to Quebec in 1759. Both Wolfe and Montcalm died on the Plains of Abraham, and with that battle and a subsequent one the following year, the French surrendered their claims to Canada. The subsequent Treaty of Paris ratified the loss of the North American French Empire. And it is that loss that is remembered and mourned by a disgruntled, French-speaking, Catholic Quebec up to the present, despite the Quebec Act of 1774 granting Quebec the French legal code, its system of land tenure, and the right to practice Roman Catholicism. Witness the slogan on the automobile license plates in today's Quebec: "Je me souviens."

For the English colonists on the American frontier, the wars carried a collective name, the French and Indian Wars. Each war in the series of hostilities had its own name honoring the English throne in whose name the war was fought: King William's War, Queen Anne's War, and King George's War. The wars, from the American point of view, are celebrated in James Fenimore Cooper's novels *The Leatherstocking Tales* and give vivid narrative to raids and killings on the frontier and the role played by Indians in the service of their French and English allies.

HOW DID CANADA GET ITS NAME?

As Jacques Cartier went west along the St. Lawrence River, he gave Canada a name that is one of history's pleasant mistakes. "What is this place?" asked the explorer, thinking of the vast river valley he was exploring. Kanata, answered the Indians, assuming he had asked about a settlement on the far side of the river!

Figure 25.2. Jacques Cartier Square, Montreal, Quebec, Canada, around 1900

WHY ARE THE PEOPLE OF QUEBEC (THE QUEBECOIS) CALLED UNMELTABLE ETHNICS?

The reference is to what Quebecois refuse to be: people who accept inclusion in an American-style melting pot. The people of Quebec fiercely guard their separate identity. It is an identity undergirded by a 250-year-old fear, the fear of cultural extinction. In 1977 the government of Quebec enacted a language law requiring that all commercial enterprises in the province operate in French. And language police are alert to stores and shops that give precedence to English names over their French equivalents.

Far more important are the referenda whereby the Province of Quebec has voted on its future—whether or not to withdraw from Canada to establish an independent nation. The most recent referendum in 1995 kept Quebec in Canada by the slimmest margin, with 49.3 percent voting for independence, and 50.7 percent rejecting it. The issue is far from dead, and the leading organized proponent of independence, the Parti Quebecois, is a powerful presence in the Parliament of Quebec. Its demand for independence is a constant presence in Canadian politics and a threat to Canadian unity. Whether the threat is real or superficial is difficult to say. Public figures in Canada's western provinces (Alberta, Saskatchewan) sometimes say, "We're tired of blackmail. If they want out, let 'em go!"

HOW STRONG ARE THE TIES OF CANADIAN UNIFICATION?

The United States fought a long and terrible war to keep its southern states in the Union. Its national government has been pulling the American states into tighter and tighter dependence since the beginning of the twentieth century. Canada, in contrast, has the second loosest confederation system in the world.[2] Canada reformed its Constitution in 1982 and, with deference to history and the special place of Quebec, inserted opt-out or escape clauses in the Constitution, giving each province the option to make national law non-binding on the province. The opt-out provisions regarding Quebec are grounded in the Constitution's Charter of Rights and Freedoms, which codified long-standing conventions (agreements and traditions), including the Constitution Act of 1867.

WHAT WAS THE EFFECT OF THE AMERICAN REVOLUTION ON CANADA?

The American Revolution created not one but two countries: the United States and Canada. Canadians often say that theirs is the country that got away—from the United States. Even before the signing of The Declaration of Independence, the thirteen American colonies were convinced that the people of the fourteenth North American colony (Canada) shared American revolutionary sentiments. In 1775 two American armies under Benedict Arnold and Richard Montgomery marched northward. Montreal was captured and Quebec besieged, but American arms were no match for Canadian resistance to independence from Britain. The invading American armies withdrew, and as the struggle for independence escalated, more than 50,000 British loyalists fled the rebellious colonies to take up residence in Canada. Thirty-two

[2] Only the Swiss give their provinces (cantons) greater independence.

thousand sailed from the eastern seaboard in British ships to take up residence in Nova Scotia. Eight thousand more went from New York and Pennsylvania to settle in Quebec along the north shore of Lake Erie.

For the English-speaking Canadians, the American Revolution was an assault on patriotism and the established social order. For French-speaking Canadians, the revolution was a threat to the liberties given them by the Accord of 1774. Worse, it stood as the threat of a Protestant nation under arms. One immediate result of the American Revolution was to bring to Canada a new contingent of English speakers. To reassure both Anglophones and Francophones of Britain's concern for their welfare, Parliament separated Canada into two provinces, English-speaking Upper Canada (now Ontario) and French-speaking Lower Canada (now Quebec).

The Revolution also set the foundation for two distinct political ideals: Canadian and American. These ideals (as components of a political culture) continue to separate Canada and the United States. The American ideals embodied in The Declaration of Independence stress equality, liberty, individual freedom, and a populist government pledged to advance citizens' pursuit of happiness. Canadian ideals stress group rights and (as in the Canadian Constitution of 1867) peace, order, and good government.

WHY IS CANADA CALLED A DOMINION?

At the outbreak of the American Civil War, Confederate leaders were convinced that Great Britain would favor their cause. English textile mills (and their owners) relied greatly on southern cotton, and the British aristocracy had strong cultural ties to the plantation elites of the South. At the war's beginning, President Lincoln was reluctant to declare a blockade of southern ports. Doing so, under international law, would give belligerent status to the Confederacy and bestow legal recognition on its government. Without declaring a formal blockade, British ships would continue to trade with the South, bringing the Confederacy needed goods and money to fight the war. The North declared a blockade of southern ports, and Britain observed the blockade, not, however, without incidents that inflamed both British and northern public opinion. For example, in 1861 the U.S.S. San Jacinto boarded a British mail steamer and arrested two Confederate officials. Fearing further hostile acts, Britain reinforced its 6,400 Canadian garrisons by over 14,000 men. Despite Britain's declaration of neutrality, northern leaders asserted that Britain was aiding and abetting the southern cause. The British Navy, said to be strongest in the world, assisted southern blockade runners to the West Indies (in the style of Margaret Mitchell's fictional hero in *Gone With the Wind*, Rhett Butler).

When the Civil War ended, aggrieved opinion leaders in the North revived an old expansionist dream: to make Canada part of the United States. Finish what had failed in 1775 (the assaults on Montreal and Quebec). Finish the unfinished business of the War of 1812 when American forces invaded Canada and burned Toronto, and then the British, in turn, invaded Washington and burned the White House. Avenge the burning of the White House.

Britain responded to the American threat by uniting its Canadian colonies to give them a common defense. So, the Dominion of Canada was established in 1867.[3] The Canadian Constitution of the same year, enacted by Parliament and proclaimed by Queen Victoria, joined Ontario, Quebec, Nova Scotia, and New Brunswick into a single dominion. In 1982 Canada became a fully independent nation. Why dominion? For Americans, the Civil War was being heralded as a rebirth of America's democratic ideals. To call the country to America's north the Kingdom of Canada would risk an affront to American public opinion. Dominion might avoid that affront, and dominion would have Biblical overtones, as promised in Genesis One and the seventy-second Psalm: "He shall have Dominion from Sea to Sea."

IS CANADA AN INDEPENDENT COUNTRY?

Canada is a freely associated member of the British Commonwealth, an organization of heads of government of Great Britain and its former colonies. Although Canada is an independent self-governing country, many forms and traditions of empire remain. The monarch of Great Britain, Queen Elizabeth II, "By the Grace of God, of Great Britain, Ireland, and the British Dominions beyond the Seas…" is Sovereign of Canada.

The Queen is represented in Canada by the Governor General of Canada, a person appointed by the Queen but always in accordance with the wishes of the Canadian government. The Governor General, as the Sovereign's representative, is Canada's head of state, whose status is essentially ceremonial (bestowing honors and awards, for example). The sometime British Empire holds to old forms and ceremonies. So, in the pleasantries of tradition, the Governor General delivers the Speech from the Throne (written by the Prime Minister on behalf of the majority party in the House of Commons), gives assent to legislation, and "appoints" Canada's Prime Minister. All the Prime Minister's cabinet are said to act on behalf of Canada's

[3] For the hundred-year anniversary in 1967, Canada staged a massive World's Fair in Montreal, one of the most popular world fairs in history. One of this book's authors, James E. Harf, spent a week at the Fair.

Sovereign. And all legislation of the national government begins with the time-honored formula: "Her majesty, by and with the advice and consent of Senate and House..."

WHAT ARE CANADIANS CALLED: SUBJECTS OR CITIZENS?

Canadians stopped being subjects of the Sovereign in 1947, when they became citizens of Canada. The march toward symbols of independence was gradual. The national flag (the red maple leaf on white field with wide red bars left and right) was adopted in 1965. The designation EIIR (Elizabeth II Regina, Latin for queen) was removed from post boxes in 1970. And a national anthem, "O Canada," was adopted in 1980.

WHAT ARE THE DUTIES OF THE ROYAL NORTHWEST CANADIAN MOUNTED POLICE?

The redcoats and brown beaver hats of the Mounties are Canada's most recognized symbols. Many have commented on policeman and cowboy as the contrasting symbols of Canada and the United States and on what these symbols say about national cultures. The cowboy is the lone rider on the prairie—fearless, independent, ready to take the law into his own hands, slow to anger, lethal in revenge. The Mountie is an agent of the government, the policeman who brings law and order to the wilderness. His slogan, "The Mountie always gets his man," reaches back to Canada's frontier days and to the Mounted Police's reputation for dogged and tireless pursuit of those who broke the law. More important to reputation, Mounties rarely drew their guns; their service was in almost equal measure law enforcement and community assistance.

The Northwest Mounted Police was established in 1873 to bring rule of law to the sparsely settled areas in the west, which today are the provinces of Saskatchewan and Alberta. More directly, the Mounted Police was created to prevent the lawlessness of the American frontier from taking root in Canada. Rogue traders were bringing alcohol to the Indians, cheating them of furs, and robbing at gunpoint. In 1898 the Mounted Police imposed civil government on the Yukon. The name Royal was prefixed by a patent from King Edward VII (1904). The Royal Canadian Mounted police today (using automobiles, airplanes, and the most modern equipment) enforce the laws of the national Canadian government, leaving responsibility for province laws to provincial and metropolitan police.

Even legends have their ironies. The Mounties achieved worldwide recognition largely through movies made on location in Hollywood, not Canada. Over 400 motion pictures have been "Mountie pictures." Chief among them is an operetta, *Rose Marie*, written by a Prague-born American composer, Rudolf Friml.

Figure 25.3. Postcard of Royal Canadian Mounted Police officer.

WHO ARE SOME OF THE BEST KNOWN CANADIANS?

Canadians are rightly proud of their countrymen's accomplishments. Many in the realms of science and technology overcame the barriers of time and space (geography as destiny?). In 1857 Frederick Gisborne invented the undersea telegraph cable. In 1878 Alexander Graham Bell obtained a patent for the telephone, sending the human voice across time and space. And in 1889 he accomplished an analogue for music, with his patent for the gramophone. Canadians invented the electronic microscope in 1937, thereby making possible the exploration of the smallest "spaces." In medical matters, Frederick Banting and colleagues received the Nobel Prize in 1923 for isolating insulin, thereby saving from certain death millions afflicted with diabetes.

Canadian inventions enrich comfort and pleasures worldwide: the snowmobile in 1922 and the game of Trivial Pursuit in 1980. In 1922 Gideon Sundback patented the zipper. And in 1891 James Naismith created the game of basketball.

Canadian authors of world renown include those writing in English and in French: Margaret Atwood, Robertson Davies, Mavis Galant, Antoine Maillet, Rohinton Mistry, L.M. Montgomery, Farley Mowett, Stephen Leacock, and Mordecai Richler. And among Canadian-born actors and public personalities are Genevieve Bujold, Raymond Burr, Glenn Ford, Michael Fox, Peter Jennings, and Raymond Massey.

WHAT IS THE CANADIAN OUTLOOK?

Some ideas are too useful ever to be discarded. When Alexis de Tocqueville toured the new American Republic in the early 1800s, he searched for an understanding of the world's first large republic. "Habits of the heart" is how he described the American outlook: widely shared ideas about the world, about fellow citizens, about civic duty and obligation, and about preferred ways of living one's life and getting on in the world. Today, "national outlook" is close in meaning to habits of the heart, what social scientists call civic culture.

Casual travelers crossing from Canada to the United States and vice versa find little to differentiate the two countries. This is especially the case if the border crossing is accomplished somewhere other than a large urban place. Dress, language, speech patterns, and body language are alike. So, too, are architecture, automobiles, and popular music. But if the border crossing is through a large city, the contrasts are striking. Windsor, Canada is an orderly, prosperous city. Its streets are well maintained, and there are no signs of urban violence and decay.

Nearby, however, Detroit's cityscape is light years away. Downtown Detroit is derelict. Its business establishments have long ago departed; storefronts are boarded up; sidewalk traffic is sparse, and pedestrians are few and shabbily dressed. The cityscape is reminiscent of a scarred battle zone. What habits of the heart can explain the differences between the lively, safe streets, excellent public transport, and striking architecture of, for example, Toronto and the American cities that cluster near the southern shores of the Great Lakes?

WHAT IS THE CANADIAN OUTLOOK ON GOVERNMENT?

History and geography mold the Canadian outlook. When Canada resisted the American Revolution, it also rejected those American habits of the heart that embraced unencumbered individualism, populism, mistrust of government, and political experiment. The American outlook mistrusts government. In constructing their Constitution, Americans tried to keep government at bay and in check by dividing power among the executive, legislative, and judicial branches and by enacting a Bill of Rights protecting citizens against their government. The American version of the American Revolution is a memory of an abused people who overthrew the tyranny of a distant government. Canadian memory of this event is of thirteen threatening and rebellious colonies to their south poised to strike at Canada's peace and tranquility.

Canada's government is patterned on the British Parliament. The Prime Minister sits in the legislature and comes to office by assembling a legislative majority. As long as he keeps that majority, his powers are unchecked by a rival branch of government. He and his (or her) majority have considerable latitude in legislating.

Americans are wary of government intruding into the workings of the marketplace. Government controls over such things as urban development, consumer-safe goods, and workplace safety have been accomplished only after protracted debate and compromise. Canadians view their government as a benevolent enterprise that uses its authority to better their lives. Government gave them free land to settle the West, built railroads to overcome geography, and used its powers to fulfill a duty (*noblesse oblige*) to monitor the marketplace. Canadian novelist Robertson Davies sees Canadian government as a paradox: a socialist monarchy. Canada is the North American pioneer in providing universal medical services for its citizens. And in contrast to the American attempts at public housing for the poor (high-rise buildings, acres of concrete and asphalt, and poverty communities in concentrated areas), Canadians offer low-rise housing for their poor and integrate them into established neighborhoods.

WHAT IS THE CANADIAN OUTLOOK ON CIVIC OBLIGATION?

Tocqueville used the word individualism to best describe Americans' view of the world and their obligations to that world. In rejecting the American Revolution, which Britons significantly call the American Civil War, Canadians continued the English and French respect for their upper classes and relied on those classes to live up to their social responsibilities (again, *noblesse oblige*). Tocqueville also observed that American individualism went hand in fist with a drive for worldly and financial success. Contemporary observers link this syndrome of individualism and success to American crime.[4] Approximately 5 percent of Americans are victims of crime each year. The American homicide rate has declined from a high of 9.2 murders per 100,000 people to a more recent statistic of 6.5 percent. Canada's homicide rate for 2010 was 1.62 per 100,000. The United States enjoys the dubious reputation of executing more convicted felons than any other country, save China. Litigation may also be an outcome of the American individualism-success syndrome. America has the reputation of being the world's most litigious society. As servants of that litigation, the United States has one lawyer per 274,000 people. In urban areas, the number is many times greater. Canada has one lawyer per 400,000 people.

Canadians are concerned about being overwhelmed by American popular culture. Legislation fixes the number of American programs that can be broadcast on TV, and the government actively encourages books by Canadian authors. One difference in the two nations' habits of the heart is Canada's more subdued patriotism. Canadian author Pierre Berton once mused that it embarrasses us to love our country out loud[5]. Americans find it strange that Canadians celebrate Queen Victoria's birthday but not that of their "founding father," John McDonald. A staple of American public discourse is to invoke God's blessing on the U.S.A. ("God Bless America"). In Canada, such invocations, if they occur at all, are reserved for formal church service.

Canadian philosopher Northrop Frye has said (no doubt with wry exaggeration) that Americans love to make money, while Canadians love to count it. "I know of no country," he said, "where accountants have a higher social and moral status"[6] Margaret Atwood, Canadian novelist, asserts that she can always tell when Americans are present in a restaurant. Their voices, she says, are loud and strident, the clothes too flashy, and ever present is their talk about money.

But however much Canadians may find to reject in the American heart, Canadians, especially young Canadians, continue to migrate to their southern neighbor, where the climate is

---

[4] Crime, according to many of its practitioners, is just a business; not getting caught is its ultimate mark of success.

[5] Wayne C. Thompson, *Canada 2013*, The World Today Series (Lanham, MD: Stryker-Post Publications, 2013), 14.

[6] John Robert Colombo, editor, *The Northrop Frye Quote Book* (Toronto: Dundurn, 2014), 22.

more benign, taxes are lower, and greater opportunities beckon. The outflow of Canadian talent is of major concern that Canadian publications have begun to combat this phenomenon by writing about why other people are choosing Canada.

CANADA IS NOW AT THE FOREFRONT OF SOCIAL REVOLUTION: WHAT IS GOING ON?

When Pierre Trudeau succeeded in changing Canada's Constitution, one purpose was to "repatriate the Constitution," that is, to take from the British Parliament a final say in judging the legality of Canadian law. To allay Quebec's fears that the new Constitution might erode its autonomy, the new Constitution included opt-out provisions. It also included a Charter of Rights and Freedoms, Canada's equivalent of the American Bill of Rights. Such charters are rarely, if ever, self-defining. Courts intervene to flesh out and give substance to such provisions as "Every individual is equal...and has the right to equal benefit of the law without discrimination...based on race, religion, sex, age or mental or physical disability." When the charter first came into effect, opponents filed what the courts dismissed as frivolous suits, such as the man who sued because his three-year-old son was denied a driver's license. But in 2003 a court decision in Ontario gave legal sanction to same-sex marriages, and the federal government announced that it would draft legislation to extend that legality nationwide.

Extending the charter's logic, the Canadian government also announced in July 2003 a plan to provide marijuana to those using it for medical purposes. Asked to comment on such compelling departures from the social policy of the United States government, Canadians respond with familiar and non-familiar replies: "We measure ourselves in our degree of difference from the United States." "We have always been closer to Europe than to the United States in our social policies." "Take universal health care, for example. We do not regard government as the enemy, but as provider of social goods." Much of U.S. social policy is a response to the political power of religious fundamentalists, but Canada keeps religion out of its politics.

HOW DID THE FRENCH DEFEAT AT QUEBEC GIVE THE UNITED STATES ITS FREEDOM?

Tennyson said, "Let the Great World spin forever, / Down the ringing grooves of Change[7]." When France ceded Canada to Great Britain, France carried its anger across the Atlantic and befriended the rebellious American colonies. Comte de Rochambeau augmented Washington's army by 5,000 French soldiers. France also gave the rebellious colonies loans and supplies. But

---

[7] Alfred Lord Tennyson, "Locksley Hall" (Poem), 1835.

after six years of fighting, the colonials were exhausted. Washington's forces were split north and south. A new British general, Lord Cornwallis, led 7,200 battle-hardened troops into Virginia to burn crops, conscript men, and crush Washington's army. As defeat loomed, word came from the French West Indies. Admiral de Grasse would arrive with ships and men. He would blockade the British fleet in Chesapeake Bay, ferry Washington's northern soldiers down to Virginia, and contribute French sailors and soldiers to Washington's command. Washington's newly consolidated army of 9,000 northern troops was augmented by 7,800 French foot soldiers, creating a land force of almost 19,000 (plus 18,000 French sailors) against Cornwallis's 7,200. The Battle of Yorktown in October 1781 was a stunning defeat for Britain. At the ceremony of surrender, the British pipes played a mournful dirge, "The World Turned Upside Down." The War for Independence was effectively over.

In a small town in the south of France stands a statue to Admiral Comte de Grasse with these telling words: "He Gave the United States its Freedom."

AFTERWORD

The word "history" comes to us from its founder, Herodotus, who tells us that the word merely means inquiry. Inquiry into what? Cause and effect. And explanation. Explanation comes from the Latin word meaning, "to lay flat." Conjoined to explanation is the Greek poet Hesiod's legacy, "Happy is he who knows the cause of things." Accordingly, our book is a search for the causes of things.

As writers of this book, we have approached our task from the perspective of professors who, between them, have taught, lectured, and traveled alone, with friends and family, and with students young and old for over a century. And in reflecting on our own education and our teaching, we arrive at the idea of "residues and remainders." When all is said and done, what stays with us? Simply put, ideas that have influenced our lives. Ideas that help us to understand cause and effect—connections between things and ideas that are the great web of history, culture, politics, and human aspirations. These are the purposes of our book. It is inspired by the idea, as Robert Browning says so well in "Andrea del Sarto" that "A man's reach should exceed his grasp." And, as the motto of Phi Beta Kappa suggests, "To the stars with aspiration."

Ideas and connections in the great web: The driving force and the goal of our book has been to give readers, in effect, the essence of a university education in the humanities—an essence that we hope will remain with readers long after the book has gathered dust on the shelves.

ABOUT THE AUTHORS

James E. Harf (Ph.D.) is Associate Vice President and Director of the Center for Global Education at Maryville University of St. Louis. He and Herson were faculty colleagues in the Department of Political Science at The Ohio State University for over 30 years. Harf is an accomplished writer, having authored/edited over three dozen academic books as well as one novel, *Memories of Ivy*. For the past thirteen years, Harf has overseen programs to every corner of the globe for over 2,000 university students and 150 faculty. He has personally led more than 1,000 students overseas.

Lawrence J. R. Herson (Ph.D.) is a well-published author in six languages who was a decorated combat meteorologist in the South Pacific Theater during World War II as a young man. Since retiring from The Ohio State University two decades ago, Herson has spent his time as a lecturer on very exclusive cruise ships calling on ports throughout the world. He has spent at least a third of the year on such ventures at sea even though he is now 90 years old and is in such demand by the cruise lines that he could spend the entire year on board such ships if he chose.

Agapy publishes a variety of books in international education. Visit www.agapy.com for more information. Readers of *The Wise World Traveler* may also be interested in the following:

Faculty-led 360: Guide to Successful Study Abroad

Leading a study abroad program can be one of the most exciting, rewarding, and pivotal experiences of a professor's career, but how to get started and sorting out the details can be daunting. Field trainers, Melanie McCallon and Bill Holmes have helped numerous universities and professors navigate the path to successful study abroad. If you are interested in developing and leading a travel-study course or an international academic program, *Faculty-led 360* is the one book that will help you get there.

Bridges: An Extraordinary Journey of the Heart

In this fictional dramatization by W. S. Williamson, the Peace Corps, along with mystery, danger, and romance, takes a young American woman, Jessie, into the heart of Africa and halfway around the world to Europe and South America. Jessie's new found love may not be what her heart seeks, while a positive-negative force, deeper and disturbing, seizes her mind. This fascinating thriller crosses into an unknown dimension of human existence. Echoing the theories of Carl Jung, a brilliant interplay between cultures, beliefs, lightness, and darkness make this book truly exceptional.

College Abroad

For students who want to travel, this book by Holly Oberle is about how to get an international education, a degree, and a new perspective on life and the world. It's for those who are interested in pursuing a diploma abroad in addition to or en lieu of a study abroad experience. It covers everything you need to know about going to college in another country, from before you leave to after you return, for both undergraduate and graduate study. Pursuing a degree abroad is a smart way for students to get a great education and a global competitive advantage for less time and money.

CPSIA information can be obtained at www.ICGtesting.com
Printed in the USA
LVOW09s0542290415

436389LV00002B/2/P

9 781938 52201